Barbara F. Reskin

Patricia A. Roos

With case studies by

Katharine M. Donato,

Polly A. Phipps,

Barbara J. Thomas,

Chloe E. Bird,

Linda A. Detman,

and Thomas Steiger

Job

Explaining

Queues,

Women's Inroads

Gender

into Male

Queues

Occupations

Temple University Press

Philadelphia

Temple University Press, Philadelphia 19122
Copyright © 1990 by Temple University. All rights reserved
Published 1990
Printed in the United States of America

The paper used in this publication meets the minimum requirements of
American National Standard for Information Sciences—Permanence of
Paper for Printed Library Materials, ANSI Z39.48-1984 ⊚

Library of Congress Cataloging-in-Publication Data

Reskin, Barbara F.
    Job queues, gender queues : explaining women's inroads into male
    occupations / Barbara F. Reskin and Patricia A. Roos ; with case
    studies by Katharine M. Donato . . . [et al.].
    p.   cm. — (Women in the political economy)
        ISBN 0-87722-743-8   — ISBN 0-87722-744-6 (pbk.)
    1. Sexual division of labor—United States.   2. Pay equity—United
    States.   I. Roos, Patricia A.   II. Title.   III. Series.
    HD6060.65.U5R473   1990
    306.3'615'0973—dc20   90-31544
                                                              CIP

For Lowell and Chip who,
by rejecting gender queues
and in countless other ways,
have made our lives better

Contents

Preface   *ix*

Part I   *Explaining the Changing Sex
Composition of Occupations   1*

1   Occupational Sex Segregation:
Persistence and Change   3

2   Queueing and Changing
Occupational Composition   29

3   Consequences of Desegregation: Occupational
Integration and Economic Equity?   69

Part II   *Case Studies of
Occupational Change   91*

Barbara F. Reskin   4   Culture, Commerce, and Gender:
The Feminization of Book Editing   93

Polly A. Phipps   5   Industrial and Occupational Change in
Pharmacy: Prescription for Feminization   *111*

Katharine M. Donato   6   Keepers of the Corporate Image:
Women in Public Relations   *129*

Chloe E. Bird   7   High Finance, Small Change: Women's
                                 Increased Representation
                                 in Bank Management *145*

Katharine M. Donato   8   Programming for Change? The Growing
                                 Demand for Women Systems Analysts *167*

Barbara J. Thomas   9   Women's Gains in Insurance Sales:
                                 Increased Supply, Uncertain Demand *183*

Barbara J. Thomas   10   A Woman's Place Is Selling Homes:
and Barbara F. Reskin   Occupational Change and the Feminization
                                 of Real Estate Sales *205*

Polly A. Phipps   11   Occupational Resegregation among
                                 Insurance Adjusters and Examiners *225*

Linda A. Detman   12   Women behind Bars:
                                 The Feminization of Bartending *241*

Thomas Steiger   13   Baking and Baking Off: Deskilling and
and Barbara F. Reskin   the Changing Sex Makeup of Bakers *257*

Patricia A. Roos   14   Hot-Metal to Electronic Composition:
                                 Gender, Technology, and Social
                                 Change *275*

            Part III   *Conclusion* *299*

                            15   Summary, Implications,
                                 and Prospects *301*

                                 Appendix: Guidelines Used for Occupational
                                 Case Studies *325*

                                 References *331*

                                 Name Index *371*

                                 Subject Index *374*

                                 About the Authors *387*

Preface

Sex segregation has a history as old as the labor force itself. By comparison, our involvement in this project has been short, although the development and fruition of this book have taken most of a decade. The immediate origins of this project lie in our association with two National Academy of Science (NAS) Committees. Patricia A. Roos served from 1978 to 1980 as research associate on the Committee on Occupational Classification and Analysis. That committee produced *Women, Work and Wages: Equal Pay for Jobs of Equal Value* (Treiman and Hartmann, 1981), a report that has played a pivotal role in the struggle for pay equity. Three of its staff members—Heidi I. Hartmann, Pamela S. Cain, and Patricia A. Roos—were instrumental in the establishment of a permanent NAS Committee on Women's Employment and Related Social Issues. As that committee's first study director, Barbara F. Reskin directed a comprehensive study of sex segregation that gave rise to *Sex Segregation in the Workplace: Trends, Explanations, Remedies* (Reskin, 1984) and *Women's Work, Men's Work: Sex Segregation on the Job* (Reskin and Hartmann, 1986). The twin foci of these two NAS committees—pay equity and sex segregation—are no accident. The pay gap between the sexes stems primarily from the segregation of women and men into different jobs and from the fact that women's jobs pay less than those men dominate. Thus, both integrating jobs and eliminating the wage penalty imposed on predominantly female jobs should reduce the pay gap between the sexes.

The two NAS volumes on sex segregation documented its extraordinary resilience. The sporadic implementation of the few mechanisms that reduced segregation did little to undermine sex segregation. In 1983, however, the Census Bureau released 1980 census data that pointed to women's marked inroads into a small number of male occupations during the 1970s. The resulting publicity in the *New York Times* and *Washington Post* captured our attention. We wanted to discover what forces in these occupations had made them more accessible to women. A cursory examination of the 1980 census data immediately established that women's gains were far from evenly distributed across occupations. Women's dramatic inroads highlighted in newspaper stories were confined to a few occupations such as typesetting and composing and insurance adjusting and examining. In most predominantly male occupations, we learned, women posted only modest gains during the 1970s. This discovery called for a study design that examined the occupations in which women made the greatest numerical headway, while also discerning the factors that affected sex composition across all 503 detailed census occupations. We decided to conduct two separate studies: case studies of occupations in which women's representation increased at least twice as much during the 1970s as it had in the labor force as a whole (the results appear in this volume), and statistical analyses of occupational-level data on all 503 detailed occupations, with the goal of identifying factors linked to changes in occupations' sex composition between 1970 and 1980 (to appear in a subsequent volume). Those statistical analyses permit us to assess the role of variables that eluded examination through case study and to test the generalizability of our findings.

We were fortunate in attracting to the project Polly A. Phipps, then a doctoral student at the University of Michigan, and Katharine M. Donato, then a doctoral student at the State University of New York at Stony Brook. Phipps undertook preliminary case studies of women's inroads into pharmacy and insurance adjusting and examining that helped establish the feasibility of the case study method. Both contributed to our early discussions and helped prepare successful proposals for research support. Phipps was instrumental in identifying useful data sources for subsequent case studies, and Donato played a major role in developing the quantitative data needed for the studies.

The labor-intensive nature of the case study method prompted us to expand our research team. Chloe Bird, Linda Detman, Thomas Steiger, and Barbara Thomas, then graduate students at the University of Illinois, joined the project after Reskin moved to Illinois. Each, along with Donato and Phipps, was the primary author of one or more case studies that appear in this volume. Without their efforts (largely voluntary, because the time the case studies took far exceeded our grant funding), this book would not exist. Equally essential were the contributions of the scores of workers in the fourteen occupations we studied who generously shared their observations and experiences. We are also grateful to our student assistants who aided us with virtually every part of this study: our warm thanks go to Barbara Kritt and Sharon Reitman from the University of Michigan; Dawn Dworak, Jamie Fetkewicz, Pauline Pang, and Georganne Rundblad from the University of Illinois; Elizabeth Chute, Elizabeth Hein, and Valerie Hilicus from the State University of New York at Stony Brook; Katharine Jones, Hei-Soo Soh, and Sarah Thompson from Rutgers University; and Susan Slater from Stanford University.

Collaborations as complex as this one require a division of labor. Reskin assumed primary responsibility for the case studies, working closely with the graduate students who conducted them. Roos took on the difficult and often frustrating task of preparing the quantitative data that we cite occasionally in the present volume and that form the basis for our second monograph. We each drafted two of the analytic chapters in this book. Roos drafted Chapters 1 and 3, Reskin Chapters 2 and 15. It goes without saying that in revising these chapters—more times than we care to remember—we both contributed to each chapter.

We incurred extensive intellectual debts in the course of this project. Some debtors we cannot acknowledge by name; they are persons who raised tough questions or offered new interpretations or useful examples at colloquia where we formally presented our ideas. Reskin presented parts of the argument that appears in Chapter 2 in colloquia at Loyola University, May 1987; the University of California at Santa Barbara, October 1987; Harvard University, December 1987; Stanford University, Fall 1987 and Spring 1988; the Center for Advanced Study in the Behavioral Sciences, April 1988; the University of North Carolina, April 1988; and the University of Arizona, October 1988. Roos presented an early version of Chapter 3 at a Rutgers Sociology Department Colloquium and at a Rutgers International Relations and Labor Markets Workshop Series. Reskin and Roos presented some of the ideas in Chapter 3 at the Conference on Ingredients for Women's Employment Policy, State University of New York at Albany, in April 1985 and later, along with ideas in Chapter 15 at the Institute for Women's Policy Research's first annual Women's Policy Conference in Washington, D.C. in May 1989. Reskin presented the formal model of queueing and its implications for changing occupational composition at the American Sociological Association meetings in August 1989.

In addition to thanking those who offered insightful comments and questions on the above occasions, we are happy to have this chance to express our gratitude for the substantial contributions of several colleagues. Paula S. England generously shared *Dictionary of Occupational Titles* data that she has updated for use with the 1980 census codes, and Randall Filer gave us his estimated rates of unionization for detailed occupations. Donald J. Treiman provided us with access to the 1970 public use microdata and patiently answered our technical questions, and Elizabeth Stephenson ensured that we received the data in a form in which we could use them. We regret that even asserting our special indebtedness to James N. Baron, Jerry A. Jacobs, and Ronnie J. Steinberg for excellent comments on several chapters fails to convey the depth of our gratitude. The book profited also from useful discussions with Francine Blau, Ross Boylan, Lee Clarke, Dorothy Sue Cobble, Paula England, Lowell Hargens, Heidi Hartmann, Mary Jackman, Toby Parcel, and Myra Strober. Strober's work with Carolyn Arnold has provided a model for occupational case studies, and the similarity of her conclusions (some developed collaboratively with Lisa Catanzarite) to our own has lent certainty to our confidence in our own findings. Finally, we appreciate the support of Temple University Press production editor Mary Capouya (with special thanks for assigning our book to copyeditor Patricia Sterling) and especially the encouragement and the patience of our editor, Michael Ames.

We conducted this project while in residence at five different institutions, all of which provided support and resources that we appreciate. Roos was on the faculty at the State University of New York at Stony Brook when she began the project, and she finished it at Rutgers University. Reskin began work on this volume while at the University of Michigan and completed it at the University of Illinois. She spent the 1987–88 academic year at the Center for Advanced Study in the Behavioral Sciences where the Center's superb staff and resources permitted her to devote much of her time to this project and other fellows—especially the members of the Feminist Seminar—provided both encouragement and diversion.

Finally, we are grateful to the National Science Foundation for its support (grants SES-85-12452 and SES-85-12586, including supplementary Research Experience for Undergraduate awards to each of us) and the Rockefeller Foundation Program on Changing Gender Roles (grants RF GA OE 8533 and RF 84036). We are happy also to have a chance to acknowledge the support of the University of Michigan Rackham Graduate College (387-895), the University of Illinois Research Board, the Rutgers University Dean of the Faculty of Arts and Sciences (2-09694) and the Rutgers Research Council (2-02079), and the John D. and Catherine MacArthur Foundation that helped support Reskin's year at the Center for Advanced Study in the Behavioral Sciences.

Barbara F. Reskin, Urbana, Illinois
Patricia A. Roos, Metuchen, New Jersey

Part I
Explaining the Changing Sex Composition of Occupations

1

Occupational Sex Segregation: Persistence and Change

Early in the 1980s the media took notice of a new phenomenon: women's marked progress into occupations traditionally reserved for men. Commenting on newly published data from the Department of Labor and the Bureau of the Census, media accounts such as Frank Prial's were quick to portray women's gains in "men's" occupations as dramatic:

> An increasing number of women in the United States are working at what used to be men's jobs. Despite the unemployment rate, the number of women working [for wages] in the United States has risen 21 million, or 95 percent, over the last two decades, according to a new study by the United States Department of Labor, and many of the jobs they have taken are in categories once largely the province of men. (Prial, 1982)

Front-page stories in leading newspapers announced women's advancement in such occupations as executive, lawyer, pharmacist, physician, veterinarian, bartender, bus driver, and baker (e.g., Prial, 1982; Herbers, 1983; Castro, 1985). By 1980, for example, women represented nearly half of all bus drivers and bartenders. Moreover, as Prial noted, women had become the majority in six formerly male-dominated occupations: insurance adjusters, examiners, and investigators; bill collectors; real estate agents and brokers; photographic process workers; checkers, examiners, and inspectors; and production-line assemblers.

Published 1980 census data indeed confirmed that women had posted

Table 1.1
Occupational Distribution over Major Occupational Groups, by Sex and Race,
Civilian Labor Force, 1980

Occupational Group	Men			Women			Percent Female
	Total[a]	White[b]	Black	Total[a]	White[b]	Black	
Executive, administrative, managerial	12.1	13.2	5.4	7.2	7.7	4.5	30.5
Professional specialty	10.5	11.2	5.6	13.7	14.4	11.2	49.1
Technicians and related support	2.9	3.0	1.8	3.0	3.1	3.2	43.8
Sales occupations	8.8	9.6	3.9	11.3	12.2	6.5	48.7
Administrative support, including clerical	6.7	6.5	9.0	30.7	31.9	25.2	77.1
Service occupations	9.4	8.2	17.0	18.2	16.4	29.3	58.9
Farming, forestry, fishing	4.3	4.2	3.4	1.0	1.0	.6	14.9
Precision production, craft, repair	21.0	21.7	15.5	2.4	2.3	2.4	7.8
Machine operators, assemblers, inspectors	10.0	9.2	15.1	9.3	8.1	13.0	40.7
Transportation and material moving	7.5	7.2	11.0	.9	.9	1.0	7.8
Handlers, equipment cleaners, helpers, laborers	6.8	6.0	12.3	2.3	2.0	3.2	19.8
Total[c]	100.0	100.0	100.0	100.0	100.0	100.1	42.5

[a] All races.
[b] Whites of Hispanic background not included.
[c] Sample sizes: 59,625,553 (total men), 49,633,442 (white men), 5,161,234 (black men), 44,092,523 (total women), 35,624,861 (white women), 5,058,243 (black women).

Source: U.S. Department of Labor, Employment and Training Administration (1982:1).

disproportionate gains during the 1970s in some predominantly male occupations (Bianchi and Rytina, 1984). But close inspection of the data suggests that media accounts of women's *progress* were exaggerated—women's representational gains exceeded their growth in the labor force as a whole in only a small number of the detailed occupations for which the Census Bureau collects data, and they even lost ground in a few occupations such as heavy-equipment mechanics, lathe and turning-machine operators, and production testers (U.S. Bureau of the Census, 1984a).

The phenomenon underlying these news stories and census data is the segregation of the sexes into different lines of work. Occupational sex segregation is one of the most enduring features of the U.S. labor market (Reskin and Hartmann, 1986). As Table 1.1 confirms, in 1980 substantial differentiation by sex existed at the level of aggregated occupational categories. Men tend to be overrepresented in managerial and craft occupations, traditionally the best paid of the white-collar and blue-collar workforces, respectively. They also predominate in transport operative and laboring occupations. Women are the clear majority in service occupations and in administrative-support occupations because of their predominance in clerical jobs. They are also slightly overrepresented in professional occupations because of their preponderance in the typically lower-paid female *semi*professions such as nursing, library work, social work, and teaching.

Table 1.1 reveals another fundamental feature of the U.S. occupational structure—its segregation by race. Blacks, whether male or female, are less likely than whites to command well-paid managerial or professional jobs.[1] Similarly, relative to white men, black men have garnered few of the better-paid blue-collar craft occupations. Compared with white women, black women are underrepresented in sales and administrative-support occupations. Instead, blacks of both sexes are overrepresented in service, operative, and laborer occupations. Like sex segregation, race segregation is problematic because it relegates blacks to the most poorly paid occupational sectors and hence helps to perpetuate the wage disparity between blacks and whites.

The segregation of the U.S. occupational structure by race and sex extends back to the turn of the century. Gross (1968), for example, found that occupational segregation by sex, as measured by the index of segregation, remained essentially constant between 1900 and 1960, reflecting the unusual persistence of this social phenomenon (see also Jacobs, 1989b).[2] Table 1.2 updates Gross's occupational segregation indexes across major census groups for both sex and race between 1940 and 1981. The data reveal that occupational segregation by race declined sharply after World War II, especially for women. Nonwhite women, 81 percent of whom are black (U.S. Department of Labor, Employment and Training Administration, 1982:1), have gone a long way

Table 1.2

Occupational Segregation Indexes across Major Census Categories for Sex and Race, 1940–1981

	1940	1950	1960	1970	1981
Segregation by sex among					
Whites	46	43	44	44	41
Blacks and others	58	50	52	49	39
Segregation by race among					
Men	43	36	35	30	24
Women	62	52	45	30	17

Sources: For 1940–70, Treiman and Terrell (1975:167); for 1981, Reskin and Hartmann (1986:19).

toward reducing the occupational gap between themselves and white women. However, *nonwhite women* continue to lag far behind *white men*.

As we show in more detail below, occupational *sex* segregation has been more resistant to change than race segregation. Despite revolutionary transformations in the industrial and occupational structures, and changes in the composition of the labor force, the degree of occupational sex segregation among whites remained essentially constant between 1940 and 1970. During the same period, with black women's movement out of domestic work, occupational sex segregation among blacks declined to the level of whites. Beginning in the late 1960s another "revolution"—the women's liberation movement—promised to improve women's position in the workplace. By challenging social values, the feminist movement fostered and reinforced antidiscrimination regulations, thus opening to women the doors of some traditionally male occupations. As a consequence of these and other factors, the level of occupational segregation declined at a faster rate during the 1970s than in any other decade in this century (Beller, 1984). Nonetheless, the labor force remained segregated: in 1981 at least 39 percent of black women and 41 percent of white women would have had to change to a different major occupational category to achieve distributions identical to those of men of their race across broad occupational categories (Table 1.2).[3]

Thus, the 1970s represented a watershed for sex segregation. For the first time in this century women made notable gains in some occupations in which men had typically predominated. However, the level of occupational sex segregation at the end of the decade remained high. In 1980 almost half of all women and 53 percent of men worked in occupations that were at least 80 percent women and men, respectively (Rytina and Bianchi, 1984). Women made inroads into some "male" occupations but little or no progress in integrating most others. White women were more likely than black women to enter customarily male occupations, but black women and men did advance disproportionately into some sex- and race-atypical occupations (Reskin and Roos, 1989; Sokoloff, 1989).

The variability in women's increased representation in male occupations during the 1970s raises three important questions. First, how can we explain women's disproportionate movement into some traditionally male or mixed-sex occupations during a decade in which their advancement into most male occupations was modest at best? In other words, what factors facilitated women's movement into the particular occupations in which they made pronounced numerical inroads? Second, what forms did occupational feminization take? Did women's entry yield genuine sex integration within these desegregating occupations so that women and men did the same kinds of work? Finally, did women's integration bring them closer to economic equity with male incumbents in occupations that became more female during the 1970s? This book provides answers to these questions.

The changing race composition of occupations since 1970 (Sokoloff, 1989) raises similar questions, and they are equally pressing. As demonstrated in Table 1.1, the continued segregation of blacks in low-paid, low-skill occupations ensures blacks' continuing economic disadvantage. At the outset we planned to examine changing patterns of both sex and race segregation, but the depth and complexity of our research methods soon convinced us that we could not encompass both in a single volume; hence, this study emphasizes the changing sex composition of occupations. Because we believe that our theoretical approach applies equally to understanding the changing race–sex composition of occupations, however, we plan to examine that question in future work.

| | | | Trends in Industrial and Occupational Structure

Broad industrial and occupational changes have transformed the U.S. economy in this century. Most striking has been its *industrial* transformation from a goods- to a service-producing economy. As the data in Table 1.3 indicate, at

Table 1.3
Industrial Employment, 1910–1980

	1910	1940	1980
Goods-producing industries	64.1%	51.4%	32.9%
Agriculture, forestry, fisheries	32.1	18.3	3.6
Mining	2.9	2.2	1.0
Manufacturing	22.8	23.9	22.1
Construction	6.4	7.0	6.3
Service-producing industries	35.9	48.6	67.1
Transportation and other public utilities	8.8	8.3	6.6
Trade	9.3	14.4	20.3
Finance and real estate	1.4	3.1	6.0
Educational and other professional service	4.6	8.0	20.0
Domestic and personal service	10.2	11.4	8.8
Government not elsewhere classified	1.5	3.3	5.4
Total N (in thousands) =	36,130	49,980	99,303

Note: Data are not exactly comparable across time. Data for 1910 and 1940 are based on "gainful workers", for 1980 on "employed civilians." Industries are named as in the 1970 census (U.S. Bureau of the Census, 1975:138). Equivalent 1980 titles are agriculture, forestry, fisheries; mining; construction; manufacturing; transportation, communication, and other public utilities; wholesale and retail trade; finance, insurance, real estate; professional and related services; services other than professional and related services; public administration (U.S. Bureau of the Census, 1986b:388).

Sources: For 1910 and 1940, U.S. Bureau of the Census (1975:138); for 1980, U.S. Bureau of the Census (1986b:388).

Table 1.4
Occupational Employment, 1900–1981

Occupation	1900	1950	1981
White collar	17.6%	36.6%	52.7%
Professional, technical, and kindred workers	4.3	8.6	16.4
Managers, officials, and proprietors	5.8	8.7	11.5
Clerical and kindred workers	3.0	12.3	18.5
Sales workers	4.5	7.0	6.4
Blue collar	35.8	41.1	31.1
Craftsmen, foremen, and kindred workers	10.5	14.2	12.6
Operatives and kindred workers	12.8	20.4	14.0
Laborers, except farm and mine	12.5	6.6	4.6
Service	9.0	10.5	13.4
Private household workers	5.4	2.6	1.0
Other service workers	3.6	7.9	12.3
Farm	37.5	11.8	2.7
Farmers and farm managers	19.9	7.4	1.5
Farm laborers and foremen	17.7	4.4	1.3
Total N (in thousands) =	29,031	58,999	100,397

Note: The data are not exactly comparable. Data for 1900 and 1950 are based on the experienced labor force aged 14 and older, for 1981 on employed persons 16 and older.

Sources: For 1900 and 1950, U.S. Bureau of the Census (1975:139); for 1981, U.S. Bureau of the Census (1982c:388–90).

the turn of the century two-thirds of the labor force produced goods in manufacturing, mining, construction, or agricultural work. The remainder held jobs in the service sector—in trade, the professions, personal services, transportation, and so forth. By 1980 the distribution had flipped, with 33 percent of the labor force employed in producing goods and 67 percent in providing services. Most of the decline in the goods-producing sector stemmed from the shrinking number of agricultural workers. In 1910 nearly a third of the labor force worked in agriculture, forestry, or fishing industries; by 1980, this proportion had dwindled to less than 4 percent. As the need for agricultural workers declined, service industries absorbed much of the slack.

With these industrial changes came the *occupational* restructuring of the labor force (see also Oppenheimer, 1970: chap. 5). Table 1.4, which shows this change, depicts the shift from a farm and blue-collar labor force to a white-collar and service one. For example, from 1950 to 1981 the proportion of the labor force engaged in professional and technical work almost doubled; from 1900 to 1981 it nearly quadrupled.[4] Although the proportion of skilled workers increased slightly, the overall proportion of workers in blue-collar jobs had declined by 1981 as technological advances eliminated the jobs of laborers.

The trends portrayed in Tables 1.3 and 1.4 reflect the economic and labor force consequences of larger processes of social change—the increasing mechanization and bureaucratization of work. During the late nineteenth and the early twentieth century, large factories replaced the small-scale production units characteristic of most of the nineteenth century (Scott, 1982). In large factories, employers sought men for heavy jobs and young, single women for lighter work, such as operating machines to manufacture textiles, paper, buttons, shoes, and watches (Scott, 1982:168). As more firms organized bureaucratically, the organization of work shifted from a personalistic system in which small producers were linked together to a more centralized production process. The latter was characterized by an elaborate division of labor, a hierarchy of jobs governed by standard operating procedures, and structured written communication. Opportunities in professional and managerial jobs in the developing bureaucracies drew educated men away from clerical jobs at the same time that bureaucratization dramatically expanded the need for clerical workers. To staff these jobs, employers favored women as a relatively inexpensive, literate labor force. Large numbers of women also found jobs in the expanding semiprofessions as teachers, nurses, social workers, and librarians (Kessler-Harris, 1982). Oppenheimer (1970) documented that these social transformations stimulated a demand for female labor, which in turn drew millions more women into the workforce. That influx had the reciprocal effect of allowing service-sector industries to expand further.

At the turn of the century, according to published census figures, fewer than one woman in five worked for wages (see Table 1.5).[5] Shortly after 1890 the increased mechanization and bureaucratization of work stimulated the growth of women's labor force participation. Between 1940 and 1986 the percentage of American women 16 years of age and older who were employed doubled, from 27 to 55 percent. Women aged 25 to 54 were especially likely to work for pay: in 1986, 71 percent of these women worked, compared with 94 percent of men in the same age group (Fullerton, 1987:21). The likelihood that a woman will be employed for wages continues to increase: by the year 2000, according to the Bureau of Labor Statistics, 81 percent of "prime working age" women will be employed, compared with 93 percent of similar men (Fullerton, 1987:21).

Married women—especially those with children—constituted the major source of this growth in women's labor force participation. A female labor force that had in 1890 been largely young and unmarried was transformed by 1960 to one that better represented the entire female population (Oppenheimer, 1970, explains this change). By 1986, 58 percent of the female labor force was married women, compared with 36 percent in 1940 (U.S. Bureau of the Cen-

Table 1.5
Women's Labor Force Participation Rates, 1890–1986

	Female Labor Force as Percentage of Female Population[a]			
Year	Total	Single	Married[b]	Widowed/Divorced
1890	18.9	40.5	4.6	29.9
1900	20.6	43.5	5.6	32.5
1910	25.4	51.1	10.7	34.1
1920[c]	23.7	46.4	9.0	—
1930	24.8	50.5	11.7	34.4
1940	27.4	48.1	16.7	32.0
1950	31.4	50.5	24.8	36.0
1960	34.8	44.1	31.7	37.1
1970	42.6	53.0	41.4	36.2
1980	51.1	61.5	50.7	41.0
1986	54.7	65.3	55.0	43.1

[a] Includes women 15 years and older, 1890–1930; 16 years and older, 1940–86.
[b] Includes married, spouse absent.
[c] In 1920 only, single includes widowed and divorced.

Sources: For 1890–1930, U.S. Bureau of the Census (1975:133); for 1940–86, U.S. Bureau of the Census (1986b:382).

sus, 1986b:382). As Table 1.5 documents, in 1890 only 5 percent of married women worked; by 1986, 55 percent did. Moreover, in 1986, 51 percent of those with children younger than age 3—the population least likely to work outside the home—were employed (U.S. Bureau of the Census, 1986b:383). As these statistics suggest, women increasingly remain in the labor force during their child-rearing years, bringing their age patterns of participation much closer to those of men (see also Waite, 1981:8; Reskin and Hartmann, 1986:4). As a consequence, between 1950 and 1980 the expected worklife of a 20-year-old woman almost doubled, from 14.5 to 27.2 years, compared with 36.8 years for a 20-year-old man (Reskin and Hartmann, 1986:3). These trends have radically reshaped the composition of the U.S. labor force. By 1985, women made up 44 percent of the civilian workforce, up from 29 percent in 1950 (Waite, 1981:4; U.S. Bureau of the Census, 1986b:375). By the year 2000, women's share of the workforce is predicted to reach 50 percent (U.S. Department of Labor, Women's Bureau, 1989).

| | | | Stability and Change in Occupations' Sex Composition

Despite these dramatic changes in labor force composition and in industrial and occupational structures, the extent to which women and men are segregated into different occupations has changed little between 1900 and 1970. Table 1.2 displays the persistence of occupational sex segregation at the level of *major* occupational groups. The indexes of sex segregation that Gross (1968) calculated for the Census Bureau's *detailed* occupation codes hovered between 65 and 69 percent from 1900 to 1960 (see also Jacobs, 1989a).[6] Thus, through 1960, approximately two-thirds of either all working women or all working men would have had to change to a detailed occupation the other sex dominated for the sexes to be identically distributed across detailed occupational categories.[7] The minor fluctuations between 1900 and 1970 in this barometer of segregation reflect both the changing sizes of some occupations and small shifts in the sex makeup of certain occupations. For example, measured segregation increased slightly in the 1950s because predominantly female clerical and professional occupations grew, and decreased slightly in the 1960s in part because of men's movement into predominantly female semiprofessions such as teacher, librarian, nurse, and social worker (Blau and Hendricks, 1979: 206). Not until the 1970s did the value of the segregation index change by more than a couple of points (England and McCreary, 1987; Jacobs, 1989a). The segregation index has continued to decline in the 1980s but at a slower pace than in the 1970s (Blau, 1989).

The Feminization of Occupations

Despite the striking stability in the extent of occupational sex segregation from 1900 to 1970, in a few occupations the majority sex and the occupations' sex label have shifted, usually from male to female. A review of these changes reveals some of the factors that may have precipitated change in occupational sex composition in the 1970s.

Clerical workers.   In the late nineteenth century, few clerical workers were women. In 1870, 2 percent of "bookkeepers, cashiers, and accountants" were female, as were 3 percent of "office clerks" and 4 percent of "stenographers and typists" (Davies, 1982: Table 1).[8] By 1900 these percentages had increased to 29, 7, and 77, respectively, and by 1930 to 52, 35, and 95. Currently, all are predominantly female jobs.[9] Thus today, as a century ago, clerical jobs are still performed primarily by one sex, but that sex is now female.

Why did clerical work feminize? One clue lies in the restructuring of clerical work and the increased demand for clerical labor. Prior to the Civil War, clerks resembled twentieth-century professional managers more than today's clerical workers. Employers responded to the increase in correspondence and recordkeeping that bureaucratization occasioned by instituting an elaborate hierarchical division of labor. This reorganization created specialized jobs, such as filing, shipping, and billing clerks (Rotella, 1981; Davies,

1982: 30).[10] At the same time, office work was mechanized through the introduction of new technology such as the typewriter, which permitted employers
to break down more skilled office work into simpler and more routine tasks
(Scott, 1982:172). Introduced in the 1870s and 1880s, the typewriter allowed
employers to consolidate the reorganization of labor and generate a new occupation—typist—that offered little hope for mobility to management positions. Many women who had been copyists in their homes moved to offices,
where they became typists (Srole, 1987). While the typewriter did not create a demand for female labor, it reinforced a trend toward hiring women
as less expensive labor. Gender ideology supported employers' preference for
women because it characterized women as "uniquely suited to boring, menial
tasks where qualities of leadership or independence were totally unnecessary"
(Davies, 1982:174).

As clerical work feminized, the wage advantage that clerical workers had
enjoyed over manufacturing workers declined, particularly for men (Strom,
1987:87). This loss in relative earnings, along with the restricted mobility that
became associated with clerical jobs, prompted educated, ambitious young
men to pursue better opportunities in sales, advertising, and administrative
work (Scott, 1982:172; Strom, 1987:93). As the supply of adequately educated
white, English-speaking men available for clerical jobs declined, employers
increasingly turned to white, English-speaking, middle-class women. These
newly opened clerical jobs attracted the growing numbers of middle-class
women entering the labor force. Moreover, such jobs offered gainful employment and some upward mobility for comparatively well-educated working-
class women; their earnings in clerical work were notably higher than those
they could command in other nonprofessional jobs. Further, the work was
respectable, and the working conditions were not so dirty or the work so difficult as in mills and factories (Rotella, 1981). But clerical work could be just as
temporary; as in the mills, many employers reserved clerical jobs for young,
single women by imposing age limits (Scott, 1982:172) and forcing women
to resign when they married. Their object, of course, was to reduce costs by
preventing women clerical workers from accumulating seniority.

Cohn's (1985) study of two British organizations that turned to women
to fill clerical jobs in the late nineteenth and early twentieth centuries—the
General Post Office and the Great Western Railway—sheds further light on
why clerical work feminized. He showed that feminization resulted from these
organizations' increasing reliance on clerical labor and their resulting need to
economize by seeking a cheaper workforce. Employers cut their wage bills by
hiring women and enforcing turnover through marriage bars.

Telegraph and telephone operators.   Telegraph companies, which had
traditionally recruited men, began to experiment with female labor toward
the end of the last century to reduce the cost of services; according to one

estimate, women telegraphists were paid 25 percent less than their male co-workers (Garland, 1901). Another benefit to hiring women was their perceived docility:

> In England and France the women are practically unorganised, whilst the men have followed the general tendency to form unions for the protection of their interests and the improvement of their position. . . . [The Italian Administration notes that] "the women do not generally concern themselves with political questions, and are strangers to the struggles of parties and interests. This endows them with the best qualities requisite for the telegraphic service, namely, patience, discipline and application." (Garland, 1901:252)

When telegraph companies first began offering telephone service in the last century, they employed boys, often former messengers, as operators (Hapgood, 1986:70). It was not long until the young men's unreliability and rudeness prompted telephone companies to switch to female operators. As one contemporary noted: "The work of successful telephone operating demanded just that particular dexterity, patience, and forbearance possessed by the average woman in a degree superior to that of the opposite sex" (cited in Hartmann et al., 1986:26). Female operators were unmarried and typically young. By requiring that women resign on marrying—a requirement they would hardly impose on men—employers maintained an inexperienced and hence low-waged labor force. Employers' images of these young women as easily trained and docile (in contrast to the unruly male tricksters they replaced) and their low wages (about one-third the male wage) explain their appeal (Hapgood, 1986:70).

Waiting occupations. Waiting work in the food-service industry was predominantly male until the 1920s.[11] In 1900 only four of every ten waiting workers were women; by 1970, over 90 percent of these workers were female, and waitressing was the sixth largest employer of women. In the first two decades of this century employers experimentally hired waitresses, because women allegedly showed "greater cleanliness, tact, efficiency and adaptability" (quoted in Cobble, forthcoming: chap. 1). A decline in the supply of waiters—attributable to military call-ups in World War I, strike activity, and the Immigration Act of 1924—furthered employers' resolve to recruit (especially native-born) waitresses. Also hastening feminization was the growth in the number of restaurants and coffee shops catering to the working and middle classes, which shifted the majority of jobs away from large, elegant hotel restaurants. Restaurant owners turned to women because they constituted a less expensive labor pool, and the emphasis on quick and informal service in these "new-style eateries" made women the workers of choice. According to Cobble:

The presence of a friendly, attractive female server suited owners perfectly. One waiter complained that men could no longer compete now that employers emphasized beauty, sex appeal, and a pleasing personality. Waiters "give more conscientious service," he insisted, "but it is hard to overcome the prejudice of the bosses regarding the small items wherein we constantly fall down, to-wit, lacking neatness in our appearance, forgetting how to smile, demonstrating our animosities toward one another for all to observe."

As waitressing gained social respectability, women flocked to it. Feminization continued into the 1930s and picked up speed in the post–World War II era, when fast-food outlets proliferated and rising real earnings plus the increase in two-earner families made eating out more popular. However, despite feminization, old patterns of occupational sex segregation persist today. Men predominate at higher-prestige restaurants, and women at coffee shops and cafeterias where both the paychecks and the tips are lower. Even when they do work in the same establishments as men, women tend to draw the less lucrative shifts.

Public school teachers.   From colonial times most public school teachers were men, but by 1870, 60 percent were women, and in 1920 women's representation peaked at 86 percent (Tyack and Strober, 1981:33; see also Strober and Best, 1979; Rotella and Margo, 1981). Public schools opened their doors to women teachers in response to a demand for literate labor that was less costly than educated men (Tyack and Strober, 1981:137). Increasing urbanization and changes in the organization of teaching eroded the occupation's attractiveness to men. Tyack and Strober (1981:140) noted that

> as the school term lengthened and professional requirements increased in Nebraska, the percentage of male teachers dropped from a majority in 1870 to only about 12% in 1910. By 1920 there were only eight states where the percentage of male teachers was more than 20% and only one had more than 30%; these were predominantly rural states where the terms were relatively short and where bureaucratic controls were scanty.

Thus, as the school year lengthened and training costs increased without compensating salary boosts, better-paying jobs attracted men, whereas educated, middle-class women—who had few opportunities for respectable, white-collar work—were drawn to teaching, where the shortage of male teachers created jobs for them.

Bank tellers.   As recently as 1935, few bank tellers were women. As Strober and Arnold (1987a) noted, this "foolish prejudice" against women vanished during the war years, when military call-ups brought a shortage of personnel. The banking community had drawn on women to staff clerical and lower-level managerial jobs during a shortage of labor in 1917. However, when the Depression created a pool of unemployed men qualified to work as bank tellers, employers stopped hiring women (Kessler-Harris, 1986:770). Nevertheless, by 1950 women constituted 45 percent and, by 1980, 91 percent of all bank tellers. According to Strober and Arnold (1987a), this reversal occurred because men migrated to more profitable work as the promotion possibilities of bank telling declined and banks' clientele was "declassed" once banks began serving a wider public during World War II. As a consequence, employers turned to women, who were attractive in their own right as a cheaper labor supply.

The Masculinization of Occupations

The occupations of clerical worker, teacher, waiter, bank teller, and others feminized because opportunities for mobility, earnings, and job autonomy declined, and native-born white men sought better opportunities elsewhere. Men voted their preferences with their feet, relocating to new occupations that offered better prospects. Their female counterparts entered these vacated jobs in large measure because they were now open to them and because they provided superior rewards compared with traditionally female jobs.

Given this common pattern underlying a shift in sex composition, one might wonder what prompts typically female occupations to masculinize. In fact, they have done so rarely. When men did replace women in an occupation, the shift was often from a native-born female to a foreign-born male workforce. As Irish immigration grew in the mid-1800s, for example, Irish men replaced native white women in U.S. textile mills when the latter were drawn to teaching and the other middle-class jobs that native-born white men were vacating (Hartmann, 1976:161). A second example, cigarmaking, illustrates an occupation's shift from female to male and back again (Hartmann, 1976:162; Kessler-Harris, 1982:266). Before 1800, U.S. farm women made cigars in their homes. After employers shifted the work to factories and competition from European cigarmakers grew, skilled men supplanted women. As in the textile mills, the new male workers were immigrants, and by 1860 only 9 percent of cigarmakers were women. However, the development of the wooden mold in the late nineteenth century offered employers the capability of cutting the workforce by 80 percent. For the few skilled jobs remaining, employers turned to experienced Bohemian women who had immigrated from Austria-Hungary—over the vociferous objections of the Cigarmakers International Union, which fought to retain the outmoded technology. The CIU's efforts were futile: by 1930 nearly 60 percent of cigarmakers were women, and 50 percent of the cigars were machine made (Kessler-Harris, 1982:266).

Occasionally, native-born men have made inroads into female-labeled occupations, especially the female semiprofessions. During the Depression and again in the 1960s, men displaced some women from positions in social work, nursing, and librarianship (Blau and Hendricks, 1979; Kessler-Harris, 1982:260), although at both times women remained numerically dominant. Such was not the case for healers and midwives, female jobs that men had appropriated, albeit under different occupational titles, by the early twentieth century (Walsh, 1977; Kessler-Harris, 1982). As Ehrenreich and English (1979: chaps. 2–3) showed, in colonial and especially rural America women provided most healing services. Using herbal remedies and lore handed down over generations, female lay healers and midwives often served as their communities' only medical practitioners. Throughout the nineteenth and early twentieth centuries, the emerging male medical establishment drove their often more experienced female competitors out of business. Professional and scientific transformations ensured that male physicians, schooled in "regular" (that is, allegedly scientific) medical schools and supported by the American Medical Association, secured a monopoly on the practice of medicine in the United States (Walsh, 1977; Morantz-Sanchez, 1987).

I I I I A Decade of Change

Notwithstanding the preceding examples, only during the 1970s did the *aggregate* level of occupational sex segregation decline by a nontrivial amount. For example, the index of segregation computed for 262 detailed occupations fell from 68.3 to 61.7 between 1972 and 1981, suggesting a rate of decline three times greater than that for the 1960s (Beller, 1984:24). The bulk of the decline occurred not because the number of workers employed in highly segregated occupations decreased but because women integrated occupations that men had dominated in 1970 (Jacobs, 1983; Beller, 1984:24; Bianchi and Rytina, 1984). Which occupations opened their doors to women in the 1970s, prompting this aggregate decline in the index of segregation? And were there any female occupations that men entered in disproportionate numbers? Table 1.6 answers these questions by listing the Census Bureau's three-digit 1980 occupational titles in which women's representation showed a disproportionate increase or decline between 1970 and 1980 (U.S. Bureau of the Census, 1984a).[12] Although our focus is on the 1970s, we also include Bureau of Labor Statistics data for 1988 to determine whether the changes continued into the 1980s.[13] For purposes of comparison, Table 1.7 lists some traditionally male occupations in which women made only limited inroads during the 1970s and 1980s.

Determining what constitutes "disproportionate" change requires an arbitrary decision. Because our interest centers on explaining why women made particularly large inroads into some male occupations and little or no headway in others, we used the criterion of a 9-percentage-point change

Table 1.6
Percent Female in Sex-Segregated Occupations, 1970–1988

Occupation Title[a]	1970	1980	1988	Change in Percent Female	
				1970–80	1980–88
Labor force as a whole	38.0	42.6	45.0	4.6	2.4

Occupations in which women's representation increased disproportionately 1970–80

Executive, administrative, and managerial

	1970	1980	1988	1970–80	1980–88
Administrators & officials, public administration	21.7	33.6	44.5	11.9	10.9
Financial managers	19.4	31.4	42.4	12.0	11.0
Managers: marketing, advertising, public relations	7.9	17.6	32.0	9.7	14.4
Administrators: education and related fields	27.8	38.1	48.9	10.3	10.8
Accountants and auditors	24.6	38.1	49.6	13.5	11.5
Personnel, training, and labor relations specialists	33.4	47.0	58.9	13.6	11.9
Buyers: wholesale and retail trade, except farm products	27.8	44.5	50.4	16.7	5.9
Inspectors & compliance officers, except construction	7.1	17.8	26.8	10.7	9.0

Professional specialty

	1970	1980	1988	1970–80	1980–88
Operations and systems researchers and analysts	11.1	27.7	39.6	16.6	11.9
Pharmacists	12.1	24.0	31.9	11.9	7.9
Designers	36.2	49.9	53.3	13.7	3.4
Public relations specialists	26.6	48.8	59.1	22.2	10.3

Sales

	1970	1980	1988	1970–80	1980–88
Supervisors & proprietors, sales occupations, salaried	13.7	28.2	33.5[b]	14.5	5.3
Insurance sales occupations	12.9	25.4	29.7	12.5	4.3
Real estate sales occupations	31.2	45.2	48.5	14.0	3.3
Securities and financial services sales occupations	9.2	18.6	27.5	9.4	8.9
Advertising and related sales occupations	20.5	41.6	47.8	21.1	6.2
Sales workers, hardware and building supplies	15.4	25.0	21.4	9.6	−3.6
News vendors	17.1	33.3	37.4	16.2	4.1

Administrative support occupations, including clerical

	1970	1980	1988	1970–80	1980–88
Computer operators	33.9	59.1	66.0	25.2	6.9
Dispatchers	14.6	31.5	45.9	16.9	14.4
Production coordinators	20.2	44.4	46.6	24.2	2.2

(*continued*)

Table 1.6 (continued)

Occupation Title[a]	1970	1980	1988	Change in Percent Female 1970–80	Change in Percent Female 1980–88
Traffic, shipping, and receiving clerks	13.4	23.6	27.5	10.2	3.9
Stock and inventory clerks	24.3	34.7	38.7	10.4	4.0
Expediters	35.4	54.1	62.8	18.7	8.7
Insurance adjusters, examiners, & investigators	29.6	60.2	72.2	30.6	12.0
Protective service					
Guards and police, except public service	4.0	13.5	13.5	9.5	0.0
Service occupations, except protective and household					
Bartenders	21.2	44.3	49.6	23.1	5.3
Waiters'/waitresses' assistants	32.1	41.6	39.9	9.5	−1.7
Janitors and cleaners	13.1	23.4	31.2	10.3	7.8
Precision production, craft, and repair					
Bakers	25.4	40.7	47.8	15.3	7.1
Machine operators, assemblers, & inspectors					
Typesetters and compositors	16.8	55.7	73.9	38.9	18.2
Transportation and material moving					
Bus drivers	28.3	45.8	48.5	17.5	2.7

Occupations in which men's representation increased disproportionately 1970–80

	1970	1980	1988	1970–80	1980–88
Service occupations, except protective and household					
Cooks, except short order	67.2	57.2	49.8	−10.0	−7.4
Kitchen workers, food preparation	91.8	78.2	73.3	−13.6	−4.9
Maids and housemen	94.3	75.8	85.0	−18.5	9.2

[a] Titles (from 1980 occupational code, U.S. Bureau of the Census, 1982b) include only those occupations in which the other sex's representation increased disproportionately between 1970 and 1980. A disproportionate increase or decrease is defined as at least twice that shown in the labor force as a whole. All 1970 estimates are based on at least 100 persons (see text).
b Supervisors and proprietors, sales occupations.

Sources: For 1970 and 1980, U.S. Bureau of the Census (1984a); for 1988, U.S. Bureau of Labor Statistics (1989).

Table 1.7

Selected Male-Dominated Occupations in Which Women Posted Disproportionately Little Progress, 1970–1988

Occupation Title	Percent Female			Change in Percent Female	
	1970	1980	1988	1970–80	1980–88
Labor force as a whole	38.0	42.6	45.0	4.6	2.4
Executive, administrative, and managerial					
Funeral directors	7.1	8.7	—	1.6	—
Professional specialty					
Electrical and electronic engineers	1.7	5.0	7.9	3.3	2.9
Mechanical engineers	1.0	2.1	3.7	1.1	1.6
Physicians	9.7	13.4	20.0	3.7	6.6
Dentists	3.5	6.7	9.3	3.2	2.6
Clergy	2.9	5.8	8.8	2.9	3.0
Sales					
Sales engineers	.7	3.2	—	2.5	—
Sales workers, parts	4.4	8.4	9.0	4.0	.6
Protective service					
Firefighting occupations	1.5	1.1	2.1	−.4	1.0
Police and detectives, public service	3.7	6.0	10.1	2.3	4.1
Farming, forestry, and fishing					
Timber cutting and logging occupations	3.3	2.5	.5	−.8	−2.0
Precision production, craft, and repair					
Automobile mechanics	1.4	1.3	.7	−.1	−.6
Heavy equipment mechanics	1.2	.8	.5	−.4	−.3
Carpenters	1.1	1.6	1.5	.5	−.1
Electricians	2.1	2.1	1.4	.0	−.7
Painters, construction and maintenance	3.1	5.8	5.8	2.7	0.0
Machinists	3.0	4.9	4.8	1.9	−.1
Butchers and meat cutters	11.4	14.6	21.2	3.2	6.6
Machine operators, assemblers, & inspectors					
Lathe and turning machine operators	11.8	8.8	5.8	−3.0	−3.0
Welders and cutters	6.2	5.9	4.9	−.3	−1.0
Transportation and material moving					
Truck drivers, heavy	1.5	2.3	2.3	.8	0.0
Railroad brake, signal, and switch operators	1.5	1.4	—	−.1	—
Handlers, equipment cleaners, helpers, and laborers					
Construction laborers	1.9	3.2	3.4	1.3	.2
Garbage collectors	1.6	3.0	—	1.4	—

Note: This table is illustrative, not comprehensive. Titles (from 1980 occupational code, U.S. Bureau of the Census, 1982b) are selected throughout the occupational spectrum where women's representation changed by 4 percentage points or fewer between 1970 and 1980. All 1970 estimates are based on at least 100 persons (see text).

Sources: For 1970 and 1980, U.S. Bureau of the Census (1984a); for 1988, U.S. Bureau of Labor Statistics (1989).

in women's representation between 1970 and 1980—roughly twice women's increase in the entire labor force during this period.

Specifying exactly how much women's representation changed during the 1970s is problematic because the Census Bureau radically altered its occupational classification scheme for the 1980 census to conform to the Standard Occupational Classification (SOC; U.S. Department of Commerce, 1980). It even moved some detailed occupations across major categories. Fortunately, the bureau has estimated the percentage of females for 1970, using the 1980 occupational codes (U.S. Bureau of the Census, 1984a); to do so, it recoded the occupations of a sample of 127,125 persons from the 1970 census according to the 1980 classification scheme (see Bianchi and Rytina, 1984; U.S. Bureau of the Census, 1989:ix). The reliability of these estimates, however, is dubious for occupations that few members of the 1970 sample pursued. Thus, the recoded data show some occupations as having had few or no incumbents or few or no female incumbents in 1970 (such as female legislators and physician's assistants) because no one in the recoded sample of 127,125 persons held these occupations. In fact, of course, had the occupations of the entire 1970 workforce been recoded, the results would have included some women in these occupations. To avoid erroneous estimates of changing percentage of females in small occupations because of sampling error in the recoded sample, we dropped 73 occupations whose estimate of percentage female in 1970 was based on fewer than 100 persons.[14]

In addition to excluding occupations vulnerable to sampling error, we also deleted 24 occupations whose titles were too vague for us to ascertain what kind of work was involved or that encompassed widely varied jobs (such as titles including "other," "not elsewhere classified," and "miscellaneous"). In most of the 397 occupational titles that remained,[15] women's representation changed only slightly. Thus, occupational sex-typing remained robust, even in a decade in which women reportedly posted revolutionary gains. In only 33 occupations did female representation increase disproportionately between 1970 and 1980; in three occupations the percent female decreased disproportionately (see Table 1.6).

The predominantly male occupations that became more accessible to women ran the gamut. Among managers, women chalked up impressive gains as wholesale and retail buyers; personnel, training, and labor relations specialists; and accountants and auditors. Among professional occupations, women's gains were strongest in public relations and in operations and systems analysis. Women also made inroads into customarily male sales, clerical, and service occupations (for example, advertisers, computer operators, insurance adjusters, bartenders). Their gains were modest at best in traditionally male blue-collar work. Within skilled and semiskilled occupations, women posted disproportionate gains only among guards, bakers, typesetters and compositors, and bus drivers. Women made almost no headway into many well-known craft occupations such as mechanics, carpenters, electricians, painters, machinists, and butchers (see Tables 1.6 and 1.7). Most of the occupations that feminized in the 1970s became even more female in the 1980s. Of the 33 occupations that feminized disproportionately in the 1970s, women's representation in 22 increased twice as rapidly during the 1980s as their representation in the whole labor force. Only in the categories of hardware and building supplies sales workers and waiter's/waitress's assistants did women lose ground after gaining disproportionately in the 1970s.

Men's representation *increased* by more than 9 percentage points in only three predominantly female occupations in the 1970s: cooks (except short order); food-preparation kitchen workers; and maids and housemen. In each of these service occupations, however, women remained the majority. In the 1980s men continued to become cooks and kitchen workers in disproportionate numbers; among cooks, men even became a slight majority. Among maids and housemen, however, the 1970s trend reversed itself, with women disproportionately increasing their share of jobs.

| | | | **Research Design**

The wide variation in the extent of change in sex composition across occupations during the 1970s affords us the opportunity to determine the conditions that foster such change, the forms it takes, and its consequences for women who move into customarily male occupations. How might we investigate these issues? Relatively little is known about the factors associated with the changing sex composition of occupations, precisely because the extent of occupational sex segregation has varied so little until recently (Blau and Hendricks, 1979; Reskin and Hartmann, 1986). Those who have studied changing sex composition have approached it either through case studies of specific occupations or through statistical analyses. Above we reviewed several excellent case studies of occupations whose sex composition has changed. In the best example of the statistical approach, Treiman and Terrell (1975) identified several factors that were implicated in changes in occupations' sex composition between 1940 and 1960. They found evidence, for example, that the proportions of women at the beginning and the end of the 1950s were positively correlated. Each sex's representation grew in occupations that it already dominated and declined in occupations that the other sex monopolized. In addition, they found that the proportion of females in an occupation in 1960 was negatively related to wage levels of both male and female incumbents.

Both the case study and the statistical approaches offer useful models for explaining changes in occupations' sex composition, and we decided to employ both in our research design to answer the questions posed above. This volume presents the results of the case studies. Most of these in-depth and labor-intensive occupational portraits, conducted by ourselves and our graduate students, took two to three years to complete. Because we studied only traditionally male or mixed-sex occupations in which women made marked progress, the case study results may not hold for occupations in which women posted more modest gains. In a forthcoming monograph reporting the results of statistical analyses we assess the generalizability of the case study results. The statistical analyses in that monograph examine the effects of a variety of occupational characteristics (working conditions, occupational requirements, unionization, education, unemployment, part-time work, earnings or income) on changing occupational sex composition during the 1970s, enabling us to identify the determinants of changing sex composition of all 503 detailed occupations listed in the census.

For our case studies we chose occupations from among the 33 three-digit 1980 occupational titles in which women's representation showed a disproportionate increase between 1970 and 1980 (see Table 1.6). Because different processes might operate at different levels of the occupational structure, we selected from all strata of the occupational hierarchy: professional, managerial, sales, clerical, service, and blue-collar occupations. To achieve enough homogeneity to permit the identification of meaningful occupational clusters, we chose to study only those occupations that comprise a small number of readily identifiable suboccupations. Sometimes we selected a single occupation within these detailed occupational categories (for example, book editors from "editors and reporters"; insurance adjusters and examiners from "insurance adjusters, examiners, and investigators"). We and the six members of our research team completed intensive case studies of eleven occupations: book editors (by Barbara F. Reskin);[16] pharmacists (by Polly A. Phipps); public relations specialists (by Katharine M. Donato); bank managers (by Chloe E. Bird);[17] systems analysts (by Katharine M. Donato);[18] insurance sales occupations (by Barbara J. Thomas); real estate salespersons (by Barbara J. Thomas and Barbara F. Reskin); insurance adjusters and examiners (by Polly A. Phipps); bartenders (by Linda A. Detman); bakers (by Thomas Steiger and Barbara F. Reskin); and typesetters and compositors (by Patricia A. Roos). These appear as Chapters 4 to 14 of this book. Barbara Reskin did partial case studies of three additional occupations: accountants and auditors, broadcast and print reporters, and bus drivers.

To ensure consistency across fourteen case studies conducted by eight persons at three different universities, we used a set of preestablished guidelines (see the Appendix). Our first order of business was to discover the occupation's duties and the settings in which workers were employed. Government documents such as the *Occupational Outlook Handbook*, the *Dictionary of Occupational Titles*, *Occupation by Industry*, and the *Selected Characteristics of Occupations Defined in the Dictionary of Occupational Titles* were invaluable in our development of these occupational profiles.

Five sets of questions guided our efforts to discover the determinants of changing occupational sex composition. First, did the nature of the occupation change, and if so, how? Our purpose here was to place the 1970s changes in a historical context. How did workers' duties change? Did the skill level change, perhaps as a result of technological change? Did the organization of work, working conditions, work setting, or industrial distribution change? Did the occupation add or lose jobs, and if so, why? Second, did the training required for the occupation expand, contract, or become more accessible to women? What happened to educational requirements? How did the numbers of women and men in training for the occupation change? Did workers come to be trained in different ways? Were licensing or certification requirements altered? Third, more broadly, did the labor market change so that persons entered the occupation in different ways, or were entry barriers lifted? Did the occupation undergo changes in the level of unionization or the strength of unions or professional associations? Did such groups change their attitudes toward women? Did regulatory agencies, the courts, or women's groups intervene in employers' hiring practices? Were sex-discrimination charges filed against industry leaders? Fourth, how did the characteristics of occupational incumbents change over the decade? Were workers younger by 1980? More or less educated? More likely to work part time? How did the men and women who entered the occupation differ from each other and from earlier entrants? Finally, how and why did occupational rewards (earnings, prestige, promotion chances, autonomy) change from 1970 to 1980?

We also asked whether women's standing in the occupation changed. By 1980 were women internally stratified within the occupation (that is, concentrated in different specialties or industries) or distributed throughout? Did women's duties differ from those of men or from those of women incumbents in 1970? Did women maintain or improve their economic position relative to their male counterparts? To help answer this last question, where 1970 and 1980 occupational codes were comparable, we compared sex wage ratios across the decade.

To answer all these questions, we examined a wide variety of sources, including published reports, scholarly analyses, government documents (including Bureau of Labor Statistics Industry Wage Surveys, the Census of Manufacturing), trade and professional journals, union publications, census microdata, and court records (see the Appendix). For example, for the relevant case studies we reviewed several decades of trade journals: *Publishers Weekly, American Printer, Bakers Digest, Public Relations Journal, American Druggist, National Underwriter, Insurance Almanac, Datamation, Banking,* and others.

For some case studies, the investigator visited workplaces to view the work process. For example, Steiger and Reskin visited bakeries in the Midwest and California; similarly, Detman observed bartenders at work, and Roos visited several locations where typesetters or their employers work (large and small newspapers, a book publishing house, employer organizations, and their homes).

To supplement the documents and data, we interviewed by phone or in person a cross section of people involved in the occupation—practitioners, gatekeepers, and industry experts. Our interview schedules for incumbents included questions on training and qualifications, the nature of the workplace, the interviewees' experience in the field, and their views about changes in the occupation and women's role in it. We asked selected respondents to comment on early drafts of the case studies and often incorporated their reactions.

Most of the case study chapters begin with a statistical picture of women's representational gains in the occupation under consideration. They then describe the tasks and working conditions the occupation involves, the industries in which it is located, and how its labor market operates. Some paint a cultural history of the occupation to give a sense of how and when it became labeled "men's work" and of how some occupations are being relabeled "women's work." By examining changes in these factors over the last few decades, the case studies account for women's growing occupational representation. By paying special attention to sex segregation *within* the occupation and to whether and how factors precipitating feminization differed across occupational subspecialties or work settings, we can account for women's increased job share in some but not other specialties or settings within an occupation. Doing so is essential, because to explain women's *varying* progress across occupations, we must look at occupations in which women's representation increased little if at all, as well as those in which it grew.

We abandoned our original plan to select matches for each of the feminizing occupations we studied, because the case studies took much longer than we had expected and because we had difficulty finding adequate matches. Fortunately, the occupations provided *internal* matching across specialties or work settings, precluding the need for control occupations. As Chapter 3 shows, women's numerical gains in most of the occupations we studied were largely confined to a few specialties or work settings. For example, women pharmacists were concentrated in retail drugstores and hospitals, women typesetters and compositors in newspaper publishing, women realtors in residential sales, and women bakers in supermarket bakeries. This variation in degree of feminization across different specialties within the same occupation permitted us to identify explanatory factors that also varied within occupations. For example, we could link changing sex composition to growth, change in work, or declining income by comparing specialties within the same occupation: residential versus commercial real estate sales, newspaper versus commercial typesetting, manufacturing bakeries versus in-store bakeries, book editing versus newspaper editing.

I I I I The Organization of This Book

The volume is divided into three parts. Part I (Chapters 1 through 3) introduces the study, addresses the broad questions it raises, and synthesizes the case study findings. Chapter 2 answers our first question—what explains the marked desegregation of a handful of customarily male or mixed-sex occupations—and uses a queueing model to show how changes in structural characteristics of the job and labor queues that constitute labor markets led occupations' sex makeup to change.

Chapter 3 addresses the form and consequences of the statistical desegregation of our case study occupations. It first shows that women's entry into feminizing occupations has brought little if any genuine integration. Instead, women's numerical gains in feminizing occupations mask their ghettoization in lower-paying, less prestigious occupational subspecialties or represent the resegregation of male occupations or occupational specialties as female work. The chapter then investigates whether women's representational gains have brought them closer to economic equity with men in the same occupation by probing the consequences of women's increased share of jobs. Here, the results are mixed: while feminization has yielded women higher salaries than they can command in traditionally female occupations, it has done little to alleviate the male–female earnings gap within occupations.

Part II (Chapters 4 through 14) presents the case studies. Separately, each one tells an interesting story of occupational feminization. Taken as a group, they constitute the data on which Part I rests.

Finally, Part III (Chapter 15) outlines our analyses' theoretical implications for sex inequality. It formalizes queueing theory as a structural approach to understanding changing occupational composition and points to the role of group power in maintaining or undermining occupational segregation. It also shows why occupational resegregation is an almost inevitable outcome of substantial occupational desegregation. It closes by discussing the prospects for future occupational desegregation and identifying policies that can facilitate genuine integration and thereby foster greater equity between women and men.

I I I I Notes

1. Black women have been more successful in getting professional jobs than black men for the same reason that white women are overrepresented in professional occupations—their preponderance in the lower-paid female semiprofessions.

2. The index of segregation is defined as:

$$\text{I.S.} = (\Sigma |x_i - y_i|) / 2$$

where x_i equals the percentage of one group (e.g., women) in the ith category of a classification, and y_i equals the percentage of the other group (e.g., men) in the same category (Duncan and Duncan, 1955). This index measures the degree of difference in the distributions of the two groups (here, women and men) across a set of categories (here, occupations). The index denotes the minimum proportion of members of one group who would have to change occupations for the two groups' distributions to be identical.

3. At the *detailed* occupation level (see n. 6 below), in 1980 approximately 60 percent of women would have had to change occupations to have a distribution identical to that of men (Jacobs, 1989a:29).

4. Sokoloff (1989) found that the professional and technical labor force grew by more than 8 million between 1960 and 1980.

5. Folbre and Abel (1988) argued that census enumerations of women's employment at the turn of the century substantially underestimated the amount of market work women actually performed. Particular areas of undercount included taking in boarders, engaging in farm labor, assisting in family-owned businesses, and performing industrial work at home. The authors' estimates, based on census and other survey data, were at least twice the published census levels.

6. "Detailed" occupations refer to those measured by the census three-digit occupational codes. For example, the major occupational categories (on which the indexes in Table 1.2 are based) include Professional Specialty Occupations and Sales Occupations; examples of detailed occupations within these categories are law and real estate sales occupations, respectively. In 1980 the U.S. Bureau of the Census used 503 three-digit codes to denote detailed occupations. The more refined the level of classification, the higher the index of segregation. However, even an index based on a three-digit occupational classification underestimates the amount of sex segregation, because detailed occupational categories aggregate smaller groupings called "jobs." This term refers to particular tasks performed by one or more people in a specific work setting such as a firm or an industry (Reskin and Hartmann, 1986:9). Bielby and Baron (1984:35) found that job-level sex segregation substantially exceeds that at the occupational level: over one-half of the 393 firms they studied were completely sex segregated by job title. For the 162 firms with some integrated job titles, the average index of segregation was 84.1.

7. We do not necessarily see identical distributions for men and women as a social ideal. Rather, identical distributions provide a benchmark against which to measure how extensively the sexes are segregated in different lines of work.

8. The first commercial typewriters were not in wide use until the 1880s (Davies, 1982), so the 1870 percentage refers almost entirely to stenographers.

9. The 1980 estimates of percent female for these occupations are not exactly comparable to those for 1930 because the census classification systems differ. We can, however, get some idea of women's predominance in modern-day clerical occupations. In 1980 women constituted 91 percent of stenographers; 97 percent of typists; 90 percent of bookkeepers, accounting, and auditing clerks; 82 percent of general office clerks; and 84 percent of cashiers (U.S. Bureau of the Census, 1984a: Table 1).

10. Edwards (1979) argued that the employers' object in establishing elaborate divisions of labor and intricate rules and procedures was also to control their workforce.

11. This section relies heavily on Cobble (forthcoming: chap. 1).

12. We employ the 1980 occupational classification system to ensure comparability across the decade, following the lead of researchers who have taken steps to maximize the comparability of 1970 and 1980 census data.

13. Given our focus on sex-segregated occupations, we restricted Table 1.6 to occupations that one sex had dominated in 1970 (i.e., those more than 60 percent male or female). Women's representation also increased disproportionately between 1970 and 1980 in nine occupations that had been between 40 and 60 percent female: educational and vocational counselors; shoes sales workers; transportation ticket and reservation agents; records clerks; payroll and timekeeping clerks; investigators and adjusters, except insurance; statistical clerks; food counter, fountain, and related occupations; and packaging- and filling-machine operators.

14. Better estimates of the 1970–80 extent of change in sex composition for all detailed occupations await further work. We are analyzing data from a 2-percent sample of the 1970 census microdata with 1980 occupational and industry codes. Treiman and Rubin (1983) developed multiple-imputation procedures for use with data sets whose classifications have changed over time; these will enable us to estimate occupational characteristics for the 1970 U.S. population using the 1980 census codes. Treiman et al. (1988) describe the analogous procedure for industry. We thank Donald Treiman for providing us access to these data.

15. We subtracted from the 503 occupational titles in the 1980 classification 24 vague titles, 9 mixed-sex titles, and 73 titles with possible unreliability in the 1970 estimates of percent female.

16. The census occupational title "editor and reporter" (census code 195) includes book editors, newspaper and magazine editors and reporters, broadcast editors and reporters, and editors employed for various profit and nonprofit enterprises. In the census category as a whole, women's representation increased by 7.7 percentage points (and hence is omitted from Table 1.6). However, women's gains vary markedly across these jobs. We selected book editors for intensive study because women made substantial gains in this sector (see Chapter 4).

17. This is the major job within the census occupation "financial managers" (census code 007).

18. The 1980 census classification codes systems analysts in two occupational categories: "computer systems analysts and scientists" (census code 064) and "operations and systems researchers and analysts" (065), depending on whether they work in computer systems and data processing or other information systems, respectively (U.S. Bureau of the Census, 1982b). In the former occupation women's representation increased 8.9 percentage points; in the latter it climbed by 16.6 percentage points. Donato's case study addresses both types of systems analysts.

2

Queueing
and Changing
Occupational
Composition

What led to the feminization of the customarily male occupations our research team studied? In answering that question, this chapter develops a theoretical model of occupational feminization. We begin our task by outlining a model of occupational composition that accounts for the uneven distribution of groups across occupations and hence, specifically, how occupations' sex compositions change. The most fruitful model sees occupational composition as the result of a *dual-queueing* process: *labor queues* order groups of workers in terms of their attractiveness to employers, and *job queues* rank jobs in terms of their attractiveness to workers.[1] Identifying how and why employers order workers within labor queues and workers rank occupations within job queues—and how these factors have changed since 1970—tells part of the story of why some customarily male and mixed-sex occupations have feminized. How the "shapes" of the two queues have changed to provide some groups with jobs that were formerly beyond their reach completes the story.

The queueing perspective is a powerful lens that makes sense of seemingly disparate results from our case studies. It encompasses a wide range of phenomena, elucidates puzzling findings, and predicts future patterns. Because we rely heavily on the queueing perspective in this chapter and the next, we begin by examining queueing processes.

| | | | Labor Markets as Queues

Lester Thurow (1969:48; see also Thurow, 1972, 1975) was the first social scientist to characterize the labor market explicitly as a labor queue. Blacks, Thurow hypothesized, experienced more unemployment than whites because employers ranked them below whites in the labor queue. In recognizing that the labor market functions as if it comprised ordered elements, Thurow formalized what others had already remarked. As early as 1929, a Women's Bureau bulletin (U.S. Department of Labor, Women's Bureau, 1929:13; cited in Strober and Catanzarite, 1988:10) stated:

> The history of . . . women workers in New England textile mills . . . show[s] a picture typical of such occupational changes. . . . The moving of the New England girls of the old stock out of the mills into higher-grade occupations, and the filling of the vacant posts by Irish women, had become common enough in the latter half of the [eighteen] forties.

In examining race differences in labor market outcomes, Thurow and his successors (Doeringer and Piore, 1971; Hodge, 1973; Lieberson, 1980) focused on the *labor* queue. Yet implicit in the New England girls' move from the mills into higher-grade occupations is a second queue—a *job* queue that represents workers' rankings of jobs.[2] Rotella (1981) and Strober (1984:150) and her colleagues (Strober and Arnold, 1987a:117; Catanzarite and Strober, 1988) recognized the importance of job queues, although they did not designate them as such. Rotella explained the feminization of clerical work partly in terms of the attractiveness of clerical jobs relative to women's alternatives, and Strober and her colleagues posited more generally that society grants men first choice of jobs and that men select the most attractive ones available. Job queues and labor queues govern labor market outcomes: employers hire workers from as high in the labor queue as possible,[3] and workers accept the best jobs available to them.[4] As a result the best jobs go to the most preferred workers, and less attractive jobs go to workers lower in the labor queue; bottom-ranked workers may go jobless, and the worst jobs may be left unfilled (Thurow, 1972:73).[5]

Historical accounts (reviewed in Chapter 1) and studies (reviewed later in this chapter) of upwardly mobile groups bequeathing abandoned jobs to groups ranked below them illustrate the role of queueing in occupational succession. Also supporting queueing theory's applicability to labor market outcomes are statistical analyses of race differences in occupational distributions and unemployment (Thurow, 1969:53–57; Hodge, 1973; Snyder and Hudis, 1976; Lieberson, 1980:300; Lyson, 1985; Olzak et al., 1988; Jacobs and Labov, 1989). Thus, the research literature is consistent with the concept of labor and job queues jointly generating the uneven distribution of groups across occupations—in other words, occupational segregation.

The Structural Properties of Queues

Queues can be characterized by three structural properties: the *ordering of their elements* (that is, jobs, groups of workers), their *shape* (the relative sizes of various elements—population subgroups in the labor queue and occupations in the job queues), and the *intensity of rankers' preferences* (whether or not elements overlap). We argue below that changes in these properties redistribute groups across occupations.

By definition, queues are composed of ordered elements (occupations, jobs; subgroups of workers), and their ordering dictates which groups end up in which jobs. As Lieberson (1980:296) put it, if employers tend to favor group X, then the Xs will be concentrated in the best jobs and the non-Xs largely relegated to the least desirable ones.

The absolute and relative numbers of elements in a queue determine its shape. Thus, the number of prospective workers in each subgroup in a labor market sets the shape of the labor queue. Similarly, the number of jobs at each level in the job queue fixes its shape. Panels A and B of Figure 2.1 show how the shapes of labor and job queues can vary while their order remains constant. This variation influences each group's probable access to occupations of varying desirability and each occupation's chance of recruiting workers from particular groups. For example, in a society with relatively few workers in the preferred group (A2) and few very desirable jobs (for illustrative purposes, we consider nonmanual jobs preferable to manual jobs; see B2), preferred groups will monopolize the generally preferable jobs. A mismatch in the relative numbers of jobs and workers at corresponding levels of their respective queues means that some workers will get better or worse jobs than persons from their group normally garner. For example, when preferred jobs sharply outnumber highly ranked workers, as in a situation characterized by panels A2 and B1, employers must fill some better jobs with workers from lower in the labor queue than usual. In contrast, when the job queue is bottom-heavy (as in B2), only the highest-ranked workers get desirable jobs, and workers moderately high in the labor queue must settle for less. As Lieberson (1980: 297) has shown, both the *absolute* and *relative* size of each group in the labor queue affects lower-ranked workers' chances of getting desirable jobs. The larger a subordinate group relative to the size of the preferred group, the harder employers find it to deny its members good jobs (Hodge, 1973).

The intensity of raters' preferences is the third property of queues. For some employers, group membership is the paramount consideration in ordering the labor queue. When group membership is overriding, rankers invariably favor persons from the group they prefer, regardless of their qualifications; for example, some employers never hire blacks to supervise whites. Yet others are almost indifferent to group membership, using it only to break ties between otherwise equally qualified prospects. Figure 2.2 illustrates variation

Panel A. Hypothetical labor queues ordered by race for predominantly white and predominantly black labor markets.

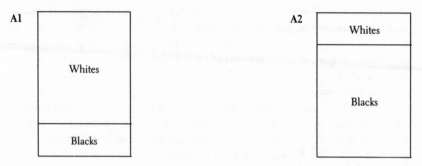

Panel B. Hypothetical job queues ordered by nonmanual–manual work for predominantly nonmanual and predominantly manual occupational structures.

Figure 2.1
Variation in the shape of labor and job queues

in the intensity of raters' preferences with respect to workers' race in three hypothetical labor queues. The space between the races in panel A depicts the ranking for employers who invariably hire the lowest-ranked white worker over the best black worker; the preferences for moderately qualified blacks over whites with low qualifications and for highly qualified blacks over whites with only moderate qualifications in panel B mean that raters' aversion to blacks, though weak, persists. Panel C illustrates an intermediate situation in which employers prefer average white workers over above-average blacks but suppress racial biases to hire very talented blacks over mediocre whites.

Of course, workers' job preferences also vary in intensity. Some workers may have a categorical preference for any job in a high-ranked occupation over any work in what they perceive as a lower occupation (expressed, for example, in rejecting all manual jobs in favor of any nonmanual work). Others

Panel A. Racial group membership is an overriding consideration to rankers. Employers hire applicants as qualified as possible but choose unqualified whites before highly qualified blacks.

Blacks	Blacks	Blacks	Whites	Whites	Whites
Low	Moderate	High	Low	Moderate	High

Level of Qualification

Panel B. Racial group membership is a minor consideration to rankers. Employers hire the most qualified applicants but, within levels of qualification, give white applicants an edge over equally qualified blacks.

Blacks	Whites	Blacks	Whites	Blacks	Whites
Low	Low	Moderate	Moderate	High	High

Level of Qualification

Panel C. Racial group membership is an intermediate consideration to rankers. Employers prefer a more qualified white to a less qualified black but will hire very qualified blacks over unqualified whites.

Blacks	Blacks	Whites	Blacks	Whites	Whites
Low	Moderate	Low	High	Moderate	High

Level of Qualification

Figure 2.2
Variation in the intensity of raters' preferences with respect to race: employers hire applicants from as far right as possible.

may be more attuned to specific job characteristics: they may occasionally appropriate more desirable jobs within lower-ranked occupations that usually go to less preferred groups (for example, male nurses); or they may eschew jobs in occupations usually reserved for the preferred group (such as physicians in isolated rural communities), thereby making them available to workers from lower-ranked groups. We expect the former behavior from the lowest-ranked members of the preferred group (among men, for example, ethnic and racial minorities, immigrants, and inexperienced youth). The latter is most likely for nominally highly ranked occupations that are for other reasons undesirable.

Changing Occupational Composition and Queue Mismatches

Changes in size—of subgroups of workers or of various occupations—that create a mismatch between the number of workers at some level in a labor queue and the number of jobs in the corresponding level of the job queue can lead occupations' composition to change. When labor becomes scarce in top-ranked groups, either through job growth or a shrinkage in the number of customary workers, employers must be less choosy. Shortages spur occupations' composition to change because they force employers to resort to lower-ranked workers than they normally hire. For example, employers gave women semiskilled factory jobs at the end of the nineteenth century because the opportunity for freeholding, with its prospects for financial security, depleted the supply of men (Abbott, 1909). Wars have often precipitated shortages of white male workers.[6] At least since the Civil War, American minorities of both sexes and white women have won jobs that white men had dominated before war service called them away (Baker, 1977:83; Anderson, 1982:83–84). Nonwhite men and white women have been the first to benefit from employers' descent down their hierarchy of preference to fill white men's jobs. During World War I the shortage of male workers gave women a start in such diverse jobs as streetcar conducting, marketing, publishing, accounting, life insurance, and personnel relations (Kessler-Harris, 1982:227; 1986:769). World War II replicated the process: employers hired women for traditionally male blue-collar jobs in retooled auto plants and for nonwar jobs such as bank telling and reporting (Milkman, 1987; Strober and Arnold, 1987a; Beasley and Theus, 1988). The jobs that white women and black men had abandoned for better opportunities trickled down to black women (U.S. Department of Labor, Women's Bureau, 1929:15; Jones, 1985; Sokoloff, 1989). For example, light manufacturing industries turned to black men only after they had "tap[ped] the reserve" of available white women, and they did not turn to black women until they ran out of black men (Weaver, 1946, cited in Strober and Catanzarite, 1988:11). Thus, labor shortages can create a chain of opportunities for progressively lower-ranked groups in the labor queue.

When a higher-ranked group expands—or the number of positions open to it shrinks—it spills over into jobs normally held by the less preferred.[7] For example, as medical-school slots became scarce early in this century, schools that had been admitting women increasingly excluded them (Starr, 1982:124). More recently, when high unemployment in the early 1980s permitted the military to meet enlistment goals among young men, it cut female recruitment (Williams, 1989:56). Queueing ensures that workers from the lowest-ranked groups, as the last hired, are usually first to be fired, even without seniority rules. A shortage of jobs in occupations reserved for preferred workers or the emergence of desirable jobs in occupations usually allotted to lower-ranked workers can lead the former to usurp the latter's jobs. This is especially likely with jobs that high-ranked workers had formerly held (Thurow, 1972:73,75). For example, white women, bumped from factory jobs by returning soldiers after World War I, displaced black women from domestic jobs (Jones, 1985). During the Great Depression men reclaimed banking, insurance, librarianship, and social work jobs that women had entered during World War I (Kessler-Harris, 1986: chap. 9),[8] and each time men have come marching home from military service, employers have restored the prewar sex (and race) composition of most occupations (e.g., Kessler-Harris, 1982:219; Milkman, 1987). However, not having held jobs in the past does not prevent higher-status groups from colonizing them if they become more attractive than "their own" jobs.[9] For example, in Great Britain men moved into women's jobs in radiography after pay and working conditions improved (Cockburn, 1988). In the United States, since Title IX of the 1972 Educational Amendment raised the budgets of women's sports programs, men have been replacing female coaches for women's collegiate sports (Acosta and Carpenter, 1988). Thus, while it is rare for men to take over female occupations, they may do so when those jobs are better than availab`. male jobs.

How Employers Rank Male and Female Workers in Labor Queues

Before tackling the question of why labor queues change, we must take a moment to consider how employers rank workers. Classical economists contend that employers rank prospective workers in terms of potential productivity and labor costs (Doeringer and Piore, 1971).[10] That these and other considerations transform the labor queue into a *gender queue* is evident in the high level of sex segregation in the workplace. Until recently, employers gave white men "first dibs" on most jobs (Strober, 1984).[11] Thus, establishments with the most "good" jobs are the most sex and race segregated (Lyson, 1985:290); occupations whose male workforce has grown faster than others pay best, offer more vocational training, demand less strength, and shelter incumbents from competition (Simpson et al., 1982:1303); and occupations' return on workers' human-capital investments is positively correlated with men's representation (Catanzarite and Strober, 1988). Of course, other factors affect employers' placement of groups of workers in the labor queue; marital and parental status also influence their evaluations of women workers, beyond any effects on women's performance.

Ever since they invented wage labor, employers have paid women less than men. Predominantly female occupations still pay less than male occupations, and men still, on average, outearn women. Recent data show that *within* many occupations women are paid about two-thirds of what men earn; in only a few does the wage ratio reach four-fifths (Mellor, 1985:54–59). These disparities within occupations result largely from the segregation of women and men in different jobs, firms, and industries. Women's lower market wage not only "endear[s] them to employers" (Rotella, 1981:162); it sometimes has been a sufficient incentive for employers to rank women ahead of men and occasionally to replace male workers (see, e.g., Garland, 1901; Rose, 1988).[12] A nineteenth-century student of industrialization explained that employers sought constantly to replace human labor altogether with machinery or to "diminish its cost by substituting the industry of women and children for that of men" (Scott, 1982). However, employers' preference for low-wage workers has seldom governed their ranking of the sexes. Instead, custom, the belief that women's lower productivity or other factors will offset their lower pay, and sex bias have led employers to place men ahead of women whom they could hire more cheaply. It is these factors that transform labor queues into gender queues. Let us examine the role each one plays.

First, sex labels that characterize jobs as "women's" or "men's" work influence day-to-day hiring and job assignments by affecting employers' notions of appropriate and inappropriate workers for particular jobs (Oppenheimer, 1968). The force of custom tends to blind employers to economically irrational decisions, at least until external events galvanize them to change.

Second, employers' difficulty in identifying productive workers leads them to resort to proxies such as educational attainment, experience, and group membership. Although various factors could generate differences in women's and men's productivity, sex often influences rankings through stereotypical beliefs that men outproduce women in "male" jobs because they are stronger, more rational, more mechanically adept, and so forth, or because women have higher absentee and turnover rates (Cohn, 1985:18; Bielby and Baron, 1986; England and McCreary, 1987:296).[13] Stereotypes supported by custom make employers reluctant to risk untried workers, especially for jobs involving uncertainty (Kanter, 1977; Konrad and Pfeffer, 1991). In occupations in which observers can easily judge workers' performance, employers are less likely to act on group stereotypes about performance (Baron and Newman, 1989).

Third, some employers worry that male workers' negative response to female interlopers will reduce productivity or raise labor costs by increasing turnover, or lead men to demand higher wages to compensate them for working with women (Doeringer and Piore, 1971; Bergmann and Darity, 1981; Bielby and Baron, 1986:791). Historically, like every group faced with competition from lower-paid workers, men have responded to the threat of female incursion with organized opposition: strikes, slowdowns, and on-the-job resistance (Hartmann, 1976; Walshok, 1981; Schroedel, 1985; Milkman, 1987).[14] Of course, anticipated male opposition need not deter employers if enough qualified women are available to replace men, but employers can rarely feminize entire work teams. Seniority rules prevent their replacing experienced men; too few qualified women may be available; and employers may be unable to train women because male unions control training or because training takes too long. Moreover, if employers believe that the pool of women cannot meet their needs, especially for jobs that require substantial on-the-job training (England and McCreary, 1987:296), they will not risk antagonizing male workers to hire women, even at bargain rates—especially if they harbor any doubt as to whether women can be as productive as men.

Fourth, some employers are not compelled to minimize wages. The level of competition they face and the share of all costs that wages constitute affect their incentive to find ways to cut wages. When labor makes up a large fraction of an organization's total costs, hiring cheaper workers can generate enough savings to compensate for opposition (Cohn, 1985; Strober, 1988). In contrast, when labor constitutes a small part of all costs or when employers are buffered from concern with costs, they can ignore potential wage savings in positioning workers in the labor queue (Stolzenberg, 1982; Cohn, 1985:18–22). Factors that buffer organizations from the need to minimize their wage bill include market dominance (Ashenfelter and Hannan, 1986), high profits, and nonprofit status. Rich enterprises may derive prestige from paying above-market wages and thus opt for costly workers over cheaper ones as "noneconomic amenities" (Stolzenberg, 1982; but see Rotella, 1987). Furthermore, as Jacobs (1989a:180) noted, employers who pay premium wages to spur greater productivity are indifferent to the cost savings that women offer.

Finally, some employers willingly accept higher wages as the price for favoring men (Becker, 1957). The effect of bias on employers' rankings of the sexes is well established. Hartmann (1976) claimed that in preferring men for customarily male jobs, male employers seek to maintain male privileges inside as well as outside the workplace. Strober (1984, 1988; Catanzarite and Strober, 1988) proposed additional reasons for employers' preference for male workers: gender solidarity preserves sex-based privileges that all men enjoy, forestalls the possibility that women will eventually challenge owners' and managers' positions, and keeps employers in the good graces of their male friends and colleagues who demand preference for male workers even if it means a higher wage bill. To the extent that all employers abide by this patriarchal norm, Strober argued, none suffers a competitive disadvantage. Reskin (1988) advanced a more general explanation for men's monopoly of the most desirable jobs: men enforce segregation partly to sustain sex differentiation because it legitimates the larger sex–gender hierarchy from which almost all men benefit. Dispensing with sex differentiation at any level threatens it at every level, so ignoring sex in the labor queue challenges the advantaged positions of male employers and managers. As Cockburn (1988:41) put it, "Behind occupational segregation is gender differentiation, and behind that is male power." Of course, when labor costs are nontrivial and cutting costs is paramount, biases are less likely to affect rankings. For example, postbellum white southerners' aversion to integration did not prevent their hiring black teachers after they realized they could pay them much less than white teachers (Jones, 1985).

When all employers share a bias—especially one that community values endorse—the disadvantage from the premiums they pay to hire preferred workers cancels out. Finally, even nondiscriminating employers can perpetuate discriminatory queues when they delegate hiring and job assignment to biased subordinates who lack the incentive to minimize labor costs (Ashenfelter and Hannan, 1986).

In sum, expectations about performance and cost, the dictates of custom, and sex prejudice influence how employers rank the sexes within labor queues. Which considerations prevail depends partly on whether employers are insulated from economic considerations, whether performance is paramount and easily assessed, the strength of employers' biases, the cost of indulging them, and men's ability to raise the cost of employing women. Because employers tend to place greater weight on custom, stereotypes about sex differences in productivity, and anti-female or pro-male biases than they place on minimizing wages, labor queues typically operate as gender queues that favor men over women.

How Workers Rank Occupations in the Job Queue

We have emphasized the labor queue to stress employers' primary role in the labor market: ultimately, employers assign and withhold jobs.[15] Obviously if we hope to explain groups' changing distributions across occupations, we must also specify how workers rank jobs—ranking expressed usually in their power to reject jobs. We devote less attention to this issue because readers—as past, present, and future workers—already understand this process. Most workers try to maximize income, social standing, autonomy, job security, congenial working conditions, interesting work, and the chance for advancement; and they rank occupations accordingly (Jencks et al., 1988). Of course, specific groups (temporary migrant workers, students) may attach more or less importance to particular job attributes (job security, benefits) or prefer activities other than those sought by the majority, and these differences may lead to inconsistent rankings across groups (Lieberson, 1980).

For our purposes, the key question is whether women and men value different job characteristics. They rank income equally highly among job rewards (O'Farrell and Harlan, 1982; Walker et al., 1982) and differ little on why they judge a job to be good or prestigious (Bose and Rossi, 1983; Jencks et al., 1988:1345; for a review, see England and McCreary, 1987).[16] Some observers contend that women place a premium on jobs that are compatible with child rearing (e.g., Mincer and Polachek, 1974, 1978), but sociological research provides little support for the thesis that women's family roles lead them to choose different occupations than men do (England, 1982; but see Berryman and Waite, 1987). Others have argued that some men value the capacity of exclusively male blue-collar occupations to confirm their masculinity (Martin, 1980; Williams, 1989). Although this claim enjoys anecdotal support, no evidence exists as to its importance relative to material rewards, and we suspect that men in low-paying or low-prestige jobs value maleness in jobs more than other men do.[17]

In sum, job queues result from how workers rank jobs on a variety of characteristics on whose importance women and men generally agree. Overall, the sexes generally rank occupations similarly. Although many exceptions do exist, for the occupations we studied there is little question that women's rankings were similar to men's; women's increasing numbers in these occupations speak for themselves.

Before turning to how the queueing approach elucidates women's disproportionate entry into several male occupations after 1970, we offer a final example by way of summarizing the operation of both labor and job queues. Throughout the 1970s the military services ranked almost all men above all women, a fact reflected in their 2 percent quota for women. Despite this gender queue, however, in the 1970s the shortage of potential male recruits with a high school diploma prompted the military services to recruit increasing numbers of women. Women responded to these initiatives because military jobs stood higher in the job queue than most others available to women: they paid 40 percent more than women could expect to earn, on average, as civilian workers (Binkin and Bach, 1977:32). Below we show that similar factors drew women to the occupations we studied.

I I I I Explaining Women's Inroads into Male Occupations

By definition, occupations' feminization results from their disproportionate recruitment or retention of women workers. Disparate recruitment and retention are the product of *changes* in the structural features of queues (how employers order workers and workers rank jobs, the intensity of either group's preferences, and the shapes of the labor and job queues): that is, the relative distributions of workers or jobs. Our case studies showed that all these factors changed during the 1970s, contributing to occupational feminization. In some occupations, job growth raised labor demand beyond the number of qualified men. In others, women constituted a greater share of the qualified labor pool because the supply of men had shrunk or the supply of women had grown as new opportunities had begun to beckon women. Jobs' rankings shifted as occupations dropped in the job queue, reflecting their declining ability to attract or retain enough men; the ordering of labor queues was transformed as employers upgraded women or downgraded men for particular occupations.[18]

The Changing Shape of the Job Queue

The continuing transformation of the American economy has reshaped the job queue by creating thousands of service-sector jobs that often outstripped the supply of qualified men. The 1970s saw the birth of more than 20 million new jobs, many in predominantly male occupations. For example, educational administration, accounting and auditing, law, real estate sales, guard duty, janitorial work, heavy-truck driving, construction labor, and carpentry all gained at least 200,000 jobs (U.S. Bureau of the Census, 1984a). Although occupational growth can open male occupations to women (Oppenheimer, 1970; Bielby and Baron, 1984; Fields and Wolff, 1989), it does so only after it has exhausted the supply of acceptable candidates from the preferred group in the United States—usually white men (Simpson et al., 1982). In expanding male occupations for which qualified male prospects were plentiful—that is, desirable occupations for which workers can easily qualify—employers had no need to resort to women. Thus, although carpentry and heavy-truck driving each added about 370,000 jobs in the 1970s, women claimed only 2.7 and 5.6 percent of those jobs. Growth is especially likely to prompt employers to resort to women for jobs whose high entry requirements limit the number of qualified prospects. Then employers "reduce their hiring standards, recruit from the disadvantaged labor force, and provide additional training to raise the productivity of the disadvantaged" (Doeringer and Piore, 1971:165). Given women's lower position in the labor queue, they are among the "disadvantaged" who benefit from shortages (Abrahamson and Sigelman, 1987; Baron and Newman, 1989). Thus, Oppenheimer (1970:99, 102) observed,

> the continuously growing demand in an industrializing society for workers with a fairly high level of general education plus some special skills has . . . resulted in a chronic shortage of "middle quality" labor. . . . In such a situation, . . . occupations . . . [that] are less successful than others in competing for middle-quality labor . . . tend to utilize female labor. Once recourse has been made to female labor to provide quality labor at a low price, employers tend to get used to relatively well-educated workers . . . [who work] for much less than men who have received a comparable education. To substitute men to any considerable extent would require either a rise in the price paid for labor or a decline in the quality of the labor, or both.

Supporting these predictions about the role of growth is evidence that sex segregation across industries dropped most during the 1970s in the fastest-growing occupations (Fields and Wolff, 1989). What about the occupations we studied? Table 2.1 shows occupational growth and women's share of new jobs. Readers must be aware, however, that the data in Table 2.1, while consistent with the idea that growth fosters feminization, are only illustrative; we cannot conclude from them that growth and feminization are statistically related across *all* occupations.[19]

As we noted above, growth supports feminization when it creates a shortfall of male workers. Growth in desirable and easy-to-enter occupations

Table 2.1
Job Growth during the 1970s and Women's Share of New Jobs

Case Study Occupation	Growth	Women's Share (%)
Financial managers	189,361	45.3
Accountants and auditors	366,367	62.0
Computer systems analysts/scientists	95,071	32.4
Pharmacists	30,093	69.8
Editors and reporters	55,385	70.8
Public relations specialists	39,735	93.6
Insurance sales occupations	91,998	89.9
Real estate occupations	354,085	57.2
Insurance adjusters, examiners, investigators	65,538	107.5
Typesetters and compositors	−16,056	—
Bartenders	102,637	93.3
Bakers	21,993	106.9
Bus drivers	128,215	81.0

Note: Percentage female in 1970 estimated for a sample of 127,125 respondents from the 1970 census, whose occupations were recoded according to the 1980 occupational classification scheme; thus, estimates subject to sampling error.

Source: Computed from U.S. Bureau of the Census (1984a).

such as truck driving and construction labor attracts more workers of the type already employed. Men pass the word about good jobs to male relatives, friends, and casual acquaintances (Granovetter, 1974). In jobs that demand hard-to-acquire credentials, in contrast, rapid growth is likely to exhaust the supply of trained workers from the preferred group. For example, as the computer industry exploited an expanding market, the demand for systems analysts skyrocketed, and approximately 64,000 men and 31,000 women found work as systems analysts, almost doubling the occupation's workforce. Accounting registered even greater expansion as American corporations grew and rationalized business functions, small firms increasingly relied on accounting services, and complex tax laws made accountants indispensable to individual taxpayers. To meet these needs, accounting recruited almost 139,000 additional men, as well as more than a quarter of a million women.

In lines of work unable to draw enough men, employers can preserve a male workforce by raising wages, but barring a strong preference for men or significant penalties for hiring women, they have no incentive to do so if prospective workers lower in the queue can do the job adequately. In residential real estate sales, for example, brokers did not raise commissions to offset declining earnings during an erratic housing market; rather, they apparently quite happily contracted with women to sell residential properties.

In small, high-turnover occupations, shortages can quickly assume crisis proportions. As a result, feminization occurs more rapidly. For instance, insurance adjusting and examining, which employed fewer than 100,000 people in 1970 and retained workers on average just over five years (Carey, 1988), flipped from a male to an overwhelmingly female occupation within a single generation. The high turnover prevalent in book editing, both insurance and real estate sales, and bartending contributed to their rapid feminization during the 1970s as well. In contrast, in large occupations, such as law and medicine, that tend to retain workers for life, women's representation has grown slowly, despite a large jump in their share of professional schools' enrollments.

In occupations in which a policy-setting body controls the labor market, anticipated labor shortages often stimulate actions to increase the pool of qualified workers. Opening the doors of educational establishments to more applicants may mean either lowering admissions standards or admitting groups formerly excluded. For professional occupations, only the latter is a viable option. For example, during World War II a shortage of physicians spurred medical schools to double their production of female graduates within four years (Jacobs, 1989a:158). More recently, faced with a decline in the number of male students after 1975, pharmacy schools graduated several thousand more women during the late 1970s than they had ten years earlier. A powerful incentive for these schools to admit women were the per capita student federal grants that the American Pharmaceutical Association won from Congress after predicting a shortage of pharmacists.

In sum, in a few of the feminizing occupations we studied, shortages of qualified men prompted employers to draw on women for nontraditional jobs higher up in the job queue (Tienda et al., 1987:263). An inadequate male labor supply not only created opportunities for women; it also undermined male workers' incentive to oppose women because growth assured them of job security and promotion opportunities.

Men's Reranking of Occupations in the Job Queue

Most of the occupations or specialties we studied experienced a shortage of male workers during the 1970s not because they grew dramatically but because their rewards or working conditions deteriorated relative to other occupations for which male workers qualified, making them less attractive to male workers. Workers rank available jobs on the basis of their relative wages, hours, working conditions, and so forth. When the rewards in typically white-male occupations decline, relative to occupations requiring similar qualifications, employers cannot attract and retain enough qualified male workers. To the lower-ranked groups to whom they turn—often white women—such jobs represent a step up. This sequence of events was evident in examples of occupational feminization reviewed in Chapter 1. Women took over schoolteaching because salaries and autonomy dropped, relative to other occupations open to qualified men (see, e.g., Oppenheimer, 1970; Rotella and Margo, 1981;

Strober, 1984), and bank telling feminized after World War II when men were drawn to occupations that offered better returns on their qualifications (Strober and Arnold, 1987a). Carter and Carter (1981) contended that declining attractiveness has swollen women's representation in several traditionally male professional occupations, including college and university teaching, medicine, and law. More generally, Simpson and her colleagues (1982:1303) found that the male labor force declined or grew slowly in low-wage occupations that required little education or specific vocational training. Several customarily male occupations we studied—insurance adjusting and examining, real estate sales, typesetting and composition, and editing—conformed to this pattern. After changes reduced the attraction of these occupations for the educated white men they had recruited in the past, employers turned to women.[20]

Often technological changes that elaborated the division of labor, deskilled work, or altered working conditions set the stage for occupational decline. Normally, jobs change because employers transform the technology of production or reorganize the work (Oppenheimer, 1970:116). Employers can seize either alternative as an excuse to cut wages and replace the workforce with less skilled and cheaper workers (Braverman, 1974; Rose, 1988). The computer industry provides an example of technological changes altering an occupation's sex composition. Early computers had no operating systems, so programmers performed craftlike tasks: for example, rewiring circuits each time they ran a program. The development of operating systems allowed programmers to store common tasks in machine memory, freeing them for higher-level projects. However, as the computer workforce grew, managers sought to contain labor costs by separating from programming two new occupations: systems analysts, who designed information systems; and coders, who translated programs into computer codes and entered data. The industry construed the latter jobs as clerical and filled them predominantly with women. Systems analysis was initially men's work; only in the 1970s did it begin to feminize. A second example of technological change facilitating a shift to a female labor force occurred when electronic advances computerized and revolutionized the work of typesetters and compositors. As high-speed electronic phototypesetters and electronic scanners diffused throughout newspaper publishing, skilled male workers rejected the transformed craft jobs as clerical work "any high school girl could do" (Rogers and Friedman, 1980:6)—especially when the wages also approached clerical pay.

Insurance adjusting epitomizes the feminizing effect of the transformation of an occupation's work process. Throughout the 1960s, "outside" adjusters—virtually all male—worked in the field, where they settled a few claims a day. They scheduled their own work, used company cars, and enjoyed reasonable prospects for promotion into managerial jobs. During the high-inflation 1970s, unstable interest rates and increased competition resulting from the deregulation of the financial industry prompted insurance companies to cut costs by standardizing work (Hartmann et al., 1986:41). Toward this end, they brought adjusting into the office, where "inside" adjusters handled a large number of claims, using telephones and video display terminals.[21] In clericalizing adjusting (one industry adviser referred to inside adjusters as "skilled desk technicians"), firms robbed the job of its autonomy, bumped it from the career ladder to management, and subjected workers to quotas and electronic monitoring—all for lower pay. With the clericalization of adjusting, the number of male adjusters dropped by 6,447 between 1970 and 1980, while the number of women increased by 73,744. Although employers may not have intended to feminize the adjuster workforce (Phipps found no evidence that firms barred men from the jobs), that outcome was inevitable after the highly routinized work and erosion of real earnings made adjusting unattractive to the kind of man who had formerly done it.

The life insurance industry, a pioneer in using computers to increase productivity and cut labor costs (Murolo, 1987), followed a similar strategy with examiners, computerizing their work so that by the early 1970s examiners were using electronic systems to verify claims and issue checks. Subsequently, major insurers fully computerized examiners' work and could monitor their performance in the bargain. In both adjusting and examining, as jobs were computerized, real wages dropped, and opportunities for organizational mobility almost disappeared.

Any change that reduces an occupation's financial rewards, mobility opportunities, or job security can depreciate its ranking in a job queue. Occupations have risen in the queue as their rewards became more tempting (examples include medicine, professional sports, and, more recently, investment banking), only to fall again as workers' values change or they become disillusioned over their prospects.[22] In the 1960s young people aspired to be artists and artisans; in the early 1970s journalism drew thousands of would-be Woodwards and Bernsteins. By that decade's end, young adults were once again seeking careers in the traditional professions of law and medicine. In the 1980s medical-school applications fell, and business administration outdrew all other college majors (U.S. National Center for Education Statistics, 1987: 148, 195, 197), reflecting young people's growing appetite for high incomes.[23]

Declining earnings and benefits.   A primary reason the occupations we studied failed to draw or retain enough men was that their earnings declined during the 1970s, relative to those of the male labor force as a whole. Not only did real relative earnings decline; so too did these occupations' level of compensation to men for each year of education, relative to the average occupation. As we indicated in Chapter 1, changes in the occupational classification system in the 1980 census rendered 1970 and 1980 data for some occupations not fully comparable. In this chapter and the next, we compare census data for only those occupations for which at least 90 percent of incum-

Table 2.2

Ratios of Earnings and Earnings per Year of Education of Men in Feminizing Occupations to Those of Male Labor Force, 1969, 1979

Case Study Occupation[a]	Earnings Ratio[b]		Earnings to Education Ratio[e]	
	1969[c]	1979[d] (in 1969$)	1969	1979
Pharmacists	1.41	1.20	1.04	.90
Editors and reporters	1.34	1.09	1.02	.86
Public relations specialists	1.40	1.26	1.08	1.01
Insurance sales occupations	1.30	1.33	1.19	1.17
Real estate sales occupations	1.44	1.33	1.34	1.17
Insurance adjusters, examiners and investigators	1.03	.93	.84	.76
Bartenders	.71	.57	.73	.60
Bus drivers	.80	.81	.97	.86

[a] Excludes feminizing occupations whose 1970 and 1980 census classifications differed too greatly to permit comparison (see text). For those listed, classification changes were small; nonetheless, they render 1969 and 1979 values not entirely comparable.

[b] Ratio of mean earnings of male occupational incumbents to mean earnings of male experienced civilian labor force.

[c] Based on mean annual earnings of males in experienced civilian labor force, aged 16 and over, who worked 50–52 weeks in 1969 (U.S. Bureau of the Census, 1973a: Table 19).

[d] Based on mean annual earnings of males in recent experienced civilian labor force, aged 18 and over, who worked full time, year round in 1979 (U.S. Bureau of the Census, 1984c: Table 1).

[e] The numerators of the ratios are the quotient of mean earnings divided by median years of education of occupational incumbents; the denominators represent the quotient of mean earnings divided by median education (12.3 years in 1970; 12.7 years in 1980) for male labor force. Median educational levels for 1970, from U.S. Bureau of the Census (1973a: Table 5); for 1980, computed from U.S. Bureau of the Census (1983a).

bents would have been classified in the same occupational title in both years (U.S. Bureau of the Census, 1989); hence, we do not compare 1970 and 1980 census data for systems analysts, accountants and auditors, bank and financial managers, typesetters and compositors, and bakers. As the first two columns of Table 2.2 show, in all the comparably coded feminizing occupations except insurance sales and bus driving, male incumbents' earnings advantage relative to the labor force declined between 1969 and 1979.[24] Moreover, all deteriorated in how well they compensated men for each year of education, as indicated by the 1969 and 1979 ratios of earnings return to education for male incumbents compared to the male labor force overall (see the last two columns). Ratios above 1 indicate that occupational incumbents received a higher return on their education than did the average male worker. Thus, of the occupations in Table 2.2, real estate and insurance sales provided workers with the highest payoff for each year of education. Except for insurance sales (where the payoff to education remained constant), the feminizing occupations compensated incumbents more poorly for their education—compared with the average male worker—in 1979 than they had in 1969.[25] Pharmacy, editing and reporting, real estate sales, and bartending suffered the sharpest erosion in how well they compensated male incumbents for each year of education. Although in 1980 most of these occupations employed men who were relatively less well educated than those they had employed in 1970, incumbents' relative incomes declined more than their relative education.

One reason men's real earnings declined in the occupations we studied was the decline in the proportion of full-time, year-round jobs. Most striking was bartending, in which the proportion of men who worked at least 30 hours per week for 50 or more weeks a year dropped from 60.7 percent in 1970 to 45.5 percent ten years later. Real estate sales and insurance adjusting and examining were at the other extreme: the proportion of men who worked full time, year round dropped by less than a percentage point during the 1970s (computed from U.S. Bureau of the Census, 1983a). The case studies in Part II chronicle the reasons earnings declined. In a few, income dropped after duties were computerized and perhaps deskilled. For example, the introduction of electronic technologies into newspaper typesetting substantially cut the relative earnings of print craftworkers. Similarly, after the major insurance firms computerized claims processing, adjusters' real earnings declined. Phipps's (1989) synthetic-cohort analysis of adjusters and examiners revealed that 35- to 44-year-old men disproportionately left adjusting during the 1970s. Older men were more likely to stay in the occupation, presumably because they could capitalize on their seniority either to retain one of the remaining better-paid outside adjusting jobs or to obtain a supervisory job.[26]

The real earnings of male pharmacists in both retail and hospital settings declined. More serious for retail pharmacy were waning entrepreneurial opportunities following the proliferation of drugstore chains and the emergence of pharmacies within discount stores, supermarkets, and health-maintenance organizations. As the number of independent drugstores plummeted, the proportion of retail pharmacists who owned their pharmacies dropped from one in two in 1956 to one in ten by 1980. This precipitous decline in retail pharmacy's ability to offer an entrepreneurial career undermined its attraction to men.

In a few of the occupations we studied, economic fluctuations and changing government regulation eroded earnings. Deregulation exposed banks to competition with savings and loan associations. This in turn led banks to emphasize performance and curtail wage growth for managers. Tax-law changes during the 1970s prompted real estate firms to eliminate salaries and benefits for sales personnel. By 1980 most residential salespersons were independent contractors rather than employees. Partly because of these changes, the 354,085 new jobs in real estate sales during the 1970s drew only about 151,389 men, and brokers hired women to make up the difference. A 1966 amendment to the Fair Labor Standards Act allowed owners of large eating and drinking places to pay "tipped workers" less than the minimum wage, which contributed to the sharp drop in bartenders' earnings.

Declining job security, occupational prestige, and mobility opportunities. Declining job security reduced some occupations in men's eyes. Industry competition brought an end to the lifetime employment that banking had traditionally offered its managers. In book publishing a spate of mergers associated with the conglomerization of publishing made editors' tenure uncertain. As newspaper publishers replaced hot-metal Linotype machines with video display terminals, technological displacement undermined the job security of typesetters and compositors.

A decline in prestige also contributed to men's downgrading of occupations. Just as a post–World War II shift to a mass and less affluent clientele hastened the feminization of bank telling by reducing its prestige (Strober and Arnold, 1987a), banks' competition with savings and loans for customers during the 1970s undermined the prestige of managers in personal (as opposed to commercial) banking. To compete, banks provided more services at more branches, creating thousands of service-oriented management jobs in personal banking. However, these jobs lacked the prestige that bank management traditionally conferred and failed to provide the skills essential for promotion to top management.

Declining prestige and autonomy also contributed to the feminization of book editing. Throughout most of this century, book publishers traded on the industry's image as a "gentleman's profession" to attract educated men. As media and nonmedia conglomerates acquired major publishing houses in the 1970s, increasingly profit-oriented publishers sought "blockbusters" rather than literary masterpieces. As a result, they transferred acquisition decisions to specialists in marketing and subsidiary rights, thereby diminishing editors' autonomy and prestige. Editorial wages remained low, and publishers—unable to attract bright, literate men to editing—turned to women. Similarly, retail pharmacists' precarious claim to professional status has atrophied during the 1980s as computer programs are taking over pharmacists' traditional task of identifying drug interactions and side effects, further routinizing their work.

Exacerbating the tendency for all these changes to tarnish deteriorating occupations in men's eyes is the tendency for feminization to reduce the prestige of male occupations (Touhey, 1974).[27] Women's entry into already declining occupations (especially those in which men prize working in an all-male setting; see Martin, 1980) brings home the message that the occupation is "on the skids" (Baron and Newman, 1990). As one male typesetter lamented to Roos about his trade, "It's a girl's job now."

Changes in occupations' skill mix. In many occupations we studied, the failure to attract men was confined to certain jobs. Baking exemplifies this pattern. In the late 1960s manufacturers found a way to freeze unbaked goods for shipment to retailers, who could bake them on the premises and sell them as fresh from the oven. This innovation created thousands of jobs at in-store bakeries and at the cookie, doughnut, and pretzel chains that now dot America's shopping malls. Although women did not increase their numbers among bakers in manufacturing in the 1970s, they have virtually taken over the new, less skilled retail "bake-off" jobs. These rarely unionized, low-wage, and often part-time jobs attract almost no men. Already they have been labeled women's work.

A white-collar counterpart to in-store baking exists among public relations specialists. Large organizations, increasingly concerned with employee relations during the 1970s, created public relations jobs for "communications technicians" who served employees (for example, by editing in-house newsletters) rather than the public and had no policy-setting responsibility. Men who sought to move up the corporate hierarchy could shun such low-paid public relations jobs because they had other options. Consequently, public relations specialists have become so overwhelmingly female that their own professional association has dubbed the occupation a "velvet ghetto" (Cline et al., 1986).

A similar pattern appears in bus driving. By 1980 there were almost as many school bus drivers as metropolitan transit drivers. But driving school buses, because it is typically part-time work for low hourly wages, has not attracted enough men; by 1980, 63 percent of those drivers were female (U.S. Bureau of the Census, 1983a). Thus, the growth of a feminizing specialty, school-bus driving, created enough jobs that went to women to raise women's representation substantially in the occupation of bus driving without dramatically altering women's representation in metropolitan transit jobs.

Most of the occupations we studied, then, feminized at least partly because their earnings, benefits, prestige, job security, autonomy, or chances for advancement failed to keep pace with those in other occupations. As a result, men were less interested in these occupations than they had been a decade earlier. In moving on to other occupations, they surrendered declining occupations or occupational specialties to women.

Employers' Reranking of the Sexes in the Labor Queue

Employers' rankings of groups of potential workers tend to be stable over the short run because stereotypes and biases change slowly and because productivity-related characteristics tend to be fixed within cohorts (Hodge, 1973:19). Nonetheless, during the 1970s employers reduced their preference for men for some occupations, or even put women first in the labor queue. The queueing perspective points to four reasons employers might have advanced women ahead of men: (1) they believed productivity or cost differentials between the sexes had changed; (2) their aversion for women or preference for men declined or disappeared; (3) the costs they incurred for indulging preferences rose; (4) new rankers entered the picture who did not routinely support male preference. All four reasons figured prominently in the feminization of the occupations we studied.

Changing presumptions regarding women's productivity or employment costs. Employers repositioned women ahead of men when (a) they believed sex differences in characteristics they assumed to be linked to productivity (such as education and experience) had shrunk or disappeared, (b) they discovered that their presumptions about men's greater productivity lacked merit, or (c) work changed in ways that employers believed would render women as productive as men, possibly at lower wages.

For some occupations, employers became more favorably disposed to women once sex differences had declined in education, experience, absenteeism, and turnover. As women closed the gap in postsecondary education and labor force attachment, more women were as qualified as men, and the best women were likely to be better qualified than many men.[28] For example, by the mid-1970s women admitted to several pharmacy schools had higher grade-point averages and qualifying-examination scores than the men who were admitted (Urban and Rural Systems Associates, 1976). Similarly, a survey of public relations specialists established that women were better educated and probably a better buy for employers than men (Nesbitt, 1986). Real estate and insurance brokers, bar and in-store bakery managers, and publishers were among the occupational gatekeepers who cited female applicants' superior qualifications to explain their occupations' feminization.

Some employers discovered that women were as productive as men after labor shortages or affirmative-action plans forced them to hire women (Kessler-Harris, 1982:219; Bielby and Bielby, 1988). Motivated to prove themselves, women pioneers reportedly outperformed their male counterparts as book sales representatives and as real estate and insurance agents. As long as male occupations select only women who top their sex's labor queue, the first women who enter male occupations are likely to outperform men. If the uncertainty of their reception spurs those women to do their best, they are even more likely to outperform male coworkers.

For some jobs a basis for employers to expect women to be more productive than men was an increase in the number of women among workers' role partners or potential customers. The belief that minority populations serve members of their own group more productively than members of majority groups do can create "restricted markets" for minority members (Lieberson, 1980; Collins, 1983).[29] This "gender-based integration" (Baron and Bielby, 1985) created occupational niches for women in public relations, book editing, insurance sales, and perhaps real estate sales as employers became increasingly oriented to female consumers or clients. Corporate recognition of women's spending power after World War II led firms to hire female public relations specialists to court prospective female customers. In explaining the growing number of women insurance sales agents, informants cited the growth of a female market in which women could outsell men. Interviewees from the publishing industry mentioned two variants of the go-between role in explaining the feminization of book editing: first, the women's liberation movement stimulated a profusion of manuscripts that in turn created editorial jobs for women; second, because most fiction readers are women, female editors can better gauge their taste.

However, many exceptions cast doubt on the hypothesis that same-sex role partners create jobs for women (Glazer, 1984:78). To cite just two, although women buy two of every five cars, more than nine of every ten car and boat salespersons were male in 1980; and women surely purchase a far greater share of burial services than their one-in-eleven representation among funeral directors suggests. Hence, we suspect that growing female markets and clientele are largely post hoc justifications for decisions that employers made on other grounds.

We have similar reservations about the effect of sex stereotypes on occupational feminization. In her pioneering study, Oppenheimer (1970) showed that work becomes labeled as female or male and that subsequently jobs are assigned accordingly. When employers alter male jobs to include tasks already labeled as appropriate for women or at which women stereotypically excel, employers *may* switch to women.[30] Of the occupations we studied, insurance adjusting, typesetting and composing, systems analysis, public relations, retail pharmacy, and retail baking took on more female-labeled tasks during the 1970s, perhaps fueling a demand for women. For example, the female label attached to clerical work meant that when newspapers replaced the old technology with typewriter-like keyboards and video display terminals, employers could easily construe typesetting as women's work. Similarly, the centrality of taking phone calls and entering data in inside adjusting reinforced its relabeling as women's work.[31]

Researchers have assigned partial responsibility for the feminization of some occupations to employers' deference to sex stereotypes or sex labels (e.g., Strober and Best, 1979). Women's increased representation in bank management, public relations, retail baking, pharmacy, insurance adjusting, typesetting and composing, and systems analysis is consistent with the influence of sex stereotypes or sex-labeled duties newly added to jobs. For example, employers disproportionately assigned women to the growing public relations specialty of communications expert, which deals with employee morale, on the basis of women's reputed expertise at interpersonal relations. Moreover, a new specialty in systems analysis geared to communicating with corporate users created jobs for thousands of women partly because employers assumed that women's superior communication skills would suit them for it. Interviewees mentioned women's stereotypically superior interpersonal and communications skills in explaining the feminization of bank management. As banks offered more services, they filled service-providing management jobs with women, who supposedly serve customers better than do men.

Since 1970 some of the feminizing occupations we studied have involved more typically female "emotional work"—work which, according to Hochschild (1983), requires the worker to generate emotions in herself and others.[32] With its object of shaping opinion, public relations seems to fit Hochschild's formulation, and informants explaining its feminization mentioned women's expertise at such interpersonal manipulation as "cooling out the public" following corporate misbehavior.[33] Although selling insurance has always involved emotional work, brokers claimed that the shift in the 1970s toward a "softer" sales technique made employers more receptive to hiring female sales agents. As a manager said of his firm's shift away from its traditionally hard-sell approach, the new "needs-based" approach is better suited to women because it does not require a domineering style. As a result, he expected to see more successful women agents (Leidner, 1989b).

The foregoing examples are consistent with the belief that sex stereotypes influence occupations' sex composition. However, if sex stereotypes exercise a more than trivial effect, why did it take so long for occupations such as book editing, residential real estate sales, and public relations, which have always involved traditionally female emotional skills, to feminize? These occupations have long drawn on such stereotypically female characteristics as patience and skill at interpersonal relations. One interviewee cited the "handholding" that service banking now requires in explaining women's headway in bank management. But editors figuratively held authors' hands when men dominated editing; by the time editing feminized, literary agents had taken over that job.

A closer look at the occupations we studied suggests that employers gerrymandered the sex labels of jobs that were feminizing for other reasons, selectively invoking sex stereotypes after they decided to hire more women. As Davies (1975:282) observed of the feminization of clerical work, transforming its nature "circumvent[ed] stereotyped ideas of the appropriate sexual division of labor." For this reason, the first step in reconstruing occupations' sex labels is transforming the labor process, usually by mechanizing it. As Oppenheimer (1970:118) observed, breaking the tradition of how work is done paves the way for reversing ideas about which sex should do it. Reconstruing altered work as appropriate for women is usually a simple matter because most jobs contain both stereotypically male and female elements. The history of the changing sex composition of bank workers illustrates this point. In 1917 wartime shortages of male workers prompted banks to paint women as exceptionally suited to low-level managerial jobs because of their "neatness, deft handling of money and papers, tact, and a certain intuitive judgment" (Kessler-Harris, 1986:770).

Fifteen years later, facing Depression-induced labor surpluses, banks justified excluding women by claiming that the public would refuse to hand money over to them. When World War II initiated another labor shortage, banks named women as ideal tellers because of their interpersonal expertise (Strober and Arnold, 1987a). We saw a more contemporary variant of this pattern in insurance trade journals, which repackaged adjusting as "women's work" during the 1970s by depicting claims adjusters as empathetic and nurturant listeners.

Our data do not establish the extent to which the introduction or growth of sex-stereotyped duties fostered the feminization of male occupations and how much employers reconstrued these occupations in stereotypically female terms after the fact. Employers can ignore stereotypes or cite them—along with occupations' sex labels and the existence of female markets—to recast formerly male jobs as women's work in order to placate male workers or even to attract women. While state laws banned women from bartending, proponents of women's exclusion explained the need to protect women from the corrupting influence of liquor-ridden men. A decade after the Supreme Court invalidated those state statutes, a union official whom Detman interviewed explained that employers preferred women to men because they were more honest employees.

Given the pervasive sex-typing of activities (Bem, 1983) and the omnipresent sex stereotypes in our cultural vocabulary, workers are primed to explain women's growing representation in customarily male occupations in terms of stereotypes.[34] As Leidner (1989a) pointed out, workers tend to interpret sex segregation in jobs as both a manifestation of differences between the sexes and evidence of the importance of such differences for performing the job. However, this does not mean that changes in work content that included sex-stereotyped tasks contributed significantly to feminization; stereotypes played a role by providing powerful justifications that legitimated altered hiring decisions.

Declining preference for men and bias against women.   Until a generation ago, the public tolerance of sex discrimination guaranteed men's top place in labor queues. Then the civil rights and feminist movements challenged white men's birthright to the most desirable jobs. Growing public disapproval of discrimination in the 1970s led some employers to attach less importance to workers' sex and deterred others from acting on biases. However, the only occupation we studied in which liberalized attitudes directly fostered feminization was bartending. Women's exclusion had depended partly on male unionists' claim that mixing drinks would corrupt women (Cobble, 1989b). The women's liberation movement and the "sexual revolution," as well as delayed marriage and the changing courtship practices of the late 1960s and 1970s, helped refute such fears and challenge traditional beliefs that women need protection. However, in the other feminizing occupations we studied, changing attitudes were of minor importance in inducing employers to hire women, compared with economic considerations and labor shortages. In general, popular sentiments about the kinds of work permissible to women change *after* rather than *before* occupations feminize (Rotella, 1981). For example, broadcasters had long barred women from reporting the news because their voices allegedly lacked authority. What opened reporting to women was not enlightenment among radio and television station managers but the risk of losing their broadcast licenses.

Direct attacks on male preference broadly supported the feminization of the occupations we studied. Feminists in colleges and universities attacked discrimination in admissions and financial aid in graduate and professional programs, thereby helping to pave the way for women's entry into professional and managerial occupations. Declining discrimination at universities contributed to women's inroads into accounting, bank management, systems analysis, pharmacy, journalism, and public relations. While it is premature to conclude that sex discrimination has disappeared in graduate and professional training programs, educators' growing indifference to students' sex has created more balanced applicant queues.

Finally, sometimes male preference declined because employers were no longer willing or able to pay the premium wages men required. For example, among the strategies some insurance firms implemented to save money during the 1970s was hiring women agents who received little or no supplemental salary before they began earning commissions. The earnings differential was also implicated in a shift away from male preference in insurance adjusting and typesetting and composing.

Changing costs associated with hiring each sex. Changes in the costs employers faced for acting on their preferences came from two sources: antidiscrimination regulations that made acting on male preference more expensive, and a reduction in men's inclination or ability to penalize employers who broke ranks and hired women for customarily male jobs.

Despite the 1963 Equal Pay Act, women's restricted labor market options continue to make them cheaper than equally productive men, giving employers an incentive to replace men with women. As we argued above, employers may fail to act on that incentive if they expect offsetting costs such as higher turnover, opposition from male workers, and the expense of revising personnel practices. Employers' apparently increased preference for women in a few male occupations by the end of the 1970s reflects a revised assessment of the economic risks entailed in hiring and not hiring women. The cost of hiring women declined in some of the occupations we studied because male resistance became ineffective or disappeared; in others the potential costs of *not* hiring women increased with the threat of sanctions by regulatory agencies or litigation.

Title VII of the 1964 Civil Rights Act—which barred sex discrimination in employment practices for firms with fifteen or more employees—and the state laws that followed limited employers' freedom to downrank women for jobs simply because of their sex. The most dramatic effect of Title VII on women's access to male occupations occurred in bartending. The federal statute was the basis for the first effective challenge of state "protective" laws that prohibited women from tending bar. In 1967 President Lyndon Johnson expanded the federal arsenal against sex discrimination when he amended Executive Order 11246 to prohibit federal contractors from discriminating on the basis of sex in employment. Nixon's 1971 revision of the order required contractors to take affirmative action to eliminate the effect of past discrimination. Even though enforcement of antidiscrimination regulations was limited during the 1970s, employers who discriminated against women risked lawsuits, the loss of federal contracts, monetary penalties, and negative publicity (Reskin and Hartmann, 1986). In a few industries, efforts by agencies charged with enforcing discrimination and affirmative-action regulations did help women enter nontraditional jobs. In 1972 the Equal Employment Opportunity Commission targeted both banking and insurance for investigation (Dunetz, 1977:78). Five years later, at the insistence of the EEOC, the Prudential Insurance Company agreed to increase its female sales force. One industry veteran commented that the effect of the settlement went beyond Prudential by serving as a warning to other companies.

In 1977 the Office of Federal Contract Compliance Programs (OFCCP) gave notice that it would view women's underrepresentation as prima facie evidence of discrimination, and the Department of Labor threatened to withhold federal contracts from banks that continued to discriminate in assigning jobs. In the same year the OFCCP also targeted federal contractors in banking and insurance, and in 1980 it earmarked substantial resources to scrutinize the insurance industry. At the state level the New York attorney general's investigation of discrimination in publishing, an industry centered in New York City, encouraged publishers to open more editorial and managerial jobs to women.

Women's groups both galvanized enforcement agencies to action and reinforced their efforts. As early as 1969 women reporters began suing newspapers for discrimination in job assignment, wages, and promotion policies. Dozens of charges followed, including suits against the *Washington Post* and the *New York Times*, each of which yielded close to quarter-million-dollar settlements. In 1973 and 1974 women sued the Bank of America and Harris Bank for discriminatory hiring and promotion practices. Subsequently, the National Organization for Women (NOW) filed discrimination charges against several more banks. Indeed, between 1974 and 1977, class-action suits charged sex bias against nine of the twenty-four banks that the Council on Economic Priorities (1977) surveyed. Women also sued insurance firms, and in 1974 and 1978 decisions a U.S. district court ruled against the Liberty Mutual Insurance Company for employing men as claims adjusters and women as lower-paid claims representatives, and for the pay discrimination that resulted (*Wetzel v. Liberty Mutual, 1974, 1978*).[35] Although some suits took years to resolve (a 1971 suit against J. Walter Thompson Advertising by Betty Harragan, a public relations specialist, dragged on for years; and the 1979 suit of *Kraszewski et al. v. State Farm Insurance* was not settled until 1988, after one of the three plaintiffs had died), they nonetheless alarmed other firms. Their visibility, combined with the continued risk of regulatory-agency action, prompted firms to increase women's access to heavily male jobs (Shaeffer and Lynton, 1979).[36] In sum, litigation and pressure by federal anti-discrimination agencies against a few industry leaders prompted banks to give an unprecedented number of women managerial titles (if not always managerial responsibilities)[37] and insurance firms to begin hiring more women to sell insurance.

Women's gains in broadcast reporting also stemmed from collective action by advocacy groups that invoked the regulatory power of a federal agency. In 1966 a civil rights group filed a challenge with the Federal Communications Commission (FCC) protesting the renewal of the broadcast license of a Mississippi station that it had charged with racist programming. By 1972, armed with the 1970 addition of "sex" to the FCC's equal-opportunity regulations, a coalition of feminist groups borrowed the strategy and began challenging license renewal applications from radio and television stations in which women were underrepresented in professional jobs (Beasley and Gibbons, 1977:126–27). Within a year these challenges had put the licenses of 143 stations in limbo (*Broadcasting*, 1973). During the same period, women employees at the networks organized to pressure their employers for equal opportunities (Lewis, 1986; Sanders and Rock, 1988). In consequence of these two campaigns, women's representation among radio and television reporters rose from 4.8 and 10.7 percent, respectively, in 1971 to 26.3 and 33.1 percent in 1982 (Weaver and Wilhoit, 1986:21).

Although most federal contractors evaded the scrutiny to which targeted industries were subject, affirmative-action regulations paired with the public relations costs of appearing to discriminate prompted many companies to espouse equal-employment practices and sometimes to increase women's representation in visible professional and managerial jobs. This concern with public image, combined with the need to report employment data by sex and race to regulatory agencies, contributed to the feminization of broadcast reporting, bank management, and public relations; in all of which, firms showcased their affirmative-action activities.

Accompanying the increase in regulatory pressures on employers was a decline in male resistance to women workers. Male opposition has played a major role in excluding women from men's jobs. Just a few men can keep women out of their jobs through harassment (Bergmann and Darity, 1981), and organized resistance can ensure women's near exclusion from an entire occupation. For instance, at the turn of the twentieth century, printing firms adopted Linotype machines with an eye to cutting wages by hiring female typists as typesetters, but the International Typographical Union's monopoly over other aspects of the printing process allowed it to thwart employers' intentions (Roos, 1986). Similarly, the Hotel and Restaurant Employees and Bartenders' International lobbied for and won state laws banning women bartenders; exclusionary practices by the Bakery, Confectionery and Tobacco Workers Union limited women's access to unionized baking jobs (Kaufman, 1987); and the American Newspaper Guild permitted contracts that set lower wages for women members (*Press Woman*, 1975:13). In some cases, men's resistance continued to limit women's access to jobs well into the 1980s.

However, excluding women from an entire occupation requires male incumbents to act collectively and to institutionalize barriers. Restricting job competition has been one of the primary goals of labor unions, and their success at excluding all women and male racial or ethnic minorities is reflected in those groups' underrepresentation in the skilled trades (Freeman and Medoff, 1984; Baron et al., 1988). Men's exclusion of women depends on a power base—usually control over the labor supply. This explains why unionized men have withstood sex integration better than unorganized men, and it accounts for women's paltry movement into unionized male craft jobs during the 1970s. Anticipated opposition from male workers can prompt employers to lower women in the labor queue (e.g., Milkman, 1987), whereas employers in occupations in which male resistance to women is low can take advantage of women's lower wages. Cohn's (1985) analysis of the feminization of clerical jobs in the British General Post Office and the Great Western Railway supports this analysis. He contended that clerical work feminized partly because the male unions were too weak to control occupational entry (see also Davies, 1975). In the 1970s the Newspaper Guild capitulated to pressure from female members to condemn sex discrimination against reporters (*Editor and Publisher*, 1970b:44): in 1971 it adjusted nineteen contracts to give women equal pay (Marzolf, 1977:103), and a year later it filed a sex-discrimination complaint against the *Cleveland Plain Dealer* (*Presstime*, 1982:3). The advent of electronic composition in the 1970s all but eliminated the unique expertise of typesetters, thereby allowing publishers of small papers and weeklies to bypass the once powerful International Typographical Union and bring women into their composing rooms. The ITU remained strong in large metropolitan dailies; in consequence, those composing rooms remain male.

More frequently in the occupations we studied, men voluntarily acceded to feminization for various reasons. First and foremost, they had begun to abandon jobs that did not seem worth fighting for. Men signaled their lack of interest in depreciated occupations such as book editing, retail pharmacy, residential real estate sales, and insurance adjusting and examining by failing to apply for jobs. For example, several informants told Roos that women first broke into typesetting in the 1960s after employers introduced teletypesetter machines; male unionists relinquished their claim to this machine in large measure because its "QWERTY" keyboard resembled a typewriter.

Second, men failed to oppose women's entry because they planned to leave or be promoted out of the jobs in question. Case study occupations with high turnover included bartending, insurance adjusting and examining, book editing, and real estate sales. Given that incumbents' median tenure in these fields during the 1980s averaged between four and six years (Carey, 1988), most had little incentive to exclude women.

Third, women who enter different jobs from those men hold within an occupation pose little threat and elicit little opposition. This phenomenon probably helped account for women's more rapid entry into male occupations within already female-intensive industries such as banking, insurance, publishing, hospitals, and the retail sector (Shaeffer and Lynton, 1979; Fields and Wolff, 1989). As Chapter 3 shows, within most feminizing occupations the sexes were so heavily segregated that women did not threaten men's monopoly of desirable jobs. Similarly, when jobs change substantially, as they did in insurance adjusting and bake-off baking, men do not define women as taking "their" jobs (Rotella, 1981:162).

Finally, as we noted above, in rapidly growing occupations such as accounting and systems analysis, women posed little threat. This was especially true because most women were confined to lower-level posts. In large organizations, male managers probably accepted women's presence in lower managerial positions as inevitable, given affirmative-action programs.

New rankers of labor queues. Until the late 1960s, men dominated the positions that rank workers in the labor queue, and neither the ideology of sex-typing nor men's right to preserve it had been challenged. In the 1970s, however, actors with different values took up some of the posts that ranked prospective workers, and different rankers can make a difference. In California, for example, Baron and his colleagues (1988) found that in large state agencies leadership turnover was associated with faster integration, and that integration progressed more rapidly in younger than in middle-aged agencies, presumably because the former were less hidebound or had been established during a period of greater sensitivity to equal opportunities.

A change in those who ranked prospective workers in the labor queue contributed to the feminization of publishing, real estate sales, and pharmacy. During the 1970s, as corporations or conglomerates acquired family-owned book and newspaper publishing firms, they transformed personnel practices in newly acquired divisions and subsidiaries. For instance, when CBS sought to reduce its vulnerability to a sex-discrimination suit, it instructed its publishing subsidiary, Holt, Rinehart & Winston, to promote women to editorial jobs.

As franchises or national chains became an important force in industries, they too altered personnel practices. In real estate sales, franchising fostered sales jobs for women because the franchises stood to gain from more sales agents. Major franchise operations such as Century 21 geared recruitment drives toward women. Also facilitating feminization in real estate and insurance sales was the increasing tendency for agents to work on commission, because commission-based pay encourages firms to recruit a large workforce (Markham et al., 1987:237). The sheer size of retail pharmacy and grocery chains allowed them to transform work practices across whole industries, structuring jobs and shaping working conditions in ways that discouraged applications from men. The organization of retail bake-off baking as mostly part-time work is one example.

Finally, the 1970s garnered more managerial positions for women, and women's involvement in assigning jobs may lead to more sex-atypical jobs for women (Kulis and Miller, 1989). Among the occupations we studied, women made marked progress into managerial slots in banking, public relations, publishing, and real estate; and informants in publishing and real estate reported that women's involvement in hiring decisions contributed to these occupations' feminization, insisting that women were more likely than men to ignore the gender queue in assigning jobs.

The Changing Shape of the Labor Queue

Throughout this century, the shape of the labor queue has steadily changed as women's share of the labor force has grown. The influx into the labor force during the 1970s of more than 13 million women raised the odds that a job assigned randomly with respect to sex would go to a woman—from 38 percent in 1970 to 42.6 percent in 1980 (and to 57.7 percent among workers new to the labor force; Rytina and Bianchi, 1984:13). Surely women's growing share of the labor queue helped to foster their movement into some male occupations.

However, we must not lose sight of the reciprocal relationship between demand and supply: employers' increasing need for women for desirable jobs helped to stimulate their growing availability. Among women showing the most sharply increased workforce participation during the 1970s were those 30 to 44 years old and currently or formerly married (see Chapter 1). Many had limited work experience, but a recordbreaking number had to maximize their earnings as the primary support of themselves and their dependents. It is likely that employers in some feminizing occupations constructed jobs to take advantage of this growing pool of potential women workers (Thurow, 1969:50). Employers sometimes design part-time jobs with a view toward using female labor (Beechey and Perkins, 1987). Certainly, grocery stores could have made bake-off baking full-time rather than part-time work if they had wished to attract men. Other occupations too took advantage of women entering the labor force in the 1970s. Indeed, a real estate broker described the perfect prospect for a residential sales job as a married woman in her thirties or forties with children. Thus, heightened demand for women stemming from occupational growth, men's revised rankings of occupations, employers' reranking of the sexes, and a decline in the intensity of employers' preference for men all stimulated an increase in the female labor supply for particular occupations.

Of course, for these jobs to have attracted women, women must have known that desirable jobs existed and have had access to any necessary training. How did so many women discover that feminizing occupations were open to them? Where did they get the skills to qualify for those jobs? In a nutshell, the majority learned about the jobs' existence and how to do them while doing sex-typical work. As Jacobs (1989a) has shown, most women employed in male-dominated occupations previously worked in sex-neutral or predominantly female occupations. Of these, the large number working alongside men who do male jobs are well placed to spot opportunities and to learn necessary skills. Thus, many women who became book editors, real estate and insurance agents, insurance adjusters, bank managers, and bartenders during the 1970s learned of job opportunities and acquired job skills from working in companion "female" occupations as clerks, secretaries, receptionists, editorial assistants, bank tellers, and cocktail waitresses. In doing typically female clerical jobs, millions of women acquired the skills necessary to work as typesetters and insurance-claims adjusters and examiners after computerization transformed those occupations. In fact, the *Occupational Outlook Handbook* (U.S. Bureau of Labor Statistics, 1974b) noted that women with clerical experience could become insurance adjusters.

For a few feminizing occupations, women learned of opportunities and mastered the jobs' duties as consumers or homemakers. Some women tried their hand at real estate sales after buying or selling a home. Others applied for jobs as bakers or school-bus drivers on the basis of skills developed in nonmarket work. The sexual division of labor at work created a pool from which employers—especially those pressured to hire women—could fill vacant jobs in male occupations. For example, with the development of the female occupation of coder ("data-entry operator"), employers had a pool from which they could recruit programmers and, later, systems analysts. In sum, doing female-typed tasks, both at home and in the workplace, prepared women for jobs in some feminizing male occupations. Ironically, the very division of labor that segregates the sexes into different but physically proximate jobs exposed women to opportunities in sex-atypical jobs—as well as to their benefits.

In contrast to occupations in which women could exploit skills acquired in "women's" jobs were a few mostly professional and managerial occupations for which workers are formally trained or certified before employment. Here, credit for women's entry goes in part to the women's liberation movement, which modified public opinion and gave women permission to aspire to occupations that had formerly been off limits to them. Legions of women,

Table 2.3
Percentage of Degrees Awarded to Women, by Degree and Field, 1971, 1981

Degree	1970–71	1980–81
All bachelor's degrees	41.5	47.9
Communications	35.3	54.7
Computer/information science	13.6	32.5
Law	7.1	30.2
Pharmacy	18.3	42.6
Engineering	.8	8.7
Accounting	11.6	45.4
Business and management	9.1	36.7
All master's degrees	39.7	49.3
Business administration	3.6	25.2
Pharmacy	18.6	32.2
Accounting	8.7	34.4
All doctor's degrees	13.4	29.8

Sources: Total bachelor's, master's, and doctor's degree data from U.S. Bureau of the Census (1986b:158,160); all other data from U.S. National Center for Education Statistics (1987), except master's degrees in accounting, which are for 1973 and 1983 from *Wall Street Journal* (1986:11D).

anticipating equal treatment, trained for traditionally male jobs. Colleges and universities exposed women students to opportunities in customarily male professional and managerial occupations and, after the 1972 Educational Amendment barred sex discrimination in educational institutions receiving federal funds, increasingly admitted them to nontraditional majors. Women's sense of entitlement to jobs and their optimism that affirmative action ensured their finding jobs encouraged them to acquire advanced degrees in traditionally male fields. As a result, during the 1970s record numbers trained for careers in systems analysis, accounting, pharmacy, journalism, and financial management. As Table 2.3 shows, women's representation increased at every degree level and in every program from which customarily male professions draw, enabling women to compete for male jobs (Jones and Rosenfeld, 1989).

Education offered women a pathway into a few nonprofessional occupations as well. The proliferation of real estate courses in community colleges allowed women to sidestep the requirement that brokers—almost all men—sponsor would-be sales agents. As one broker said of these classes, "We set up a mechanism for people to get into this business that worked for men and women, and there were a lot more women out there who wanted to get in." Similarly, the development of vocational printing courses enabled women to bypass the lengthy and exclusionary union apprenticeship programs once necessary for employment in typesetting and composition. Bartending schools apparently played a similar function in the 1970s, but by the 1980s few bartenders were using them to learn their trade.

Assuming that talent is equally distributed across the sexes in labor queues, women's growing share of a labor queue increased the number of women who were as qualified as many men and better qualified than some. Employers then chose between (1) paying prime wages to attract the men ranked highest in an occupation's labor queue, (2) settling for men who were less qualified than some available women, or (3) hiring women. The insatiable appetite during the 1970s for trained recruits in accounting or systems analysis meant—given women's growing share among degree holders—that many employers made the third choice.

The foregoing discussion assumes that women and men within' labor queues for the same occupations are equally talented. We may question this assumption, however. If the most promising candidates of each sex pursue the highest-ranked jobs that are open to them, as long as male jobs are more desirable than female jobs and are not fully accessible to women, many female candidates for desegregating male jobs will be *better* qualified than male candidates. Some evidence indicates that this situation occurred in pharmacy, residential real estate, book editing, and baking. We should not be surprised to find that the pattern holds more broadly across all feminizing occupations: when more attractive occupations tempt away the best men from the top of the labor queue, the remaining men are competing with the most qualified women, to whom many desirable male jobs are not fully open.

This analysis leaves unanswered a key question: why should women move into occupations that men have rejected in favor of greener pastures? The answer is simple: because they are preferable to most female occupations. Confined to a limited number of traditionally female occupations, women have been queued up to enter better jobs as they came along. During the 1970s the customarily male jobs that opened their doors more widely attracted women in droves: deteriorating or not, most of such jobs outranked traditionally female occupations that required similar qualifications.[38] Table 2.4 demonstrates this point with respect to earnings. The first two columns show the ratio of female occupational incumbents' real mean annual earnings in 1969 and 1979 (in 1969 dollars) to those of all female workers. All but bartending and bus driving paid more in 1969 than the average woman worker earned, attracting women during the 1970s. Though this advantage in real earnings declined during the 1970s in all these occupations except bus driving, most still paid better than traditionally female occupations.[39] The last two columns of Table 2.4, showing the ratio of the return in earnings to years of education, provide a second index of how well these occupations compensated female incumbents for their education compared with the entire female labor force. In 1969 all but two of the occupations that feminized during the 1970s rewarded women better for their education than did the labor market as a whole. By the

Table 2.4
Ratios of Earnings and Earnings per Year of Education of Women in Feminizing Occupations to Those of Female Labor Force, 1969, 1979

Occupation[a]	Earnings Ratio[b]		Earnings to Education Ratio[e]	
	1969[c]	1979[d] (in 1969$)	1969	1979
Pharmacists	1.60	1.55	1.21	1.18
Editors and reporters	1.45	1.33	1.14	1.07
Public relations specialists	1.60	1.37	1.35	1.13
Insurance sales occupations	1.28	1.15	1.26	1.17
Real estate sales occupations	1.50	1.46	1.45	1.45
Insurance adjusters, examiners and investigators	1.18	1.00	1.14	1.03
Bartenders	.83	.69	.89	.73
Bus drivers	.70	.88	.72	.94

[a] Excludes feminizing occupations whose 1970 and 1980 census classifications differed too greatly to permit comparison (see text). For those listed, classification changes were small; nonetheless, they render 1969 and 1979 values not entirely comparable.

[b] Ratio of mean earnings of female occupational incumbents to mean earnings of female experienced civilian labor force.

[c] Based on mean annual earnings of females in experienced civilian labor force, aged 16 and over, who worked 50–52 weeks in 1969 (U.S. Bureau of the Census, 1973a: Table 19).

[d] Based on mean annual earnings of females in recent experienced civilian labor force, aged 18 and over, who worked full time, year round in 1979 (U.S. Bureau of the Census, 1984c: Table 1).

[e] The numerators of the ratios are the quotient of mean earnings divided by median years of education of female occupational incumbents; the denominators represent the quotient of mean earnings divided by median education (12.4 years in 1970; 12.7 years in 1980) for female labor force. Median educational levels for 1970 are from U.S. Bureau of the Census (1973a: Table 5); for 1980, computed from U.S. Bureau of the Census (1983a).

end of the 1970s, with the exception of real estate sales and bus driving (note that the 1979 value for bus driving is based on the 11 percent of female bus drivers who worked full time, year round), these occupations' relative advantage had dropped slightly, reflecting the changes that had rendered them less attractive to men.

Comparing the median 1979 earnings for women employed full time in feminizing occupations to other specific occupations illustrates the attraction of the former. Women selling real estate averaged $6.97 per hour, compared to $4.64, $4.90, and $6.33 for typists, general office clerks, and teachers, respectively (U.S. Bureau of the Census, 1987a:Table 11). Financial managers averaged $6.95 and computer systems analysts $8.84, compared to $4.11 hourly for bank tellers. Insurance adjusters and examiners made $5.40, compared to $4.92 for data-entry keyers. Female accountants grossed $6.45 per hour, compared to $4.98 for bookkeepers and accounting clerks. Pharmacists averaged $7.91, almost a dollar per hour more than registered nurses, who made $6.98. Even bartenders' paltry $3.37 an hour exceeded waitresses' $3.10. In 1979 public relations specialists averaged 2 to 16 percent higher pay than nurses, librarians, and social workers. Systems analysis and operations and systems research were among the highest-paid occupations for women. Our interviews confirmed the attraction that earnings represented: women frequently explained that they entered one of the occupations we studied because it paid more than they could earn elsewhere. Women in real estate and insurance sales spontaneously mentioned the additional attraction of commission-based pay: equal pay for equal work. These economic attractions, as well as the higher prestige these occupations command in comparison with traditionally female jobs, were sufficient incentives to induce women to migrate into declining occupations.

Despite the similarity of men's and women's preferences for rewarding, well-paying jobs, they may differ in their responsiveness to an occupation's compatibility with domestic responsibilities. Women still do the lion's share of domestic work; as a result, women with families may attach more importance than do men to part-time work or flexible hours (Gerson, 1987). Indeed, the case studies indicated that residential real estate sales, retail baking, bartending, and school-bus driving offered some part-time work or permitted flexible hours. A few women in real estate said that one of the occupation's attractions had been their belief that selling houses would fit into their family obligations, though they soon learned that customers' schedules often required them to work during "family" times—evenings and weekends. Ironically, in the still male-dominated specialty of commercial real estate sales, agents work regular hours.

In fact, however, between 1970 and 1980 women's opportunity to work part time declined in five of the occupations we studied: editing and reporting, insurance sales, real estate sales, insurance adjusting and examining, and bus driving. It rose by almost 12 percentage points in bartending and by 1 to 2 percentage points in pharmacy and public relations (see Table 2.5; U.S. Bureau of the Census, 1973b, 1983a). Except for bartending, these results are inconsistent with the case study occupations' feminizing because they offered women greater opportunities for part-time jobs. The chance for flexible working hours may have drawn women to some of the feminizing occupations, but it was not sufficient for their feminization. Without the labor shortages or external pressures that required employers to turn to women, neither women's presumed greater interest in part-time or flexible work nor the occupations' capacity to provide flexible or part-time schedules was sufficient for their feminization.

Summary

This section has shown that the factors facilitating women's inroads into the feminizing male occupations we studied conform to queueing processes.

Table 2.5

Percentage of Employment Full Time, Year Round in Feminizing Occupations, by Sex, 1970 and 1980

Occupation	Female		Male	
	1970	1980	1970	1980
Pharmacy	51.8	50.1	80.7	78.2
Editing/reporting	50.0	51.9	74.5	70.4
Public relations	56.6	55.4	81.0	74.5
Insurance sales	64.2	68.5	80.9	79.7
Real estate sales	40.1	45.4	70.6	70.1
Insurance adjusting/examining	66.1	71.1	82.9	82.0
Bartending	47.7	35.9	60.7	45.5
Bus driving	6.7	12.9	57.9	50.7

Note: Excludes feminizing occupations whose 1970 and 1980 census classifications differed too greatly to permit comparison (see text). For those listed, classification changes were small; nonetheless, they render 1969 and 1979 values not entirely comparable. Full-time, year-round employees are those who worked at least 30 hours per week and at least 50 weeks per year.

Sources: For 1970, computed from U.S. Bureau of the Census (1973b: Table 11); for 1980, computed from U.S. Bureau of the Census (1983a).

Although most employers continued to structure the labor queue around a gender queue, when the supply of men was inadequate—either because rapid job growth exhausted the supply or because men spurned jobs as inferior to accessible alternatives—employers turned to women. They also did so when economic considerations made hiring women cheaper and regulatory agencies made *not* hiring them potentially costly. Women's influx into better jobs than those to which they have long been relegated is neither new nor surprising. What is new since 1970 is how often employers have been pressed to turn to women to fill customarily male jobs.

| | | | Notes

1. Although we sometimes speak of *a* labor market, *a* labor queue, and *a* job queue, contemporary American society comprises numerous labor markets that serve specific occupations, communities, and regions. Employers hire day laborers in local labor markets of unskilled workers, teachers in statewide markets of teaching-certificate holders, and physicists in a national scientific labor market. Each of these labor markets consists of job and labor queues (see Boylan, 1988).

2. Given Thurow's and Hodge's focus on unemployment, job queues were irrelevant.

3. Doeringer and Piore (1971:168) argued that queueing is less prevalent among secondary-sector employers who treat workers as an undifferentiated labor pool.

4. Indeed, employers are suspicious of workers who will settle for jobs that are "beneath them" and often reject such applicants as "overqualified."

5. Blau et al.'s (1956) explanation of how individual workers end up in particular jobs and White's (1970) vacancy-chain model are individual-level analogues to our model.

6. A dwindling influx of workers into the labor market (e.g., after immigration laws had stemmed the tide of immigrant workers, or in the aftermath of the "baby bust") also induces shortages that can transform occupations' composition (Lieberson, 1980; Kessler-Harris, 1982:238).

7. However, as Thurow (1969:50) noted, growth in a lower-ranked group can lead demand to shift to exploit that growth, thereby expanding the group's employment options and affecting those of higher-ranked groups as well. When less preferred groups increase their labor force share—as southern-central-eastern Europeans did during the Great Migration and southern blacks did in northern labor markets early in this century—some from their ranks advance into better jobs than their group usually commands, concentrating the more privileged groups into still better jobs (Hodge, 1973:24; Lieberson, 1980:297).

8. The onus of this bumping process has fallen on African Americans. For example, in 1865, when southern white men scorned skilled construction work, blacks held 80 percent of such jobs, but Depression-based unemployment in the 1930s led whites to appropriate 83 percent of them (Silberman, 1978:175–76).

9. But if the available jobs are seen as too far below a group's normal jobs, some members may opt instead for temporary nonemployment. Many men did just that during the Great Depression rather than take female-labeled clerical jobs (Milkman, 1976).

10. It is the preference for cheap, tractable, and productive workers that has led some employers to put machines at the head of the labor queue. Mark Twain sought to do that in his printing business because the automatic typecasting machine could "work like six men and do everything but drink, swear and go out on strike" (Zimbalist, 1979:106). Employers who cannot replace human labor with machines try to substitute cheaper for more expensive workers (Braverman, 1974; Scott, 1982).

11. Of course, employers rank women ahead of men for certain jobs, such as that of receptionist.

12. Other stereotypically female attractions are greater docility and the ability to "civilize"—and thus help employers control—an unruly male workforce (see Reskin and Padavic, 1988).

13. In fact, sex differences in absenteeism and turnover result from the different jobs in which women and men typically work. Moreover, some evidence suggests that women work harder and are as committed as men to their jobs (Lorence, 1987:121–42; Bielby and Bielby, 1988), and that employers forced to use women in men's jobs have been satisfied with their performance (Milkman, 1987; Reskin and Padavic, 1988).

14. Although white men have often had recourse to this tactic—for example, between 1882 and 1900 they struck at least fifty times to protest working with blacks (Lieberson, 1980:347–48; Cohn, 1985:223)—they are hardly alone in its use. White women have reacted similarly when their employers hired black women (Anderson, 1982; Milkman, 1987).

15. To highlight the role of employers, we speak of "employers ranking workers"

rather than "jobs seek[ing] people" (Thurow, 1972:68) or "occupations compet[ing] for workers" (Simpson et al., 1982).

16. Filer (1985) claimed that women get, and presumably prefer, a larger fraction of their total compensation in nonpecuniary rewards than do men. However, Jacobs and Steinberg (1991) cast doubt on Filer's thesis by showing that taking nonmonetary rewards into account actually increased the total compensation gap between the sexes. Moreover, analyses of the 1979 and 1982 National Longitudinal Survey samples of women found no clear pattern of preference for characteristics typical of predominantly female occupations, and some evidence that women preferred the nonpecuniary dimensions characteristic of men's work over those common in women's work (Reed and Holleman, 1988).

17. Similarly, a predominantly male workforce can lead women to downrank an occupation if they expect it to provide an uncongenial environment, but Padavic and Reskin (1990) found that neither a job's predominantly male workforce nor hostility from male workers affected women's inclination to transfer to a blue-collar plant job.

18. The rest of this chapter and Chapter 3 draw heavily on the case studies without formally citing authors and chapter titles. For more details and support for our claims, turn to the appropriate chapter in Part II.

19. We show below that shrinking occupations feminized for other reasons. In fact, typesetting and composing feminized during the 1970s despite an apparent loss of about 16,000 jobs (its 1970 and 1980 classifications are not sufficiently comparable for us to determine exact job loss). Our ongoing work tests the link between growth and feminization through statistical analyses of all 503 three-digit detailed occupations.

20. An unchanged occupation can fall or rise in a job queue if other occupations that compete for the same workers become more or less attractive. Take the current shortages of nurses and teachers: the increased accessibility of traditionally male professions to educated women has all but depleted what had been a captive labor pool of educated women on which teaching and nursing had drawn. In effect, educated women downgraded the female semiprofessions once they had access to greener pastures.

21. Facilitating this transformation was a shift of some of the work of adjusters to customers, who were called on to do more paperwork in making claims. Shifting work to women customers is another way work can feminize (Glazer, 1984, 1988).

22. The clergy, for example, drew more men during the Vietnam war; subsequently, that occupation's attraction for men has plummeted (Nesbitt, 1989).

23. The proportions of female and male college freshman who sought to be "very well off financially" climbed from 32 and 54 percent in 1969 to 57 and 69 percent, respectively, ten years later (American Council on Education, 1979).

24. The census asks for total earnings for the year before the decennial year in order to obtain total calendar earnings.

25. Data limited to feminizing occupations do not establish that change in relative income is correlated with changing sex composition, much less the causal order of any relationship. In subsequent work we address these questions by statistically analyzing the relations among these and other variables for all detailed occupations.

26. Undoubtedly, pension plans or uncertainty about their ability to compete with younger men in other lines of work constrained some older men from leaving

adjusting. Nor were independent adjusters directly affected when insurance companies brought adjusting inside.

27. For example, the National Academy of Sciences report,*Computer Chips and Paper Clips* (Hartmann et al., 1986:38) noted that the 1980 census had reclassified accountants and auditors—down from 85 percent male in 1950 to 62 percent male in 1980—from professional workers to "management-related occupations," suggesting a "reorganization of job content and perhaps some downgrading of the occupation as the proportion of females has increased."

28. As Hodge (1973:19) recognized, the more heterogeneous the lower-ranked group on qualifications, the more members it will have who outqualify the preferred group—and women's qualifications, like those of men, vary widely.

29. Occupational niches for minorities in atypical occupations emerge when groups prefer to obtain products and services within their own group or when the majority fails to provide adequate services (Hout, 1986). The dominant group sometimes creates niches by using minorities as intermediaries between the dominant and the minority community (Lieberson, 1980; Collins, 1983). Protected markets created jobs for blacks in race-segregated jobs such as personnel specialist and in "go-between" roles in social service (Collins, 1983:379). Hicks (1988:30C) credited black investment bankers' concentration in municipal bonds to big-city black mayors' insistence on dealing with investment brokers of their own race.

30. A rare instance of a switch in the other direction occurred during the nineteenth century when cotton-industry employers substituted more costly male for female workers because they thought that men could operate new, heavier, and faster equipment more productively than women (Abbott, 1909:95–96).

31. However, although the automation of wholesale production baking (through continuous-processing equipment, high-speed mixing, and pneumatic-handling systems) made the work less physically taxing, it did not open production jobs to women. Instead, between 1950 and 1980 employers replaced 35,625 mostly male production workers with machines. As a result of its reducing male but not female jobs, mechanization left production baking less male dominated without creating new jobs for women.

32. Leidner (1989a) introduced a similar concept of "interactive service work" in her comparison of predominantly female counter workers at McDonald's with overwhelmingly male insurance sales agents. As Leidner pointed out, however, despite their interactive-service component, the insurance agents construed their jobs as masculine by emphasizing the need for "manly" traits such as control and self-direction.

33. A. H. Robbins used a spokes*woman* to respond to charges of corporate malfeasance in marketing a dangerous intrauterine device (IUD), and Union Carbide followed suit after the Bhopal disaster.

34. This is not to deny that occupations' sex labels and sex stereotypes influence workers' expectations of doing some jobs but not others.

35. Despite the Liberty Mutual suit, the timing of women's gains in insurance adjusting and examining suggests that enforcement played a minor role in women's increased representation in that occupation. Once they had clericalized adjusting and examining jobs, employers did not need any external pressure to hire women.

36. In one dramatic instance, when employees hit NBC with a sex discrimi-

nation suit, CBS—figuring it could be next—immediately implemented changes to reduce sex segregation.

37. The leeway the EEOC gave employers in reporting jobs' sex and race makeup across broad occupational categories enabled employers to circumvent the spirit of the regulations through "job-title" promotions that were largely nominal. Beller's (1984) data on the earnings of financial managers are consistent with banks' assigning some women managerial titles without managerial salaries.

38. The declining demand for workers in many traditionally female occupations probably accelerated some women's shift to male occupations (Blau, 1989).

39. The 1969 earnings data are for women who worked year round, either part or full time, whereas the 1979 data are limited to full-time workers. Including part-time workers lowered the 1969 mean earnings, so occupations' incomes may have declined more during the 1970s than these data suggest.

3

Consequences of Desegregation: Occupational Integration and Economic Equity?

To what extent has desegregation yielded occupational and economic opportunities for women? This chapter focuses on the two parts of that question. First, did women benefit occupationally from moving into the desegregating occupations we studied? In other words, did occupational-level desegregation translate into sex integration at the level of jobs, or did sex segregation persist within these nominally desegregated occupations?[1] Second, did occupational-level desegregation reduce the earnings gap between men and women within these occupations? Obviously, the answer to the second question depends on the first: if women experienced genuine occupational integration, their progress toward economic equity would be greatly enhanced. Because the passage of the 1963 Equal Pay Act has made equal pay for equal work a legal requirement for most employers, women's inroads into the full range of male jobs within occupations should have the consequence of reducing the earnings gap. If, on the other hand, occupational desegregation did not bring full job-level integration, and the occupational specialties to which women were relegated ranked lower and paid less than male specialties, we would expect systematic sex differences in earnings to persist.

The observation that job-level integration may not accompany occupational desegregation is not meant to understate women's job gains. During the 1970s and into the 1980s women made dramatic headway into thirty-three occupational titles that had traditionally been men's work. These gains were in sharp contrast to the relative stability in occupational sex segregation that segmented the labor force during the first seven decades of this century. The purposes of this chapter are to specify the nature of these gains and to examine the extent to which desegregation yielded women opportunities in desegregating occupations. To do so, we once again rely on evidence from our case study occupations.

I I I I Integration, Ghettoization, or Resegregation?

As we showed in Chapter 1, during the 1970s large numbers of women moved into almost three dozen occupations traditionally thought of as "men's" domain. We developed a schema to better understand the patterns underlying women's gains by drawing on theoretical models constructed to explain desegregation by race. Pettigrew (1969:58), for example, distinguished real and nominal racial integration by examining two major ways in which segregation by race can diminish.[2] He argued that genuine integration would be achieved only if the races moved from racial separation to racial togetherness *and* if in the process blacks achieved true personal and group autonomy. He contrasted this state with a second form that reductions in racial separation could take— mere desegregation. By the latter he meant declines in segregation that are not accompanied by increased personal and group autonomy for blacks—in other words, only nominal declines.

Other students of racial segregation recognized that another outcome can follow increased interracial contact—resegregation. In analyzing residential desegregation by race, for example, Duncan and Duncan (1957) described the influx of blacks into formerly all-white neighborhoods that led in turn to white flight and eventually to the neighborhood's resegregation as black (we elaborate this argument below). Thus, what appeared to be integration was sometimes only a temporary stage in a longer process of resegregation from white to black neighborhoods.[3]

The important distinction between real and nominal integration, or the various forms desegregation can take, calls our attention to the difference between a minority group's full involvement in society's institutions and "institutionalized biracial settings [including] both races but little cross-racial acceptance and often patronizing legacies of white supremacy" (Pettigrew, 1969:58). There is little doubt that nominal desegregation, while reducing racial segregation in some respects, perpetuates it in others.

Following the same line of reasoning, we ask whether sex desegregation in the occupations we studied was real or nominal. In other words, during the 1970s did women integrate all levels of the case study occupations, or did sex segregation persist within them? In addition, is there any evidence that the post-1970 integration was only a stage in a process that will culminate in these occupations' resegregation as female? We cannot expect occupational resegregation to enhance women's occupational equity relative to men, since the integration involved is only temporary.

To answer these questions we conceptualize three forms of occupational desegregation by sex: genuine integration, ghettoization, and resegregation. Women made *genuine progress* in traditionally male occupations if they integrated all specialties within a desegregating occupation and if they found work in all industries in which the occupation is located and all establishments that employ occupational incumbents. Genuine integration should bring women occupational equity with male coworkers of equivalent experience. It should also enhance the economic equity between the sexes, assuming that equal-pay laws are adequately enforced. However, we found no clear-cut examples of such integration in our case studies. Rather, the second form of desegregation, *ghettoization*, was the modal outcome in the feminizing occupations we studied. Ghettoization occurs when women and men in the same occupational title typically perform different jobs. In ghettoized occupations, women and men work in different firms or industries and hold different job titles and ranks. As a result, they usually perform different tasks. The third form of desegregation, *resegregation*, occurs when an entire occupation or a major occupational specialty switches from a predominantly male to a predominantly female labor force. Our case study data revealed two instances of resegregating occupations and several resegregating occupational specialties.

Although we distinguish between ghettoization and resegregation in examining the degree to which desegregation has created opportunities for women, these are not mutually exclusive outcomes. They reflect different faces of the same edifice and occur for the same reasons. The latter denotes women's replacement of men in formerly male lines of work and hence taps both women's entry into a formerly male occupation and their subsequent extreme concentration in that line of work. As noted above, resegregation can occur at the level of an entire occupation but applies as well to occupational specialties. Ghettoization highlights a different dimension, the segregation of women and men into different jobs within the same occupation. This segregation need not be so extreme as to make some jobs overwhelmingly female and others overwhelmingly male. Thus, both ghettoization and resegregation can occur in the same occupation if sex segregation exists across jobs or specialties and if one or more specialties that men formerly dominated become overwhelmingly female.[4] Both resegregation and ghettoization represent limited progress for women; indeed, they point to the perpetuation of segregation by sex.

It is important to clarify one point before describing our findings in detail. When we look at the changing sex composition of occupations between 1970 and 1980, or from 1970 to the present, we must remember that the change recorded in that period may be continuing. We focused on the years between 1970 and 1980 because census data showing large changes in occupational sex composition during that decade commanded the attention of researchers, the media, and policymakers. Restricting our conclusions to the 1970s, however, limits the inferences we can draw as to whether sex desegregation represented ghettoization, resegregation, or true integration. Change in an occupation's sex composition is a *process:* what appears to be integration at the end of some interval may give rise to complete resegregation at a later time. These two outcomes in turn have very different implications for women's job and earnings prospects.

Ghettoization

The workplace is replete with instances of ghettoization by specialty, task, and firm. When women first broke into typesetting, for example, they clustered in the book sector, where they specialized in typing straight, unbroken lines of text. Composing headlines, justifying columns, and integrating photos and other nontext material remained the purview of skilled men (Hartmann et al., 1986:29). Despite women's influx into law, they are overrepresented in legal clinics, where work is routinized and opportunities for advancement inferior (Epstein, 1983). Blau (1977) found substantial intraoccupational sex segregation of office workers (such as accounting clerks) across firms; Reskin and Hartmann (1986:12–13) offer additional evidence of occupational sex segregation across and within firms. In a recent study of screenwriters, Bielby and Bielby (1987) found that employers hired women to write situation comedies but not action shows.[5] Baron and Bielby (1985:239–40) observed another form of job-level ghettoization in their California industry data: spatial or temporal desegregation in multilocational establishments in which women and men in the same job titles worked on different shifts or in different locations. In one real estate office, for example, women managers supervised female clerical workers in one location, while male managers supervised salespeople in a different location.

Women and men were concentrated in different jobs in every feminizing occupation we studied. This occupational ghettoization took many forms: women and men worked in different subspecialties in these desegregating occupations, for different clients within firms, in different industrial sectors, and at different ranks. Men retained most of the more desirable jobs; women were disproportionately relegated to lower-status specialties, less desirable work settings, lower-paying industries, and part-time rather than full-time work. Thus, the answer to our question of whether occupation-level desegregation translated into job-level integration is a resounding no. Women and men tended *not* to work alongside one another in the same jobs in these newly desegregating occupations. The occupation-level desegregation we observed masked a substantial amount of persistent internal segregation.

The queueing perspective, developed in Chapter 2, reveals why these forms of intraoccupational segregation remain so prevalent. In Chapter 2 we focused on explanations for occupational feminization; in this chapter we apply the queueing approach to explain the feminization of particular occupational specialties. Both labor and job queues exist *within* occupations, dictating women's and men's distributions across jobs as well as occupations. Employers maintain distinct labor queues for different occupational specialties and select workers on the basis of these queues. Similarly, employees rank occupational specialties in job queues and select jobs accordingly. These queues operate to reserve for men the occupational specialties that offer the highest rewards, are most attractive relative to the alternatives available, and hence are implicitly highest within occupation-specific queues. As a consequence, less desirable specialties feminized faster and more attractive specialties more slowly.

In this section, we examine two sets of explanations for women's concentration in certain specialties within desegregating occupations. First, men disdained jobs they deemed undesirable, and employers in turn resorted to workers lower in the labor queue—female labor. Second, employers sometimes recruited women for visible jobs for which hiring women yielded a public relations or equal-opportunity payoff, or in other jobs in which there existed a sex-specific demand for female labor.

Specialties that men rejected. Men eschewed or abandoned particular specialties within the occupations we studied because the specialties' relative earnings declined between 1970 and 1980. They also rejected specialties that became less desirable for nonmonetary reasons, including declining autonomy, fewer entrepreneurial opportunities, reduced availability for full-time work, and a shift in work content away from "masculine" toward more "feminine" tasks. As a consequence, employers turned to women to staff these positions, ensuring the ghettoization of women in the occupation's lowest-ranked jobs.

Underlying women's dramatic gains as bakers, for example, was their ghettoization in supermarket bakeries in which low-paid workers finish baking already prepared products and package them for sale. As bake-off baking emerged to become a new part-time and low-paid specialty in the 1970s, men refused these jobs.[6] This job concentration of women mirrors their greater predominance at the retail end of the production process. When women work in production baking, they are in low-paying, monotonous jobs toward the end of the line, loading and unloading machines that package the goods. Men monopolize high-paying production jobs, including mixing, blending, and baking goods from scratch.

Similarly, women's growth among typesetters and compositors occurred primarily in newspapers, the sector that suffered the sharpest decline in relative earnings and that is most threatened by technological displacement.[7] Men continue to predominate as typographers in the better-paying commercial sector. One informant whom Roos interviewed described a two-tiered system in his unionized workplace that ghettoized women as a secondary labor force: his employer hired women as "trainees" to work alongside better-paid union members doing identical work. The employer maintained this vertical segregation by requiring the trainees to relinquish their jobs within four years, with the same effect as the ban on married women at Britain's Great Western Railway and the General Post Office (Cohn, 1985): women were stuck in low-paying and less desirable positions. Another reason for women's growing predominance as typesetters and compositors in the lower-paid newspaper sector was that production first shifted to electronic typesetting there, thus threatening male unionists' monopoly over the composing room. The job autonomy that the powerful International Typographical Union had once guaranteed its members declined precipitously. With the standard "QWERTY" keyboard, the job became relatively more open to anyone with typing skills. Reinforcing the more rapid feminization of newspaper typesetting is that work content switched to skills sex-typed as female. Smaller newspapers were among the first work settings to adopt computerized typesetting, and also the first to feminize. Concomitant with adopting the new technology, newspaper publishers reorganized their composing rooms into more typically white-collar—and hence "female"—environments.

Feminization also accompanied declining wages in insurance-adjusting specialties (Phipps, 1989:115). The specialty with the least deterioration in wages experienced the smallest influx of women. Between 1965 and 1980, real weekly wages deteriorated only $5 for insurance adjusters working in the medical/health sector, whereas in life insurance and property/liability, real earnings declined by $7 and $15, respectively, and the percentage of females in these specialties increased by 12 and 8 percent. Phipps (1989: chap. 5) observed that as adjusting and examining became mostly female jobs, the real wages of both women and men declined dramatically, and men's wages approached those of female clerical workers; thus, new male adjusters and examiners began at lower wages than their predecessors. The shift to a computerized claims system also reduced the autonomy and discretion traditionally held by insurance adjusters. The increased routinization and standardization of claims processing has radically transformed the work of adjusters and examiners. Women are most concentrated in the most routine and standardized jobs, as examiners; slightly more males are inside adjusters, and men dominate the remaining jobs in outside adjusting.

In real estate sales, real earnings dropped most in the residential and least in the commercial sector. As a consequence, men left residential sales to move to more lucrative commercial sales. A shift to independent-contractor status for residential salespersons also helped reduce the job's desirability for workers requiring a secure, full-time income. Once recruits to real estate sales could circumvent traditional barriers to occupational access through community-college courses, women became available to meet the increased demand for their services in residential real estate.[8] The sexes remained differentiated vertically, with the traditionally higher-paid brokers disproportionately male: men were four-fifths of the brokers but only 38 percent of salespersons.

Ghettoization also exists in bus driving, where women are hired primarily for relatively lower-paid, part-time positions as school-bus drivers, which men avoid. We found that women were more than half again as likely as men to drive school buses (61 compared to 39 percent) and that 29 percent of male school-bus drivers worked full time year round, compared to only 7 percent of women.

In public relations, women are overrepresented as lower-paid "communications technicians," and men are more likely to be promoted to higher-paying management posts. Moreover, women typically made their first major forays into public relations in female industries—elementary and secondary education and hospitals. Responding to a shortage of men, employers in these industries were more likely to accept women's breaking of sex-typing barriers, thereby contributing to ghettoization by industry. Even in systems analysis—a rapidly growing occupation—men and women are segregated by job. As one of Donato's informants noted, women predominate among low-paid analysts whose daily tasks involve interacting with users, while men are more likely to work in high-paid jobs in which they make decisions about information systems and interact with analysts, programmers, and managers.

When conglomerization robbed book editors of their traditional autonomy in selecting and working with authors, fewer men chose editing. But they did not entirely abandon the occupation, choosing instead to retain the top editorial positions and the university press jobs, where commercial pressures are lower and autonomy higher. Women, in contrast, are concentrated in trade presses, where the opposite characteristics obtain.

In pharmacy, women are concentrated in hospitals, which offer the lowest salaries, while men predominate in the higher-paying retail settings. Managers in all sectors and owners of retail pharmacies are disproportionately male. With the proliferation of chain pharmacies and a concomitant decline in the number of independently owned drugstores in the 1970s, however, retail pharmacy offered decreasing entrepreneurial opportunities. As men eschewed nonmanagerial chain-store jobs, women pharmacists necessarily came to predominate in them.

To the limited extent that black women disproportionately entered male occupations (Reskin and Roos, 1989; Sokoloff, 1989), they have also been confined to the least attractive specialties. Although between 1970 and 1980 their representation among insurance adjusters, investigators, and examiners grew from 2.2 to 8.2 percent, black women disproportionately work as examiners or claims processors, performing routine low-paying clerical jobs in which workers enter data into computerized programs. Other sources have shown that women of color have been ghettoized after entering traditionally white female occupations such as retail sales, some backstage clerical jobs, teaching, and practical nursing. Occupations in which black women have become newly overrepresented include prekindergarten teacher, keypunch operator, file clerk, calculating-machine operator, social-welfare clerical assistant, and the female semiprofessions in general (Malveaux and Wallace, 1987:282; Sokoloff, 1989). Despite the notion that African-American women particularly benefit from affirmative action, evidence increasingly documents what observers have long recognized: the joint effects of racial, ethnic, and sex segregation have made black women the last to profit from the opening of any doors into male lines of work (Anderson, 1982; Sokoloff, 1987; Leonard, 1988; Strober and Catanzarite, 1988).

The flip side of feminizing jobs, then, are specialties that have remained predominantly male. In some feminizing occupations, unionized settings continue to exclude women, thus reserving the higher-paying and more desirable jobs for men. For example, the resistance of unionized male workers contributes to women's lack of headway in production baking and municipal transit, despite women's strong gains in the nonunionized sectors of retail baking and school-bus driving. Women have made substantially smaller inroads into typesetting and composition in large metropolitan dailies where union strength remains strong. Women reportedly first gained access to bartending in nonunionized settings, where male employees were unsuccessful in keeping them out (Cobble, 1989a). In other occupational specialties, male opposition remains an effective force for exclusion, even without unions. For example, women have made few inroads into commercial real estate sales, where brokers still reportedly hesitate to hire women; contributory factors include the fear of adverse reactions from male developers and men's desire to monopolize the lucrative commercial jobs.

Sex-specific demand for female labor.   In addition to hiring women for the less desirable jobs that men abandoned, employers sometimes specifically recruited women to fill job openings in occupational specialties when they perceived a sex-specific demand. Chapter 2 showed that employers chose women for some visible occupational specialties because regulatory agencies or vocal employee groups pressured them to do so; thus, employers sometimes targeted women for recruitment because of outside pressure rather than in response to a decline in the male labor supply. Though placing women in visible positions showcased employers' responsiveness to affirmative action, these positions were more often than not staff jobs with little opportunity for upward mobility. This pattern was apparent among the public relations specialists we studied. One specialist whom Donato interviewed remarked that firms were using women as spokespersons to publicize themselves as equal-opportunity

employers, but "spokespersons are usually powerless puppets, having little autonomy when speaking to others . . . so that using women this way is just a
management ploy." This suggests that firms seek a public relations payoff for
hiring women in sex-atypical jobs but place them where they are not a competitive threat to highly placed men. As public relations managers, women
are less likely to be on managerial career ladders. Similarly, as managers in
customer-service banking, posts that do not generate profits, women rarely
accumulate the experience or connections to threaten men's prerogative for
top management posts, but they are highly visible and satisfy EEOC goals.

Another example of this strategy occurred among broadcast reporters.
Pressured to hire women in professional or managerial slots lest the FCC
deny license renewals, stations concentrated women in soft-news positions,
while men continued to report the hard news and to anchor news programs.
Although women's representation among print reporters did not increase disproportionately during the 1970s, women's representation did rise sharply in
two newspaper chains, Gannett and Knight-Ridder. Their corporate commitment to advance women in reporting and editing jobs substantially increased
women's representation in affiliated newspapers (Wilson, 1989). This example
illustrates that commitment to equal-employment opportunity by top leadership is strongly associated with women's progress in sex-atypical jobs (Shaeffer
and Lynton, 1979).

Employers have also hired women to work with female clients, perpetuating female ghettos within desegregating occupations in what Baron and
Bielby (1985) called gender-based desegregation. Thus women were hired as
editors in part to work specifically with a growing number of authors writing
books about women. Employers have also hired women in public relations
and in insurance sales to tap the emerging female market. Notably, women in
insurance sales have had their greatest success in the female market and the
family market, or in selling tax-sheltered annuities to teachers and nurses—
professions made up mostly of women.

Sometimes employers justify hiring women for certain specialties because of perceptions of women's greater productivity, given their stereotyped
expertise in specific skills. For example, bankers hired women in retail and
branch banking when increased competition led them to emphasize interpersonal skills, long seen to be "female" characteristics. Brokers recruited women
for residential real estate because of their presumed knowledge about housing,
their neighborhoods, and local schools. Of course, these reasons may also be
merely post hoc justifications for hiring women to fill jobs left vacant by an
undersupply of men.

A partial success story?   Examining the occupation in which we found
the least ghettoization—bartending—is instructive. Bartending is relatively
unsegregated because, unlike the other occupations we investigated, it lacks

the differentiation that segregation requires. Four-fifths of all bartenders work in a single industry, food and beverage service; often only one or two bartenders work on a shift, and their duties usually do not involve enough differentiation to support a division of labor by sex. Moreover, although some bartenders become managers, the occupation lacks a developed job ladder that can support vertical segregation. Prior to 1970 the union excluded women from mixing drinks and relied largely on formal exclusions through state laws to preserve their turf. After courts struck down those laws, male bartenders lacked any means to segregate women within bartending.

Resegregation

Occupational *resegregation* occurs when an underrepresented group replaces the former majority as the predominant group in an occupation. Historical accounts offer a few instances of women replacing men—as telephone operators, teachers, clerical workers, and bank tellers (see Chapter 1). This process of occupational change resembles Duncan and Duncan's (1957) classic analysis of residential desegregation (see Chapter 15). As they recognized, the process of succession occurs over a period of years; it can be interrupted for some time, or it can remain incomplete. The recognition that resegregation—or any changing composition—is an ongoing *process* makes extrapolating outcomes inherently risky. What appears to be resegregation can halt or even reverse with changing labor market conditions. Recall how men reclaimed feminizing occupations during the Great Depression and after both world wars; a replay of such reversals is conceivable. For example, in residential real estate a booming housing market could attract men back to this sector; indeed, it had reportedly done so in the Los Angeles market by 1990 (Kinchen, 1990).

With this caveat in mind, we nevertheless found evidence of occupational resegregation in two of our case studies. Women's representation among insurance adjusters, examiners, and investigators doubled, from 30 to 60 percent, between 1970 and 1980; in 1988, women constituted 72 percent of this occupation. Similarly, female typesetters and compositors increased from 17 to 56 percent during the 1970s, and by 1988 three out of four were women (Table 1.6; U.S. Bureau of Labor Statistics, 1989).

Within some case study occupations, resegregation turned certain specialties over to women, while others remained predominantly male. In insurance, examining and inside adjusting became primarily female. Typesetters and compositors were more likely to be female in newspapers and corporate in-house shops, while commercial typesetting remained predominantly male. Women constitute a strong majority of residential real estate salespeople and the plurality of trade book editors; women retail bakers are well on their way to following suit; and 1980 census data show that women constituted 63 percent of elementary and secondary school-bus drivers.

Many of the occupations we studied continued to feminize into the 1980s. For example, by 1988 bartending was 50 percent female, and public relations 59 percent (U.S. Bureau of Labor Statistics, 1989). The professional association for public relations specialists has already characterized itself as a velvet ghetto (Cline et al., 1986). In Duncan and Duncan's (1957) terminology, women have "invaded" these occupations, perhaps paving the way for their eventual resegregation as predominantly female occupations; however, it is too early to tell how much more they will feminize.

| | | | Did Desegregation Benefit Women Economically?

A primary objection to sex segregation is that it lowers women's wages by confining women to lower-paying lines of work. We have assessed the existence and extent of women's gains in the case study occupations in four ways. First, we examined women's earnings relative to those of their male coworkers. Second, to estimate how well women in desegregating occupations are doing relative to those who remain in traditionally female occupations, we compared these women's earnings with those of all women. Third, we observed the earnings of women in the desegregating occupations relative to those of the average male worker. Finally, we briefly considered women's nonincome progress toward occupational equity.

The data presented in the previous section temper our optimism as to whether occupational desegregation has enhanced sex equality within feminizing occupations. Given the extent to which women predominate in lower-paying, less desirable jobs within feminizing occupations and the tendency of formerly male occupations or occupational specialties to resegregate as female, one should not expect substantial increases in women's relative earnings. Occupational ghettoization and resegregation do not indicate that women are achieving meaningful economic gains relative to their male coworkers.

Researchers have generally used the ratio of female to male earnings to measure women's economic status relative to men's. They typically calculate this ratio for the median annual earnings of full-time, year-round workers in the experienced civilian labor force.[9] Changes in the earnings ratio can derive from shifts in both men's and women's annual earnings. Thus, fully understanding changes in the ratio requires decomposing it into these components. Feminization between 1970 and 1980 could have increased women's earnings relative to men's if both men's and women's real earnings increased but women's did so at a faster rate; if both men's and women's real earnings decreased but women's did so at a slower rate; if women's real earnings increased while men's remained steady or declined; or if women's remained steady while men's declined. Note that though any of the four conditions would lead to an increase in the earnings ratio, they imply very different underlying changes in the relationship between men's and women's earnings within an occupation. We must thus examine not only changes in ratios but also changes in the real earnings of men and women over time.

To put our case study occupations into context, consider how the aggregate male–female earnings ratio has changed over time. When the Census Bureau began to track women's relative annual earnings in 1955, women employed year round and full time earned 63.9 percent as much as men. Between 1955 and 1981 the ratio fluctuated but ultimately hovered around 60 percent. In 1985 it reached 64.6, a record high, then dropped again in 1986 to 64.3 (U.S. Department of Labor, Women's Bureau, 1983: Table III-1; U.S. Bureau of the Census, 1987b: Table 7). The National Committee on Pay Equity (1987:3) has calculated that one-quarter of the increase in the earnings ratio between 1979 and 1986 is attributable to a *decline* in men's wages.[10] Between 1970 and 1980, the decade on which our case studies focus, the ratio fluctuated, registering a net increase from 59.4 in 1970 to 60.2 percent in 1980.

Occupational Feminization and Earnings

Traditionally, "women's" jobs have been both lower paid and less valued than "men's." Occupational incumbents have thus been chagrined to learn that their occupation is feminizing, fearful that women's influx will lead to a deterioration in wages and prestige. For example, a recent study from the University of Maryland reporting that women's influx into journalism and related professional careers threatened to turn these occupations into "pink-collar ghettos" with lower status and salaries drew a spate of hostile and alarmist reactions (Beasley and Theus, 1985).

This fear has a valid empirical basis: the percentage of female workers in an occupation *is* negatively correlated with occupational earnings (Treiman and Hartmann, 1981). This negative association does not necessarily imply that women's entry *causes* earnings to drop; the observed negative relationship is equally consistent with causality running in the opposite direction, from earnings decline to women's entry. Certainly, the evidence that many of our case study occupations feminized because they dropped in men's job queue lends support to the latter causal ordering. As we noted in Chapter 2 and in the preceding section of this chapter, men often abandon occupations or specialties for better-paying alternatives when faced with declines in wages; employers then hire women to fill the resulting labor vacuum. Chapter 2 also showed that men's real earnings declined during the 1970s in every feminizing occupation (except insurance sales) for which we had comparable 1970 and 1980 data. Given their lower average earnings, women's greater representation in the occupation (or specialty) may also lower its median earnings.

A third possible causal sequence that could lead occupational earnings to be negatively correlated with percentage female involves outside factors that influence both. Two possibilities for the occupations we studied are employment discrimination and reorganization of the work process. Discrimination that assigns women predominantly to lower-paying specialties and lowers women's earnings relative to men's would produce a negative correlation between earnings and sex composition. Similarly, when employers restructure and deskill the work process, they often use the occasion to lower wages and to replace male with female workers.

The historical record supports the contention that the causal relationship between feminization and earnings runs primarily from declining earnings to female entry. Strober and Arnold (1987a:146) argued that the shift of bank telling from male to female reinforced a deterioration in earnings that hastened its feminization. The earnings of male bank tellers relative to all male wage and salary workers dropped 14 percent in the 1950s and 18 and 32 percent, respectively, in the 1960s and 1970s. During the same period, women's representation in the occupation increased from 45 to 91 percent. Similarly, relative to manufacturing workers, clerical workers lost ground in the early part of the twentieth century: the wages of manufacturing workers increased by 29 percent between 1890 and 1926; those of clerical workers grew only 3 percent. As wages declined, clerical occupations feminized, and the earnings gap between men and women narrowed from between 25 and 45 percent in the early part of the century to between 15 and 20 percent in the 1960s and 1970s (Strom, 1987:87).

While bank telling and other clerical work no longer provided men their previous level of economic return, they did offer women entrants better economic opportunities than other occupations open to them, given their education level. Strober and Arnold (1987a: Table 1) found that in 1950 women bank tellers earned 38 percent more than all women wage and salary workers; by 1970 their wage advantage still existed but had dropped to 14 percent.[11] Clerical work also paid women higher wages than did other jobs to which they normally had access.

> From a working-class or middle-class woman's (or her family's) point of view, the salaries paid for office jobs must have looked good. . . . Since some high school was now compulsory for everyone, a daughter could receive free business training and move right into an office job, where she made higher wages than women in any other line of work except the professions. Moreover, if she could advance into the middle ranges of clerical work—stenographer, bookkeeper, statistical clerk, or supervisor, for example—she could earn more than most other working women and even as much as some men. . . . The Census of 1950 still showed that median yearly incomes for women clerical workers put them closer to managers, proprietors, and professionals of the same sex than any other occupation. (Strom, 1987:87)

Of course, these historical data are not inconsistent with a continuing decline in occupational earnings *because* of women's entry. The very fact that employers turn to women when faced with shortages of male workers allows them to downgrade pay scales, because they can generally hire women at lower salaries than men. Strober and Arnold's (1987a) data speak to this issue. The authors found that women bank tellers' earnings relative to those of all women wage and salary workers continued to decline between 1950 and 1980, as women constituted an increasingly larger portion of all incumbents. Strober and Arnold (1987a) speculated that employers turned to women because a drop in earnings and promotion prospects reduced the supply of men, and that the ensuing feminization justified further wage cuts.

The real usefulness of these historical data, however, is to serve as a baseline for evaluating the occupations that feminized in the 1970s. In the next section we use our case studies to examine whether these historical processes held true across the more diverse set of occupations feminizing since 1970.

Feminization and Earnings in the 1970s: Case Study Results

Tables 3.1 and 3.2 present earnings and earnings ratios for eight of our case study occupations. The data, taken from 1970 and 1980 censuses, represent earnings for the preceding calendar years, 1969 and 1979. Table 3.1 indicates that between 1969 and 1979, all women increased their earnings relative to all men by 3.8 percentage points, suggesting a modest increase in economic equity across all occupations over the decade (see column 11). The first row of Table 3.1 reveals that over all occupations both men's and women's real earnings increased between 1969 and 1979 (columns 7 and 8): for women, the increase in real earnings was $637, compared with $491 for men. Because women's earnings increased slightly more than men's, the earnings gap narrowed across the decade.

The picture differs, however, within the feminizing occupations for which we could find comparably coded data. The earnings ratio for the sexes increased in every occupation but insurance sales, reflecting a narrowing of the within-occupation wage gap between women and men. The interdecade change in the earnings ratio ranged from a decrease of almost 3 percentage points for insurance sales to an increase of less than one percentage point for insurance adjusters, examiners, and investigators to an increase of 15 percentage points for bus drivers. Despite the reduction in wage inequality in most of the case study occupations, these indicators of women's economic status relative to men remain low. At one extreme, women in insurance sales earn only 48 cents to every dollar men earn. At the other extreme, among pharmacists, women earn 72 percent as much as men. Most ratios hover around 60 percent, which is only slightly better than the overall ratio of 55.4 for all occupations.[12]

Table 3.1
Mean Annual Earnings, and Earnings Ratios for Year-Round Workers, by Sex, 1969, 1979

| Occupations[a] | 1969[b] | | 1979[c] | | 1979 (in 1969 $)[d] | | 1969–79 Change in Real Earnings (in 1969 $)[d] | | Female/Male Earnings Ratio | | 1969–79 Change in Earnings Ratio |
	Men (1)	Women (2)	Men (3)	Women (4)	Men (5)	Women (6)	Men (7)	Women (8)	1969 (9)	1979 (10)	(11)
All occupations	$9,580	$4,944	$19,943	$11,051	$10,071	$5,581	$491	$637	.516	.554	.038
Pharmacists	13,475	7,897	23,876	17,178	12,058	8,675	–1,417	778	.586	.719	.133
Editors and reporters	12,830	7,151	21,718	14,742	10,968	7,445	–1,862	294	.557	.679	.122
Public relations specialists[e]	13,420	7,908	25,115	15,193	12,683	7,672	–737	–236	.589	.605	.016
Insurance sales occupations[e]	12,430	6,308	26,491	12,666	13,378	6,396	948	88	.507	.478	–.029
Real estate sales occupations[e]	13,749	7,401	26,531	16,171	13,398	8,166	–351	765	.538	.609	.071
Insurance adjusters, examiners, and investigators	9,898	5,820	18,576	11,064	9,381	5,587	–517	–233	.588	.596	.008
Bartenders	6,787	4,122	11,346	7,584	5,730	3,830	–1,057	–292	.607	.668	.061
Bus drivers	7,667	3,477	16,056	9,693	8,108	4,895	441	1,418	.454	.604	.150

[a] Only those occupations with comparable occupation codes between 1970 and 1980 were included (see Chapter 2).

[b] Based on mean annual earnings of persons in experienced civilian labor force, aged 16 and over, who worked 50–52 weeks in 1969 (U.S. Bureau of the Census, 1973a: Table 19).

[c] Based on mean annual earnings of persons in recent experienced civilian labor force, aged 18 and over, who worked year round, full time in 1979 (U.S. Bureau of the Census, 1984c: Table 1).

[d] Deflation coefficient = .505.

[e] Occupation's title changed between 1970 and 1980, but classifications were sufficiently similar to permit comparison. Equivalent 1970 titles: "public relations men and publicity writers," "insurance agents, brokers, and underwriters," and "real estate agents and brokers."

Table 3.2
Ratios of Female Earnings in Case Study Occupations to Earnings of All Men,
1969, 1979

Occupation[a]	1969[b]	1979[c]
All occupations	.52	.55
Pharmacists	.82	.86
Editors and reporters	.75	.74
Public relations specialists[d]	.83	.76
Insurance sales occupations[d]	.66	.64
Real estate sales occupations[d]	.77	.81
Insurance adjusters, examiners, and investigators	.61	.55
Bartenders	.43	.38
Bus drivers	.36	.49

[a] Only those occupations with comparable occupation codes between 1970 and 1980 were included (see Chapter 2).

[b] Based on mean annual earnings of persons in experienced civilian labor force, aged 16 and over, who worked 50–52 weeks in 1969; men's mean earnings, $9,580 (U.S. Bureau of the Census, 1973a: Table 19).

[c] Based on mean annual earnings of persons in recent experienced civilian labor force, aged 18 and over, who worked year-round, full time in 1979; men's mean earnings, $19,943 (U.S. Bureau of the Census, 1984c: Table 1).

[d] Occupation's title changed between 1970 and 1980, but 1970 and 1980 classifications were sufficiently similar to permit comparison. The equivalent 1970 titles are "public relations men and publicity writers," "insurance agents, brokers, and underwriters," and "real estate agents and brokers."

Decomposing the earnings gap into its component parts reveals three distinct patterns of change in these feminizing occupations. First, in only two—insurance sales and bus driving—did the real earnings of both male and female year-round workers increase between 1969 and 1979. Among bus drivers, women's earnings rose faster than men's ($1,418 to $441), thus increasing the earnings ratio. Of course, this finding is deceptive, since the vast majority of women bus drivers work only part time. Among insurance sales occupations, men's earnings rose faster than women's ($948 to $88), thus leading the earnings ratio to drop. Interestingly, among our eight feminizing occupations, insurance sales remained the most predominantly male in 1988 (only 29.7 percent female; see Table 1.6). Evidently, this occupation's rewards did *not* deteriorate and lead to male flight. In this context, men's more rapid wage advancement widened sales agents' wage gap. Second, among pharmacists, editors and reporters, and real estate salespersons, men's real earnings declined while women's increased. Third, in the remaining occupations of public relations specialist, insurance adjuster/examiner, and bartender, *both* men's and women's real earnings declined, but the earnings ratios rose because women's earnings fell less than men's. Thus, while the earnings ratios rose in seven of the eight occupations, they did so primarily because male earnings declined. For example, fully 81 percent of the increase in the female-to-male earnings ratio among editors and reporters was attributable to men's loss in real earnings. Similarly, 56 percent and 21 percent, respectively, of the rise in the earnings ratios for pharmacists and real estate salespersons resulted from men's wage loss.[13]

Thus women fared better relative to men in 1979 than they had in 1969 because men's earnings eroded during the 1970s in the occupations we studied. This erosion in male wages is probably attributable in part to that fact that the men who remained in these deteriorating occupations in 1980 were those most poorly qualified. Although the second and third patterns we describe above had the consequence of enhancing women's economic position relative to that of men, the results do not suggest that the economic prospects for women entering these formerly male occupations are particularly bright. A drop in real earnings for men or for both sexes no doubt denotes a declining occupation that does not offer women the prospects of a lucrative working environment.

Women's economic progress relative to other women workers. According to the queueing perspective developed in Chapter 2, women took jobs in customarily male occupations because they offered better rewards or opportunities than the occupations to which most women had been relegated. Indeed, the ratios of female earnings in our case study occupations to all female earnings (see Table 2.4) showed that in 1969 most feminizing occupations provided higher pay than the average woman worker received. We used those data to show that these feminizing occupations attracted women because they offered economic opportunities superior to those typically available in traditionally female occupations.

Of course, the implication is that women benefited economically from entering these occupations, and in six of the occupations—pharmacists, editors and reporters, public relations specialists, insurance sales, real estate sales, and insurance adjusters and examiners—female incumbents did earn from 18 to 60 percent more than the average woman worker in 1969. Despite declines in relative earnings from 1969 to 1979, if we can assume that women migrants who entered these occupations during the 1970s did as well, they earned notably more than women earned on average in the traditionally female occupations to which women had ready access. Two exceptions exist: both bartending and bus driving in 1969 paid women less than the average woman worker. However, if we compare women in these occupations to women in other service occupations, we find a similar earnings benefit: the earnings ratio of women bartenders and bus drivers to waitresses, for example, were 1.16 and 1.48, respectively (computed from U.S. Bureau of the Census, 1984c: Table 1).

While women did benefit economically from entering these feminizing occupations, their wage advantage over the average woman worker declined notably during the 1970s. The relative earnings of women in seven of the eight desegregating occupations dropped over the decade, indicating once again the occupations' deteriorating economic conditions.[14] The decline in relative earnings was small in some occupations (pharmacy, real estate sales), appreciable in others (public relations, insurance adjusting), but sufficient in most to cost women monetarily.

Women's economic progress relative to the average male worker. To what extent did women's inroads into our case study occupations improve their economic position relative to the average male worker? Were women entrants able to reduce the earnings gap between themselves and the average man? Our results (see Table 3.2) do not indicate much progress in this regard. Women posted small earnings gains relative to the average male worker in only three of the occupations (pharmacy, real estate sales, and bus driving); in the rest, the earnings ratio either declined or remained essentially stable. Although feminizing occupations provided women with better economic opportunities than those available to most of their sex, women who entered them did not significantly narrow the earnings gap between themselves and the average male worker.

Women's nonincome progress toward occupational equity. However slight women's *economic* gains in desegregating occupations, did desegregation benefit women in other ways? For example, did pioneering in desegregating occupations allow them greater access to full-time work or enhance their opportunities for promotion? Unfortunately, the case study evidence does not offer much support for these possibilities.

In Chapter 2 we investigated whether an increase in part-time work (and hence an increased flexibility to accommodate family and work responsibilities) may have prompted women to pursue these newly desegregating occupations (see Table 2.5). The findings suggest that part-time work opportunities increased for women in only three of the comparable case study occupations. Among bartenders, the proportion of women working part time increased by nearly 12 percent; among pharmacists and public relations specialists it rose 1.7 and 1.2 percent, respectively. In the remaining occupations, women had greater access to full-time employment than they had in 1970. However, in 1980 the proportion of women working full time in most of our case study occupations remained far below that of men. Women in bartending came closest to men in the likelihood of working full time (35.9 percent were employed full time, year round, compared to 45.5 percent of men). At the other extreme, only 12.9 percent of women bus drivers worked full time, compared to 50.7 percent of their male counterparts (see Table 2.5). As we noted, much of this difference is attributable to women's overrepresentation in school-bus driving and men's in urban transport.

Further, the case study data do not support the suggestion that women enhanced their promotion prospects by moving into desegregating occupations. One of Phipps's interviewees noted that as chains have become a larger proportion of all retail pharmacy outlets, the career ladder from pharmacy management to store management has disappeared; thus, women who finally began to break into pharmacy management found their upward mobility blocked. Similarly, women in reporting have encountered few prospects for advancement to editorial jobs, although several women have moved into top management in book publishing. In bank management, women reportedly confront "glass ceilings" when they attempt to move up the career ladder. As one of Bird's informants noted:

> You literally didn't know that there was a glass ceiling there, and you thought you were just going to keep moving up and developing and [then] you ram into it. . . . You go through quite a traumatic time until you start to realize . . . that your experience is not exceptional, and in fact is typical, and [that] it is not likely to change in the short run.

Finally, in lower-prestige service occupations such as bartending, bus driving, and baking, the work itself is not organized to allow upward mobility. Career ladders are almost nonexistent, and incumbents have little opportunity to move up.

| | | | Summary

This chapter has asked two questions: did women benefit occupationally from moving into the desegregating occupations we studied, and did they gain economically? A single short answer applies to each: not much. Women's progress relative to men, both occupationally and economically, was disappointing. Though women did make progress in desegregating traditionally male occupations, by the time women gained access to them, the occupations had lost much of their attraction to men and were becoming less advantageous for women as well. Women's success in these occupations was in large measure hollow.

The best way to measure women's progress is to evaluate it relative to the most positive scenario possible: genuine sex integration across jobs. Women would have made genuine progress integrating typically male occupations if they had gained access to all or even most jobs within desegregating occupations. In concrete terms, this implies that women would have been represented across the industries in which the occupation is located, in the full range of jobs that compose the occupation, and across the establishments that employ incumbents. True integration would have enhanced women's prospects for both occupational and economic equity relative to their male coworkers and perhaps to all male workers. As this chapter has documented, however, we found no signs of true integration in our case study occupations. Rather, ghettoization and, in a few instances, resegregation better describe the forms desegregation took in the 1970s.

Ghettoization occurred when women and men held the same occupational title but worked in different specialties in an occupation. Specialization took many forms: sometimes the sexes worked in different industries or work settings; sometimes they held different ranks and performed different tasks. In all cases, we found women concentrated in the lower-paying, less desirable, and dead-end positions. Resegregation occurred in a few occupations and occupational specialties as they switched from being predominantly male to predominantly female.

The outlook for women in these desegregating occupations, then, is not particularly promising. Although women made more headway in entering male occupations during the 1970s than in any previous decade, ultimately not much genuine integration occurred. More genuine integration, with more real economic payoff for women, may have occurred in male occupations in which women's numerical gains were more modest; perhaps occupations that feminize more slowly can more readily incorporate female entrants (see Chapter 15). We pursue this possibility in our ongoing work on the determinants of changing sex composition over the full range of detailed occupations.

Ghettoization and resegregation are not indicative of increased economic gains accruing from feminization. Thus, not unexpectedly, women in desegregating occupations failed to reduce substantially the wage gap between themselves and male workers. When the wage gap did narrow, it was largely because of declines in men's real earnings, and not increases in women's; women thus seemed to gain by default. One beneficial outcome that did accrue from feminization, however, is that women bettered their earnings relative to the average woman worker. Women in these desegregating occupations generally earned more than did those in the occupations to which women have traditionally had access—although this benefit too eroded between 1970 and 1980.

I I I I Notes

1. Recall the distinction we made in Chapter 1 between "occupation" and "job." We measure "occupation" by the Census Bureau's three-digit codes. These occupational categories are aggregates of the smaller groupings that are called "jobs."

2. Pettigrew's (1969) model applies to racial separation across all of society's institutions: neighborhoods, schools, churches, and workplaces.

3. Pettigrew (1969:58) noted a third outcome of racial desegregation: the "hypothetical black power ghetto," which allowed racial separation to coexist with true personal and group autonomy for blacks. In one respect, this theoretical outcome corresponds to resegregation in that it represents a return to racial separation. It differs

from resegregation, however, in that it represents, at least hypothetically, desegregation that is truly separate and equal.

4. Since we rely on census occupational codes, this distinction between ghetto-ization and resegregation is an important one. The 1980 census classification routinely combines jobs involving related tasks into the same detailed occupation. Five of the occupations we studied included combinations of jobs in the census occupational title: accountants and auditors; insurance adjusters, examiners, and investigators; editors and reporters; typesetters and compositors; and bank and financial managers. Almost all our case study occupations contained different jobs (or specialties) not obvious from the titles. In real estate sales, agents work in either residential or commercial sales; some pharmacists work in retail stores, others in the health-care sector, and still others in industry.

5. They also found that employers hired black writers primarily for shows fea-turing black families.

6. Steiger and Reskin found several women in part-time baking jobs who wanted but were denied full-time work because their in-store jobs were designed for part-time workers.

7. Compositors in the newspaper sector suffered much sharper declines in their relative earnings than those in the commercial sector. U.S. Bureau of Labor Statis-tics (1985) data confirmed that between 1950 and 1986, the average weekly earnings of newspaper production workers, expressed as a percentage of the weekly earnings of all print production workers, fell from 106 to 89 percent. Three-quarters of this drop occurred between 1970 and 1986, the period of greatest dissemination of elec-tronic technologies and the period experiencing the most rapid influx of women into newspaper composing.

8. This illustrates the role that demand plays in generating supply. Blau (1989), for example, pointed to supply-side factors, such as lowered training requirements or technological change, that spurred women's initial entry into traditionally male occupations.

9. Researchers present this either as a proportion (e.g., in 1980 the ratio of women's earnings to men's was .602) or as a percentage (e.g., in 1980 women earned 60.2 percent of men's earnings).

10. Recent government statistics on trends in the wage gap may misleadingly overestimate improvements in women's earnings relative to men's. While earlier re-ports used *annual* earnings, more recent reports have relied on *weekly* or *hourly* wage data, which yield higher earnings ratios (National Committee on Pay Equity, 1987).

11. By 1980, women bank tellers were earning 18 percent *less* than all female wage and salary workers (Strober and Arnold, 1987a: Table 1). Interestingly, the earn-ings ratio between women and men tellers remained constant between 1950 and 1980, reflecting a corresponding decline in men's relative earnings.

12. The overall ratio for all workers (55.4) is a conservative estimate, since employers disproportionately assign men to year-round jobs.

13. By way of example, we estimated the 81 percent figure for editors and re-porters by first calculating what the ratio would have been if women's real earnings had changed between 1969 and 1979 but men's had not declined ($7,445/$12,830), then subtracting the resulting ratio (.58) from the actual 1979 earnings ratio (.679). Finally,

we divided the difference (.099) by the change in the ratio between 1969 and 1979 (.122), and multiplied the quotient (.81) by 100. For details and additional examples, see National Committee on Pay Equity (1987:4).

14. The one exception—bus driving—is misleading because only a small minority of women bus drivers worked full time, year round in 1980.

Part II
Case Studies of Occupational Change

Barbara F. Reskin

4

Culture, Commerce, and Gender: The Feminization of Book Editing

For centuries book editing was a "gentlemen's profession" (Tebbel, 1972: 207), yet in the 1970s women made such large gains in the occupation that some have speculated that editing is becoming a women's ghetto (Geracimos, 1974:25). How can we explain women's gains? This chapter examines the changes in the publishing industry and the editorial role that have led to women's increasing representation among editors.

Culture and commerce, art and business—these disparate concerns shaped the book publishing industry (Coser et al., 1982). Its origins in medieval monasteries and universities (Dessauer, 1974:2) bestowed on publishing a special status. As literature and literacy came to enjoy public esteem, their prestige spilled over onto those who contributed to their production. But though books were cultural objects, they were also objects of commerce. As early as the twelfth century, stationers duplicated and sold books (Dessauer, 1974:2), and until the nineteenth century, publishers' primary activity was printing books for sale (Bingley, 1972:1). The gradual democratization of education expanded the market. During the eighteenth century, two million titles were published worldwide; in the nineteenth, the total was four times as large. The universal literacy movement in the United States created a huge reading audience (Tebbel, 1972:207), and by the twentieth century publishing was big business. After World War II, firms began to go public, and during the 1960s and 1970s nonpublishing conglomerates purchased many old publishing houses (Powell, 1982:33). In the late 1970s the president of a major house admitted, "Whether you like it or not, [publishing] is an act of commerce" (Snyder, 1977:38).

Traditionally, its "high cultural mission" (Coser, 1975:17), links to literacy and the arts, and low pay shielded publishing from the stigma attached to commerce (Weber 1978:936; see also Lane 1975:42) and raised its status relative to most commercial endeavors. In England the first editors came from upper-class families and were connected to the academic, artistic, and political elites. Normally, such men would have eschewed commercial careers, but noblesse oblige encouraged some "to act as arbiters on behalf of persons outside their circle" (Lane, 1975:39,42). Thus, three factors—the links between publishing, knowledge, and culture; the high socioeconomic status of early editors; and wages too low to offer an economic incentive—made editing books a socially acceptable activity for the privileged classes (Lane, 1975: 39,42).

The American publishing industry retained this cultural image (Tebbel, 1972:207). Publishing houses recruited editors from Ivy League schools (Caplette, 1979), and as recently as the 1970s most editors, especially in trade houses,[1] came from the higher socioeconomic classes (Coser et al., 1982:105–6). The elite origin of editors reflects both the traditional disdain for commerce among the upper classes and their access to other sources of income, since surviving on a publishing salary is difficult (Tebbel, 1981:727). People did not expect nor were they supposed to seek commercial success in publishing. As publisher William Ellsworth said seventy years ago,

> Nobody should seek to be a publisher unless he loves books. . . . If one wants to make money, let him go into the steel business or into something in which there is money to be made, for there is little in books . . . unless they are pushed in a purely commercial spirit, and if they are— why, then it were much better not to publish them at all. (Quoted in Bechtold, 1946:13)

Added to its association with culture was the prestige that famous authors gave the entire publishing industry (Coser, 1975:19). Editing books meant access to the creators of culture, and editors enjoyed entree into literary circles (Powell, 1982:48; James, 1987). For example, through editing their books, Maxwell Perkins became the intimate of such celebrated authors as F. Scott Fitzgerald, Ernest Hemingway, Thomas Wolfe, and Marjorie Kinnan Rawlings (Berg, 1978). As publishing historian John Tebbel (1987) explained, "Upper-class kids from good schools [came] to publishing because they thought it was glamorous [and] they wanted to meet authors." He added, "When they got there, they learned it's a lot of work for low pay."

The image sketched above is that of trade publishing. Scholarly publishing enjoys esteem based on its links with the production of knowledge; other major sectors of the industry differ in image as well as in their goals and structure (Coser et al., 1982). To understand editing, one must take these differences into account. Next to U.S. government publications, educational publishing represents the largest share of the industry, followed by trade books. Mass-market paperback publishing assumed a growing importance during the 1970s and 1980s. Finally, university and scholarly presses make up a small but significant segment of the industry (Grannis, 1985:13).[2]

| | | | Women in Publishing

Until the 1960s, publishing was "predominantly a business of middle-aged and older men" (Tebbel, 1975:101), but between 1963 and 1968, women accounted for 62 percent of employment growth in publishing (compared with 52 percent for the printing and publishing industry overall and 35 percent for all manufacturing), and during this period the numbers of men and women employed in the industry rose by 19 percent and 41 percent, respectively (U.S. Bureau of Labor Statistics, cited in *Publishers Weekly*, 1971:69). By 1980, publishing's sex composition had changed (Tebbel, 1981:728), and observers were calling it a "women's business" (Caplette, 1982a:148). By the late 1970s and early 1980s, estimates put women's employment share at about two-thirds of the industry's workforce (Association of American Publishers, 1977:27; Cornelius, 1983:34; U.S. Bureau of the Census, 1984b: Table 4).

Sex Segregation in Publishing

Even when men dominated the industry, publishing employed women for some jobs. While college publishing was predominantly male, scholarly publishing was so to a lesser degree (university presses could take advantage of the captive labor market that faculty wives represented). Women were concentrated in children's publishing, in mass-market paperbacks (Coser et al., 1982)—which enjoyed little status and lacked a "cultural" image because these houses reissued hard-cover editions and published lightly edited genre books, such as mysteries and historical romances—and in certain jobs in trade publishing.

Men dominated marketing and management,[3] the highest-paying jobs in the industry, and except in paperback publishing the majority of editors—particularly acquisitions editors—were men (Strainchamps, 1974:133; Caplette, 1982a:157). Women were typically relegated to lower-level editorial jobs (copyeditor, editorial assistant), normally behind-the-scenes positions (Caplette, 1982a:154). Most began their careers as manuscript readers, secretaries, or editorial assistants, jobs whose low pay and clerical duties could attract few men (Tebbel, 1981:728).

Other female ghettos were the noneditorial "service" jobs of publicity and subsidiary rights (Geracimos, 1974:27; Caplette, 1982a:158). Selling subsidiary rights is complex, detailed work but—until recently—not especially profitable (Tebbel, 1975:140). A former subsidiary-rights director described it as "a pro forma job: . . . sending out notes, keeping track of things, and then the [male] editor-in-chief would step in to do the razzle-dazzle deal" (*Publishers Weekly*, 1979). Publicity, according to a former publicity director, "was naturally a female job" because it involved "lots of handholding, nurturing, socializing," and like subsidiary rights it was not considered a moneymaking function until the 1970s.

Until 1970, publishers rarely hired women as sales representatives,[4] the traditional entry-level job for college editors; before that, "it was almost inconceivable that a woman should go on the road alone" (Strainchamps, 1974:159–60). Publishers feared, informants explained, that women would find the books too heavy, would not be able to find the colleges, or would get raped— or that professors would feel insulted if a woman called on them (Strainchamps, 1974:155). One editor recounted that a university press denied her a sales job in 1964, although she had six years editorial experience, because they "couldn't allow a pretty young lady to travel alone" even two or three days a month. Another interviewee recalled that when her employer transferred a woman to college sales in the mid-1960s, the male representatives "tormented her" until she quit. She added, "It was an object lesson to us all."

The Sex Composition of Editors

Although women were underrepresented in editorial jobs until the late 1960s and early 1970s, they have held some editorial positions since early in the century. About the time of World War I a survey of 82 publishing firms revealed that 14 percent of the 1,400 female employees were working in editorial jobs (Tebbel, 1975:177). Yet a world war later, publisher Henry Holt still described editors as male (Bechtold, 1946:14). Industry histories (Cerf, 1977; Tebbel, 1978) rarely mentioned women editors. Bechtold (1946:14) noted that women editors earned less than men and had to wait longer and work harder to succeed. Women with editorial titles usually copyedited or styled manuscripts for publication. Only in children's books was editing fully open to women (Laskey, 1969:13); indeed, men rarely held these jobs through the early 1960s (Tebbel, 1978).

Many female secretaries and editorial assistants did editorial work without the title, including screening the thousands of unsolicited manuscripts that swamped publishers (see, e.g., Caplette, 1982a:152–54). The secretarial and editorial assistant jobs were in a secondary labor market with a nonexistent or weakly defined career ladder to full editorial positions (Caplette, 1979), though finding a promising book in the "slushpile" of unsolicited manuscripts sometimes meant a step up the editorial ladder. Moreover, the ratio of aspirants to openings was—and remains—enormous. It took women extraordinary effort to get out of the secretarial–assistant ghetto, and few female editorial assistants became editors (Caplette, 1982a:161; Tebbel, 1987). In contrast, the few men who began as assistants moved up rapidly (Caplette, 1982a:154). Thus, the considerable sex segregation across editorial jobs revealed in a survey made by Chicago Women in Publishing (1973:2) probably reflected the industry as a whole.[5]

The educational sector of the industry did not resemble trade publishing with respect to women's access to editorial jobs. College publishers required sales experience of editors because of the importance of marketing in college sales; sales representatives acted as "field editors" who scouted out potential authors (Coser et al., 1982:20, 102). As a result, men's monopoly over sales jobs ensured that editing was also their preserve (Caplette, 1979:5). No large college firms employed women as acquisitions editors in major disciplines until early in the 1970s, and late in the decade three-quarters of college editors were still men (Coser et al., 1982). In school publishing the sex ratio was more balanced because firms hired former teachers as editors.[6] Scholarly—particularly university—presses employed relatively more women than did other sectors (Powell, 1985:30).

Women's Increased Representation among Editors

By 1970 just under half the editors employed in book and periodical publishing were women (U.S. Bureau of the Census, 1972: Table 8), but only 5,025 of these 26,745 workers edited books (Association of American Publishers, 1977:24). Unfortunately, no data enumerate book editors by sex, but by all accounts women were underrepresented, and female editors were concentrated in school and paperback publishing or in low-level editorial positions in trade, college, and scholarly houses. During the 1970s women made considerable strides in editing in most sectors of the industry; by mid-decade their number had increased so much that a *Publishers Weekly* article (Geracimos, 1974:25) called 1974 "the year of the woman" in trade publishing (see also Tebbel, 1975:101), and in 1978 a survey of 117 publishing employees showed women outnumbering men two to one in editorial acquisitions and manuscript editing (Caplette, 1982a:155). However, the wage gap in one large publishing house, in which women editors averaged 54 cents for each dollar men received, indicates that although two-thirds of its 195 editors were female, they either held lower-level positions or were paid less than male editors in the same jobs (Osterman, 1979). Nonetheless, by 1980 women made up more than 57 percent of the 36,161 editors employed in book and periodical publishing (U.S. Bureau of the Census, 1984b: Table 4), although again we do not know their proportion among the approximately 10,000 *book* editors (Wright, 1984:589). Caplette (1982b:158) observed that "the gradual increase of women editors in the last decade has, within the last few years, become an upsurge—nearly half of trade and mass-market paperback editors are now women." Confirming her impressions are those of more than forty industry informants who agreed that the 1970s brought dramatic progress for women in editing and other publishing jobs.

| | | | Explaining Women's Progress in Editing

Although women advanced in many occupations in the 1970s, their gains in editing outstripped those in most other occupations. To account for their progress, I used a variety of documentary data and published sources, including memoirs of editors and publishers, scholarly analyses of the publishing industry, articles from *Publishers Weekly* between 1968 and 1987, and forty-one interviews, including eleven that Michele Caplette (1981) conducted in 1978.[7] I found that changes in the publishing industry and the editorial role set the stage for women's gains by altering both the supply of male would-be editors and the demand for women.

Industrial Growth and Change

First in the chain of events that transformed publishing was its pronounced growth over fifteen to twenty years, beginning about 1960 (Lofquist, 1970:6, 9; Powell, 1985:5). Rising personal income and educational levels, unprecedented federal investments in public education, and the information explosion (Powell, 1982:33) stimulated record book sales. Profits led existing firms to expand their lists and attracted new firms to the industry (Altbach, 1975:11; Dessauer, 1982:34). At least three hundred new firms set up shop between 1967 and 1978 (Noble, 1978:35); between 1972 and 1977 the number of firms increased by almost half (Gilroy, 1980:8, 11), and between 1954 and 1977 the number more than doubled (Powell, 1985:213). Both title output and sales volume showed increases of 50 to 100 percent between 1959 and 1980 (Powell, 1985:4).[8]

These two decades of expansion set the stage for dramatic changes in the culture of publishing. Rapid growth and solid profits led to a spate of mergers in the late 1960s and again in the late 1970s and middle 1980s (Gilroy, 1980:12) and inevitably drew the interest of nonpublishing firms and conglomerates looking for profitable acquisitions (Tebbel, 1981:733). Conglomerization, which hit publishing in the early 1970s, transformed the industry (Navasky, 1973b); it "became less of a gentleman's industry and more of a business" that emphasized "the bottom line" (Galassi, 1980:28).

Although concern with profits was not new, according to industry analyst John Dessauer (1982:36), "it has become more virulent [as] opportunities for making a quick buck have increased with a growing market, and the big-money ownership that has entered the field is more easily tempted by the quick buck than were the other-worldly types that used to constitute the industry's core." As Powell (1985:6) noted, "Outside ownership brought modern management practices that fundamentally altered the craftlike nature of book publishing." Commercialization eroded publishing's reputation as an industry outside the fray, and in so doing, transformed editorial work. As a result, it also transformed the publishing workforce.

Changes in Editorial Work

To understand the changes in the role of editor that figure importantly in women's gains in the occupation, I begin by examining the traditional editorial role. The predecessors of modern editors were readers—often established writers or academicians (Lane, 1975:38)—whom publishers paid to evaluate manuscripts and help writers improve their work (Sifton, 1985:43). Twentieth-century editors perform similar functions: acquisitions editors select manuscripts and work with authors in completing them, and manuscript editors concentrate on the production side (Lane, 1975:35). Of the two functions, producing books enjoys less status and lower wages than the more exciting job of acquiring them (Carter, 1984:24).[9] However, acquisitions can be demanding work in many sectors of the industry. Editors typically handle upward of forty books a year, a few of which are culled from thousands of unsolicited manuscripts (Rawson and Dolin, 1985:28). A book's existence and ultimate success depend on its editor's efforts to sell the manuscript to the editorial board and the marketing people (Rawson and Dolin, 1985:25).[10] As the publishers' representatives, editors work closely with authors to negotiate contracts, monitor progress, suggest revisions (Sifton, 1985:43–45), and offer encouragement. The last function may extend to serving as friend, cheerleader, confessor, and psychotherapist (Giroux, 1982:55; Dong, 1984:22); some (Canfield, 1969:27; Rawson and Dolin, 1985:23) have characterized editors as surrogate parents "You hear from authors on weekends, . . . they may even end up living in your house" (Dong, 1984:26). Editorial responsibilities include looking out for an author's interests within the firm: translating royalty statements, arranging advances, touting the book. Some editors also emphasize the importance of subordinating their egos to "literature" and to authors: "An editor . . . must be willing to play second fiddle" (Lehman, 1987:89; also see Evans, 1979:31).

Editors have written extensively about the qualifications their work demands. Common themes depict the ideal editor as charming, sophisticated, and willing to take risks; as a person with taste, intuition, and empathy who can be persuasive yet tactful in dealing with "difficult" authors and who is willing to make her- or himself an "agreeable nuisance" (Association of American Publishers, 1977:22; Galassi, 1980:29; Giroux, 1982:55; Carter, 1984:24–25).

Besides all this, in most sectors of the industry, editors must be willing to work long hours for sometimes notoriously low salaries.

The shift to outside ownership strained the traditionally amiable relations between publishers and editors and profoundly altered editorial work. The pursuit of the blockbuster in large trade houses sharply circumscribed editorial autonomy in acquisition decisions (Wendroff, 1980): "Editors could no longer simply sign a book and then tell their house to sell it" (Powell, 1982:47).[11] By 1973, "fewer and fewer editors [had] the right to commission books without first securing the approval of a Publishing Committee, and most often it [was] the editor-in-chief who [made] the presentation to the committee rather than the editor" (Navasky, 1973a). The new emphasis on packaging and sales gave publicity, marketing, and subsidiary-rights people much more sway in editorial decisions (Phalon, 1981:253; Powell, 1982:47), thereby eroding editorial autonomy. Bringing the views of the corporate boardroom into the editorial side also discouraged creative risk taking (Tebbel, 1981:733),[12] an important source of satisfaction in editorial work. Instead, editors were under pressure to sign up best sellers or, in the smaller and still-independent houses, to acquire more books (Powell, 1982). An editor who noted that publication committees' choices are based largely on budget considerations wondered "whether editors have as much power as they once did, whether their power is more circumscribed, and . . . who controls what editors do" (Geracimos, 1974:25).

A second consequence of outside ownership was the deterioration of the traditional close relationship between editors and their authors. With more money at stake, authors changed houses frequently in pursuit of better deals and hired agents or lawyers to represent them in negotiating with editors (Powell, 1982). The growing role of literary agents in getting books published (Bannon, 1972:102; Doebler, 1978:27) further circumscribed editor–author contacts. Agents are more influential than editors in acquiring books and have assumed other traditional editorial functions in the publication process (Gabriel, 1989). Besides having less close contact with authors, editors interact less with other editors, thus fragmenting "the old sense of a community of bookmen" (Powell 1982:49).[13]

The absorption of book publishing by other media also altered editors' duties. Arranging the fat subsidiary-rights agreements or movie tie-ins essential for big trade profits meant that editors "had to change their habits and spend more time working on deals." In his insightful analysis of the impact of outside ownership on book publishing, Powell (1982:48–49) quoted an editor whose small firm had been acquired by a large diversified publishing corporation: "After[ward] I never had time to see authors. I spent all my time in meetings with various corporate executives and 'selling' our imprint within the parent company." After being promoted to head the trade department in a large house, another editor Powell interviewed, who had formerly helped his authors develop their work, said that he was "in danger of becoming simply a well-paid retailer of ideas and entertainment."

New ownership patterns also threatened editors' job security, the only economic compensation for publishing's low wages. The frequent mergers of the 1960s and 1970s often precipitated corporate shake-ups that cost editors their jobs (Evans, 1978:45; Carter, 1983:8). The corporate focus on performance further eroded job security (Tebbel, 1981:733) and forced editors to compete with corporate executive staff from outside the publishing industry for the only top-level positions to which senior editors could aspire—publisher and director.

Changes in the Supply of Would-Be Editors

For most of this century, publishing's glamour and its image as a "gentlemen's profession" were sufficient to attract more than enough qualified recruits. Then, although industrial expansion heightened the demand for editorial workers, the concomitants of that growth reduced the industry's attractiveness to its traditional workforce: talented young men from high socioeconomic backgrounds.

Dwindling attraction for men. Publishing's primary draw for such men had been entree into the world of culture without the taint of commerce. But commerce is exactly what outside ownership meant. At the same time, as we have seen, editorial work lost many of the features that had compensated nonwealthy workers for low wages. To make matters worse, commerce was supplanting culture without conferring the usual economic incentives of commercial careers. Although editorial wages had always been low, there were other compensations. One editor said, "I consider the right to publish books which don't make money a part of my salary" (Navasky, 1973a). Just as some editors lost that right, wages may have actually declined (Tebbel, 1981:728; Rosenthal et al., 1986). In 1982, entry-level pay for editorial assistants was as low as an $9,000 a year (Powell, 1985:225), and several people I interviewed noted that it is increasingly difficult, perhaps impossible, to survive—much less support a family—in Manhattan on editorial wages. An industry expert said, only partly in jest: "Only college graduates with rich parents willing to subsidize them can afford to work in editorial jobs any more" (Tebbel, 1981: 728).[14] In the face of society's growing emphasis on a fashionable life-style and the increasing tendency to use income as "the measure of a man," publishing's low wages further deterred men from pursuing editorial jobs (Tebbel, 1987). Better-paying media jobs (technical writing for high-tech companies, corporate public relations, film) and graduate school lured away talented men interested in communications.[15]

With declining opportunities for mobility (Coser et al., 1982:112) and challenges to the traditional promotion practices that had given men a fast track to the top (Strainchamps, 1974), little remained to draw men to editorial work. A woman editor whom Caplette interviewed in 1978 remarked, "The average man thinks that he has a God-given right to start in as an editor." To the extent that this was true, entry-level jobs as editorial assistants (often a euphemism for secretary when these were women's jobs) attracted few men, and the industry increasingly relied on women as editorial assistants.

Increasing supply of women.   The gentility that had rendered publishing jobs appropriate for upper-status men did so too for "respectable" women whom traditional values encouraged to pursue cultural and aesthetic pursuits (Veblen, 1899). As a long-time assistant at Harper & Brothers said, "Young women getting out of college were so anxious to get a job in something they could be proud of that they would go into publishing and work for practically nothing" (Caplette, 1982a:151). Gender-role socialization further enhanced women's qualifications for publishing by schooling them in verbal and communications skills that equipped them with the facility and inclination to work with words and predisposed them toward the interpersonal work that editing often involved. One female holder of a master's degree said of her secretarial job in the mid-1950s, "I thought it was an honor to read books and write . . . flap copy" (Caplette, 1982a:169). Working in an intellectual and cultural industry situated in one of the metropolitan publishing "capitals" offered an added incentive to women graduating from prestigious eastern colleges, particularly before the 1970s, when few alternatives presented themselves to career-minded women.

The massive influx of women into the labor force during the 1970s expanded the pool of women available for editorial jobs, and the women's liberation movement encouraged women to consider occupations customarily reserved for men. Publishing attracted women also because it reputedly presented fewer obstacles than many other industries. Moreover, male occupations in predominantly female industries—particularly growing industries— tend to be more hospitable and hence more attractive to women (O'Farrell and Harlan, 1984). Thus, although women knew they faced discrimination in publishing, they probably realized that other commercial fields were worse (Dessauer, 1974:42). Publishing's low wages were less likely to deter women than men because their socialization had not encouraged them to maximize income. Because women lacked access to many better-paying jobs, they did not have to forgo more lucrative opportunities for jobs as assistants or editors, and their limited alternatives presumably also explained their willingness to accept the changes that were making editorial work less desirable to men.[16] As a result, the supply of female applicants remained unabated or grew, while that of males declined.[17] Moreover, several interviewees contended that because publishing could no longer attract the most qualified men, female applicants often had better credentials than the males who did apply. If publishers chose the best applicant (as the new emphasis on profits dictated), it would probably be a woman.

The operation of the publishing labor market enhanced women's gains in editing. Several prestigious colleges close to the industry's centers in New York and Boston generated a supply of qualified women eager to work in publishing. The proliferation of publishing training programs (the first was established at Radcliffe) augmented that supply—by 1980 the director of the popular Denver Publishing Institute estimated that three-quarters of its students were women (Caplette, 1982a:169)—and helped women make contacts with employers. Most women began in entry-level positions on the editorial ladder. For years, sex discrimination and the high ratio of assistants to editors kept most secretaries and assistants from advancing. When the barriers to women began to crumble, however, most houses had a large number of talented, experienced women ready and able to edit books (Geracimos, 1974:25).

Even in college publishing, in the 1970s women successfully challenged both their exclusion from sales and the job ladder that made sales the only route to acquisitions (Association of American Publishers, 1977:16). Some companies began hiring women sales representatives, and others promoted to acquisitions one or two women who lacked sales experience. An early female sales representative speculated half-jokingly that her activity in a women's caucus at her firm may have won her a sought-after transfer to sales. The success of these first saleswomen who, as she said, "tore up the territory" eased the way for others, as well as putting women on the editorial ladder. Once college sales and acquisitions were recast as jobs to which women could aspire and the career ladder was restructured, a supply of women became available to work as acquisitions editors.

The Growing Demand for Women Editors

Two decades of growth in the publishing industry created a demand for additional personnel; nonproduction (white-collar) employment increased by approximately 50 percent during the 1970s.[18] High turnover generated further demand for new editorial assistants and editors (Dong, 1980; Dessauer, 1982:34).[19] Previously, publishing had never had trouble finding "eager bodies" to fill openings (Association of American Publishers, 1977:19), but as editing became less attractive to men, the demand for women grew. Publishing had long relied on women for many jobs, for reasons that are easy to understand. For one thing, gender-role socialization and a liberal-arts education qualified women for editorial jobs by encouraging literacy, deftness in interpersonal relations, and attention to detail—skills valued in an industry whose stock in trade is communicating ideas. As editor Elizabeth Sifton put it, "We all knew how to type, we were good work horses, and we were willing to learn the ropes" (quoted in Lehman, 1987:43). Moreover, their low profit margin restricted publishers to workers who would settle for low wages because either they had another source of income, placed low priority on earnings, or lacked better-paying alternatives. In fact, industry analyst John Dessauer (1974:64) contended that women won managerial-level jobs partly because publishers knew they could pay them less than men.

In addition to across-the-board growth, several traditionally female sectors grew disproportionately. The growth of subsidiary rights particularly benefited women. Long confined in a female ghetto, women who had developed expertise in rights rose to positions of power when rights directors began making million-dollar movie and paperback deals in the 1970s (*Publishers Weekly*, 1979). Editors consulted them in acquisition decisions, opening a path from subsidiary rights to editorial positions (Coser et al., 1982:104) and later to top management jobs. The detailed, technical nature of the work probably prevented inexperienced men from invading this "empty field" (Tuchman and Fortin, 1984), although Powell (1988) has pointed out that men with legal degrees are now entering subsidiary rights.

When the paperback industry exploded in the late 1960s and the 1970s (Benjamin, 1981:42; Tebbel, 1981:738) and paperback publishers began to acquire and publish original manuscripts, they needed more editors. Massive federal spending on education led to the expansion of school publishing, a sector in which the sexes were already integrated at the editorial level. Public interest in social issues spurred growth in the social sciences, a disproportionately female specialty in both college and mass-market houses. The women's movement gave birth to women's studies, creating jobs for editors knowledgeable about the women's movement and sympathetic to it. Finally, in order to cut costs, the industry increasingly contracted work out, fueling the demand for freelance editors—a predominantly female specialty.[20]

A highly sex-differentiated society creates a demand for workers (such as coaches, counselors, and prison guards) who are the same sex as their occupational role partners (Bielby and Baron, 1984). Once women made up the majority of the fiction-reading and -buying public (*Publishers Weekly*, 1974:25), publishers sought female editors for insight into women's taste (Geracimos, 1974:23). Women also compose a growing percentage of authors[21] and the majority of the literary agents who are playing an increasingly important role in getting books published (Lane, 1975:41–42; Doebler, 1978:27), so the likelihood that the editor's role partners will be female has increased. To the extent that authors or literary agents prefer same-sex editors, the demand for female editors may have grown accordingly.[22]

In other words, women became attractive to publishers because of their literary and interpersonal skills, their presumed ability to read for a largely female readership, and their expertise in growing segments of the industry—

and because they would work cheap. These factors, combined with their avail-ability as a surplus labor pool that could be readily drawn into the workforce, made women an acceptable solution to publishing's economic fluctuations (Caplette, 1982a:151).

Declining Sex Discrimination

Early in this century the feminist movement prompted publishing "to open its doors to [women], however reluctantly" (Tebbel, 1975:176). This process was repeated on a larger scale in the 1970s. Inspired by the women's libera-tion movement to reject the low-level jobs to which most women had been relegated, some women mobilized against sex discrimination and pressed for better opportunities in publishing (Dessauer, 1974:42; Strainchamps, 1974). Their efforts included both pressure from within and litigation.

By 1970 a group of women had formed Women in Publishing, an organization that carried out actions against some publishing houses, partly in conjunction with labor-organizing issues (*Publishers Weekly*, 1970), and women's groups soon emerged at publishing houses (Strainchamps, 1974:154; Caplette, 1987). When these groups confronted their employers with evidence of wage and job discrimination, some houses began to rectify disparities. For example, after a year-long campaign for job posting by Boston Women in Publishing, five houses posted openings (Reuter, 1976:18). In 1974 the presi-dent of Harper & Row, in a letter to *Publishers Weekly* (Knowlton, 1974:12), described that firm's efforts to provide equal opportunities for women, includ-ing salary reviews and broader job posting. The industry reclassified secretaries as "editorial assistants"—although their duties did not change (Coser et al., 1982:108); and many firms eliminated separate career ladders for men and women, giving women greater access to senior-level editorial jobs and tem-pering their preference for men in certain jobs.

Other firms were less receptive. In 1974 New York state's attorney general challenged several companies privately and brought suit against Macmillan (Geracimos, 1974:27; Maryles, 1974; *Publishers Weekly*, 1975a), which subse-quently established an affirmative-action plan (*Publishers Weekly*, 1976b). In 1975 a sex-discrimination suit by women editors in Houghton Mifflin's school division led to a cash settlement and to Houghton Mifflin's expansion of its job-representation goals (Smith, 1981:19). In the same year the publishing committee of the Boston chapter of the women's rights organization called 9to5 charged Addison-Wesley and Allyn & Bacon with race and sex discrimi-nation (*Publishers Weekly*, 1975b; 1976a). As a result of these suits, "wages [rose] and management practices . . . changed," according to Massachusetts Attorney General Francis X. Bellotti (Mello, 1980; Reuter, 1980).[23]

The spate of actions against other media giants, including *Newsday*, Time-Life, and NBC, heightened the impact of the suits against book publishing firms. A former editor at Holt, Rinehart & Winston claimed that a three-million-dollar suit against NBC prompted CBS (Holt's parent company) to implement a broad program to recruit and promote women and minorities: "You cannot imagine the amount of [management activity] there was around here [right after the NBC suit] in getting women up to speed."

A minority publisher claimed that no enforcement agency "is really after book publishers" and added, "If somebody zeroed in, there'd be a difference" (Weyr, 1980:31). However, most observers claimed that pressure from women's groups, litigation, and the risk of government intervention had companies running scared and that the pressure from women's groups had led publishers to curtail sex discrimination (Geracimos, 1974:25). For example, according to an editor in college publishing, "The threat of litigation made a difference. One major responsibility of the personnel director at [a large firm] that especially feared being sued was to keep the company out of trouble by encouraging the hiring of blacks and women."

Another observer commented, "They were worried primarily about the legal costs—not the loss of creative input, because they had gotten along without that." Educational publishers were especially vulnerable to government action in the early 1970s because they held large government contracts. A Harper & Row vice-president for personnel confirmed that affirmative action occurred because publishers—especially large trade and educational houses—had to implement affirmative-action regulations in order to get or keep government contracts (*Publishers Weekly*, 1980).

The women's liberation movement in conjunction with changing social values helped to alert gatekeepers who "consider[ed] themselves *avant garde*" to the contradiction between their behavior and their liberal values. One school publishing editor recalled that after the National Organization for Women (NOW) protested sex stereotyping in some materials she had developed, she and her male boss found stereotyped material in many of their other books. She said, "To have [NOW] protest has a consciousness-raising effect—whether you're a man or a woman." She believed that such experiences had helped men to recognize sex inequality in publishing employment.

The opening of management positions to women further enhanced women's access to editorial jobs.[24] When men dominate management, hiring decisions for desirable jobs tend to favor men (Kanter, 1977). My interviews with women in top-level positions suggest that women's attaining organizational power fostered opportunities for women in lower ranks without necessitating preferential treatment of women. The presence of a few women who had finally attained top-level positions encouraged decisionmakers to ignore sex in filling lower-level editorial positions (see also Caplette, 1979:17). It also conveyed to women below that they could hope to advance. For example, Sherry Arden (quoted in Geracimos, 1974:23) recalled how moved the secretaries were when she was made a vice-president: "They felt . . . they had a chance at this point." Thus, "the notion that women [couldn't] be acquisitions editors gave way before the insistence of women" (Strainchamps, 1974:159–60; also see Tebbel, 1981:728), and the knowledge that opportunities existed generated a supply of applicants for them (Reskin and Hartmann, 1986).

| | | | Conclusions

In sum, the factors that facilitated women's increased representation in editing and the decline in sex segregation across editorial roles began with outside ownership and conglomerization, which tarnished the industry's image and reshaped the editor's role—especially that of the trade editor—robbing it of autonomy and the chance for creative risk taking. Job security declined, and wages failed to rise and may have declined. As a result of these changes, publishing could no longer attract the caliber of men it desired because they had better alternatives.

The decline in the number of qualified men seeking editorial careers paired with industrial growth to increase the ever present demand for editors, and the growth of several female-dominated specialties led the industry to turn to the large number of women who continued to seek work as editors. Women's availability at lower wages than men commanded no doubt contributed to their attractiveness to publishers. By the time these changes were under way, publishing was already a predominantly female industry, with women monopolizing the lower rungs on the editorial ladder. Pressure by women's groups and fear of government action encouraged publishers to modify their personnel practices to eliminate sex discrimination, creating opportunities for women in editorial jobs. Although sometimes women simply got titles to match the jobs they had been doing all along, many were promoted into senior editorships in trade and college houses. Publishing historian John Tebbel (1987) concluded, "Corporations were virtually forced to give women more opportunities, and women took advantage of [them]." Indeed, women now hold some of the top jobs in the industry (McDowell, 1987)—although they still report to the men who run the corporations that have come to control publishing.

In 1981 Michael and Susan Carter subtitled an article on women in the professions "Women get a ticket to ride after the gravy train has left the station." Although book editing has never been a gravy train, for most of this century its nonmonetary rewards compensated practitioners for low wages. Now, as many of those rewards have diminished, so too has the pool of male would-be editors on whom the industry formerly drew. The result has been both a higher proportion of female editors and a breakdown of sex segregation among editors. Most editors with whom I spoke indicated that male and female assistant editors now do the same jobs. A few expressed concern that editing is becoming resegregated as a female job (e.g., Geracimos, 1974:25)—

an outcome consistent with the findings of other studies in this volume. But as Powell (1982) and others have pointed out, trends in publishing are fickle: mergers were common at the turn of the century, then ceased, only to re-appear in the 1960s and 1970s; some conglomerates have sold their publishing houses, and others may look for greener pastures; firms may effectively resist takeovers (see, e.g., Glabberson, 1987). In short, the changes in the editorial role need not be irreversible. The data are not all in, and the final chapter remains to be written. What seems likely is that women will edit it.

| | | | Notes

Acknowledgments: I completed this chapter while I was a fellow at the Center for Advanced Study in the Behavioral Sciences, where I was supported in part by a grant from the John D. and Catherine T. MacArthur Foundation. I am happy to acknowledge the assistance of many individuals—particularly Michele Caplette, who generously lent me her dissertation data; John Tebbel, who explained changes in the publishing industry; Miriam E. Phelps, research librarian at R. R. Bowker, who provided articles and indexes for back volumes of *Publishers Weekly*; Barbara Kritt of the University of Michigan, who did the spade work for this chapter; and Pauline Pang, who as an undergraduate at the University of Illinois provided valuable research assistance. This chapter benefited from the comments of Lowell Hargens, Walter Powell, Patricia Roos, and Kathleen Much, who also provided editorial assistance. My greatest debt is to the thirty overworked members of the publishing industry who generously shared their experiences and impressions.

1. Books intended for sale to the general public are referred to as "trade books," a legacy of the eighteenth-century practice of calling London booksellers "the Trade" (Bechtold, 1946:6).

2. In 1977 educational publishers employed 38 percent of the industry's non-production (or nonmanufacturing) workforce, followed by trade (24 percent), technical and scientific (20 percent), religious (8 percent), and reference (3 percent). Book clubs and mail-order firms make up even smaller sectors (U.S. Department of Commerce, 1977b).

3. Men monopolized managerial jobs for the same reasons that they do so in other industries: the use of informal networks to recruit (Roos and Reskin, 1984), the reluctance to share power, and concern over women's unpredictability (Kanter, 1977). A woman publishing executive illustrated the third point: "Women were allowed [more] latitude in creative areas [because] there was the notion that [at those levels men would] be able to keep [women's] hormonal tendencies under control should [they] go completely berserk."

4. Of 2,074 names *Publishers Weekly* listed in 1969 in "Who's Who among Travelers," fewer than 3 percent were women. The occupational association, which first admitted a woman in 1970, called itself the Brotherhood of Sales Representatives until 1980 (Chaney, 1984:23, 50).

5. The index of segregation across editorial positions in the Chicago firms they studied was .47 (.66 for small firms), representing the minimum proportion of members of either sex who would have to shift to another position in order to achieve total integration.

6. Nevertheless, the career ladders that led to the editors' jobs were segregated. The career path for men was through sales; women began as "consultants" who traveled to schools, demonstrating new teaching materials to their former colleagues.

7. I identify by name only editors whom I quote from published sources and industry experts whom I interviewed.

8. I computed sales rates from statistics of the Association of American Publishers, which appear annually in *Publishers Weekly*.

9. In 1980 associate and assistant editors, copyeditors, and editorial assistants earned $11,000 to $25,000, whereas acquisitions editors earned $25,000 to $50,000 (Wright, 1984:594).

10. This includes preparing written description for sales and publicity departments and drumming up enthusiasm for the book within the publishing house (Sifton, 1985:57).

11. This was not true in the lower-stakes world of scholarly publishing, in which editors retain considerable autonomy (Powell, 1985).

12. This was particularly true in college publishing because of its higher costs. According to one college editor, "One serious mistake could put you out on your ear."

13. Powell's use of the term *bookmen* in this context was apt.

14. This conclusion no doubt applies as well to people with rich spouses. Kathleen Much (1988) suggested that in the 1960s and 1970s publishing probably attracted married women of "good" families because their salaries were too low to threaten the belief that good husbands supported their families.

15. According to one industry observer (Much, 1988), school publishing still attracts teachers especially to sales because it pays marginally better than teaching.

16. Several commentators also suggested that the relatively flexible working schedule and the opportunity (indeed, necessity) to work at home may have attracted women with children (Cornelius, 1983:34; Lehman, 1987:43).

17. One house that kept statistics indicated that in 1976 and 1977 two-thirds of the applicants were women (Caplette, 1982a:169).

18. There were 40,900 nonproduction employees in 1970 (Lofquist, 1970:6,9), 46,200 in 1977 (U.S. Department of Commerce, 1977b: Table 1a) and an estimated 66,000 in 1980 (Wright, 1984:589).

19. In the early 1980s publishing experienced a 30–33 percent turnover, compared to 15–22 percent over all industries (Cornelius, 1983:33; see also Wright, 1984: 590). Most observers attribute high turnover to low wages and limited mobility opportunities (Dong, 1980).

20. Women freelance editors outnumber men by two or three to one, according to most observers (Tebbel, 1987). The membership of the Editorial Free Lance Association is two-thirds to four-fifths female, and 72 percent of 211 persons listed as editors in the 1986 *Literary Marketplace* were women. Freelance editing is predominantly female because it permits women to combine market and domestic work; it is supplied by former (mostly female) editorial assistants and copyeditors who left in-house jobs

because of blocked opportunities; and most men will not accept low freelance wages or work in predominantly female jobs.

21. Their representation among writers increased from 25 percent in 1960 to 44 percent in 1980 (Bielby and Bielby, 1987).

22. A highly respected editor alleged that most male authors, too, prefer working with female editors because "they are less threatened than if challenged by a man" (Geracimos, 1974:24).

23. Unfortunately, some progress was only nominal. After being charged under Title VII, an unnamed publisher promoted several female editorial workers to "staff editor" positions, while simultaneously promoting several male editors into a new job title: "senior staff editor" (Osterman, 1979).

24. Women's gains in top-level positions occurred after they had made gains in senior editing positions and were in part a result of the larger pool of senior editors that those advances produced. Many insiders still contend that "the higher up you go, the fewer women there are," and that "men are still not comfortable with [them]" (Charnizon, 1987:27), but most would agree that women have made major strides in top-level management in the 1980s (Charnizon, 1987; Lehman, 1987). The effect of outside ownership on women's access to top positions remains unclear. One female executive suggested that conglomerate ownership may have contributed to a less supportive climate for women at managerial levels, because the conglomerate managerial people "aren't very kindly disposed to the notion of women as heads of the houses they own." She added, "The bigger the stakes, the fewer women [who] are allowed any latitude at all." Another highly placed woman pointed out that women are underrepresented at the managerial level in conglomerates. She added that her firm's parent company "is a traditionally very male-oriented company, so I have a funny feeling that at some point I might be blocked." This may be particularly true of the conglomerates of the 1980s, which tend to be owned by foreign media companies.

Polly A. Phipps

5

Industrial and Occupational Change in Pharmacy: Prescription for Feminization

Women's representation in pharmacy has increased dramatically over the past few decades. In 1950 and 1960 women accounted for approximately 8 percent of all pharmacists (see Table 5.1). Between 1970 and 1980 their representation rose from 12 to 24 percent. Overall, the occupation itself grew 31 percent, from about 110,000 pharmacists in 1970 to more than 143,000 in 1980. This represented a net growth of some 21,000 women pharmacists compared with men's increase of more than 12,000. Thus, by 1980 there were about 34,000 women and 109,000 men practicing pharmacy. By 1988, women constituted 32 percent of all pharmacists (U.S. Bureau of Labor Statistics, 1989).

Women's movement into pharmacy was greatest during the 1970s, but understanding that dramatic jump requires knowledge of earlier events.[1] Therefore, I provide an overview of pharmacists' (including women pharmacists') work and the retail and hospital settings in which they perform it. I show how these have changed and describe the projected labor shortages and concomitant increases in federal funding that paved the way for increased female entry. Finally, I show that women's numerical advances in pharmacy resulted primarily from changes in the industrial structure, including the decline of the independent retail sector (which lessened men's attraction to the occupation) and expansion of the hospital sector (which increased opportunities for women). These changes, combined with federal monies for pharmacy education in the 1970s, created more slots in pharmacy schools, attracting women

111

Table 5.1
Employed Pharmacists, by Sex, 1950–1980

	Women	Men	Total	Percent Female
1950	7,295	81,028	88,323	8.3
1960	7,129	85,026	92,155	7.7
1970	13,032	96,610	109,642	11.9
1980	34,249	109,241	143,490	23.9

Sources: U.S. Bureau of the Census (1963d: Table 202; 1972: Table 8; 1984b: Table 4).

seeking well-paid professional jobs that they could attain with a moderate expenditure of time.

The practice of medicine originally included pharmacy among its other healing activities.[2] Although these activities separated in Europe in the thirteenth century, as late as the seventeenth and eighteenth centuries many physicians passed exams in pharmacy as well as medicine. Apothecaries appeared in the fourteenth century: some served physicians; others also practiced medicine. By the eighteenth century, apothecaries had established themselves as medical–pharmaceutical practitioners. At the beginning of the nineteenth century, chemists and druggists, who had been encroaching on the pharmaceutical duties of apothecaries, took over the dispensing of drugs and became community pharmacists (Carr-Saunders, 1966; de Haen, 1971). In North America, healers practiced both medicine and pharmacy until the two professions separated during the Revolutionary War. Historically, the separation of these professional groups involved considerable struggle, and pharmacists continue to struggle for public recognition and professional status today in response to physicians' ultimate control over the dispensation of drugs (de Haen, 1971; Ritzer and Walczak, 1986).

Most pharmacists work in either retail sales or professional services (see Table 5.2). In 1980, retail pharmacies—independently owned stores and drugstore chains—employed 72 percent of all pharmacists and professional services employed about 25 percent. Of the latter, 95 percent worked in hospitals and the rest in educational institutions (U.S. Bureau of the Census, 1984b)—a pattern reflecting the continuing trend in hospital growth. Government institutions, manufacturers, and wholesalers employed the remaining 3 percent of all pharmacists.

| | | | Retail Pharmacy

As early as the 1850s in the United States some pharmacists were making drugs to supply other pharmacists, and the years from 1855 to 1876 saw the

Table 5.2
Industrial Distribution of Pharmacists, by Sex, 1970–1980

Sector	Total	Female	Male	Percent Female	Industrial Distribution Total	Female	Male
1970							
Retail	93,722	8,861	84,861	9.5	85.5	68.0	87.8
Professional[a]	13,913	3,693	10,220	26.5	12.7	28.3	10.6
Other[b]	2,007	478	1,529	23.8	1.8	3.7	1.6
Total	109,642	13,032	96,610	11.9	100.0	100.0	100.0
1980							
Retail	103,296	19,284	84,012	18.7	72.0	56.3	76.9
Professional[a]	37,317	14,264	23,053	38.2	26.0	41.7	21.1
Other[b]	2,877	701	2,176	24.9	2.0	2.0	2.0
Total	143,490	34,249	109,241	23.9	100.0	100.0	100.0

[a] Includes hospitals and educational institutions.
[b] Includes all other 2-digit SIC industries, but primarily government, manufacturing, and wholesale trade.
Sources: U.S. Bureau of the Census (1972: Table 8; 1984b: Table 4).

founding of such companies as Stearns, Squibb, Wyeth, and Lilly, which would become giants of large-scale drug manufacturing. As manufacturers became the exclusive preparers of drugs, the retail pharmacists' role changed accordingly: rather than compounding medications themselves, they began selling already manufactured pills or elixirs to customers. In eagerly stocking manufactured products, pharmacists in the late nineteenth and early twentieth centuries weakened the link between themselves and physicians. Pharmacies became storehouses of drugs, and pharmacists' birthright as caretakers of the sick and assistants to physicians eroded. Pharmacies began to expand into other merchandise in the 1860s. With the appearance of soda fountains, which peaked during the Prohibition era, this non–health-related role further eroded pharmacists' standing as health professionals (de Haen, 1971).

With large-scale manufacturing of drugs firmly in place by 1940, the activities of retail pharmacists moved a step farther from those of physicians and from drug preparation. Pharmaceutical manufacturers produced the drugs, and their sales representatives—"detailmen"—introduced and sold their products to physicians and retail pharmacists (U.S. Bureau of Labor Statistics, 1948).[3] Pharmacists, whether they owned their drugstores or worked as salaried employees, assumed the dispensary role of filling prescriptions along with sales and managerial duties (U.S. Bureau of Labor Statistics, 1948; 1957; 1963; 1972).

In 1928 the Supreme Court wrought another change in the structure of pharmacy in the United States. In *Liggett v. Baldridge*, the Liggett Company, predecessor of the Rexall Division of Dart Industries, successfully challenged a Pennsylvania law that restricted pharmacy ownership to pharmacists (*American Druggist*, 1973b). The court's ruling cleared the way for the growth of chain drugstores, which resulted in the slow but inevitable decline of independent pharmacies. In 1972, in *North Dakota State Board of Pharmacy v. Snyder's Drug Stores, Inc.*, the Supreme Court overturned the 1928 decision, ruling that state legislatures could restrict ownership of pharmacies (*American Druggist*, 1974), but by that time the chains' economic power was too great for independent retail pharmacies to reverse the trend. In 1972 corporate chain drugstores controlled 60 percent of national drug sales (*American Druggist*, 1973b). Increasingly mobile consumers who could travel to shopping centers where the chain stores were located no longer depended on neighborhood drugstores. Corporate purchasing power meant that the chains could buy in bulk and hence offer lower prices, thus increasing their market share. Large independent pharmacies weathered the rise of chains better than small stores (Kleinfield, 1987), and some of the independents remained competitive by forming cooperatives (*American Druggist*, 1968c; 1969b). Nonetheless, the chains' share of retail sales and employment steadily increased, although the drop in individual ownership of pharmacies that accompanied the growth and popularity of chain drugstores has stabilized (Kleinfield, 1987). In 1966, according to U.S. Department of Health, Education and Welfare data, 68 percent of pharmacists worked in independent retail stores and 14 percent in chain drugstores; by 1978 employment of pharmacists in independent retail stores had dropped to 43 percent, and chain employment had increased to 29 percent (Schlegel et al., 1981). Thus, the trends in retail pharmacy included a decline in individually owned pharmacies and a concomitant growth in employment in chain drugstores.

Women in Retail Pharmacy

Early community pharmacies in the United States were a male domain. Both the professional and commercial aspects of the industry discouraged women's entry. Society traditionally reserved business operations, with their financial and entrepreneurial details—including generating capital—to men, and pharmacy was no exception (*American Druggist*, 1968a; Bolger, 1971). As a result, women's early involvement in retail pharmacy was limited. According to a survey of women who graduated from the University of Colorado College of Pharmacy from approximately 1910 to 1939, employed graduates expressed the belief that women should enter hospitals and medical technology rather than retail stores; the women surveyed felt that much routine drugstore work was too heavy and that working conditions were aesthetically unpleasant (Sprowls, 1940). Of the few women who ran or owned pharmacies, most had inherited them from fathers or husbands (Urban and Rural Systems Associates, 1976).

As recently as 1970, when women made up almost 12 percent of all pharmacists, they were only 9.5 percent of retail pharmacists (see Table 5.2). One reason for this underrepresentation was discrimination by male pharmacists. Several women I interviewed reported encountering resistance from male pharmacists in finding retail jobs and believed that women had to prove themselves more than men did. One interviewee who finished pharmacy training in the late 1960s said that the few women in her class were steered to hospital pharmacy. A survey of students at three pharmacy schools in the mid-1970s suggested continued barriers for women in retail pharmacy. Women students described difficulty getting internships with male retail pharmacists, some of whom blatantly stated that they did not hire women (Urban and Rural Systems Associates, 1976). Of 8,861 women pharmacists who worked in retail settings, the 1,608 self-employed women accounted for only 6.6 percent of all self-employed pharmacists (U.S. Bureau of the Census, 1973a). Most women in retail pharmacy held staff positions (Schwirian, 1973; Kirk, 1976), and 36 percent worked less than 20 hours per week.

More than 10,000 women entered retail pharmacy during the 1970s. Though the sector's overall employment share decreased during this time, the number of pharmacists it employed grew by 9,000 (see Table 5.2). Thus, the new jobs that retail pharmacy created during the decade went to women, and the number of male retail pharmacists declined slightly. As a result, women pharmacists' share of retail jobs almost doubled, from 9.5 to 18.7 percent. Indeed, expanding job opportunities in retail pharmacy accounted for half of women's increased representation in pharmacy during the 1970s. Nevertheless, women pharmacists were more underrepresented in retail jobs, relative to their proportion in pharmacy as a whole, in 1980 (5.2 percentage points of difference) than in 1970 (2.4 points). Self-employment remained relatively stable for women between 1970 and 1980: women constituted the same proportion of all self-employed pharmacists in 1980, 6.5 percent, as in 1970 (U.S. Bureau of the Census, 1973a, 1981a). As in 1970, women in the retail sector were concentrated in staff positions in both independent and chain drugstores in 1980, although there is some evidence that they made inroads into chain management over the decade (Schwirian, 1973; Shepard and Kirk, 1981; *Florida Pharmacy Today*, 1989). However, women are not moving from pharmacy management in chain stores to posts as store managers. One female manager in California indicated that when the chains took over, male pharmacists moved up the corporate ladder from pharmacy management to store and company management, but now that women have finally made their way into pharmacy management, the rules have changed: the chains are hiring men with business degrees for higher managerial positions rather than promoting female pharmacy managers.

Changes in Duties

Long before women entered pharmacy in large numbers, pharmacists' responsibilities had shifted from compounding drugs to dispensing them, and this routinized dispensary work—combined with declining opportunities for store ownership—lessened men's attraction to retail pharmacy. This probably contributed to the personnel shortages that the *Occupational Outlook Handbook* (U.S. Bureau of Labor Statistics, 1957, 1963) referred to in the 1950s and 1960s.

Further job routinization, associated with increasing administrative and clerical tasks, occurred during the 1970s. As health insurance became widespread, pharmacists' administrative tasks multiplied. To increase productivity, stores adopted new technology, and pharmacists working at computer terminals became commonplace. The new technology automatically printed labels, recorded refills, and produced claims for insurance companies (*American Pharmacy*, 1980). The ability of computer programs to detect drug interactions further automated professional functions (*Nation's Business*, 1985), thus relieving pharmacists of one of their traditional responsibilities. In addition, the intense pressure to fill prescriptions quickly, combined with long hours and few breaks, has earned the chains low ratings on quality of work conditions and job satisfaction among pharmacists (Schering Laboratories, 1988). The emergence of increasingly routine administrative and clerical work—the latter customarily considered female work—without the income and status benefits of ownership made practicing retail pharmacy a less desirable occupation for men.

| | | | Hospital Pharmacy

Closely aligned with educational institutions, hospital pharmacy has traditionally been the "service sector" of the profession. The differing interests of hospital and retail practitioners have kept them separate; each sector has its own publications and professional organizations, and conflicting interests have long caused tension between the service and entrepreneurial sectors.[4]

Hospital pharmacists work as administrators or staff in hospital pharmacies and as clinical pharmacists providing direct patient health care. In the 1960s and 1970s, their primary duties resembled those of their retail counterparts. They also advised the hospital medical staff on the selection and effects of drugs, made sterile solutions, ordered medical supplies, taught in nursing schools, and performed administrative duties (U.S. Bureau of Labor Statistics, 1957, 1963, 1972). Since the mid-1960s hospital pharmacy has grown dramatically, both in the numbers of pharmacists employed and in their visibility within the profession. As Table 5.2 shows, professional services (95 percent of which are in hospitals) employed twice as large a share of all pharmacists in 1980 (26 percent) as in 1970 (12.7 percent). This gain of over 23,000 additional pharmacists was composed of more than 10,000 women and nearly 13,000 men.

Technological Change and New Roles

Hospitals led the way in introducing technological innovations in pharmacy in the late 1960s (Knight and Conrad, 1975). Computerization automated routine administrative tasks such as accounting and tabulating usage data (Knapp and Knapp, 1968); the Drug Products Information File, established in 1971, automated drug pricing, compiled drug use by nursing unit, and generated patients' medication profiles (Knight and Conrad, 1975). During the 1970s these systems became more sophisticated: they printed information labels for prescriptions, provided detailed patient profiles, noted contraindications, and alerted medical staff to drug sensitivity (Greenlawn and Zellers, 1978). The new systems allowed pharmacists to enter physicians' medication orders along with patients' diagnosis, drug history, and allergies into a programmed terminal that printed labels and monitored refills and billing (Knight and Conrad, 1975). Although pharmacists checked each order for allergies and contraindications, later systems detected even these problems automatically.

Hospital pharmacies also took the lead in using pharmaceutical technicians as aides in clinical settings.[5] As early as 1968, several hospitals began formal technician-training programs (*American Druggist*, 1969a), and a Michigan community college developed the first associate degree program in pharmaceutical technology in 1972 under a Health, Education and Welfare grant (*American Druggist*, 1972b).[6] Community colleges increasingly offered such programs during the 1970s and early 1980s. As a result, technicians were in wide use in hospitals in the 1970s (U.S. Bureau of Labor Statistics, 1978b). Between 1978 and 1981 the use of full- and part-time technicians increased nearly 50 and 75 percent, respectively (calculated from U.S. Bureau of Labor Statistics, 1980a, 1984c). Although state regulations for their responsibilities vary, most technicians work under pharmacists' supervision filling carts for nursing stations. This involves prepackaging and labeling drugs and intravenous (IV) solutions (*American Druggist*, 1969a, 1971b, 1979).

Retail stores also employed pharmaceutical technicians, but their retail employment has generated considerable controversy. The rationale was that the use of technicians would upgrade pharmacists' status by freeing them from their dispensary duties to assume other responsibilities (*American Druggist*, 1969a), but unions and guilds representing retail pharmacists resisted, believing that technicians threatened their jobs (*American Druggist*, 1976a).[7]

Another specialty developed out of discussions during the 1960s and early 1970s about the role of hospital pharmacists in the greatly expanding health-care system (Tyler, 1968; *American Druggist*, 1970, 1971b) and the direction and professional status of the pharmacist. For some time the profession had sought to keep up with the knowledge of new drugs, and in 1961 the American Pharmaceutical Association had increased the educational requirements for a bachelor's degree from four years with an optional fifth to a mandatory five years (Fletcher, 1971). This increased training, coincident with the elimination of functions such as compounding drugs, led to concerns about overeducated professionals and an image problem (Tyler, 1968; Youngken, 1968; Brewer, 1969).

The proliferation of drug products and the expansion of the health-care industry led pharmacy leaders in the late 1960s to define a new role, the "clinical pharmacist," who would serve as the drug specialist in the health-care team that provided direct patient care. Many saw clinical pharmacy as the "salvation" of the profession (Tyler, 1968) in that it presented the pharmacist as an information source for other health professionals. How many hospital pharmacists practice clinical pharmacy is unclear. Although there are no exact numbers on the employment of clinical pharmacists, the number of hospitals monitoring drug therapy increased from 15 to 62 percent between 1978 and 1987 (Holcomb, 1988).

Growth in the health-care system in the late 1960s also prompted the U.S. Public Health Service's Bureau of Health Professions and Manpower Training to seek better use of existing professionals (*American Druggist*, 1970). Singling out pharmacists, whom it considered overtrained and underutilized (Tyler, 1968; Urban and Rural Systems Associates, 1976), in 1970 the bureau instituted grants to encourage the exploration of new roles for pharmacists; educational institutions used these to implement training in clinical pharmacy. Instruction included therapeutics, pathophysiology, and clinical experience in counseling and assessing patients and monitoring drug therapy.

In sum, in the 1970s hospital pharmacy underwent large-scale growth and the implementation of advanced technology. Automation and pharmaceutical technicians have relieved pharmacists of some traditional dispensary duties. Pharmacists, in turn, created a clinical specialty that participates directly in patient care as part of the profession's efforts to upgrade pharmacists' status.

Women in Hospital Pharmacy

As early as 1940, women pharmacists and pharmacy educators mentioned hospitals as providing the best employment prospects for women pharmacists, particularly for those who planned full-time careers (Sprowls, 1940; Kirk and Ohvall, 1972). In 1957 the *Occupational Outlook Handbook*, a government publication for career counselors and job seekers (U.S. Bureau of Labor Statistics, 1957:12), noted that hospital and laboratory work offered women pharmacists the best job opportunities. Some of the acceptance of women in hospital pharmacy may have come from the service of Roman Catholic nuns, who worked as pharmacists in religious hospitals and often administered hospital pharmacies.[8] In general, hospitals were seen by women, educators, and vocational counselors as providing good opportunities for women, no doubt because they featured regular hours, did not require the practitioners to generate the capital necessary to purchase an independent pharmacy, were disproportionately female work settings, and had a service orientation.[9] In consequence, at least since 1940, women pharmacists have disproportionately worked in hospitals (Sprowls, 1940; Austin and Smith, 1971). In 1970 hospital and clinic pharmacists were 26 percent female, more than twice women's overall representation in the profession (see Table 5.2). Women pharmacists' disproportionate entry during the 1970s further feminized this setting. In 1980 women remained overrepresented in hospitals, where they constituted 38 percent of hospital/clinical employment, compared to their 24 percent overall representation in pharmacy. As with the retail sector, women were concentrated in staff positions. However, women and men were much more evenly distributed at lower (staff) and upper (managers, directors, owners) levels of the hierarchy in hospital pharmacy than in retail chains and independent pharmacies (Schwirian, 1973; Sheperd and Kirk, 1981).

In hospital settings the advent of clinical pharmacy and the employment of pharmaceutical technicians ostensibly upgraded pharmacists' skill. The potential to utilize pharmaceutical knowledge through direct participation in patient care attracted both men and women to clinical pharmacy in the 1970s and 1980s. Yet though clinical positions may have increased, most hospital pharmacists do not practice clinical pharmacy. Only 8 out of 132 hospital pharmacists surveyed in a five-county midwestern metropolitan area practiced clinical pharmacy; 87 held staff jobs, and the remaining 37 worked in administrative positions (Johnson et al., 1977).

Clinical pharmacy remains an ideal rather than a reality, and given the push to cut hospital expenses, its future is unclear (Mesler, 1989). Although staff pharmacists in hospitals, outpatient clinics, and health-maintenance organizations (HMOs) consider patient education one of their activities, they have little opportunity to interact directly with patients (Schering Laboratories, 1988) and spend most of their time using automated technology similar to that on which retail pharmacy depends.

| | | | "Manpower" Shortages and Federal Funding

The *Occupational Outlook Handbook,* noting shortages of pharmacists in some localities between 1948 and 1972, concluded that supply generally balanced demand, but it did forecast upward trends in employment for pharmacists. Moreover, it assured individuals with appropriate qualifications that they stood a good chance of admission to pharmacy training because schools were not filled to capacity (U.S. Bureau of Labor Statistics, 1948, 1957, 1963, 1972).

Pharmacy grew slowly in the 1950s but more rapidly in the 1960s, when it added more than 17,000 new jobs. By the 1960s, policymakers and pharmacy educators were expressing concern about health manpower. In 1968 the American Pharmaceutical Association's Committee on Future Enrollment Problems, observing a ratio of 60.6 pharmacists per 100,000 of U.S. population that year, in contrast to 67 per 100,000 in 1960, predicted a shortage of 10,000 pharmacists (Brewer, 1969). The committee anticipated a time when pharmacists would be unable to meet prescription demands. Three years later a shortage of pharmacists did exist. Fletcher (1971:65–68) attributed it to industrial growth, a one-year lag in the production of new pharmacists after degree programs were extended to five years, enrollment drops due to increased educational requirements, an increase in the number of states requiring internships, the reluctance of graduate pharmacists to relocate, and some states' refusal to enter into reciprocal licensing agreements.

In 1963 the federal government had already foreseen a problem: concerned in part with the additional work that Medicare and Medicaid would generate, Congress passed the Health Profession Educational Assistance Act (HPEAA) to increase the number of health-care professionals.[10] The act dramatically augmented pharmacy schools' budgets by providing student per capita grants, special project grants, student assistance, and construction programs (Hugill and Watzman, 1973). The 1971 Health Manpower Act authorized capitation grants of $800 per pharmacy student up to a minimum mandatory number, plus $320 for each additional student.[11] Several observers estimated that these grants accounted for 20 to 30 percent of pharmacy schools' budgets in the early 1970s (*American Druggist,* 1973a; *American Journal of Hospital Pharmacy,* 1973). Between 1965 and 1979, pharmacy schools received $246 million under the HPEAA and related acts administered by the Bureau of Health Professions (U.S. Department of Health and Human Services, Bureau of Health Professions, 1981:6), mostly from formula capitation grants and awards for student loans and scholarships received after 1970.[12]

Table 5.3 shows student enrollments in the last three years of undergraduate (bachelor's degree) programs between 1965 and 1985, and in doctor of pharmacy (as a first degree) programs from 1970 to 1985. Federal funds, which peaked for pharmacy in 1975, account for the dramatic enrollment increases in the 1970s. The largest growth in both bachelor and doctoral enrollment occurred between 1970 and 1975; thereafter, undergraduate enrollment declined, especially from 1980 to 1985, though doctoral enrollment showed steady increases through 1985.

Thus, federal funding increased pharmacy school enrollment substan-

Table 5.3
Pharmacy School Enrollments, by Sex, 1964–1985

	Bachelor of Science, Final Three Years			Doctor of Pharmacy, Total		
	Female	*Male*	*Percent Female*	*Female*	*Male*	*Percent Female*
1964–65	1,674	10,287	14.0	—	—	—
1969–70	3,029	12,068	20.1	216	615	26.0
1974–75	6,675	16,013	29.4	394	926	29.9
1979–80	9,631	12,929	42.7	720	946	43.2
1984–85	10,165	8,481	54.5	1,115	859	56.5

Sources: Sprowls (1967:91); Orr (1970:98); Schlegel et al. (1975:348); Schlegel et al. (1980:180); Chasin (1985:191).

tially in the 1970s, and the schools produced graduates in large numbers. Jobs were readily available in both hospitals and chain drugstores when the influx of students brought in under federal aid programs graduated.[13] In particular, openings were widely available in hospitals, a setting where women pharmacists have been traditionally overrepresented.

| | | | Explaining Women's Entry into Pharmacy

In addition to the factors that decreased men's attraction to the profession, the precondition of women's inroads into pharmacy was the steady occupational growth from the 1960s that left pharmacy with a potential shortage of practitioners. Rising standards of medical care, implementation of Medicare and Medicaid, and increased group-insurance coverage all contributed to the expansion of health services and helped to generate almost 34,000 new jobs for pharmacists during the 1970s.

Federal financing of pharmacy education, spurred by actual and projected increases in the demand for health services, was probably the most important factor in increasing women's representation in pharmacy. Colleges and universities offer the only path of entry into pharmacy.[14] In the late 1950s and 1960s the schools were unfilled, presumably because pharmacy had become less attractive to the professionally and entrepreneurially oriented men upon which it had previously drawn, yet few women entered training for a pharmacy career. It was federally funded capitation grants that gave schools an incentive to recruit qualified applicants from nontraditional groups.[15] Further, federal financing became available just when more women were looking seriously at professional careers. Dramatic increases in female enrollment resulted (see Table 5.3). As one pharmacist stated, "The timing was right, and changes and concurrent upgrading in pharmacy made the occupation an attractive choice for women." Compared with traditionally female health professions that required similar educational investment, such as nursing or physical therapy, pharmacy offered higher status and better pay.[16]

Pharmacy's Reduced Attraction for Men

Federal funding did not lead to feminization in all health professions.[17] What made the difference was men's decreasing interest in becoming pharmacists. A 1976 study prepared for the U.S. Department of Health, Education and Welfare (HEW) found that men often saw pharmacy as a fall-back option if they were not admitted to medical or dental schools. With the expanded numbers of slots that federal funding created in training programs for *all* health professions, however, pharmacy often lost highly qualified male candidates, according to one pharmacy educator. Thus, although many men entered pharmacy during the years of federal financing, other medical professions may have drawn away the best qualified, contributing to large numbers of better qualified women students. The HEW study confirmed the impression of pharmacists I interviewed that the women admitted into pharmacy programs in the 1970s had better credentials than the men. Female applicants accepted by three schools in the mid-1970s averaged 459 for SAT verbal and 513 for SAT math scores, compared to men's averages of 433 and 501. Women's undergraduate grade-point averages also topped men's: 3.24 compared to 3.09 (Urban and Rural Systems Associates, 1976). Thus, while federal financing helped bring women into pharmacy schools by creating a larger number of openings, the scholastic abilities of the female "pioneers" helped women gain credibility and firmly established their presence by the late 1970s. Indeed, between 1965 and 1975 the percentage of female students doubled. When federal funding declined in 1975, male enrollments dropped sharply and immediately—suggesting that men's attraction to pharmacy diminished with fewer opportunities for scholarships or loans—but female enrollments continued to grow through 1985. As a result, by the early 1980s female students were outnumbering male students; in 1985 they made up approximately 55 percent of the advanced undergraduates in bachelor of science programs and 57 percent of those in doctor of pharmacy programs as a first degree.

Men's loss of interest in studying pharmacy was a result not only of declining financial aid but of reduced entrepreneurial opportunity. An important attraction of pharmacy for men in the past had been the chance to own a business, a traditional route to upward mobility for many individuals. In 1956 retail pharmacies employed 99,000 pharmacists—89.2 percent of all pharmacists—half of whom owned their own stores alone or with a partner (U.S. Bureau of Labor Statistics, 1957). By 1970 only about one in five pharmacists was self-employed. Between 1970 and 1980, self-employment declined further, from 22 to 10 percent (U.S. Bureau of the Census, 1973a, 1981a). Chain pharmacies with their corporate buying and advertising power, rising rents (*American Druggist*, 1969b), and declining profit margins forced many independents to merge or go out of business. With this change in industrial structure, entrepreneurs faced difficult times. The number of pharmacists who owned their own stores declined from 24,000 in 1970 to 14,000 in 1980 (U.S. Bureau of the Census, 1973a, 1981a). Because male pharmacists who owned their own stores substantially outearned male pharmacists employed in other settings—in 1980 their mean earnings (computed from U.S. Bureau of the Census, 1983a) were $25,383, or $7,000 more than the average income of pharmacists employed in retail drugstores—the decline of independent pharmacies meant a substantial drop in potential earnings. In addition, retail pharmacy lost 850 male pharmacists during the 1970s (see Table 5.2). At the same time, women entered retail pharmacy in large numbers. The available data suggest that although the retail sector grew by 10 percent, the proportion of both sexes employed in independent pharmacies dropped (Schwirian, 1973; Sheperd and Kirk, 1981). Thus, the proliferation of retail drugstore chains eroded the occupations' entrepreneurial opportunities and reduced men's interest in retail pharmacy, while increasing job openings in chain drugstores expanded women's opportunities in retail pharmacy.[18] The shift from self-employment to employment in chain pharmacies has continued, fueling the feminization of the retail sector. In 1979, 26.7 percent of pharmacy graduates found jobs in chain drugstores, 30.5 percent in independent pharmacies; in 1987, chains hired 42.4 percent of graduates, and independents only 16.5 percent (*American Druggist*, 1987).

Decreasing entrepreneurship and an increase in routinized work settings tarnished pharmacists' professional image. As noted above, the work of retail and hospital pharmacists changed as pharmacists' expertise was programmed into computers. Moreover, the location of retail pharmacies in discount stores and grocery stores—next to the "bread, butter and bananas" (Schering Laboratories, 1988)—under the supervision of nonprofessionals hardly enhanced pharmacists' professional standing. Added to these status insults was the economic injury of slightly declining real earnings for male pharmacists during the 1970s (see Table 5.4). Although the drop was just over $600 (in 1967 dollars), it put male pharmacists even further below men who had entered dentistry and medicine.

In contrast to men's experience, women pharmacists' real earnings actually grew in the 1970s, albeit very slightly. The mean real earnings of women pharmacists who worked full time, year round increased just over $700 from 1969 to 1979. As a result, the ratio of women's to men's mean earnings increased from 58.6 in 1970 to 71.9 percent in 1980 (women's median was 78.3 percent of men's median; see Table 5.4).

Table 5.4
Mean and Median Earnings for Full-Time Pharmacists, by Sex, 1969, 1979

	Mean Earnings (in 1967 $)			Median Earnings (in 1967 $)		
	Women	*Men*	*Ratio*	*Women*	*Men*	*Ratio*
1969	7,194	12,275	58.6	—	—	—
1979	7,902	10,983	71.9	8,126	10,375	78.3

Sources: U.S. Bureau of the Census (1973a: Table 1; 1981a: Table 281; 1984c: Table 1).

Pharmaceutical wages differ across work settings, and these differentials have remained steady over time. Hospitals—where women are overrepresented—offer the lowest salaries; retail pharmacies—where women are underrepresented—pay higher salaries, especially for managers and owners, who are disproportionately male. The decline in the number of independent retail pharmacies has probably helped reduce the wage gap between the sexes: men's and women's salaries exhibited the greatest inequality in independent drugstores because of the high salaries of mostly male owners and women's greater likelihood of working part time. The closer approach to wage equality also reflects the growth in hospital employment, since hospital incomes vary little by sex (U.S. Bureau of Labor Statistics, 1974b, 1978b, 1980a).

Thus, one of pharmacy's greatest attractions for women may be that they can expect compensation closer to men's than in many other professional occupations. The 78 percent earnings ratio indicates that inequality between men's and women's incomes persist, but it is far better than the 1979 average of 59 percent for all occupations or the level in most other occupations (see Chapter 3).

Part-Time Work

Throughout the 1970s, recruiters, administrators, faculty, pharmaceutical journals, and trade magazines frequently cited the opportunity to work part time in order to attract women. Pharmacy observers (*American Druggist*, 1969c, 1971a, 1977; *Pharmacy News*, 1970; Urban and Rural Systems Associates, 1976; American Pharmaceutical Association Task Force, 1981) depicted pharmacy as a "flexible" occupation that permitted part-time schedules and facilitated combining a family and a career. While most retail pharmacies offered both full- and part-time work, their representatives described women as indispensable because of their flexibility and availability (Bolger, 1971). By the mid-1970s some observers (Kimble, 1975; *American Druggist*, 1977) were criticizing pharmacy professionals for this portrayal, suggesting that it might deter women who sought full-time careers from entering the profession. They also suggested that this stereotyped view tracked women into jobs where they primarily dispensed drugs (*American Druggist*, 1977). Were opportunities to work part time tied to women's increasing numbers in pharmacy? Women pharmacists with preschool and school-age children do work fewer hours than other women, and mothers in independent pharmacies work the fewest hours (Sheperd and Kirk, 1982). However, concomitant with the increased percentage of female pharmacists between 1970 and 1980 was a *decrease* of approximately 4 percent in the proportion of women in part-time jobs—although women still averaged fewer hours than men: in 1980, 35.5 hours per week compared to men's 44.6 (U.S. Bureau of the Census, 1983a). Nevertheless, pharmacy may attract some women students because they believe it offers a way to combine family and career, and women who want to work part time may be able to do so more easily than in other professions (Kirk and Henderson, 1975). For example, approximately 32 percent of women pharmacists worked fewer than 35 hours per week in 1980, compared to 29 percent of female registered nurses and 18 percent of female medical doctors (U.S. Bureau of the Census, 1981a).

| | | | Conclusion

Several factors have contributed to women's increased participation in pharmacy. First, for several decades, women have been overrepresented in hospitals, a sector that added more than 20,000 jobs during the 1970s. Second, men's attraction to retail pharmacy weakened as real earnings dropped and entrepreneurial opportunities declined with the growth of chain pharmacies. The view that pharmacy is a less attractive occupation than it was a generation ago is reflected in the fact that four out of ten pharmacists say they do not want their children, particularly their sons, to follow in their footsteps (Schering Laboratories, 1988). Third, the proliferation of chain stores created a large number of retail jobs that (as men eschewed them) recruited women. Fourth, federal capitation grants requiring full enrollment increased the schools' incentive to admit women. Fifth, the clinical curriculum and growing service orientation of the profession have attracted women seeking a professional role and a good income for which they could qualify in just five years. The image of pharmacy as allowing women to work part time so that they can combine family and career has probably also drawn some women.

Since 1970 women have claimed a growing share of both the bachelor's and the doctor of pharmacy degrees (see Table 5.3). In 1987 women constituted 60 percent of students enrolled in pharmacy schools (Schering Laboratories, 1988), and enrollment patterns portend continuing feminization.[19] Continued transformation of retail and hospital pharmacy may further reduce

the ability of those sectors to attract men. For example, recent drug manufacturers' campaigns that directly targeted consumers (Miller et al., 1989),
computer programs that allow consumers to learn about the side effects of prescription drugs without asking their pharmacists (Kato, 1989), and physicians'
dispensing of drugs (Schwartz with Hager, 1987) have further circumvented
the retail pharmacists' role. Indeed, Dean Jere Goyan (1988) of the School
of Pharmacy at the University of California, San Francisco, has argued that
pharmacy chains have turned retail pharmacists into "human dispensing machines" and will use automation to try to eliminate them altogether. However,
the current oversupply in other health professions, including medicine and
dentistry, and a new shortage of pharmacists (Rodowskas, 1988) may restore
the occupation's attractiveness to men, and women may once again face tough
competition for slots in pharmacy schools and desirable positions.

| | | | **Notes**

Acknowledgments: Special thanks go to Barbara F. Reskin for her assistance
with this chapter. I also appreciate the comments of Marilyn Standifer Shreve, the cooperation of the pharmacists I interviewed, and Sheila Pelichoff's prompt and careful
typing of the manuscript. I presented an earlier version at the annual meeting of the
American Sociological Association, August 1987. The conclusions here are my own
and do not necessarily represent the views of the U.S. Bureau of Labor Statistics.

    1. I used government documents and trade and educational journals to trace
women's changing role in pharmacy. To identify patterns of change, I reviewed the following journals from 1968 to 1981: *American Druggist, American Journal of Hospital
Pharmacy, American Journal of Pharmaceutical Education, American Journal of Pharmacy,* and the *Journal of the American Pharmaceutical Association.* I also interviewed
ten practicing pharmacists.

    2. This paragraph and the first paragraph of the next section rely substantially
on de Haen (1971).

    3. Even as recently as 1980, few women were working as "detailmen." Only one
in six of the sales representatives in mining, manufacturing, and wholesale (which includes drug manufacturing) and in drugs, chemicals, and allied products was a woman
(U.S. Bureau of the Census, 1984b).

    4. The expansion of the hospital industry and decline of entrepreneurial oppor-
tunities in the retail sector have exacerbated this split. Hospitals have gained power
in the profession, and independent pharmacists increasingly view hospital and clinic
pharmacies as impinging on retail sales (*American Druggist,* 1972a; Neumann, 1972).

    5. Pharmaceutical technicians are included in the census detailed occupational
category "health technologist and technicians, not elsewhere classified," which was 54
percent female in 1970 and 63 percent female in 1980 (U.S. Bureau of the Census,
1984a).

    6. This grant was part of a U.S. Bureau of Manpower program to transfer pro-

fessionals' routine duties to technicians so that professionals could devote themselves to primary care.

7. As early as 1968 the American Pharmaceutical Association's fear that drug chains and discounters would employ technicians at wages lower than those of pharmacists led it to challenge a 1966 Alabama statute that permitted the licensing of assistant pharmacists (*American Druggist*, 1968b). At this writing, a battle over the use of technicians is raging in California.

8. In the early 1960s, when 25 percent of all hospital chief pharmacists were female, half of those women belonged to religious orders (Austin and Smith, 1971:28). The proportion of women pharmacists and pharmacy directors dropped in the 1970s (Schwirian, 1973; Sheperd and Kirk, 1981), probably because of hospitals' increasing business orientation.

9. These characteristics are probably associated with the large number of female pharmacists in Europe and Latin America (*American Druggist*, 1968a).

10. The federal legislation's objectives included using health-care professionals more efficiently by (1) reallocating routine tasks to technicians and reserving primary-care duties for professionals, (2) expanding the number of professionals, and (3) redistributing them to rural and inner-city shortage areas (Rodowskas, 1988).

11. Educational institutions did not receive any money if minimum enrollments were not met.

12. Policymakers considered pharmaceutical manpower shortages less critical than those in medicine and dentistry; thus, some monies were not available to pharmacy until 1970 (U.S. Department of Health, Education and Welfare, 1970:31).

13. The period 1976–78 may have been an exception. Some pharmacists expressed concern about a labor surplus (*American Druggist*, 1976c, 1978), accusing educators of overenrolling to get capitation money (*American Journal of Hospital Pharmacy*, 1973; *American Druggist*, 1976a, 1976b).

14. Every state has licensing requirements. To practice, pharmacists must graduate from an accredited school of pharmacy; license applicants must also have had one year of practical experience and pass a state board examination (U.S. Bureau of Labor Statistics, 1957).

15. I found no evidence of any affirmative-action effort.

16. Several pharmacists I interviewed suggested that women entering pharmacy were looking for a higher-status career than nursing.

17. Capitation grants did increase women's numbers in other health–professional schools, particularly medicine, dentistry, and veterinary medicine, all of which experienced large increases in women practitioners. Pharmacy exhibited this impact earlier because of its shorter training time.

18. Entrepreneurship was not a key factor in women's choice of a pharmacy career, partly because the difficulty women faced in obtaining loans discouraged them from attempting to purchase a business.

19. The 1989 entering class for doctor of pharmacy (as a first degree) at the University of California, San Francisco, was 74 percent female.

Katharine M. Donato

6

Keepers of the Corporate Image: Women in Public Relations

The tasks of public relations specialists are many. To manage public opinion, practitioners may write newsletters and speeches, lobby for organizational interests, collect news items about corporations, organize media and fundraising events, and inform the public about corporate activities. Interestingly, many women have become the visible actors who convey their employers' image. For example, when the *Challenger* space shuttle disaster occurred in 1986, the National Aeronautics and Space Administration (NASA) turned to a woman to handle the subsequent media pandemonium. The Long Island Lighting Company hired a woman as its major spokesperson to respond to politicians, activists, and residents who challenged its plan to open a local nuclear facility (*Newsday*, 1985). Althea T. L. Simmons recently replaced a male chief lobbyist for the National Association for the Advancement of Colored People (Williams, 1987). Even the Reagan administration deemed it advantageous to hire several women to fill key posts in legislative, intergovernmental, and media relations (*Ms.*, 1988).

These events represent only a few of the more recent and visible examples of a trend that began early in the post–World War II period. In 1950, 9.4 percent of all public relations workers were female (U.S. Bureau of the Census, 1963d).[1] Between 1950 and 1960 the number of women in public relations increased by over 200 percent, compared to a 40 percent increase for men (Weber and Seifert, 1966). This trend toward women's greater representation in public relations continued unabated during the 1960s and 1970s.

In 1970, women comprised 27 percent of 80,302 public relations specialists; in 1980 they made up 49 percent of 120,037 (U.S. Bureau of the Census, 1984a).[2] During the 1970s women's representation had grown dramatically (by 174 percent), while men's numbers increased very little (4.3 percent).[3]

What is interesting about this shift is its timing. Although, early in the century, public relations was considered a "man's" job (Tedlow, 1979; Cutlip et al., 1985),[4] the field drew small numbers of women during the 1920s and 1930s. For example, the Ku Klux Klan hired Bessie Tyler and Edward Y. Clarke, whose efforts contributed to the KKK's membership spurt from several thousand to about 3 million in three years. Several wife-and-husband teams also demonstrated that both sexes could succeed in public relations (Smith, 1968).[5] Nevertheless, public relations remained closed to most women until the 1970s.

This chapter seeks to explain the recent shift in the sex composition of public relations specialists, using evidence from government documents, trade publications, the social science literature, and interviews with public relations workers.[6] I begin by showing how public relations work has changed over time and by briefly describing the current state of the occupation. I then examine explanations for women's entry.

| | | | The Rise of Public Relations

Deadheading and Puffery

Shaping public opinion has been important throughout American history (Bernays, 1952). During the seventeenth and eighteenth centuries the British government and the American colonies expressed their opinions to the public in free newspapers and pamphlets. By the nineteenth century, however, newspaper advertising had become so substantial a source of income that advertisers began to play an important role in the newspaper business. They not only announced their wares in paid newspaper space, but they were also given free "puffs"—advertisements written by corporate personnel but disguised as news items. Corporations also sought publicity through "deadheading," the practice of giving reporters gifts, in exchange for which they were expected to puff their benefactors.[7]

As paid newspaper advertising greatly expanded (Bernays, 1952:60), the distinctions between advertising, free publicity, and news items remained blurred. Though formal public relations did not exist prior to the turn of the twentieth century (Tedlow, 1979), as advertising grew, so did the number of press and publicity agents whom corporations hired to pursue free publicity.

In the early years of the century, corporations—growing at an unprecedented rate—hired public relations workers to shape public opinion in their struggles with regulatory agencies, politicians, and organized labor (Tedlow, 1979). By the 1920s, big business had become more concerned with managing public opinion. Corporations hired public relations workers to refute propagandists who opposed corporate interests and to encourage positive public response to corporate activities.

During the 1930s, corporate public relations efforts focused on influencing government officials to protect business from New Deal reforms and the rallying labor movement (Tedlow, 1979). Conflict between business and the federal government existed for much of the decade. The Great Depression devastated businesses, whose leaders felt that their financial problems originated in public misunderstanding of their services. Responding to these concerns, small and medium-sized businesses and the National Association of Manufacturers (NAM) hired experts to persuade the public that its interests were safe in the hands of business and that U.S. workers, even during a depression, enjoyed a better life than workers in other countries. By the end of the 1930s, with an improving economic climate, public relations efforts had successfully conveyed a positive business image to the public. Specialists also advised executives about trends in public opinion, so they became concerned with sampling opinion and conveying the results to their employers. Having salvaged the image of big business, public relations became an important staff function in corporations.

The threat of World War II reduced the antagonism between government and big business. Public relations programs during this period emphasized the natural harmony between workers and employers. By promoting employee relations, corporate public relations workers encouraged company loyalty and tried to dissuade working women and men from joining unions. Moreover, public relations programs kept customers happy through tactics such as answering customers' letters and creating institutional advertisements that favorably depicted the company's history and operating procedures (Tedlow, 1979:135–40).

The post–World War II public relations effort was primarily one of expansion. An Opinion Research Center study reported that in 1946, for example, nine out of ten companies increased their expenditures in public relations (Tedlow, 1979:151). While employees were their main target, others included consumers, the communities in which corporations located, stockholders, the general public, and the government (Cullen, 1964). Many chief executives and their families became personally involved in public relations efforts, especially in community activities. In fact, the community involvement of wives became an important consideration when employers evaluated male public relations workers for promotions.

The postwar entry into civilian life of approximately 75,000 men and women who had worked in military public relations dramatically increased the field's workforce. It also fostered interest in establishing professional standards for public relations personnel (Tedlow, 1979; Cutlip et al., 1985).[8] In 1948, two professional associations, the American Council on Public Relations and the National Association of Public Relations Counsel, merged to form the Public Relations Society of America (PRSA).[9]

Public Relations Today

The modern public relations job involves managing public opinion and representing the employer's interests to the public. The major objective of specialists in the field is to help organizations "build and maintain a positive public reputation" (U.S. Bureau of Labor Statistics, 1986). Public relations work thus involves what Hochschild (1983:155) has called "emotional labor": workers "represent decision-makers, not simply in how they look or what they say, but in how, emotionally speaking, they seem." Indeed, Ghiloni's (1984) field research in the public affairs department of a Fortune 500 corporation showed that the most important criterion used to assess a manager's work was the effectiveness of his or her emotional labor.

Postwar expansion brought increasing specialization. Public relations professionals now work in either internal or external relations. Internal specialists, often editors of corporate newsletters, are the corporation's voice to its employees. Most perform technical tasks such as writing, editing, interviewing, and clipping news items. With increasing bureaucratization and growing recognition of the importance that communication plays in organizations, this specialty expanded dramatically during the postwar period and has become "the fastest-growing area of [public relations] practice" (Cutlip et al., 1985: 315).[10]

External public relations workers represent the organization to a variety of publics, a responsibility that allows them more creativity. They may specialize in media, government, community, or investor relations. They may identify and communicate with shareholders to help maximize the market value of stocks and other financial securities (National Investor Relations Institute, personal communication, 1987). Other specific tasks include acting as spokespersons to the media and general public, conducting press conferences, representing employers at community gatherings, and lobbying for employers' interests in state and federal government (U.S. Bureau of Labor Statistics, 1986); in fact, government lobbying is a rapidly growing public relations specialty (Schmidt, 1986; Deutsch, 1987a).

Lobbyists.   In the past, public relations specialists were reluctant to embrace lobbyists as their own, partly because they saw lobbying as an evil "excess of power" (Gray, 1986), and because many lobbyists were lawyers, accountants, and managers (Evans, 1983a). Despite these attitudes, they (and the Census Bureau) have recently incorporated full-time lobbying as part of the public relations occupation, and some public relations specialists now promote lobbying as part of the field (Evans, 1983a, 1983b; Gray, 1986).[11] Interestingly, this defense of lobbying occurred precisely when "lobbying [was] growing exponentially because more special-interest groups [were] taking an active part in the legislative process" (Schmidt, 1986).[12]

At the turn of the century, lobbying was considered an art that company executives carried out in private meetings (Evans, 1983a). In contrast, clients now hire lobbyists to represent their interests to lawmakers. Lobbyists need thorough knowledge of the legislative process. Using data processing, evaluation, and research, they must identify key people and objectives, marshal information, examine how issues affect the general public, and plan for the timing of legislative action (Evans, 1983b). As I suggest below, employers hired women as lobbyists in the 1970s because they wished to advertise their affirmative-action policies.

| | | | Explaining Women's Entry into Public Relations

Women's substantial inroads into the public relations field reflect both employers' growing preference for female public relations specialists and the occupation's increasing attractiveness to women.

The Sex-Specific Demand for Women

During the 1970s, as the number of public relations specialists grew substantially, the number of women increased much faster than that of men (174 and 4 percent, respectively). Table 6.1 shows that men accounted for only 6.4 percent of the additional 40,000 public relations jobs between 1970 and 1980. The failure of the occupation to attract more men reflects in part the fact that

Table 6.1
Employment in Public Relations, by Sex, 1950–1980

	Total	Male	Female	Percent Female
1950	18,565	16,607	1,958	10.5
1960	30,363	23,358	7,005	23.1
1970	80,302	58,906	21,396	26.6
1980	120,037	61,442	58,595	48.8
Percent growth				
1970–80	49.5	4.3	174.0	22.2

Sources: U.S. Bureau of the Census (1963d, 1984a).

the real earnings of male practitioners declined during the decade. In 1970, male public relations specialists averaged 40 percent more than the mean earnings for all male workers. In 1980, they averaged only 26 percent more.

With few men available to meet the growing demand for public relations specialists—the field drew only about 2,500 additional men during the 1970s but had almost 40,000 new jobs to fill—employers increasingly turned to women. They were especially likely to favor women in growing female-intensive work settings such as hospitals and schools. Some saw women as a better bargain than men; others preferred women to reach new publics; still others were predisposed to hire women because of affirmative-action regulations. Finally, some employers hired women because public relations involved "emotional" work, for which they believed women were better suited than men.

Women as a "better buy."   The demand for women in public relations parallels its growing specialization, a process that shaped both the types of workers available for these occupations and the types of workers employers preferred. Postwar job specialization, as noted above, expanded the technical role of public relations practitioners. Recent research has shown that women are disproportionately represented as *technicians* and men as *managers* (Broom and Dozier, 1985). In a 1985 survey, 52 percent of 47 women described themselves as "communication technicians"; 81 percent of 159 men classified themselves as managers. Moreover, evidence suggested that women remained in the technician role longer than men. Only about half the women, compared to 80 percent of the men, were able to expand their work roles to include other tasks, such as problem solving (Broom, 1982).

With the overrepresentation of women as technicians, certain public relations fields are becoming "ghettos within ghettos" (Cline et al., 1986:X-2). The first ghetto results from employers' practice of assigning women to managerial positions only in public relations departments (discussed below), the second from the segregation of men and women specialists *within* the occupation. The segregation of women in technical jobs and men in managerial jobs plays an important part in maintaining the wage gap between female and male public relations workers (Dozier et al., 1983). Table 6.2 (line 3) shows that the ratio of female to male earnings barely changed during the 1970s; women continued to earn just 60 percent of the male wage. Men's earnings may exceed women's for a variety of reasons, but "women earn[ed] less than men . . . of equal education, professional experience, and tenure" (Broom and Dozier, 1985:37). Women are thus a cheaper supply of public relations labor than men.

A study by the International Association of Business Communicators (IABC) confirmed that sex segregation exists and described public relations as becoming a "two-tier system of status" (Cline et al., 1986:X-2). The authors

Table 6.2

Mean Earnings of Public Relations Specialists and Earnings Ratio to All Workers in the Labor Force, by Sex, 1969 and 1979

	1969[a]	1979[b]
Mean earnings of female public relations specialists	$7,908	$15,193
Mean earnings of male public relations specialists	$13,420	$25,115
Ratio of female to male earnings	.598	.605
Earnings ratio of female public relations specialists to all women workers	1.60	1.37
Earnings ratio of male public relations specialists to all male workers	1.40	1.26

[a] Mean earnings of members of the experienced civilian labor force, aged 16 and over, who worked full time.
[b] Mean earnings of members of the experienced civilian labor force, aged 18 and over, who worked full time, year round.

Sources: U.S. Bureau of the Census (1973a: Table 19; 1984c: Table 1).

argued that women's concentration in the technical ranks is attributable in part to their greater representation in entry-level positions. Women were approximately 77 percent of 25- to 29-year-olds entering the field, and almost 66 percent of those 30 to 34 years old (*PR Reporter*, 1985:2). Thus, women may be overrepresented as technicians because these are the jobs open to newcomers, most of whom are women.

Employers may also consider women a better buy than men because of the skills women bring to their jobs. Data from IABC panel studies show that women in public relations are better educated than their male counterparts (Nesbitt, 1986:34). By 1983, female public relations specialists were more likely than men to have graduated from college, completed some postgraduate work, and earned a master's degree.

New publics. A demand for specifically female labor originally emerged in the postwar period when public relations departments sought to influence new segments of public opinion. Edward Bernays (1945:17) argued that public relations needed women to reach the female public and interpret female views to manufacturers, distributors, and retail merchandisers. Because women constituted half the population and controlled a substantial portion of the country's wealth, buying power, and voting strength, he contended that the woman's point of view regarding the food, clothing, and other products that women purchase had "commercial value."

A variety of articles published in the *Public Relations Journal* between 1945 and 1955 emphasized the importance of women as both consumers and molders of public opinion (McLean, 1946; Pentland, 1948; Mosier, 1949). With women's expanding consumer role, some saw a corresponding need to employ women practitioners whose "natural" intuition and skill could attract female consumers (Campbell, 1947). For example, Mosier (1949:35) argued that women, "with their graciousness and charm, persuasive powers of speech, unaggressive inquisitiveness, and ability to meet with a 'soft voice' the 'big stick requirements of business' can do well in public relations."

The expansion of women's consumer roles made them targets for advertising in wider spheres. For example, a pioneering 1960 study first recognized female stockholders as important targets (Rosenthal, 1961). In addition, food corporations concerned with promoting their standards of quality considered women influential targets, either individually or through their organizations (Taylor and O'Shea, 1970). Later, recognizing they had too long ignored "the potential of the women's market," banks began pursuing women customers (Gee, 1975:14). Initially, employers assigned women public relations specialists to traditionally female products, such as foods, furnishings, and fashion (Flanley, 1946). Within ten years, however, the trade literature was supporting broadened efforts to reach women and the development of women's departments as part of public relations programs (Flanley and Woodward, 1955). In the 1970s and 1980s, corporations continued to target women and their buying power.

Female-intensive industries.   Sex segregation within public relations is further compounded by the fact that female-intensive industries such as banks and financial service companies, hospitals, educational institutions, and local governments employ the largest share of women in public relations (*PR Reporter*, 1985). The distribution of public relations specialists by industry and sex shown in Table 6.3 reveals that professional services employ by far the most public relations practitioners—in 1980, approximately 21 percent of the men and 30 percent of the women.[13] Moreover, 59 percent of all public relations workers employed in professional services are women. According to Table 6.4, which breaks down the professional-service industry into more detailed categories, women's representation is greatest in elementary and secondary schools (75 percent) and hospitals (71 percent), industries whose total employment is projected to increase by the year 2000 (Personick, 1987). Indeed, the most female-dominated industries employ the highest percentage of female public relations specialists (Spearman's $r = .909$). Thus, employers in female-intensive industries, who are more receptive to employing women in nontraditional jobs than are those in male-intensive industries (O'Farrell and Harlan, 1984:280), hire the majority of public relations specialists. Interviews I conducted also suggested that the characteristics of female-intensive settings are likely to attract women. As one interviewee put it, these settings "offer flexible hours and fewer sexist barriers than the corporate world."

Affirmative action.   In the 1970s, employers faced affirmative-action pressures to hire women in professional and managerial jobs. Women had

Table 6.3
Industrial Distribution of Employed Public Relations Specialists, by Sex, 1980

Industry	Women (%)	Men (%)
Agriculture, forestry, and fishing	0.4	0.6
Mining	0.4	0.9
Construction	0.8	1.6
Manufacturing, nondurables	7.2	10.0
Manufacturing, durables	4.6	8.5
Transportation, communications, other public utilities	8.0	11.7
Wholesale trade, durable goods	1.0	2.0
Wholesale trade, nondurable goods	1.4	2.2
Retail trades	6.5	3.4
Finance, insurance, and real estate	9.3	7.3
Business and repair services	13.1	13.6
Personal services	2.1	1.3
Entertainment and recreation services	4.9	3.7
Professional and related services	29.5	21.0
Public administration	10.8	12.2
Total	100.0	100.0
N =	3,296	3,181

Source: Calculated from a subset of 6,477 public relations specialists who worked in 1980 (U.S. Bureau of the Census, 1983a).

Table 6.4
Public Relations Specialists in Professional and Related Services by Selected Detailed Industry Groups, 1980

	PR Specialists		All Workers
	Total	Percent Female	Percent Female
Hospitals	204	71.1	76.6
Health services, not elsewhere classified	70	64.3	69.7
Elementary and secondary schools	134	75.4	70.0
Colleges and universities	440	51.8	51.2
Social services, not elsewhere classified	147	68.0	71.7
Membership organizations	338	47.9	53.9
Total	1,638	59.3	49.0

Sources: For all occupations, U.S. Bureau of the Census (1984b: Table 4); other figures calculated from a subset of 6,477 public relations specialists who worked in 1980 (U.S. Bureau of the Census, 1983a).

been relegated to staff positions, particularly in public relations and personnel departments, because employers resisted hiring women to perform line
functions. Reports from women lobbyists provide evidence that one reason for
women's influx into public relations in the 1970s was "mounting federal pressure on employers to hire more women for responsible positions" (Louviere,
1978:82). With almost one of every five lobbyists a woman (estimated by the
American League of Lobbyists) and the increasing membership of Women in
Government, Inc., which grew from 12 in 1975 to more than 600 in 1985
(Sabo, 1985), employers may have found it useful to place women in visible
positions to advertise affirmative-action policies. One retired female public
relations specialist I interviewed suggested that employers use women in the
visible role of spokesperson because they want to publicize that they are equal-
opportunity employers. My informant added that "spokespersons are usually
powerless puppets, having little autonomy when speaking to others . . . so that
using women this way is just a management ploy."

Under the 1972 amendments to Presidential Executive Order 11246,
federal contractors had to engage in affirmative action to increase women's
representation in male-dominated occupational groups and provide statistical evidence showing progress toward preestablished goals. Corporations
were instructed to report to the Equal Employment Opportunity Commission (EEOC)—which monitors compliance with the executive order—the
sex, race, and ethnic composition of their employees across nine broad occupational categories. Relegating women to public relations and personnel staff
positions, employers may boost the number of female professionals and managers they report to the EEOC and thus appear to meet affirmative-action
goals and reduce any risk of sanctions or litigation.[14] Thus, to compensate
for women's underrepresentation in professional and managerial positions,
employers recruited women for public relations, a staff function, to fulfill
affirmative-action guidelines.

Although employers may have many motives for placing women in
highly visible public relations positions, in 1978 a *Business Week* analyst suggested that one was to compensate for the limited number of women in the
professional and managerial positions that lead to top management. By placing
women in public relations, corporations confine even those titled "managers"
to staff positions that usually involve various internal functions—hiring, benefits, safety, employee relations—rather than line positions, which involve
making policy decisions and are on a managerial career ladder. The analyst
argued that the skills of public relations specialists "are not viewed as readily
transferable" because these workers fill staff positions that are not usually on
the promotional path to top management; hence, women in corporate public
relations may be on "a fast track [to] a short career" (*Business Week*, 1978:
122). Indeed, the *New York Times* recently reported that blacks and women
in staff management positions in personnel and public relations departments

were losing their jobs as businesses cut back to "super-lean headquarter staffs" (Deutsch, 1987b).

Adding to affirmative-action pressures on employers was the publicity generated by a 1971 sex discrimination suit. In the late 1960s, Betty Harragan sued the J. Walter Thompson Advertising Company after it promoted above her eight men with less experience, tenure, and qualifications. Harragan argued that women were not given equal access to promotional tracks. Although she dropped the action (which took almost ten years to reach federal court) and received no cash settlement, Harragan believed that many companies promoted women because of her lawsuit (Hunter, 1983).

In sum, one reason some employers hired disproportionate numbers of women in public relations was that affirmative-action regulations put pressures on corporations receiving federal funding. By hiring women in public relations, a staff job, employers could enhance their affirmative-action statistics without integrating women into the more desirable line positions that can lead to top management; moreover, staff positions are least threatening to male control of top management, where pressures remain to exclude outsiders (Kanter, 1977).

Gender ideology. The prevailing gender ideology views emotional work as "women's work" (Hochschild, 1983). Like flight attendants, an occupation Hochschild studied, public relations specialists engage in emotional labor by managing emotions and by being "nice" to others. It is exactly these tasks that are important in public relations. To the extent that public relations work increasingly involves emotional labor, employers prefer women.[15] This demand may be due both to employers' beliefs that women are more likely to have the skills necessary for good public relations work and to gender-role socialization that renders some women more skillful than men at emotional labor.

The need for emotional labor may be particularly strong after firms admit to engaging in hazardous or socially callous behavior, such as dumping toxic chemicals or selling unsafe intrauterine devices. Public relations specialists must defend such an employer, convincing others that the organization is dependable, responsive to community needs, and operating in the public's best interest. Thus, any propensity to hire women for public relations work because of growing job specialization or affirmative-action pressure is reinforced by employers' belief that women are better able than men to persuade the public it is not at risk and to defuse opposition during crises. As one interviewee put it, "Because corporations are facing greater scrutiny from the public . . . there is a greater demand for interpersonal skills in corporations, and . . . women are better than men at implementing these skills." As one public relations manager declared, "Public relations is an occupation in which women are stronger than men." In addition, men may not want the "flak catching" aspect of public relations (Wolfe, 1970), since it involves low-prestige and undesirable job tasks. Or some employers may believe that women will be more effective than men because adversaries may be easier on them.

Another aspect of public relations that requires emotional work is fund raising. A common task in nonprofit organizations, such as colleges and universities, fund raising, or development, requires cultivating donors. One specialist described it as "finding out who can give you money and *getting them to feel positive enough about you* so that they actually give the money" (emphasis added). Because a successful fund-raising effort involves many personal interactions at social gatherings, employers may believe that women are better at using traditionally female social skills to lure contributors successfully.

Changes in the nature of the occupation and affirmative-action pressure, then, have led employers to hire increasing numbers of women for public relations jobs. This demand for women is supported by gender ideology suggesting that public relations work increasingly involves "women's work." Traditionally, women have been seen as sensitive to their environment, naturally empathetic (Ireton, 1967), and uniquely capable of dealing with human problems (Bates, 1983). The preference for women in public relations is further encouraged by the rapid growth of service industries (Oppenheimer, 1970), which may have fostered a demand for women because many of the jobs in these industries require the emotional characteristics traditionally typed as female. In response, employers invoked stereotypes to justify hiring women during the 1960s and 1970s.

Women's Attraction to Public Relations

Recognizing that public relations increasingly offered them good opportunities, growing numbers of women entered the educational programs that prepare persons for public relations jobs. Soon after World War II, colleges took part in the push to professionalize public relations practitioners (Cutlip et al., 1985). By 1946, about half of the fifty-nine major institutions of higher education surveyed were offering public relations courses (Lee, 1947)—mostly in journalism departments, which emphasized technical skill (Sussman, 1948). As a result, beginning public relations workers are increasingly likely to have a college degree, usually with a journalism major (U.S. Bureau of Labor Statistics, 1986; PRSA Education Department, 1987), or a background in English or liberal arts.

With growing opportunities in public relations, women are entering the undergraduate majors that serve as pipelines to entry-level technical jobs. Their presence in journalism schools has increased; since 1977 women have outnumbered men (Beasley and Theus, 1985). By 1980, 60 percent of all journalism majors in fifty-four U.S. colleges and universities were female (Peterson, 1985). As a result, a large pool of female journalism majors now

Table 6.5
Earnings Ratios of Public Relations Specialists to Selected Professional
Occupations, by Sex, 1979

Earnings Ratios of Public Relations Specialists to:	Women	Men
Elementary school teachers	1.13	1.43
Secondary school teachers	1.12	1.42
Librarians	1.10	1.44
Nurses	1.02	1.31
Social workers	1.16	1.54

Note: Figures show ratios of mean earnings of female and male public relations workers who work full time, year round to mean earnings of comparable workers in selected professional occupations.

Source: U.S. Bureau of the Census (1984c).

exists for entry-level public relations jobs, and women now often outnumber men among practitioners in those jobs.

An important attraction of public relations for women is that its occupational rewards are competitive with those of other accessible occupations. Although women in public relations earned only 60 percent of what men did in 1980, the occupation paid women better than the average female job. In 1970, women in public relations averaged 60 percent more than the median for all women workers; in 1980, they did 37 percent better. Moreover, though both male and female public relations specialists' earnings advantage over the average worker declined between 1970 and 1980, public relations continued to be more monetarily attractive to women than to men. More to the point is how well public relations work pays compared with the other professional occupations that women usually enter. The earnings ratios of public relations specialists to the female semiprofessions (Table 6.5) are instructive. Overall, the traditionally female semiprofessions pay women less than public relations work.

In sum, public relations attracts women because it pays as well as or better than many of the alternative occupations open to women, even though it is not among the most lucrative of the integrating occupations.

| | | | Conclusion

Women's increasing representation in public relations during the 1970s was a continuation of a trend that began after World War II. Women's representation grew partly because the supply of men was not adequate to meet the increasing demand for public relations specialists, and partly because employers

preferred to hire women for certain roles as a result of occupational specialization, an increasingly female clientele, and federal pressure. Recognizing
the purchasing power of women, for example, employers demanded female
public relations specialists to reach female consumers. All of this occurred in
an ideological context within which the emotional tasks of public relations
were considered appropriate for women. Sex labeling of tasks influenced the
choices of employers and employees alike.

In the 1970s, many young women realized that the profession was accessible to them and that it offered higher pay than many comparable occupations
open to women. In response to perceived opportunities, thousands of young
college women became journalism majors, thereby preparing themselves for
entry-level public relations jobs.

The gains women made in the field during the 1970s have attracted
still larger numbers of female students to careers in public relations. Between
1968 and 1987 the sex composition of the Public Relations Student Society
of America (PRSSA) changed from 37 percent to approximately 80 percent
female (Teahan, 1987). In addition, women captured more than three-quarters
of all advertising and public relations jobs that went to the 1985 journalism
and mass communications graduates surveyed by the Dow Jones Newspaper
Fund (Gersh, 1986). These data suggest the continuing feminization of the
occupation.

Women's involvement in fund raising, organizing special events, and
other public relations tasks is not new; women have long been active in charity
and volunteer work. What is new is that they are being paid for such work and
that their presence in public relations is growing in what was a male occupation before the 1970s. However, though these facts denote progress, women's
positions in the field—especially as technicians—are often extensions of their
traditional work roles. Moreover, the current segregation of women as technicians and men as managers represents a relatively stable form of sex inequality
that can lead to sex differences in promotion (DiPrete and Soule, 1988).
Hence, while women's entry into public relations may be a sign of progress,
sex segregation and inequality within the occupation mean that women still
have far to go.

| | | | Notes

1. In 1950, the census included public relations workers in the category "editors
and reporters" (code 036); in 1960 and 1970, they were "public relations men and
publicity writers" (code 163).

2. These figures are from the detailed 1980 census category "public relations
specialists" (code 197).

3. Note that women's representation among "managers, marketing, advertising, and public relations" (code 013) also increased between 1970 and 1980, from

7.9 percent in 1970 to 17.6 percent in 1980 (U.S. Bureau of the Census, 1984a). In theory, public relations managers should be so coded; however, according to Census Bureau personnel (Priebe, 1988), most public relations managers were coded as "public relations specialists" (code 197).

4. The first corporate public relations department began when George Westinghouse hired E. H. Heinrichs as his personal press representative during the famous battle of electric currents. Rex Harlow, Ivy Lee, and James Drummon Ellsworth also pioneered with their efforts to promote *Harlow's Weekly*, the Pennsylvania Railroad, and the American Telephone & Telegraph Company (AT&T), respectively.

5. For example, Evart G. and Mary Swain Routzahn were hired to publicize social work in the 1920s. Doris Fleischman and her husband, Edward Bernays, also worked together on numerous public relations efforts. In 1933 the husband-and-wife team of Leone Baxter and Clem Whitaker founded the first public relations agency specializing in political campaigns. For more information on women pioneers, see *Public Relations Journal* (1951) and Smith (1968).

6. Much of the literature I reviewed focused on the effects on earnings of the increase of women in the field (e.g., *PR Reporter*, 1985; Theus, 1985; Cline et al., 1986; and see Nesbitt, 1986, for a review).

7. Railroads pioneered in developing corporate press relations by these means (Tedlow, 1979); the gifts were usually railroad passes.

8. Steps to professionalize public relations had begun as early as the 1920s, when Edward Bernays (1952) used the term "counselors" to describe their professional status, but the professional association movement began in earnest in the 1930s and 1940s.

9. Currently, the PRSA is chiefly a service organization with a code of ethics and the power to use disciplinary measures against members who violate it. In 1970, the American Association of Industrial Editors and the International Council of Industrial Editors merged to form the International Association of Business Communicators, including public relations specialists and editors. The IABC, also a service organization, recognizes the increasing importance of communication as a function of top management (International Association of Business Communicators, 1988).

10. Although internal specialists are in fact public relations workers, if they reported their job title as editor, the Census Bureau classified them as editors (code 036).

11. In 1970 the Census Bureau coded lobbyists as managers and administrators, not elsewhere classified (code 245), in 1980 as public relations specialists (code 197).

12. The *Washington Representative 1986*, an annual compendium of who's who in lobbying, lists more than 10,000 Washington lobbyists.

13. I calculated these statistics and others presented below from a 1980 census microdata subset of 6,477 public relations specialists working in 1979 (5 percent, A sample; U.S. Bureau of the Census, 1983a). For technical documentation, consult U.S. Bureau of the Census (1983b).

14. Employers are free to classify public relations workers in any of the nine major occupational groups (Equal Employment Opportunity Commission, 1987).

15. To assert that emotional labor explains the increasing feminization of public relations specialists, I would need evidence that public relations work has increasingly involved emotional work since 1970—evidence I do not have at present.

Chloe E. Bird

7

High Finance, Small Change: Women's Increased Representation in Bank Management

Women have worked in banking since early in the century, but their numbers did not become large until the 1940s, when banking began relying on women to fill clerical positions (Shulsky, 1951). By 1970 women constituted two-thirds of the workforce in banking, but most of them held clerical positions: for example, 86 percent of the tellers were women (Strober and Arnold, 1987a). The few women managers were concentrated in retail banking, which emphasized consumer relations; male managers dominated higher-status positions as officers and executives. In the 1970s, an increase of 738,107 nearly doubled the number of women working in banking (U.S. Bureau of the Census, 1984a:7). Almost four-fifths of female bank employees still held administrative-support positions in 1980, but between 1970 and 1980 women did post strong gains in bank management: they increased their share of managerial jobs from 19.4 to 31.4 percent of bank and financial managers (see Table 7.1).[1]

In this chapter I seek to explain women's recent gains in bank management and to understand the significance of these gains. Although bank and financial managers work in a cross section of industries, I focus on the over 85 percent employed in banks and in savings and loan institutions (U.S. Bureau of Labor Statistics, 1987b:288).[2] My data come from a variety of published sources, plus interviews with ten bank managers. I discuss changes in the banking industry and the role of bank manager, then trace the consequences of these changes on women's representation.

Table 7.1
Numbers of Bank and Financial Managers, by Sex, 1970, 1980

	1970[a]	1980
Men	177,667	281,218
Women	42,816	128,626
Percent Female	19.4	31.4
Total	220,483	409,844

[a] Estimates based on a sample of 120,000 persons in the civilian labor force whose 1970 occupations were reclassified according to the 1980 occupational classification system.

Source: U.S. Bureau of the Census, 1984a:7.

| | | | The Banking Industry

In the last several decades the banking industry has undergone a dramatic transformation.[3] Prior to federal deregulation, banks enjoyed virtual oligopolistic control over much of the financial market. In the 1970s state and federal governments began repealing regulations that had previously shielded banks from competition. This, along with the growth of the industry, forced banks into a competitive environment typical of the service sector. A bank manager I interviewed described the change:

> We're not just competing with banks now, we're competing with everybody. . . . [Before,] we served people who walked in. Bankers sat back and greeted them, and got a lot of business because that was the only game in town. That is no longer the case, and we're out there actively soliciting . . . to try to attract a higher market share or just to retain a market share that we have because market shares are slipping for banking as a whole because of all the competition.

In response to this increasing competition banks rationalized their organizations, changing their organizational structure. Fluctuations in the prime interest rate made banking riskier, and inflation caused operating costs to skyrocket. Consequently, a rising pressure to contain labor costs became an incentive to automate. These changes inevitably affected employment practices across the industry.

Regulation

To protect public interests, state and federal governments have long regulated banking. In the early 1930s, in response to the alarming number of bank failures, the Roosevelt administration reformed the financial system to institute economic recovery and ensure the stability of banks. Many existing regulations restricting competition among banks originated at that time (Fry and Williams, 1984). To protect depositors, in 1935 Congress enacted legislation requiring all members of the Federal Reserve system to insure their deposits with the Federal Deposit Insurance Corporation (FDIC). Since consumers favored insured banks, most state banks found participation essential and, as a result, became subject to the FDIC's regulatory authority (Golembe and Holland, 1986).

The Roosevelt administration also imposed regulations on entry into banking, placed a ceiling on interest rates on savings accounts, and prohibited banks from paying interest on demand deposits. In effect, these rules eliminated price competition within the industry, making banking unique in the otherwise highly competitive service industries. As a result, banks competed mainly through providing services to customers. *New York Times* financial analyst Robert A. Bennett (1986:8F), observed:

> Before deregulation, [banks] had a near monopoly on low-interest deposits, and borrowers had to come to them for the low-rate loans. They could lend at relatively low rates only to the most credit-worthy individuals and corporations, and make profits. The risky, high-interest loans, and the marketing hustle, were left to the finance companies.

Federal regulations allowed only banks to offer all financial services, thereby insulating them from competition with other financial institutions. Traditionally, banks served commercial customers and left consumer accounts to thrift institutions, though banks' disdain for retail accounts declined after World War II, when traditional commercial bank markets deteriorated while the market for thrift institutions flourished.[4] However, the regulations that helped banks and savings and loan associations to prosper in the 1940s and 1950s limited their ability to compete with nonbank financial services—such as the credit-card industry—during the 1960s when interest rates were high (Nadler, 1970).[5]

Industrial Growth

In 1970, banking and other finance firms employed nearly 1.7 million people. By 1980 this had increased by 50 percent, to almost 2.6 million (U.S. Bureau of the Census, 1981b: Table 669; 1986b: Table 682).[6] Over the same period the number of bank managers in all employment settings grew 86 percent (see Table 7.1). Much of the added employment of bank managers resulted from a rapid increase in the number of banking offices (see Table 7.2). While the number of banks increased by only 8 percent between 1970 and 1980, the number of bank offices increased by 82 percent in the same period with an additional 19,000 branches (U.S. Bureau of the Census, 1984e: Table 820). The trend toward larger banks, more bank holding companies,[7] and more

Table 7.2
Number of Operating Bank Offices, 1930–1980

	1930	1935	1940	1945	1950	1955	1960	1965	1970	1975	1980
Banks	22,172	15,869	14,895	14,713	14,693	14,285	13,999	14,324	14,199	15,130	15,330
Branches	3,522	3,284	3,666	4,168	5,158	7,391	11,106	16,634	22,967	32,109	41,902
Total	25,694	19,153	18,561	18,881	19,851	21,676	25,105	30,958	37,166	47,239	57,232

Sources: U.S. Bureau of the Census (1966:449, Table 613; 1975: 1035, 1037; 1981b:510, Table 844).

branch banking increased the organizational complexity and hence inflated the ranks of middle management in banking.

Between 1970 and 1980, 200 to 330 mergers and absorptions occurred annually (U.S. Bureau of the Census, 1984e: Table 823). Consequently, by 1982 the 100 largest banks employed approximately one-third of the nation's banking personnel (*ABA Banking Journal*, 1982). These changes in the structure of the banking industry directly affected employment in management occupations. Initially, larger banks offered managers longer job ladders, while growth in the industry expanded opportunities at every level (Spaeth, 1988). By the late 1970s, however, increased competition between firms led banks to trim jobs; in attempting to rationalize their organizations, they cut back the growing layer of middle management.[8]

Deregulation

Regulations preventing price competition among banks were established during a period of concern for the stability of individual banks. By the 1960s the tide had turned, and the federal government sought to reintroduce market forces to foster competition. Customers, shielded by the FDIC from the risk of bank failure, wanted financial institutions to compete in terms of interest on savings and checking accounts. Beginning in 1980, with the passage of the Depository Institutions Deregulation and Monetary Control Act, federal deregulation allowed banks to compete in interest rates on loans and money-market accounts, and it permitted savings and loan associations to offer checking accounts and other banking services as well as mortgages (McCall and Peterson, 1980). The increased costs squeezed profits, and fluctuations in the prime interest rate made banking riskier because profits depended on anticipating fluctuations in the prime rate, inflation, and the value of the dollar.

During the 1980s, Congress further deregulated finance, allowing a wide range of institutions—including Sears and American Express—to compete with banks for various types of investments.[9] Still standing regulations that prohibit banks and bank holding companies from providing certain financial services, such as selling stock, gave the less restricted nonbank providers of financial services a distinct advantage. As a result of patchwork regulation that placed different restrictions on different types of organizations, banks and nonbanks began to develop elaborate corporations to circumvent the restrictions on the services a single firm could offer.

Competition forced many small banks to close and many larger ones to reorganize or to merge with other institutions (Wright, 1984). Consequently, the single-office bank virtually disappeared. As banks have reorganized, grown, or merged with other institutions, the division of work within them has become more elaborate, modifying career ladders by creating new levels in the hierarchy and redefining old positions (Bowden, 1980).

Automation

Competition gave banks the impetus to automate check and information processing to cut costs and offer more specialized customer services (Newhouse, 1966). Advances in computer technology in the 1960s and 1970s reduced the cost of storing, analyzing, and retrieving customer data. By reducing the costs of transactions, automation accelerated industrial growth. And because the demand for banks initially outpaced the gains in efficiency from new equipment, bank employment continued to increase (Brand and Duke, 1982).

Automation marked a major change in the banking industry. To evaluate the advantages of automating, banks examined the costs of various transactions and services. Such cost accounting, which included assessing the productivity of workers, contributed to the rationalization of banking. Competing for profits compelled banks to trim jobs (Caruth, 1984) and to redistribute work: "With college trained male recruits scarce, personnel officials discover[ed] that one female service assistant [could] free 25 percent more time for four male executives handling work that demands special knowledge" (Van Breems 1969:57). Work measurement encouraged banks to set quotas, giving rise to speedups. Most banks reduced jobs by not filling vacated positions or encouraging early retirement, but by 1977 they had resorted to firing workers to trim staff more rapidly (Nadler, 1977).

New technology, computerization, and advances in communication hardware and software also facilitated the growth of large banks, in part by allowing customers to choose whatever branch was most convenient (Jacobs, 1980). However, the increased use of credit cards, automatic teller machines (ATMs), and direct deposit of paychecks, which meant that customers no longer needed to enter the bank regularly to conduct business, reduced the profitability of and need for full-service offices. In response, banks established ATMs and small branches at shopping malls and airports, facilities that do not require the same management or staff as traditional branches.

Advances in technology also increased the ability of nonbank financial services to compete with banks. Because credit cards, direct deposit, and ATMs reduced the number of direct contacts with a customer—and the opportunity for the bank to sell additional services (Berry, 1979)—the quality of remaining bank–customer interactions became increasingly important. Thus banks came to recognize the importance of employees who dealt personally with customers.

Summary

Federal regulations passed in the 1930s reduced competition in the banking industry, but changes in the makeup of bank customers by the 1950s prompted banks and other financial institutions to compete for consumer accounts. Subsequent changes in the economy and deregulation of the industry heightened competition and transformed the organization of banks. Although some single-office banks remain, larger banks and holding companies now dominate the industry. Bank deregulation and the ensuing increase in competition have affected employment, individual bank occupations, and the organization of work within banks and across the finance industry. As automation reduced direct contact with customers, banks recognized the increasing importance of the quality of each personal interaction. Prior to the emergence of intense competition, banks could afford a cold image (Nadler, 1970); as a vice-chairman of the Marine Midland Bank put it, "A decade or two ago we didn't have the same intensity for profitability as we do today. In those days, profits just fell into our laps" (Bennett, 1986:8F). But since deregulation, banks have been forced to improve their public image by catering to customers (Cole, 1982). In the words of a former Citicorp chairman who led the banking industry into deregulation, "We had a monopoly and it was lovely; now there's a market and we're losing market share." The competition for consumer loans resulted in an increasing emphasis on customer service. Banks needed, simultaneously, to sell harder to maintain their share of the market and to replace aggressive sales techniques with a service-oriented image. We can see the effects of these changes in the employees banks look for.

| | | | The Role of Bank Manager

Traditionally, banks hired management trainees with some college education, although they occasionally promoted outstanding clerks or tellers to management positions. Some banks invested in specialized off-the-job training, but most training occurred on the job. The Baby Boomers who entered the labor market in the late 1960s constituted a more educated labor pool than had previously been available, so banks were able to transfer some of the cost of advanced training to potential employees. This fact, along with pressure to rationalize their operations, led banks to abandon the policy of seeking lifetime employees in order to recoup their investment in training.

By 1970, banks were seeking as management trainees college graduates who had majored in finance or business administration (Splaver, 1973). A decade later, banks were recruiting trainees with even more education. One manager I interviewed commented on the change:

When I started to work for the bank [in 1974], having an M.B.A. was very unusual. People were hired with a B.A. degree in anything. . . . If it was anthropology, we didn't care. If you had a degree, it proved something to us, and they put them in and made them bankers. Now to get a position in a bank from the outside you virtually have to have a business degree of some sort. The bank is less willing to spend money to train someone who hasn't done something on their own to prove that banking is what they want to do.

According to the 1980–81 *Occupational Outlook Handbook* (U.S. Bureau of Labor Statistics, 1980b), the ideal education is a master's degree in business administration following a bachelor's degree in the social sciences. One senior vice-president I interviewed denied that an M.B.A. is required but granted that lacking it hinders a manager's opportunity to advance.

Bank managers work at all levels, from supervisor of junior bank officers and clerical staff to senior and executive vice-president. The 1980 census category "financial manager" includes facility and department managers, bank cashiers, treasurers, comptrollers, and credit officers (U.S. Bureau of the Census, 1982b). Managers' jobs range from computerized analysis of the banks' financial affairs and current economic conditions to commercial and retail sales of bank products and services. Within bank operations alone, managers specialize in customer services, electronic data processing, and internal services. Similarly, managers in trusts, investments, and lending specialize in either commercial or consumer (retail) accounts. These different positions vary in terms of salary and necessary education and credentials. For example, a loan officer must be familiar with the principles of economics, production, distribution, and merchandising, as well as the fundamentals of commercial law (U.S. Bureau of Labor Statistics, 1970). Unlike other bank managers, managers in lending are typically paid on commission; hence, those in commercial lending have a significantly higher earning potential than managers who market consumer loans.

As banking became more complex, banks required an increasingly specialized workforce. Consequently, the career ladders for branch management and senior management began to diverge during the 1970s. A banking consultant and faculty member of the Graduate School of Retail Bank Management, noted:

> Perhaps there is an irreconcilable void between a corporate banker in the main office performing specialized services for major corporate customers and a branch manager meeting the financial service needs of a given community. . . . A person who has the attributes to succeed in branch management may not have the personality or skills required to succeed in corporate banking, and vice versa. (Metzger, 1982:46)

The reorganization within large banks reduced branch managers' authority over personnel and business. Branch managers no longer control all branch employees; senior lending and operations officers often report directly to their respective vice-presidents (Metzger, 1982). In a field where profits are an indication of success, the centralized system disadvantages branch managers. In addition, as many customers no longer need to enter banks to obtain services, branch managers often do not meet all their retail customers, thereby losing some of their traditional status in the community.

I I I I The Changing Sex Composition of Bank Management

Patterns of Sex Segregation

Banks have repeatedly turned to women workers during periods of labor shortage. In 1917, shortages of male workers during World War I prompted banks to seek women for clerical and lower-level managerial positions. Alice Kessler-Harris (1982:219) quoted a contemporary observer: "It was not until our men were called overseas that we made any real onslaught on the realm of finance, and became tellers, managers of departments, and junior and senior officers." Although by 1928 there were 2,000 women in executive positions, one noted that women had "not yet penetrated the innermost precincts" (Kessler-Harris, 1982:236). When the Depression eliminated labor shortages, the industry cut back on women employees. Faced again with a shortage of male labor during World War II, banks once more began hiring women as tellers, explaining that women make ideal tellers because they are good at dealing with people (Kessler-Harris, 1986:770). Strober and Arnold (1987a) contended that after 1940, changes in banking technology and an increased number of part-time jobs helped attract more women to banking as secretaries and tellers. In 1945 a professor of business administration wrote:

> An overwhelming majority of the jobs in banking are routine and technical in character, and the main prerequisites for successful work are accuracy, speed and dependability. Many of these tasks can be performed capably by girls and young women of intelligence who, while not planning to make banking a career, nevertheless wish pleasant, congenial jobs under good working conditions . . . until they get married. (Griffin, 1945:15)

During the 1950s and 1960s, banks preferred female high school graduates as tellers, jobs that normally offered little opportunity to advance. However, banks placed male college graduates in teller jobs as officer trainees and paid them more than women in anticipation of their advancement to management. This practice persisted until sex discrimination lawsuits filed under the Equal Pay Act in 1969–70 challenged separate promotion ladders (Strober and Arnold, 1987a).

By 1970, women held 86 percent of teller positions and had begun to breach the next level in the hierarchy—management. Banks did not admit women to their management-training programs until the late 1960s, and until the mid-1970s women made up only a small percentage of the trainees (Bernstein, 1982:84). And even as more women gradually gained access to managerial positions, they were concentrated in retail banking and operations (Council on Economic Priorities, 1977). White men continued to dominate commercial banking; for example, a National Association of Bank Women (NABW) study found that only 19 percent of female managers had worked in commercial lending, compared to 61 percent of male managers (Bryant, 1980). This is significant because when larger banks divided the functions of bankers, the most prestige went to activities that generate profit, those of commercial bankers and, to a lesser extent, retail bankers who handle large personal loans. One interviewee summarized: "In banking, commercial lending . . . is the elite, and they tend to control the direction of the bank. They have a higher salary, greater opportunities for career changes, [and are more] recognized in the community." Banks typically assigned women managers to branch supervision, data processing, and personnel (Bryant, 1980). For example, in one major bank, although 41.2 percent of the officers were women, women were 51.8 percent of the branch managerial staff (Jackall, 1978). In 1980, according to Patricia Reuss, executive director of the Women's Equity Action League,

> women managers in line operations still tend to be branch managers. If staff, they tend to be in personnel or other "traditional" women's jobs. Women managers tend to have the title but not the power that should go with it. Rarely are they at the top, where policy is made, where power is. (Quoted in Bassi, 1980:5)

In the late 1970s Bette B. Anderson, former president of the NABW, pointed out that even banks that accepted nearly equal numbers of men and women graduates for management training tracked women into the traditionally female areas of operations and personnel rather than commercial banking (Holubowich, 1977:41). Many women managers I interviewed a decade later echoed this complaint.

Vertical Segregation—The Glass Ceiling

Another expression of sex segregation is women managers' concentration in lower-level positions such as managing female employees, including tellers and filing clerks. A 1976 study by the Council on Economic Priorities (1977) found that women constituted 15 to 20 percent of entry-level managers, 5 percent of middle managers, and one percent of top executives. More recently, Jane Sasseen (1986:35) summarized the predicament of female bank managers:

> By 1983 . . . women held just 2% of the senior jobs, despite the fact that we represented more than 70% of the banking work force. . . . Five years ago, women senior vice-presidents nationwide could have been counted on two hands; today, the National Association of Bank Women estimates that over 200 women have reached that rank, scattered at banks around the U.S. But with tens of thousands of male senior vice-presidents still running the show, the gender gap at the top remains.

According to several women managers I interviewed, many women who entered banking on the crest of new affirmative-action plans and early court settlements saw few barriers to their banking careers until they approached the vice-president level. As one female senior vice-president described the situation:

> You literally didn't know that there was a glass ceiling there and you thought you were just going to keep moving up and developing and [then] you ram into it. . . . You go through quite a traumatic time until you start to realize . . . that your experience is not exceptional, and in fact is typical, and [that] it is not likely to change in the short run.

She recounted the experience of another senior woman who had come to the bank five years before her and had also been fast tracked:

> It was basically very rapid promotion and growth within the company to the senior vice-president level and then hitting what we all refer to as the "glass ceiling," where it is obvious that the next level up or even maintaining key strategic roles within the company at the divisional level is not supported.

Sex-segregated job assignments, personnel practices, and top-level managements' discomfort with women produce this vertical segregation. Officers who hope for promotion to senior positions must have extensive experience, especially in commercial lending, but until very recently, lending departments have been closed to women (except as clerks and secretaries), thus effectively excluding them from upper-level positions (Council on Economic Priorities, 1977:41). Women's specialized training results from the banks' view of them as temporary employees. Paul Nadler (1977:13), a professor of business administration at Rutgers University, described such narrow training as "a good way to handle the question of providing job training to women who might leave to start families." In addition, during the 1970s banks were more likely to recruit women than men as specialists (Council on Economic Priorities,

1977), and though specialization can lead to middle management, it rarely leads to senior positions. Thus, many women became proficient in a single area of banking, but few were exposed to a broad range of situations where they could learn from coworkers and superiors (Holubowich, 1977).

Banks have traditionally promoted workers from inside rather than hiring new staff for middle- and upper-management positions. Because banks did not advertise these openings, managers could impose subjective definitions of the pool of promotable workers. Moreover, in the absence of institution-alized procedures for hiring and allocating workers, and the lack of objective criteria on which to base managerial recruitment and promotion, employers can indulge discriminatory preferences, which tend to reproduce the existing segregation (Szafran, 1984) even when, as has often been the case, being male was not a requirement.

Women's limited training and lack of access to information about open-ings within their own or other banks reduced their ability to compete for jobs. A female senior vice-president I interviewed reported that her bank posts some jobs, but not senior-level positions: "What you start to find is that . . . the new opportunities come and . . . they are filled by men." Until the early 1970s, bank training programs did not include management education, so women who had not acquired the credentials for senior management elsewhere were unable to obtain the skills or experience to allow them to advance (Bryant, 1980). However, according to Joseph O'Shields (1977:53), division president of a major executive-search firm, the need for specific banking skills and ex-perience at the top level of management is more imagined than real. He described banks' reluctance to treat specialized recruits as important elements of the institution: "The tendency is to consider operations managers as, in effect, 'second class citizens.'"

David Maxwell, chief executive officer of the Federal National Mort-gage Association, explained the resistance to assigning women to senior-management posts: "Chief executives who are my age [fifty-seven] or even a little younger still feel uneasiness dealing with women. . . . They're much more comfortable dealing with other men." A woman who did reach senior vice-president confronted the personnel director when her career "started to go lateral." Echoing Rosabeth Kanter's (1977) thesis of tokenism,[10] he candidly explained: "What the chairman and presidents want are people that they are comfortable with, and they are not . . . comfortable with women. It doesn't even get to the . . . level of you as an individual and [your] personality; it is the skirt that's the problem." Another interviewee put the problem at the senior vice-president level: "The chairman, vice-chairman, and president are not comfortable with women in [the] executive decision-making circle. The chairman basically admits it . . . in private."

Sex segregation in job assignment contributed to women's underrepre-sentation in top management jobs and ensured that the jobs to which women

Table 7.3
Mean Earnings of Full-Time, Year-Round Financial Managers, 1969, 1979

	1969			1979		
	Men	Women[a]	Ratio[b]	Men	Women	Ratio[b]
Financial Managers	$14,667	—	—	$27,897	14,899	.534
Managers and administrators	13,733	7,006	.510	27,624	14,203	.514
All workers	10,150	5,146	.507	19,943	11,051	.554

Note: Occupational categories in 1970 and 1980 are not comparable because of reclassification for the 1980 census.
[a] Because the 1970 census reports do not give information on the same occupational categories, data are not available on the earnings of women employed as financial managers in 1969.
[b] Female–male earnings ratio.

Sources: U.S. Bureau of the Census (1973c: Table 1, Table 7; 1984c: Table 1, Table 2).

tended to be relegated added little to their status and productivity (Council on Economic Priorities, 1977). Horizontal and vertical segregation together generated sex differences in performance, prestige, and income. As a result, the earnings gap in 1979 between male and female bank managers exceeded the gap between all men and women who were employed full time (see Table 7.3). To a large extent this overall gap reflects women's concentration in low-level management positions. A final consequence of sex segregation is that the few women who do succeed to higher-level management may lack female role models or mentors and face isolation among equal-status colleagues.

ⅠⅠⅠⅠ Explaining Women's Gains in Bank Management

The Growing Demand for Managers

Much of women's progress during the 1970s resulted from the enhanced demand for bank managers that followed growth and changes in the banking industry. Organizational change facilitates sex integration, although it does not ensure it (Baron and Bielby, 1985). An unprecedented 82-percent increase in the number of bank offices between 1970 and 1980 provided opportunities because each branch required a facility manager and one or more assistant managers. These facts translated into more than 200,000 new jobs in bank management, to which the industry was able to attract only about 100,000 men. Thus, sheer growth—between 1970 and 1975 banking experienced the largest increase in total employment of managers and officials of any industry group (Shaeffer and Lynton, 1979)—weakened many of the barriers to women in bank management. By the late 1960s the demand for management trainees had already outpaced the supply (van Breems, 1969:57). Two-thirds of the banks responding to a 1966 survey by *Banking* magazine reported difficulties in finding qualified personnel, and almost half mentioned difficulties in hiring and retaining management trainees. An officer of one large bank said: "The present military call-ups have made our situation quite difficult. Our needs were increased because we lost a few men to military service who were in our management trainee program. This, plus the fact that other companies were experiencing the same situation, made the recruiting season very competitive" (Riday, 1966:51). In response, according to a former president of the American Institute of Banking, banks increasingly looked to women to fill their growing need for executives (Foster, 1969:47).

Later, banks' image as employers began to suffer. One analyst claimed that banks failed to attract enough qualified applicants because of the perception that they were not compensating high-level management as well as other industries (O'Shields, 1977). In the past, high job security had made up for lower salaries, but this was no longer the case. As keepers of finance, bankers traditionally enjoyed power and status in the community. They not only controlled people's opportunities to own a home or open a business, but prior to World War II they primarily served the upper classes, from whom bankers derived social status. But the war accelerated the trend toward mass banking, and the industry's postwar shift to serving the general public "declassed" bank work, contributed to a deterioration of status among lower- and perhaps middle-level managers in jobs that involved contact with customers, and thus (according to Strober and Arnold, 1987a) facilitated women's movement into bank telling. In view of reduced status and the erosion in banks' commitment to permanent employment,[11] bank management's relatively low wages became problematic. One interviewee summed up the problem: "Based on the salaries you are paid, [banks] are attracting a woman workforce that is not the primary breadwinner of the family. A man could not support a family if [he] were the sole provider on the kind of income that is paid in those [lower managerial] levels." The trend toward larger banks with centralized management increased the number of lower managerial positions. In a small, single-office bank all managers were within a few steps of the president's position; in the new and larger banks, many formerly powerful managerial positions, such as branch manager, have moved far down the organizational ladder.

In short, several factors combined to reduce the attractiveness of bank management to young men, compared with similar white-collar jobs available to them. Banking's image as high-status and secure employment deteriorated, as did the earnings advantage that male bank managers enjoyed relative to other managerial workers, and the increased number of branch banks and organizational changes such as centralization robbed branch managers of organizational power as well as status in the community. Just when industrial growth was creating more jobs, banks were suddenly thrown into a buyers' market, in which they found it increasingly difficult to attract a qualified male workforce. As a result, they opened their doors to female workers.

The Decline in Sex Discrimination

Becker (1975) argued that noncompetitive markets exacerbate labor market discrimination and competition weakens it. Consistent with this claim, a study of sex discrimination and market competition in banking (Ashenfelter and Hannan, 1986) found a positive relationship between the level of competition among banks and the employment of women in high-level positions. Banking became more competitive after deregulation, and resulting economic pressures discouraged banks from discriminating against women. A study of twenty-four large U.S. banks (Szafran, 1984) found that those showing the greatest growth in managerial positions also had the greatest increase in women and minorities in the managerial ranks.[12]

Other pressures to eliminate discrimination came from federal antidiscrimination regulations. In December 1971 the Office of Federal Contract Compliance issued Revised Order No. 4 of Executive Order 11375, which required most federal contractors to implement affirmative-action programs. Most banks hold government contracts, and after the Office of Federal Contract Compliance targeted banking in 1978 for special enforcement efforts, banking probably experienced more regulatory pressure to employ female managers than most other industries (Ashenfelter and Hannan, 1986:156). Under contract-compliance regulations, the conspicuous lack of women in upper-level positions, given their overrepresentation in the lower levels, constituted evidence of discrimination that rendered banks at risk of losing federal contracts.

The Equal Employment Opportunity Commission (EEOC) began to pressure banks to advance women and minorities in 1971.[13] Banks and the American Banking Association responded by protesting that the pool of "qualified" women was too small and that there were not enough women in the pipeline to meet the needs of all banks and other organizations (Mathis and Jones, 1974:95). They could justify this claim by arguing that new hires should have graduated from college with certain majors in which women were underrepresented. In the middle 1970s, by raising the credentials necessary for employment to include the M.B.A., banks defined a primarily male pool of qualified applicants.

Although antidiscrimination agencies rarely enforced regulations during the Nixon and Ford administrations, affirmative-action pressures increased sharply during the Carter administration (Ashenfelter and Hannan, 1986). In 1977 the Labor Department threatened to bar discriminatory banks from holding government contracts unless they changed their hiring policies (*Wall*

Street Journal, 1977). Meanwhile, such women's organizations as Women Employed in Chicago, Women's Rights at Crocker Bank, and the National Organization for Women began to press sex-discrimination charges against banks. Between 1974 and 1977, class-action suits charged nine of the twenty-four banks studied by the Council on Economic Priorities (1977) with sex bias in recruiting, hiring, training, pay, and promotion practices. Litigation under equal-employment regulations affected the industry as a whole, as banks saw the potential costs of discrimination. An executive vice-president I interviewed observed:

> I bet when the woman sued Harris bank [in 1974], within a week most of the major banks in the country met with their legal council and looked at women and their positions in banks. The federal government has taken—not really an active role—but some role in this. I think some pressure has to be there.

The agreements that the Bank of California signed in the early 1970s and the 1974 consent decree in which the Bank of America committed itself to spend nearly $4 million to develop and train women employees were particularly important in influencing other banks (Povall, 1986), which viewed the financial consequences as threatening; perhaps more important, they sought to protect their public image. As a result of these concerns, survey data indicate, many banks trained and promoted nonmanagerial female employees into management posts (Council on Economic Priorities, 1977).

However, some banks tried to circumvent affirmative-action requirements by redefining the officer and manager category to include lower-level positions with few or no changes in duties (Council on Economic Priorities, 1977); others gave women managerial titles without the authority that normally accompanied them. The Senate Banking Committee's oversight hearings in August 1977 concluded that "category [job-title] inflation" may have inflated estimates of women's representation in bank management, a conclusion based in part on the fact that the proportion of all bank workers in the officer and manager category increased 16 percent in three years, while that of office and clerical workers dropped 8 percent (Kulczycky, 1977). Category inflation is also consistent with women's concentration in lower levels of management and their lower average salaries (Beller, 1984). Thus, though pressure by the federal government and women's groups encouraged banks to employ women as managers, some of women's gains in the occupation may not reflect real progress in eliminating sex discrimination.

Service Banking and Sex-Role Stereotypes

As increased competition forced banks to improve their public image, bank management became more service oriented. The pressure to improve customer relations led banks to seek managers with good interpersonal skills and to develop consumer-oriented techniques such as "relationship" or "humanized" banking, oriented toward gaining an emotional involvement with the consumer that would generate allegiance to the bank (Grossack, 1970; Berry and Thompson, 1982); banks cast retail sales employees in the role of helpers to assist people in finding the right accounts for them—an orientation reminiscent of what Hochschild (1983) called "emotional work." Sex stereotypes that construe women as interpersonally more adept than men probably contributed to banks' attraction to women managers. A female executive vice-president told me:

> The real asset [women] have is they're patient, and they're willing to go that extra step for the customer. . . . They're very customer-oriented. . . . I do many things . . . that make me popular with my customers that my husband [also in business] wouldn't [do]. That's a difference of personality, but it's the personality of a woman.

Thus, changing competitive conditions caused banks to seek to compete in terms of services, and sex stereotypes made them see women as better at providing services.

To some extent, however, banks turned to women because they could not attract enough qualified male managers and then justified hiring them by citing sex stereotypes, just as they had done when faced with labor shortages in the 1930s and 1940s (Kessler-Harris, 1986). In the 1970s, banks characterized women as well suited to selling the wide variety of their products and services.

The Increased Supply of Qualified Women

The availability of bank management jobs produced a large supply of female would-be bankers that fueled women's gains in the 1970s. The feminist movement of the 1970s had oriented women to professional and managerial education and careers. This growing pool of women interested in and educated for such careers supplied thousands of women who were qualified for bank management. Previously, when banks had trained managers on the job rather than recruiting already trained managers, women could not signal their interest in management by pursuing training independently. As affirmative-action pressure encouraged banks to advance women and as banks increasingly required the M.B.A., women had both the opportunity to show their interest in bank management by getting the degree and the incentive to do so because they knew that banks were hiring women M.B.A.'s for management jobs. Several of the younger women I interviewed reported entering banking during the mid-1970s specifically because of recent increases in women's opportunities in management. One female branch manager described her career choice:

Table 7.4

Number and Percentage of Business Degrees Awarded to Women, 1970, 1980.

	1970		1980	
	Number awarded to women	Percent of total	Number awarded to women	Percent of total
Accounting				
Bachelor's degrees	2,063	9.3	15,417	36.1
Master's degrees	103	9.4	957	38.3
Banking and finance				
Bachelor's degrees	165	2.8	2,828	25.7
Master's degrees	40	2.3	808	22.4
Business and management				
Bachelor's degrees	10,467	9.1	62,719	33.6
Master's degrees	1,038	3.9	12,305	22.3

Sources: U.S. National Center for Education Statistics (1972: Table 114; 1982: Table 108).

I narrowed it down to banking for a couple of reasons: the working environment, including the kind of facilities you're in and the hours of the day, and . . . [which] industries [were] promoting women at that time. We're talking about 1974, and at that point there had just been a major trust suit in the Bank of America, and they were trying to get some significant advances for women. So I looked at the various banks and who was doing what and how well they were doing it.

By the late 1970s banks were responding to discrimination cases in court with efforts to increase the number of women with M.B.A.'s or commercial experience in their management training programs. Within a few years these women were able to join the lower ranks of management. Once women learned that such opportunities existed, the number of women preparing for financial management careers skyrocketed, as evidenced by the numbers in Table 7.4. Consequently, in the late 1970s some banks reported that women constituted up to half of their management trainees (Povall, 1986). One analyst claimed that the changing policy toward hiring women stemmed in part from changes in the quality of the applicant pool: "It's a common refrain from bank executives these days that the best MBAs they can hire are female" (Bernstein, 1982:84).

The high earnings that bank management jobs offered college-trained women probably accounted for banks' attracting women in such large numbers. As Table 7.3 indicates, in 1979 female bank managers typically outearned other women, including other managerial workers. In 1970 women bank and financial managers had slightly outearned women managers in other occupations, but by 1980 their relative advantage had grown slightly. In 1982 women bank and financial managers outearned all managers and administrators by about $41 per week, and 18.2 percent of bank and financial managers earned over $520 weekly, compared to 14.9 percent of all managers and administrators (Mellor, 1984:25). Thus, as many of my interviewees confirmed, the relatively high incomes possible in financial management ensured a large pool of female applicants from whom banks could recruit managers.

The feminization of the banking industry also enhanced women's access to managerial jobs. In general, women hold a larger share of typically male jobs in female-intensive than in male-intensive industries: between 1970 and 1975 they gained more managerial jobs in the former (from 17 to 28 percent) than in the latter (from 2 to 3 percent) (Shaeffer and Lynton, 1979:11, 14). One reason why banking's largely female white-collar workforce spurred women's gains in management was the existence of a pool of potential female managerial recruits. Affirmative-action regulations encouraged banks to promote from this pool of nonmanagerial employees whose experience made them promising candidates for managerial training and promotion. Banking's tradition of training managers internally facilitated these promotions, as did the fact that some older male bank managers lacked advanced degrees.

I I I I Conclusions

Traditionally, men have claimed a preponderance of bank management jobs. The industry drew on women only as a reserve workforce when the supply of men temporarily shrank; it returned to men when their numbers again increased. Rapid growth in the demand for bank managers during the 1970s weakened many of the barriers to women in bank management. The increase of over 200,000 new management jobs in the 1970s created unprecedented opportunities. Although banking attracted over 100,000 men to these jobs, various factors reduced its attractiveness to men, encouraging the industry to look to women. These included changes that reduced the prestige, authority, and flexibility of bank management. One branch manager I interviewed described the changes:

> There are more women managers, but then again they have reduced the size of many branches and in fact closed many branches. So that the branch manager responsibility . . . today may be what the operations manager was [ten years ago]. The responsibilities are less. When I was in my first job as operations officer I had more authority in hiring, firing, promoting, giving raises . . . than I do now [as a branch manager].

In addition, more elaborate divisions of labor within banking have separated branch managers from traditional career ladders.

Federal pressure for affirmative action forced the industry to employ women in management jobs or risk costly litigation. In response to growing competition and federal pressure, rationalization of the industry restructured internal labor markets to provide greater opportunities to women and minorities. In addition, the greater competitiveness that characterized banking in the 1970s further inclined banks against sex discrimination because banks could simply no longer afford to ignore talent wherever they found it.

While women have made real gains in bank management, some of their progress is more apparent than real. Sex discrimination and informal barriers hamper women's progress, and barriers to senior management remain strong. Women in commercial banking still sometimes encounter customers who insist on seeing a man, one branch loan officer asserted. According to another female manager, commercial banking productivity depends in part on networking, and this handicaps women because networks are themselves sex segregated. A female senior vice-president described her effort to enter this informal circle:

> I took those damn golf lessons. I don't like the game, and I did it with [a] "by George, I'm gonna beat this" [attitude], because in banking golf is the game. I would have looked like a fool out on the golf course. Of course, that would be no way for me to impress anybody. In any case, the invitations will not come.

Moreover, what it means to be a manager has changed: middle managers have less authority and status than in the past. Women's segregation into retail banking, operations, and branch management and their exclusion from the commercial side of banking have hampered their progress into higher-level management, because experience in profitmaking functions is necessary to advance up the career ladder. Retail banking, particularly branch management, has become a female ghetto for many women whose chances to advance depend on the opportunity to get experience in other areas of banking.

Under present conditions the rapid gains women made in middle management during the 1970s will not be easily duplicated at the senior-management level. Since 1980 competition has increased, and continued high interest rates have further eroded profits, resulting in slower growth in bank management. The earlier growth in banking and in multiservice finance corporations created new middle-management jobs, but the current financial situation has fostered mergers that have meant staff cutbacks (Quinn, 1987).

In addition, barriers to the boardroom are more difficult to break. The Reagan administration's disarming of the EEOC has limited women's ability to combat sex discrimination. Unless women acquire equal access to career ladders, their gains in lower and middle management will not lead to even small changes at the top.

| | | | Notes

Acknowledgments: I am grateful to Barbara Reskin and Patricia Roos for their comments and support. I thank all the bankers I interviewed for sharing their experiences and giving me their time. I am indebted to Beverly Fremont, Georganne Rundblad, Gray Swicegood, Joe Spaeth, and especially Allen Fremont for reading earlier versions of this paper. Earlier versions of this paper were presented at the Annual Meeting of the American Sociological Association in 1989 and at the Illinois Sociological Association Annual Meeting in 1988.

1. The 1970 census category "bank officers and financial managers" included both low-level positions (head cashier, loan supervisor, trust officer) and senior executive positions (bank president, board chairman, budget director, vice-president) not included in the 1980 census category "financial managers." Only 47.5 percent of persons coded as bank officers and financial managers in 1970 would have been classified as financial managers according to the 1980 scheme, and only 68.1 percent of those who would have been so coded in 1980 were classified as "bank officers and financial managers" in 1970. Thus, one cannot directly compare the percent female in 1970 and 1980 (17.6 and 31.2 percent) across these two census classifications. Although data broken down by industry are also not fully comparable, the representation of women financial managers in the banking industry (banks, savings and loans, and credit agencies) similarly increased, from 18.6 percent of bank officers and financial managers (1970) to 37.1 percent of financial managers (1980). These data suggest that women financial managers apparently advanced more in banking than in other industries.

2. The remaining 15 percent work in other industries as comptrollers and treasurers, and in retail-trade organizations as account supervisors.

3. The banking industry includes commercial banks as well as savings banks, and savings and loan institutions. According to the Bank Holding Company Act of 1956, a bank is any institution that *both* accepts demand deposits and makes commercial loans. Demand deposits are funds that depositors have a right to withdraw on demand, such as checking accounts. Thrifts include credit unions, mutual savings banks, and savings and loan associations. Prior to deregulation, the major distinction between thrifts and banks was that banks offer checking accounts and short-term commercial and consumer loans, while thrifts offer savings accounts and long-term mortgage loans (Bowden, 1980:8). Bank managers include all managers in any of these institutions.

4. The banks' largest corporate customers turned for loans to the more effective and often cheaper commercial-paper market; see Rose's (1987) excellent analysis of the transformation of the banking industry.

5. In 1979 banks issued only 15 percent of American's 600 million credit cards, while a single retailer had 25 million active cardholders, more than half again as many as all VISA and MasterCards (Webster, 1979:13).

6. Banks added another 464,000 new jobs between 1980 and 1984.

7. A bank holding company owns stock in one or more commercial banks. The reorganization of banks through holding companies began before 1970, when there were 121 such companies. In 1975 there were 1,821; in 1982, the 4,285 holding companies owned 82 percent of all commercial banks (U.S. Bureau of the Census, 1984e: Table 823).

8. For example, the Wells Fargo and Crocker National Corporation merger in June 1986 resulted in the elimination of 5,000 jobs (Quinn, 1987).

9. In 1982 the first franchised bank opened (Luxenberg, 1985:248).

10. Kanter (1977:232) described a tendency of male managers and administrators to encapsulate women and develop special roles for them, setting them apart from their male colleagues.

11. As banks decreased their demand for lifelong employees, they began to view women as an attractive labor pool. This did not require them to change their perception of women as lacking long-term commitment to the labor force—a belief that continues to handicap female bank managers.

12. Multicollinearity prevented testing the impact of labor supply on the employment of managerial women, but Szafran (1984) found that banks in areas with low unemployment hired more female professionals.

13. The amended version of Executive Order 11246 required government contractors including banks to have a written affirmative-action plan for each of their establishments.

Katharine M. Donato

8

Programming for Change? The Growing Demand for Women Systems Analysts

Since 1960 the use of computers has increased tremendously, and computer occupations have grown apace. Because of advances in computer technology, the expanding use of electronic data-processing systems, and the proliferation of computer centers that serve individual clients (U.S. Bureau of Labor Statistics, 1970, 1974b, 1984b), the number of systems analysts increased by 88 percent between 1970 and 1980 (U.S. Bureau of the Census, 1984a). Operations and systems researchers and analysts increased by a more modest 24 percent.

Because computer occupations do not have a legacy of sex segregation and because they are experiencing rapid growth, one might expect women to have greater access to these than to occupations requiring similar qualifications that men have long dominated. And in fact, during the 1970s the number of women in systems analysis and operations research more than tripled. In 1970, 14,658 female systems analysts and scientists accounted for 13.6 percent of all systems analysts; by 1980, their numbers had risen to 45,511, and they made up 22.5 percent of all systems analysts (see Table 8.1). Furthermore, in 1970, 7,235 women accounted for 11.1 percent of all operations researchers and analysts; by 1980 their numbers had also more than tripled, to 22,441, or 27.7 percent of all incumbents. Women have since increased their representation also in computer programming, from 24.2 to 31.2 percent (U.S. Bureau of the Census, 1984a), and their share of jobs within systems analysis has continued to increase, to 30 percent in 1986 (U.S. Bureau of the Census,

Table 8.1
Employment in Systems Analysis and Operations Research, by Sex, 1970–1980

	Total	Male	Female	Percent Female
Computer Systems Analysts and Scientists				
1970	107,580	92,922	14,658	13.6
1980	202,651	157,140	45,511	22.5
Percent growth				
1970–80	88.4	69.1	210.5	8.9
Operations and Systems Researchers and Analysts				
1970	65,008	57,773	7,235	11.1
1980	80,876	58,435	22,441	27.7
Percent growth				
1970–80	24.4	1.1	210.2	16.6

Source: U.S. Bureau of the Census (1984a).

1987a). This chapter examines the reasons for women's disproportionate gains in two computer occupations: "computer systems analysts and scientists" (code 064) and "operations and systems researchers and analysts" (code 065) (U.S. Bureau of the Census, 1983a).

After outlining the history of computer occupations, documenting the technological changes that have occurred since 1945, and highlighting women's role as computer programmers, I describe the nature of systems analysis and women's current status in the occupation and go on to explain women's gains in computer occupations.

| | | | Women, Technological Change, and the History of Programming

Computer programming occupations are a very recent phenomenon. First appearing in the late 1940s (Kraft, 1977), programming work encompassed everything that was necessary to ensure the efficient operation of the computer, from analyzing problems to operating and maintaining hardware. Programmers acted independently on the job, regulating their own tasks rather than working under controls set by management (Greenbaum, 1979).

Since the first modern computers were built in the 1940s, their relevant technology has changed dramatically. Vacuum-tube or "first generation" computers were replaced in 1958 by computers with solid-state transistor hardware. Transistors offered the benefits of speed, reduced size, and enhanced reliability—important advantages for the acceptance of computers in the business community. Expanding business markets in the 1960s and the success of early models prompted efforts to develop less expensive and more reliable hardware. The technological breakthrough of integrated circuit components permitted a "general purpose" computer that could be programmed to do several tasks at the same time. Integrated circuits composed of transistors further enhanced computer speed and reliability and substantially cut consumer prices (Greenbaum, 1979:28). More recent developments include the large-scale combination of integrated circuit components, in which thousands of transistors are packed onto tiny chips that store data or process thousands of instructions per second.

Not only computer hardware but systems software has changed markedly since the 1940s. Lacking operating systems or any other support programs, early programmers performed craftlike activities on first-generation machines (Kraft, 1977, 1979; Greenbaum, 1979). Each time they ran a program or entered a new calculation, programmers had to start up the hardware and rewire circuits. The slow tedium of this task, complicated by inefficient vacuum-tube hardware, led to the development of operating systems, in which preprogrammed tasks were stored in computer memory for later use.

Operating systems and other support programs first appeared in second-generation machines. Although the software offered greater efficiency, most programs required so much memory to run efficiently that they left little or no room for users' programs. Also, because many new operating systems were incompatible with other computers, the development of software support systems lagged behind hardware development (Greenbaum, 1979).

As hardware and software developed during the 1960s, the number of computer workers grew rapidly. Concerned about containing the costs of this burgeoning labor force (Greenbaum, 1979:16), upper management shifted the costs of software development from computer manufacturers to consumers and implemented a hierarchy that subdivided programming labor into three suboccupations: coders, programmers, and systems analysts (Kraft, 1977). As the most skilled programming workers, systems analysts are responsible for "designing whole, complex data-processing systems rather than parts of larger ones as programmers do" (Kraft, 1977:16). Programmers solve data-processing problems through designing, debugging, or documenting programs. Coders, who are essentially clerical workers, translate these programs into computer language.

Women's involvement in computer work began in the 1940s with the first electronic computer—the Electronic Numerical Integrator and Computer, or ENIAC (Kraft, 1977).[1] Known as "ENIAC girls," these young college graduates with a mathematics or science background were hired "to perform ballistic shell trajectory calculations" (Greenbaum, 1979; Kraft, 1979:2; Strober and Arnold, 1987b). Women were originally accepted as programmers because the work seemed to resemble simple clerical tasks. In fact, however, programming demanded complex skills in abstract logic, mathematics, electrical circuitry, and machinery, all of which the ENIAC women used to perform their work. Once programming was recognized as "intellectually demanding," it became attractive to men (Kraft, 1979:3). Many of the early women remained in computer programming, but employers recruited few new women, and the sex composition of programming shifted in favor of men.

By the mid-1960s, when programming was being redefined and split into relatively more and less skilled specialties, an increased demand for computer personnel again prompted employers to recruit women (Greenbaum, 1979). As employers subdivided programming so that tasks became more narrowly defined, women began to reenter computer occupations.[2] During the 1970s, when most employed women were relegated to clerical and service work and the semiprofessions, computer occupations offered women the opportunity for professional and technical jobs. Reports abounded of firms hiring women as computer specialists (*Electronic News*, 1979). A 1974 *Computerworld* survey found that 13 and 20 percent of business systems analysts and programmers, respectively, were women—as were 99 percent of keypunchers (Greenbaum, 1979).

Recently, however, an advertisement in the classified section of the *New York Times*—showing a woman plugged into an electric socket while sitting at a video display terminal, under the caption "Hire a programmer"—suggests that women's entry into computer occupations has not necessarily meant progress. A closer look at women in computer specialties shows that despite their increased representation, they do not have equal access to all computer occupations. Male computer specialists are better represented in the higher-paid and more prestigious systems analysis and programming jobs than in other computer occupations.

Recent evidence confirms that computer occupations are not sex integrated (Strober and Arnold, 1987b). Despite their gains in programming and systems analysis, women still constitute less than one-third of all workers in these occupations. Among systems analysts, programmers, operators, and data-entry operators, the higher the status and pay of the occupation, the lower is women's representation (Strober and Arnold, 1987b). Data from the 1980 census showed, for example, that women comprised 23 percent of systems analysts, 28 percent of operations researchers and analysts, and 31 percent of computer programmers (U.S. Bureau of the Census, 1983a).[3] In addition, although 59 percent of computer operators were female, women remained vastly overrepresented (92 percent) as data-entry workers in 1980 (U.S. Bureau of the Census, 1984a; Strober and Arnold, 1987b).

Sex-segregation by rank persists in the managerial levels of computer occupations. Men are three times as likely to be upper-level managers as women are (10 percent of men, 3 percent of women); moreover, male software specialists' supervisors are likely to be men, but women supervise women (Kraft and Dubnoff, 1983).

I I I I Systems Analysts Today

Job Description

The Census Bureau classifies all systems analysts as professional workers, although their specific occupation codes depend on whether they work with electronic data-processing systems (U.S. Bureau of the Census, 1982a). Computer systems analysts and scientists analyze business procedures to convert data for electronic data-processing and other computer-information systems. They confer with management on the nature of data-processing problems and design systems using cost-accounting, sampling, and mathematical models. In addition, they prepare flowcharts and diagrams to describe the system to both managers and users, determine the hardware and software needs of the new system, and draw up specifications to allow programmers to debug these systems (U.S. Bureau of Labor Statistics, 1984b). Operations and systems researchers and analysts analyze the operational problems of management for purposes *other* than designing electronic data-processing and computer systems. They define problems in terms of the information available to management and develop mathematical models of these problems, using computers and other methods. They also prepare business reports on the definition, evaluation, and solution of problems (U.S. Department of Labor, Employment and Training Administration, 1977). I refer to workers in both occupations as systems analysts unless I specify otherwise.

Because data-processing problems vary and their solutions are so complex, systems analysts generally specialize in scientific, engineering, or business applications (U.S. Bureau of Labor Statistics, 1970, 1974b, 1984b). Systems analysts may forecast sales for a manufacturing firm, improve existing data processing in a university by developing a new payroll system, or develop a local area network in a publishing firm to offer users quick access to current sales information. Operations researchers who work in scientific or engineering organizations may develop systems to predict the flight path of a satellite or to monitor nuclear fission in a power plant. One operations researcher I interviewed worked for a national retail sales corporation, where he forecast the labor needed to handle sales calls made to the corporation's four telephone service centers around the country.

In estimating the complexity of the work done by systems analysts and scientists in data processing, the fourth edition of the *Dictionary of Occupational Titles* (U.S. Department of Labor, Employment and Training Administration, 1977) classified the occupation at the next to highest level of complexity with respect to data but at a low level of complexity with regard to people and things. The *DOT* classification for operations-research analysts is quite similar except that they "synthesize" data, the most complex data task. Thus, systems analysis in general is viewed as being highly complex with respect to data but quite simple with respect to people and things.[4]

Employment Settings

The distribution of systems analysts across various industries yields insights about their working environments. In 1980 manufacturing industries were their modal employer, accounting for 33 percent of workers in both occupations (U.S. Bureau of the Census, 1984b). Business and repair services employed another 25 percent of computer systems analysts but just 8 percent of operations and systems researchers. Public administration had the second largest number of employers of operations researchers and analysts, followed by the finance, insurance, and real estate industries. Thus, about two-thirds of both types of systems analysts work in three industries: manufacturing, business services, and public administration.

Table 8.2, which presents the industrial distribution of systems analysts by sex in 1979, shows that female computer systems analysts were concentrated in manufacturing and business service industries, while women operations and systems researchers were concentrated in manufacturing, public administration, and the finance, insurance, and real estate industries. Furthermore, female computer specialists were twice as likely as males to work in finance, insurance, and real estate.

Relative to the index of industrial sex segregation for men and women in all occupations, I find that males and females in computer specialties are more similarly dispersed across industries. While at least 13 percent of women in computer systems analysis and at least 16 percent of women in operations research would have to change industries to achieve an industry distribution similar to men's, 32 percent of all women workers would have to change their industry location to make their distribution identical to that of all male workers.[5]

Earnings

In 1979, computer systems analysts and scientists and operations and systems researchers and analysts averaged annual wages of $23,405 and $23,584, respectively (U.S. Bureau of the Census, 1984b). Among the factors that affect these earnings are organizational size, industry, and workers' sex. Women systems analysts and operations researchers averaged approximately 72 percent of men's earnings (Donato and Roos, 1987: Table 2). A recent study of 677 software specialists showed that organizational size affects earnings but does

Table 8.2

Distribution, by Sex and Industry of Employed Persons in All Occupations
and Two Computer Occupations, 1979

Industry	All Occupations		Computer Systems Analysts and Scientists		Operations and Systems Researchers and Analysts	
	Men	Women	Men	Women	Men	Women
Agriculture, forestry, and fishing	4.3	1.3	0.2	0.1	0.1	0.1
Mining	1.6	0.3	1.2	0.8	1.1	1.0
Construction	9.4	1.2	0.7	0.7	1.3	0.9
Manufacturing	26.6	16.8	34.7	25.5	36.5	23.8
Transportation, communications, and public utilities	9.5	4.2	6.1	7.7	8.8	8.8
Wholesale trade	5.5	2.7	4.5	4.3	2.8	1.8
Retail trade	13.8	19.2	2.5	3.1	2.4	2.2
Finance, insurance, and real estate	4.4	8.2	7.5	14.3	11.3	21.3
Business and repair services	4.8	3.3	24.0	20.6	8.6	6.8
Personal services	1.6	5.2	0.1	0.2	0.1	0.1
Entertainment and recreational services	1.1	1.0	0.1	0.2	0.2	0.2
Professional and related services	11.9	31.6	7.0	9.6	7.5	10.7
Public administration	5.4	5.1	11.4	12.7	19.3	22.3
Total	99.9[a]	100.1[a]	100.0	99.8[a]	100.0	100.0
N (in 1000s) =	56,005	41,635	156	45	58	22
Index of segregation	32.5		13.2		16.2	

[a] Error due to rounding.

Source: U.S. Bureau of the Census (1984b: Table 4).

so in opposite directions for male and female workers (Kraft and Dubnoff, 1983). Women do better in bigger organizations: in those with fewer than 100 employees women earned about 50 percent of what men made, compared to approximately 80 percent in organizations employing at least 500 workers.

Women systems analysts, like other women workers, are disproportionately employed in low-paying industries. The correlation between earnings and percent female across major industry groups is −.60 for all occupations, and −.52 and −.36 for computer systems analysts and for operations researchers and analysts, respectively (U.S. Bureau of the Census, 1984b; data not shown).

Table 8.3 shows 1979 earnings by industry and sex separately for the two analyst occupations. Columns 3 and 6 show that the wage disparity between the sexes in many industries is approximately the same for systems

Table 8.3

Mean Earnings by Sex and Industry of Employed Persons in Two Computer Occupations, 1979

Industry	Computer Systems Analysts and Scientists			Operations and Systems Researchers and Analysts		
	Men (1)	Women (2)	Female/ Male Ratio (3)	Men (4)	Women (5)	Female/ Male Ratio (6)
Agriculture, forestry, and fishing	$22,838	$13,686	59.9	$18,570	$11,422	61.5
Mining	26,031	19,909	76.5	27,220	16,262	59.7
Construction	22,661	15,781	69.6	23,179	14,418	62.2
Manufacturing	24,093	16,713	69.4	24,069	16,408	68.2
Transportation, communications, and public utilities	23,812	19,406	81.5	23,693	19,467	82.2
Wholesale trade	22,840	18,325	80.2	23,703	14,669	61.9
Retail trade	22,195	15,836	71.3	20,974	14,621	69.7
Finance, insurance, and real estate	21,381	16,657	77.9	20,877	15,052	72.1
Business and repair services	21,969	15,790	71.9	22,083	15,330	69.4
Personal services	18,928	9,734	51.4	17,387	9,104	52.4
Entertainment and recreational services	19,456	17,581	90.4	25,799	21,126	81.9
Professional and related services	20,296	13,816	68.1	21,899	13,109	59.9
Public administration	24,991	18,655	74.6	25,049	18,655	74.5

Source: U.S. Bureau of the Census (1984b: Tables 2, 4).

analysts and for operations and systems researchers. Mining, construction, wholesale trade, entertainment and recreational services, and professional and related services are the exceptions. In these industry groups, women systems analysts fared better relative to men than did women operations and systems researchers. Moreover, among the five largest employers of computer systems analysts and scientists (see Table 8.3), women fared best relative to men in the finance and insurance industry, where they earned 78 percent of men's earnings. With respect to the largest industrial employers of operations and systems researchers and analysts (see Table 8.3), women fared best relative to men in transportation, communications, and public utilities, where they earned 82 percent of men's wages. Finally, the industries that paid men well tended to pay women well. The rank-order correlations between the mean earnings of men and women in computer systems analysis and in operations research are .68 and .79, respectively.

| | | | Explaining Women's Gains in Systems Analysis

Industrial Growth and Occupational Demand

Expanding electronic business markets and growing computer information systems heightened the demand for computer specialists. During the 1970s, job opportunities in this field increased dramatically. As noted in Table 8.1, the number of systems analysts increased from 107,580 in 1970 to 202,651 in 1980, and operations and systems researchers increased from 65,008 to 80,876 (U.S. Bureau of Labor Statistics, 1984a). The Bureau of Labor Statistics projected continued growth for the 1980s, ranking systems analysis as one of ten occupations expected to grow fastest over the decade (U.S. Department of Labor, 1986b).

Much of the demand for systems analysts resulted from increases in computer technology, advances in hardware and software, and users' heightened expectations (Rooney, 1975; U.S. Bureau of Labor Statistics, 1984b), all of which reflect the expansion in computer industries. Indeed, between 1972 and 1982, employment in high-tech industries outpaced all other wage and salary employment (Riche et al., 1983).

This dramatic growth has been an important attraction to women workers. While presumably it created a demand for systems analysts of either sex, industrial growth generated job opportunities for women in particular because it outpaced the existing supply of trained men. There is also evidence that some men left the field during the 1970s as a result of declining economic conditions and limits on occupational mobility.

During the 1970s, salaries for computer professionals did not keep pace with inflation. Since most workers in the field were men, this translated into lower rewards for male computer specialists. For example, the Bureau of Labor Statistics calculated a 30 percent increase in expenses between 1970 and 1974; among computer professionals only data-processing managers received salary raises large enough to offset that increase (McLaughlin, 1975). Data from a private survey of 80,000 workers in business, data processing, and government work showed that the average starting salary of systems analysts, in constant 1967 dollars, ranged from $148 to $210 a week, while experienced systems analysts averaged $236 a week (U.S. Bureau of Labor Statistics, 1970). Four years later, in 1974, the relative salaries of systems analysts had declined, with entry-level jobs paying an average of $156 to $169 a week in 1967 dollars, while experienced systems analysts earned $203 to $227 a week (U.S.

Bureau of Labor Statistics, 1976). By 1982 the earnings of systems analysts had dropped even further: entry-level systems analysts averaged $154 a week in 1967 dollars, while the experienced earned $166 to $190 a week (U.S. Bureau of Labor Statistics, 1984b).[6] Thus, systems analysts earned relatively less in 1982 than in 1970.

Among the obvious consequences of declining occupational earnings are that some incumbents leave in pursuit of higher rewards elsewhere and that the occupation may be less able to recruit qualified workers who have other opportunities. Indeed, a 1972 article cited declining economic conditions as one reason computer "men" were leaving the field. But this was not the only reason. Men left also when they realized that their occupational mobility was blocked. Observing the distinction between line and staff positions (the latter are those that do not directly yield profit for the corporation), employers defined systems analysis as a staff responsibility. As a result, one systems analyst reported feeling like a dependent, like "the women and children of the company." He concluded that although computer work "is a favorable route to a reasonably high corporate level, [it is] strangely dead-ended" (*Datamation* 1972:81). With men leaving or failing to enter the field and demand for computer specialists soaring during the 1970s, employers increasingly turned to women.

Affirmative Action

Women's representation among systems analysts grew in part because employers were pressured to hire women. Articles in the trade literature suggest that some employers were responding to an increasing emphasis on fulfilling affirmative-action goals during the 1970s. In 1972, for example, the chairman of Xerox sent a letter to its U.S. managers, stating that "a very high priority . . . is to improve significantly the position of both minority groups and women" (Goldman, 1974). Southern California Electric (SCE) also sought out women and minorities by advertising openings through women's organizations and in newspapers read by minorities and women, by using personnel and social agencies to solicit new recruits, by offering in-house management training, by implementing affirmative-action awareness programs for all workers, and by providing educational assistance (*EDP Analyzer*, 1976).

IBM recruited its first female programmers by advertising under Help Wanted in the women's section of the *New York Times* (Walsh, 1978). IBM hired these women in part because doing so helped the corporation fulfill its affirmative-action goals. One consequence of these preferences, as reported by executive-search firms specializing in recruiting data-processing specialists, was a substantial number of requests for women during the decade (N. Miller, 1977).

Occupational Change

Changes in systems analysts' work also enhanced the demand for female computer specialists. In the early 1970s the Bureau of Labor Statistics described systems analysts' work as analyzing problems, devising data-processing systems, recommending equipment, preparing instructions for programmers, and sometimes interpreting the final results to management, specialists, or customers (U.S. Bureau of Labor Statistics, 1970:244). Despite the last task of communicating with managers and other users, and although systems analysts "worked in teams on large projects" (U.S. Bureau of Labor Statistics, 1976:109), the *Occupational Outlook Handbook* (*OOH*) and the *Dictionary of Occupational Titles* (*DOT*) did not consider working with people an important characteristic of the occupation until the 1980s.[7]

Currently, the Bureau of Labor Statistics views the ability to work effectively with people as an important aspect of systems analysts' work. "Systems analysts must have good communication skills, and like working with ideas and people . . . they must be able to communicate effectively with technical personnel, such as programmers and managers, as well as with people who have no computer background" (U.S. Bureau of Labor Statistics, 1984b:59). The trade literature also recognizes the importance of "people" skills. As early as 1972, management researchers noted that the lack of uniformity in systems analysis meant that "the systems analyst should be more people than systems oriented" (Judd, 1972:120). Systems analysts sell the systems they develop, and thus computer "systems are much more dependent on people than upon machines" (Mason, 1975:29). Given traditional stereotypes about women's relational skills, this emerging emphasis on people skills was probably both cause and consequence of women's entry into systems analysis.

Indeed, the greater emphasis on the ability to work with people interacts with employers' beliefs. One employer of support analysts in sales and marketing corporations declared that women are "better [than men] at the soft sell of systems." He hired men to make the aggressive hard sell and women to explain the use of new systems to prospective buyers, claiming that women are "more perceptive at predicting the emotional and psychological effects of computer systems on users." Another male manager of forty analysts asserted that women make good analysts because their verbal orientation and reading skills are better than men's. Other employers I interviewed believed women to be more organized than men, better at detailed work, and superior in social skills.

The duties of systems analysts have thus begun to extend beyond expertise with the business computer (F. Miller, 1977). Systems experts now play a variety of roles: practitioner, analyst, businessperson, technician, staffer, educator, salesperson, and consultant. No longer are systems analysts expected only to analyze information systems. They must also use other business marketing and communications skills to develop optimal information systems. In large organizations a number of systems analysts share these multidimensional roles, resulting in two types of specialists: manual systems specialists who emphasize input operations (that is, programming), and computer systems specialists whose job follows through from input to the production of output (that is, systems analysis). Hence, the expanding roles of systems analysts led to increased job specialization, which restricted some systems analysts to their own departments but allowed others to expand into many departments. One reason for women's gains is that employers increasingly prefer women for some new job specialties in the field, especially technical specialties (Kraft and Dubnoff, 1983). Their tendency to reserve other positions for men, such as those of generalists who make managerial decisions regarding software and hardware purchases, perpetuates sex segregation within systems analysis.

Technological Change

As technological advances increasingly transform the work of computer specialists, a profusion of research has sought to identify the impact of technological change on the nature of jobs (see Attewell and Rule, 1984). In addition to identifying changes in systems analysis, we must examine how technological advances may affect women's representation in the occupation.

A trend toward job fragmentation and increasing specialization in computer occupations has been well documented (Kraft, 1977; Greenbaum, 1979). Much of the research available on computer occupations points to how deskilling modified job content, although evidence supporting the claim that computer occupations have been increasingly deskilled is disputable.

Proponents of the deskilling position assume that changes in computer technologies combined with management's singular concern with profits to change the skill hierarchy of jobs. For example, Greenbaum (1979) argued that technological changes revised the division of labor in the computer field. In 1950, the original division of labor consisted of three overlapping classes of workers: operators, programmers, and technicians. The advent of programmable memory in computers in the early 1960s, the use of transistor hardware, and a seller's market for labor enabled management to reorganize the division and reduce the costs of labor. The new technologies relieved programmers of the time-consuming, craftlike maintenance tasks the first computers required (Kraft, 1977; Greenbaum, 1979). The reorganization of programming involved changes in who programs and in how and where they do it. Managers introduced structured programming into the workplace, which reduced the number and type of logical procedures each programmer used and thus restricted "the ability of programmers to make independent decisions about the organization of their programs" (Greenbaum, 1979:81).[8] This type of programming facilitated the breaking down of large logical tasks into smaller, more simplified and routine tasks. Thus, a distinction emerged between programmers who think and those who do everything else.

The trend toward programming that included less technical and analytical work and more clerical tasks directly benefited systems analysts, whose duties encompassed the analytical and technical skills necessary to design information systems. In contrast, programming duties ranged from clerical to technical tasks.

Greenbaum (1979) suggested that in addition to eroding the skill content of programming jobs, advances in silicon-chip technology will eliminate software components; as new hardware replaces them, she predicted, cheap but reliable pieces of equipment will replace more of the human labor of programming. Then, as software components are eliminated, employment opportunities for systems analysts should increase while those for applications and systems programmers and/or coders decline. If Greenbaum is correct in her expectation, the greater employment opportunities for systems analysts than for programmers are likely to draw women to systems analysis, especially since men have other occupations that are economically more attractive and open to them.

Recognizing changes in the content of computer occupations, the Census Bureau revised the way it classifies them. In 1960 the bureau had no occupational codes for computer specialists; in 1970 it distinguished within managerial and professional occupations four detailed computer specialties: those of computer systems analysts and scientists; computer programmers; computer programmers, not elsewhere classified; and operations and systems researchers and analysts—all within the broad occupational group of professional, technical, and kindred workers. It classified other workers, such as computer operators and keypunchers, as having clerical occupations. In 1980 the bureau's substantially revised classification included two computer occupations: systems analysts and scientists, and operations and systems researchers and analysts (U.S. Bureau of the Census, 1983b). It classified programmers— as well as computer operators and data-entry keyers—in technical, sales, and administrative-support occupations.

These changes reflect the increasing specialization within systems analysis and the emergence of a division of labor that has subdivided computer programming into complex and clerical tasks. Within this context, it is likely that as more women have entered programming occupations in clerical, entry-level positions, the number of women with programming experience has increased. These women then swell the existing labor pool for systems analysis.

Factors Attracting Women to Systems Analysis

The actual existence of new job opportunities, projections for continued growth, and the awareness of affirmative-action programs combined to spur women's interest in systems analysis. Their growing interest can be seen in their increasing representation in educational programs that prepare persons for jobs in the field. Employers of systems analysts may require a bachelor's degree, a graduate degree, and/or experience in mathematics, science, engineering, accounting, business, or computer science (U.S. Bureau of Labor Statistics, 1970, 1974b, 1984b). Many employers prefer a computer-science, information-science, or data-processing degree (U.S. Bureau of Labor Statistics, 1984b), and most prefer some programming experience.

A clearly defined institutional structure shapes the education of computer workers (Kraft, 1977, 1979). Training for computer programmers operates in a three-tiered system: research universities or science institutions, four-year engineering colleges, and two-year institutions. Two-year community colleges prepare the least-skilled programmers—coders and applications programmers—for technicians' jobs. Four-year engineering colleges train more skilled programmers, those who work on complete programs rather than only parts of programs. Elite science and research universities train highly skilled programmers, such as systems analysts, who design entire computer systems or languages (Kraft, 1977).

Sex differences in access to or distribution across these training programs may contribute to determining women's positions in systems analysis. For example, if women interested in computer careers are overrepresented in two-year colleges or four-year engineering schools, they may disproportionately enter lower-level programming occupations. However, as women have increasingly enrolled in science and engineering courses, including those in the elite science universities, their representation in systems analysis has increased as well. Data are not available on enrollments in programs that prepare male and female students for systems analysis positions, because there are no universal requirements for employment in this field.[9] Nor do we have trend data on women's share of all degrees that qualify systems analysts. The number of women receiving master's and Ph.D. degrees in computer science, however, has increased. In 1969–70, 13 percent of those with bachelor's degrees in computer science were female; ten years later the comparable figure was 30 percent. Similarly, women's share of graduate degrees in computer science climbed from 9 percent in 1969–70 to 21 percent in 1979–80. Only 2 percent of computer science Ph.D.'s were female in 1969–70; ten years later women claimed 11 percent (Berryman, 1983).

Women's greater numbers in higher education resulted in part from corporate fellowships offered to women pursuing doctoral degrees in computer science (see *Computers and People*, 1978). In addition, colleges and universities actively sought to attract women by sponsoring career-awareness programs for those interested in computer science (Rose and Menninger, 1979). Thus, women's representation in training programs increased sharply during the 1970s, producing a pool of women prepared for jobs in systems analysis. Although men still outnumber women in computer-science programs, the greater number of women with computer-science or related degrees has increased the supply of women for programming occupations.

An important reason for women's attraction to systems analysis is that it pays more than most other occupations open to them. In 1981, computer systems analysis and operations and systems research and analysis were the two most highly paid occupations for women, with median weekly earnings of $422 and $420, respectively (Rytina, 1982)—an improvement over 1969, when these two occupations ranked only eighteenth and twenty-second in pay (Sommers, 1974). Hence, systems analysis has attracted women in increasing numbers because of its high pay relative to other occupations open to them.

A final reason for women's attraction to systems analysis is the narrowing wage gap between men and women in the field: between 1979 and 1986, the earnings ratio increased from 79 to 83 percent (U.S. Bureau of the Census, 1987a).

I I I I Conclusion

Women's greater representation in systems analysis resulted from employers' growing demand for more women, which stemmed in turn from the shortage of personnel caused by the dramatic growth of both systems analysis as an occupation and high-technology industries during the 1970s. It also resulted from a shortage of men able to meet the growing demand for computer specialists. Women's entry was spurred by sex stereotypes about male and female workers and by changes in the nature of the occupation and its technology that appear related to declining occupational rewards. Men responded to the last of these by leaving the computer field, thus helping to accelerate the demand for women workers. Furthermore, the occupation changed in ways that encouraged employers to hire women. Increases in the need for "people" skills probably inclined employers toward workers with interpersonal skills, traditionally thought to be more common among women than men. The transformation of some programming tasks into clerical tasks meant that employers were more likely to see women as appropriate workers for entry-level positions. This in turn created a pool of female employees from which employers could recruit systems analysts.

Women were attracted to systems analysis by growing job opportunities and projections of continued growth and by the rewards that the occupation offers. Systems analysis pays women more, relative to what they can earn elsewhere. As a result of these attractions, a growing number of women are participating in the educational and training programs required for systems analysts, thus expanding the number of qualified women.

Although women have undeniably made progress in systems analysis, their progress has not been unequivocal. As women increasingly entered the field, they tended to be segregated into lower-paid specialties, while men monopolized the higher-paid jobs. Indeed, one employee who worked for a large publishing company described the segregation there between mostly female low-paid analysts whose daily tasks involve interacting with users and mostly male high-paid analysts who make decisions about information systems and interact with analysts, programmers, and managers. Consistent with evidence that male and female computer workers do different tasks, my research suggests mixed progress for women computer specialists.

| | | | Notes

1. Women pioneers in computer science include Grace M. Hopper, who helped develop the first electronic computing systems and COBOL (a computer language); Jean E. Sammet, who developed and chronicled programming languages; and Frances Allen, who worked on computer translation.

2. Although the direction of causality is far from clear, the field may have opened up to women again precisely because the occupation was undergoing deskilling (see Donato and Roos, 1987).

3. I calculated these statistics from the 1980 census microdata (5 percent, A sample) on a subset of computer specialists who worked in 1979. For technical documentation, see U.S. Bureau of the Census (1983b).

4. The purported low level of complexity with respect to people appears to be changing, however, according to recent reports by the Department of Labor (U.S. Bureau of Labor Statistics, 1984b).

5. This finding is due in part to the fact that few systems analysts work in three highly sex-segregated industries: agriculture, construction, and retail trade.

6. Recent data suggest that the relative earnings of junior systems analysts continue to decline. A *Datamation* survey reported that the average salary of junior systems analysts ($22,769) was 9.4 percent lower in 1986 than in 1985 (Hodges, 1986).

7. Indeed, the third and fourth editions of the *DOT* (U.S. Department of Labor, 1965; U.S. Department of Labor, Employment and Training Administration, 1977) reported that the occupation is not people oriented. Both editions characterize systems analysts as "speaking with" and "signaling to" people, tasks it rates low in complexity. This discrepancy between the fourth edition *DOT* and the 1980 *OOH* (U.S. Bureau of Labor Statistics, 1980b) is likely due to the fact that the job analyses for the former were completed in the early to middle 1970s (see Miller et al., 1980).

8. Greenbaum (1979:81) described structured programming as a "method of using a language" so that "a programmer is told what instructions to use, what logic to follow, and what routines to insert in the program."

9. The occupation also lacks a central professional organization that could collect information about all systems analysts (Kraft, 1977).

Barbara J. Thomas

9

Women's Gains in Insurance Sales: Increased Supply, Uncertain Demand

Throughout this century women's representation among insurance agents and brokers has varied with the socioeconomic conditions of the nation. Between 1910 and 1930, when women were struggling for suffrage and economic opportunity, the proportion of women selling life insurance increased more than fivefold (see Table 9.1). Indeed, before 1920 an insurance executive recruited high school girls to insurance sales, assuring them that it offered the "surest as well as the most convenient means of providing for an old age" (Kessler-Harris, 1982:227). However, the Depression of the 1930s reduced women's opportunities, and the proportion of women in the occupation increased only modestly (Hooks, 1947). Shortages of male labor during World War II provided women with a renewed opportunity: in 1943 women accounted for 13 percent of life insurance recruits. After the war women's representation again dropped, and the proportion of female incumbents remained low for twenty-five years (Boynton et al., 1977). Then, during the 1970s, women's increased entry into insurance sales and their retention in the occupation nearly doubled their share of jobs. At the beginning of the decade some 13 percent of salespersons were women; by 1980 women's representation had risen to just over 25 percent (U.S. Bureau of the Census, 1984a), and in 1988 it was 29.7 percent (U.S. Bureau of Labor Statistics, 1989:184).

Despite women's numerical gains, they remain underrepresented in insurance sales (U.S. Bureau of the Census, 1984a), a fact at odds with their predominance in the insurance industry, in sales jobs overall, and in the ser-

183

Table 9.1
Number, Increase, and Percentage of Employed Women Insurance Agents, 1910–1980

Year	Number	Percent Increase	Percent Female
1910	2,537	—	2.9
1920	5,083	100.4	4.2
1930	12,953	154.8	5.0
1940	13,081	1.0	5.5
1950	26,700	104.1	8.8
1960	35,287	32.2	9.7
1970	56,469	60.0	12.4
1980	140,717	149.2	25.2

Note: The decennial census changed the jobs included in the occupational category over time: insurance agents in 1910 and 1920; insurance agents and brokers in 1930; insurance agents, brokers, and underwriters in 1960 and 1970; and insurance sales in 1980.

Sources: U.S. Bureau of the Census (1923: Table 4; 1933: Table 13; 1943: Table 58; 1956: Table 3; 1963d: Table 201; 1973b: Table 223; 1984d: Table 276).

vice sector. In order to explain women's low but growing representation in insurance sales, after first describing the occupation, I examine the barriers to their employment. Then I identify recent changes that have weakened these barriers and altered the supply of and demand for male and female workers.

⏐⏐⏐⏐ Insurance Agents and Brokers

Because agents and brokers make up most of the workers the Census Bureau classifies in the insurance sales occupations, this chapter concentrates on these two sales jobs.[1] The term "agent" refers narrowly to employees of insurance companies or broadly both to employed and independent sales agents and to brokers. Brokers are independent businesspersons who sell for multiple companies (U.S. Bureau of Labor Statistics, 1972, 1982a). Since the time of ancient Greek civilization, entrepreneurs have sold insurance to protect against the loss of property (Phipps, 1989). Today, agents and brokers sell policies that protect individuals and businesses from financial losses in three major areas: life, property-liability ("casualty"), and health. Life insurance pays survivors when a policyholder dies, and some policies provide funds for retirement or children's education. Casualty insurance protects individuals from losses resulting from automobile accidents, fire, and theft and provides businesses with workers' compensation, product-liability, and medical-malpractice coverage. An agent may sell one or more of these types of insurance (U.S. Bureau of Labor Statistics, 1972, 1982a; U.S. Department of Labor, Employment and Training Administration, 1977).

Insurance is sold through either "agency" or "managerial" (also known as branch-office) systems. Under the older agency system, a company appoints as its area representative a general agent, who in turn may hire salespersons to help cover the territory.[2] These salespersons, whose income depends on commission rather than salary, are not employees of the company, and the general agent receives an "override"—a percentage of their commissions. Under the managerial system, the company employs managers to run its branch offices and supervise its salespersons, who are known as agents (Rosler, 1966).

Although most insurance companies favor applicants who have college degrees, high school graduation usually fulfills the minimum educational requirement for sales. Male agents averaged 13.4 years of education in 1970; in 1980 they averaged 14.2 years (U.S. Bureau of the Census, 1973c, 1983a). All agents and brokers must be state licensed in each area (life, liability, health, and group) in which they sell policies. In most states, licensees must pass a written examination on state insurance laws (U.S. Bureau of Labor Statistics, 1982b). Employers screen prospective agents through interviews, background checks, and tests designed to predict success in the field (U.S. Bureau of Labor Statistics, 1982b). Those accepted become trainee agents—the entry-level sales position (*Kraszewski et al. v. State Farm*, 1985)—whom their local agency and the company's home office train (U.S. Bureau of Labor Statistics, 1982b). At State Farm Insurance, for example, trainees complete approximately thirty hours of supervised self-study concerning company products, the legal requirements of sales, and selling techniques.

Companies often "finance" their trainees with a monthly salary as well as commissions on sales beyond a set level. Salaries "serve as a cushion for agents in recognition [of] peaks and valleys in [the early years]" (*Kouba aka Hogan v. Allstate Insurance*, 1981:22110). Some agencies require trainees to maintain a monthly sales minimum, schedule work hours, or call on a quota of prospects—or risk dismissal (Rosler, 1974; *Kraszewski et al. v. State Farm*, 1985). While time spent in this entry-level position varies, State Farm requires at least two years before a trainee can become a career agent (*Kraszewski et al. v. State Farm*, 1985). Insurance companies usually pay career agents only commissions. Because insurance agents must persuade clients to renew policies, the commission system in insurance differs slightly from that of other sales occupations: agents earn "renewal commissions," which are partially deferred to future earnings (Rosler, 1974).

| | | | Stereotypes and Discrimination

Women were working in sales occupations at least as far back as medieval times (Kaplan, 1984) and are overrepresented in sales work in modern society. In 1950 women accounted for 28 percent of the workforce but nearly 34 percent of all sales workers (U.S. Bureau of the Census, 1960b). Their representation in sales occupations increased over the next three decades so that by 1980 nearly half of all sales workers were women (U.S. Bureau of the Census, 1963c, 1984d). However, sex segregation exists within this broad occupational group (Talbert and Bose, 1977). For example, women dominate retail sales (48.8 percent and 73.4 percent in 1950 and 1980, respectively), but remain tokens in wholesaling (4 percent and 13.2 percent in 1950 and 1980, respectively) (U.S. Bureau of the Census, 1960b, 1984d); they became well represented in real estate sales during the 1980s but are largely confined to residential sales (see Chapter 10).

Ann Myers (1984:12), training development manager of Nationwide Life, contended that stereotypes of salespersons and of men and women have limited women's participation in sales occupations. But we have seen that this is not true of all sales jobs. Societal norms allowed women to enter retail sales, usually dealing with relatively low-cost items and selling to female customers. The sales positions that employ the fewest women often involve high-pressure sales trying to sell things to people who have not already decided to buy, traveling, and large commissions.[3]

Employers' stereotypes about the characteristics workers need for a job influence their hiring practices. They are naturally reluctant to hire persons who they believe lack the characteristics necessary for high productivity. This constitutes statistical discrimination when employers' stereotypes about a group's attributes influence whether they hire individual members of that group (Arrow, 1972; Phelps, 1972). In the past, selling insurance was a highly sex-stereotyped activity. According to the U.S. Department of Labor, Women's Bureau (1961), "aggressiveness" was second to "a genuine liking for people" among desirable personality traits for life insurance agents; nevertheless, in hiring practices for insurance sales jobs, stereotypical male characteristics tended to outweigh feminine attributes. Although in the 1960s Coy Eklund, then vice-president in charge of agencies for the Equitable Life Assurance Society of the United States, emphasized a sense of empathy as well as a strong ego for salespersons, he did not hire any women as agents. He clung to traditional sex roles to the extent that he "would not hire an agent whose wife worked outside the home" (Riley, 1989).

A study of the Combined Life Insurance Company found that agents and their instructors continued to describe sales in terms of sex stereotypes in the late 1980s. Interviewees saw the agent's job as a "contest of will . . . [that] required determination, aggressiveness, persistence, and stoicism," and because men are believed to possess more of these attributes than women, employers thought women would be less productive than men at selling insurance.[4] For example, a male agent at Combined Life claimed, "Most girls don't have what it takes. They don't have the killer instinct" (Leidner, 1989a:15–16).[5] Undoubtedly, this attitude is related to the company's traditional sales approach that requires door-to-door sales, a lot of travel, and controlling interactions with prospective customers—duties for which male managers and agents thought women ill suited (Leidner, 1989b). This attitude toward women's ability to sell insurance was not limited to Combined Life. James A. Ballew (1978a:46), an insurance-relations consultant, recounted that

> in many a formal meeting, class, and bull session of general agents and managers I sat in on during the 1950s, whenever the topic of hiring women agents came up, it was quickly dismissed. There was general agreement that women are difficult to supervise, they don't produce much, and they can't sell to men.

Jane Howell and Evelyn Dwyer ran into this kind of resistance when they decided to enter the field. In 1954 six companies turned Howell down before one took a chance on her (*National Underwriter*, 1981). In the 1960s Dwyer, a claims-department employee, became a licensed agent—against her employer's advice.

Stereotypes about the occupation also probably deterred some women from entering insurance sales. In his film *Love and Death*, Woody Allen (1975) captured many people's feelings when he said: "There are worse things in life than death. If you've ever spent an evening with an insurance salesman, you know exactly what I mean." This negative image may have helped make the occupation unattractive to women as well as to some men. Diane Russell (1980), an insurance agent who started as a secretary, confessed that she had such a negative attitude toward insurance that she never would have taken the secretarial job if she had known that the prospective employer interviewing her was an insurance agent. Robert Brown (1981), a life insurance department manager, suggested that many business-oriented women have not entered insurance sales because they perceive it as "hard sell." Anna Levine (quoted in Riechers and Kane, 1979:12) explained that because of the negative image, agents "face a lot of rejection. People will be very rude to you." One female agent I interviewed thought that fifteen years ago people ranked insurance salesmen just above used car salesmen.[6] Thus, the stereotype of the aggressive salesperson contributed both to the job's bad image and to its label as "men's work," and hence to women's low representation.

In addition to sex stereotypes, other factors shaped employers' preference for male agents. In *Men and Women of the Corporation*, Kanter (1977: Chap. 3) claimed that top managers respond to the uncertainty of their work by practicing "homosexual reproduction"—selecting successors who resemble themselves. According to Kanter, managers preferred men because they were used to working with them in such positions. Male insurance agents and officials illustrated Kanter's thesis in recruiting insurance salespersons. For example, an industry analyst asked, "Could the reason that so few women are agents have anything to do with the fact that there are virtually no women in management? Does like tend to perpetuate likeness?" (Dunetz, 1977:77–

78). As early as 1961 the Department of Labor (Women's Bureau, 1961:6) attributed women's low representation to restrictive hiring practices by agency managers: "Few company-authorized representatives make a positive effort to recruit women agents." A saleswoman I interviewed classified male managers into three groups with respect to their attitudes about hiring women agents: some support hiring qualified women; others believe that female agents require extra attention that makes them too much trouble; and still others claim to be open-minded about hiring women but really are not. These last, she added, "put on a front because [they] know that it's the thing to do." [7]

Women's exclusion from informal male groups has also contributed to their low representation in insurance sales. Personal contacts play a key role in men's obtaining professional, technical, and managerial jobs (Granovetter, 1974). Female exclusion from the networks to which male insurance agents belong, such as the Rotary Club, contributes to their low representation. A marketing services officer for Mutual Life of Canada argued that male agents play a major role in perpetuating insurance sales as men's work because agents—themselves mostly males—recommend the best recruits, but the persons they recommend are usually other men (Ballew, 1978b:57).

Men in the industry may hesitate to recommend women already employed in other office jobs because they are reluctant to give up effective subordinates. Just as Kanter (1977, chap. 4) found that corporate secretaries experienced low mobility because managers disliked losing a good secretary, some insurance managers discouraged women from becoming agents in order to retain them in other capacities. Female office managers and secretaries often run the agency when the boss is away, giving rise to managers like the one at State Farm who told female employees who wanted to become agents that "he could not take a good secretary away from an agent" (*Kraszewski et al. v. State Farm*, 1985:37566). Other male agents may resist promoting women staff members in order to reduce competition from women and preserve their own monopoly over desirable jobs. One woman told me that male agents discouraged her from accepting their manager's offer to transfer her to sales: "All the other agents in the agency were real happy with the job [as claims adjuster] I was doing. They knew if I left that position and became one of them, I would be competition."

When unsuccessful at excluding a woman from sales, some male agents try to undermine a female agent by shunning her. A female agency manager for the Equitable indicated that "the initial years in the business are tougher for a woman, and she should expect to [face] more rejection from peers than from clients" (*Life Association News*, 1986). Another female agent confessed, "There are some situations when I wished I might be a male agent so I could listen and perhaps participate in the bull sessions that are held at our company conventions" (Landon, 1974:59). Undoubtedly, the isolation felt by these female agents hurt women's recruitment, production, and retention in insurance sales.

Some employers view women as a disruptive influence in a predominantly male office (they seem to forget the presence of female secretaries). According to Mary Fort (1974:135), a forty-year insurance veteran, some general
agents believe that female agents might "upset the customary order of things."
Reskin and Hartmann (1986) argued that fear of sexual relations contributes
to occupational segregation. A British study found insurance recruiters who
assumed that "the very presence of women in work contexts inevitably stimu-
lates men's 'sexual drives,' thus deflecting them from commercial interests"
(Collinson and Knights, 1983:21). Ironically, women's sexuality kept them
from insurance sales jobs because employers viewed them as both potential
seducers and potential victims. Some managers claimed that insurance sales
was a dangerous job for women because it often involves calling on prospects in the evening: "How does a lady cope with that if she calls on a man's
house at night?" (Collinson and Knights, 1983:28).[8] Two agents at Combined
Life echoed this paternalistic concern for women's safety: "They wouldn't
want their wives doing this work because of the unpleasant and potentially
dangerous places agents must sometime visit" (Leidner, 1989a:16).

Some managers believe that women will sell less because of their exclusion from social networks at male clubs, lodges, sports and civic affairs
where information is leaked that can lead to sales (Karene and Anderson,
1967:5). To Kathy Meldrum, a perennial member of the elite high-sales organization called the Million Dollar Round Table, a major advantage men have
is being able to take male clients hunting or fishing or to play racketball or
golf. She added, "I am envious of men who can control business through
more social freedom. . . . I cannot do this. So I have to work harder and
earn the client's trust. I have to try harder to be more professional" (quoted in
McLean, 1978). Other industry observers (Hurlahe et al., 1980; Shaw, 1980;
Benton, 1981; Schuster, 1981) fear that customer discrimination will hamper
women's performance. Supposedly, "some men do not like to discuss financial
affairs with a woman. They have a feeling that no woman can know as much
as a man might" (Karene and Anderson, 1967:5). General agent Marguerite
Martin (1982:101) advised female agents to ask prospective clients whether
they minded doing business with a woman, adding, "If a woman doesn't ask
this, she's probably going to be wasting 80 percent of her time." An experienced woman agent claimed that saleswomen must walk a fine line in order to
prove their competence without threatening men who hesitate to buy from a
woman "when it's apparent that she knows a bit more about finance than he"
(Fort, 1974:139).

Given many managers' reluctance to hire women in sales, the policy of
a firm's executive staff often determines whether a company does so. Joseph P.
McCarthy (1977:70), who conducted equal-employment-opportunity (EEO)
seminars for insurance managers, believed that support by top management is
needed for compliance with equal-employment laws: "The executive staff will
always set the policy and the tone for line management. Their support has to

be sincere and broadly communicated and should entail a regular review of the status of EEO efforts."

Women executives might be more likely than men to take such a stance, but there have been few women managers, directors, and vice-presidents. State Farm Insurance did not have a single woman in any of these decision-making posts until late in 1981. In other companies, women's entry into executive positions also helped their representation in sales. For example, in 1960 the Equitable Life Assurance Society of the United States had no women officers or board members. Then Eklund reversed his opposition to hiring women and spearheaded a recruiting program (Riley, 1989). By the late 1970s the Equitable had employed a number of female officers, including a vice-president and several assistant vice-presidents in its agency department, and their recruiting efforts paid off—probably because women agents got "a lot of moral support from women in home office management as they . . . [built] a career in what has traditionally been a man's field" (Ballew, 1978b:57).

Until the 1970s insurance companies were able to attract and retain enough men to fill their sales force: the occupation's workforce increased by over 51,000 and 85,000 men during the 1950s and 1960s, respectively (U.S. Bureau of the Census, 1960b; 1963c). Potentially high earnings and the opportunities for entrepreneurship and advancement to managerial or executive positions attracted men: insurance salesmen at every educational level except those with postgraduate education outearned both the average male worker and the average male accountant in 1969 and 1979 (U.S. Bureau of the Census, 1973c, 1984c). For example, in 1969 the mean earnings for insurance salesmen with four years of college were $14,892, compared to $14,041 for all men and $13,795 for accountants who were equally educated. In 1979, these earnings (in 1969 dollars) were $14,020, $11,650, and $11,372, respectively.[9] Because insurance salesmen's earnings depend on the policies they sell, they lost less real income to inflation during the 1970s than many other workers. Moreover, insurance sales offer lucrative white-collar employment to men without college education. In 1970, over 45 percent of insurance salesmen had no college, compared to 19 percent of male accountants. Although the number of college-educated salesmen grew during the 1970s, in 1980 three out of ten salesmen still had not attended college (U.S. Bureau of the Census, 1973c, 1984c).

Many Americans dream of being their own boss. According to a Life Insurance Marketing and Research Association (LIMRA) study, 71 percent of male recruits gave "the quest for independence and the income potential" as the primary reasons for becoming life underwriters (*National Underwriter*, 1982). This dream has come true for one-quarter of insurance salesmen (U.S. Bureau of the Census, 1980), compared to only 9 percent of all male workers (U.S. Bureau of the Census, 1984d).

Insurance salesmen also have the opportunity to advance to managerial or executive positions. One managing general agent explained the benefits of his position: "I both sell insurance and manage. Last year I was the leading producer in my agency. I did not come to a fork in the road that said you stay in sales or go into management. My road just got wider." Insurance salesmen have also climbed their companies' corporate ladders. For example, the recruiting brochure for the nation's largest personal property and casualty insurer pointed out that most of its top people started out as agents (*Kraszewski et al. v. State Farm*, 1985). Thus, the position of insurance agent was not only desirable in itself but also served as a route to managerial positions. As a result, men had a stake in protecting their share of insurance jobs from interlopers. Firms had an adequate supply of male labor and did not have to turn to women.

| | | | Sex Segregation in Insurance Sales

Although women are overrepresented in the insurance industry—which was 43.1 percent and 56.7 percent female in 1970 and 1980, respectively—the industry is highly segregated by sex. Most women (83.2 percent in 1970 and 84.1 percent in 1980) hold clerical positions, while a majority of men (56.9 percent in 1970 and 52.0 percent in 1980) work in sales (U.S. Bureau of the Census, 1972, 1984b). Moreover, few women occupy leadership positions. Until the mid-1970s many companies had no women agency managers or general agents, jobs that are labeled as male (*Equinews*, 1975; Martin, 1982:99; *Kraszewski et al. v. State Farm*, 1985). One female agent, formerly a manager at another firm, related an incident that illustrated women's limited promotional opportunities: when a district position opened up, the company passed over her to promote a man she had trained. A vice-president explained to her, "We had to do something with [him]."

In contrast, women dominate low-level jobs within insurance sales occupations, such as that of solicitor, an agent's representative who seeks insurance applications (Davids, 1977; *Kraszewski et al. v. State Farm*, 1985). As an assistant editor of *National Underwriter* observed, some agencies allow women to sell, "but only over the phone" (Friedman, 1984:8). Still others assign female sales assistants to their male salespersons to service existing accounts while the men handle "more important work, like face-to-face sales." The comment of a top executive in a national brokerage to a seminar illustrates the different uses firms made of men and women: he explained that "if he were starting a new agency, he would hire three male producers and nine female insiders" (Strazewski, 1982:26).

Men and women are also concentrated in different sales markets. While male agents sell policies to men, married couples, and persons in higher income brackets (King, 1984:132), according to industry observers (Bolton, 1976;

Kent, 1977; Martin, 1982), many general agents believe that women can succeed only in the women's market, the family market, or tax-sheltered annuities for teachers and nurses. Marguerite Martin (1982:102) asked fellow general agents, "[Are those the markets] where you're directing that hotshot male you just hired? No. You're directing him to where he can make money." According to a LIMRA study of life underwriters, women's lower average policy size and premium per policy probably in part reflect the different markets in which men and women work.[10] Both male and female interviewees claimed that few women sell in the commercial market. One woman who does mentioned that she had just come from a sales meeting with fifty commercial-sales representatives of whom only two were women.

At the beginning of the 1970s, few women worked in either commercial or group markets. In Canada the first female group representative was appointed in 1973, and in 1978 only six women held such positions in the Canadian group insurance market. Similarly, in the United States few women specialized in group sales (Riechers and Kane, 1979). However, group health insurance is a fast-growing market—health policies almost tripled the premiums that sector paid to insurance companies between 1970 and 1980 (Insurance Information Institute, 1972; Health Insurance Association of America, 1983)—and women are entering it. By the mid-1980s, observers claimed, a substantial number of women were selling group medical insurance (Baldwin, 1986:52). Most of the agents I interviewed agreed that more women than men are drawn to the group-health market, partly because they can work daytime hours.

Several factors have limited women's entry into group and commercial sales, however (Stone, 1978). First, these markets require additional licensing, ostensibly because of their more technical nature. As a commercial agent explained, commercial sales require "all sorts of calculations." Second, earnings in group and commercial sales are far above average, so men are unlikely to give up these positions. Third, both insurance and real estate salespersons I interviewed felt that men enjoy going after big sales more than women do, perhaps in part because of their higher expectation of success. Fourth, group and commercial markets have tight networks. "Those selling in [them] tend to be a small close-knit *fraternity* with a grapevine and language all [its] own" (Stone, 1978:8; emphasis added). Finally, virtually all employers who negotiate and purchase group and commercial insurance are male. "A woman entering [these] markets [can] rarely count on sales from fellow females," as a man can from other men (Stone, 1978:9). Indeed, women agents felt that their lack of business contacts hindered them in moving to the advanced commercial and group markets (*National Underwriter*, 1982).

In summary, women in insurance sales are concentrated in the low-level sales jobs and in the less lucrative markets. Many managers still endorse the pattern of men selling outside the office while women play supporting sales roles inside the office (Strazewski, 1982), and they view women who have been able to become agents as women's-market specialists (Martin, 1982). Female agents have found that the women's market may provide a way to enter the occupation but that success comes primarily from the men's market (*National Underwriter*, 1973). Furthermore, the "soft" sales approach stereotypically associated with women may limit the positions available to women; for example, at Combined Life the soft approach was adopted by the life and health division but not the much larger accident division (Leidner, 1989b). Therefore, the majority of agent positions could be viewed as inappropriate for all but a few exceptional women. To succeed, women agents must overcome two barriers: those against their entering the occupation and those against their selling in men's markets.

| | | | Factors Increasing Women's Representation in Insurance Sales

In 1971 women accounted for only 2 percent of the recruits in life insurance. However, by mid-decade over 9 percent of the recruits were women (Boynton et al., 1977). During the 1970s the proportion of female agents more than doubled; between 1977 and 1979 alone, women's representation increased from 3 to 7.5 percent (Dunetz, 1977; Christenberry, 1979). Women's increasing share of insurance sales jobs occurred both because demand for workers increased and because that demand was increasingly sex neutral. The growth of the industry and the occupation, the shrinking pool of men interested in selling insurance, changes in the way firms compensated their agents, governmental pressures, litigation, the emergence of a women's insurance market, and possibly the development of a "softer" sales approach all made female applicants more attractive to managers. In response to job opportunities, women flocked to an occupation that offered potentially high earnings and the possibility of a flexible work schedule but required little specialized training.

The Growing Demand for Women Sales Agents

From 1958 to 1982, as the population with the greatest insurance need grew—persons aged 25 to 59 years—insurance sales volume increased, and the insurance industry steadily expanded (U.S. Bureau of Labor Statistics, 1982b, 1984a). Annuities and health insurance, two markets that general agents viewed as appropriate for women, were among the fastest-growing insurance lines (Health Insurance Institute, 1961, 1973; Health Insurance Association of America, 1983). In consequence, between 1970 and 1980 the number of insurance sales workers increased 19 percent, from 475,866 to 567,864 (U.S. Bureau of the Census, 1984a). Growth often creates job opportunities for sex-atypical workers (Rosenbaum, 1979; O'Farrell and Harlan, 1984); it unquestionably did so in insurance sales during the 1970s.

Although insurance sales did not deteriorate as much as many of the other occupations examined in this book, changes in the 1970s did reduce the economic attractiveness of the occupation and demoralize male agents. Inflation and commission cuts threatened agents economically. Double-digit inflation in the latter half of the 1970s cut agents' profits—one industry analyst warned that "agents [cannot] indefinitely outrun their own rising costs by simply writing more business generated partly by inflation" (Clark, 1976:92)—and insurance companies further reduced agents' earnings by cutting commissions to compensate for underwriting losses. A study by the National Association of Casualty and Surety Agents showed that after adjusting for inflation, premiums grew 46 percent more than commissions (*National Underwriter*, 1979). Two-thirds of the independent agents and brokers who responded to a trade journal's survey indicated that between one and three of the companies for which they sold insurance had cut commissions, and commission incomes had dropped 15 to 25 percent (Ackerman, 1975).

During the 1970s changes in marketing practices also reduced the attractiveness of selling insurance. Many insurance companies developed mass-marketing plans that limited the expansion of their sales forces and reduced agents' importance. The *Occupational Outlook Handbook* (U.S. Bureau of Labor Statistics, 1978c) anticipated that the number of insurance sales workers would not keep pace with the expanding volume of sales; it predicted that the growing number of group-insurance contracts and multiple-line policies covering many different risks previously covered by separate policies would reduce the need for salespeople. Indeed, according to a 1979 LIMRA study, the number of agents that life companies recruited declined during the last half of the 1970s (Christenberry, 1979).

Carter and Carter's (1981) argument that women have been integrated into the more routinized jobs in male professions applies to insurance sales. The executive vice-president of sales for J. C. Penney Insurance indicated that his company relied equally on mail and phone solicitors and salaried agents working in the stores. Given the decline of the importance of the agent in such companies, a senior executive vice-president of Allstate Insurance, part of the Sears Financial Network, "stopped just short of predicting the demise of the independent agent as a force in the personal-lines market." He believed that independent agents might continue to serve the rural and "service-conscious shopper," but found it "difficult to understand why a price-conscious shopper would seek out their services" (Friedman, 1985:2). Moreover, new advances in computer technology have increased an agent's clerical duties; one property and casualty carrier eliminated many policy typists, raters, and underwriters' assistants by passing some of their duties on to local agents (Hartmann et al., 1986:41). Some companies also provide a standardized sales pitch for their

Table 9.2

Employed Insurance Agents, Brokers, and Underwriters, by Sex, 1970–1982

	Number Employed (in 1000s)			Percent	Percent
Year	Men	Women	Total	Change	Female
1970	399	56	455	—	12.3
1972	390	51	441	−3.1	11.6
1977	417	83	500	13.4	16.6
1978	437	111	548	9.6	20.3
1979	407	127	534	−2.6	23.8
1980	398	134	532	−0.4	25.2
1981	453	142	595	11.8	23.9
1982	476	169	645	8.4	26.2

Note: All data are from Current Population Survey, except 1970 data which are from the U.S. Census.

Sources: U.S. Bureau of the Census (1973b:1–741, Table 223; 1978:420, Table 681; 1979:417, Table 687; 1980:419, Table 697; 1981b:402, Table 675; 1982c:388, Table 651; 1983c:419, Table 696).

agents. At Combined Life it was so routinized, a trainer claimed, that foreign-born agents could sell insurance even before they could speak English by learning their presentations phonetically (Leidner, 1989a). In sum, in the 1970s insurance sales changed in ways that made retaining agents problematic. Although the number of men selling insurance declined by only .2 percent, high turnover plagued the industry (U.S. Bureau of the Census, 1984a; Leidner, 1989a). The director of education and training systems for State Life reported that although 65 out of 100 agents survive their first calender year, five years later only 12 remain (Baldwin, 1979). Thus, recruitment was a continuous problem for firms, and men were responding less enthusiastically than in earlier decades. Insurance sales had added approximately 85,000 men to its rolls in the 1960s, but its male workforce increased by only 9,254 men in the 1970s (U.S. Bureau of the Census, 1963c, 1984a).[11]

The industry's failure to attract and retain enough men during this period of industrial growth made women more attractive job candidates. Beginning in the mid-1960s, the competition for new male college graduates grew more intense each year. At a large university business school in the mid-1960s, every graduate had at least eighteen job opportunities (Karene and Anderson, 1967). The decline in the number of men interested in insurance careers (Dunetz, 1977) led insurance-industry analysts to characterize the "existing—even worsening—manpower shortage [as] perhaps the most compelling reason of all why women should earnestly be considered" (Karene and Anderson, 1967:102–3). In 1979 and 1980 the declining supply of men caused the total number of insurance agents to drop and thus the percentage of female agents to increase (see Table 9.2). The executive vice-president of

Federated Guaranty Life, whose sales force was 37 percent female in 1979, explained that "there are more qualified women available for hire than men" (Christenberry, 1979:10).

During the same period, incentives for hiring women emerged. Women were cheaper, at least through the 1970s when they still received lower compensation than men. Since agents' productivity determines their earnings, companies had little to lose in hiring high-risk trainee agents if they required little or no financing—as was the case for women through the 1970s (*Insurance Salesman*, 1977). In fact, as early as the mid-1950s, a general agent identified this as a major advantage of hiring women (Boynton et al., 1977).

Federal enforcement of antidiscrimination laws provided the insurance industry with another incentive to employ women in nontraditional jobs. In 1972 the Equal Employment Opportunity Commission (EEOC) targeted the insurance industry for investigation (Dunetz, 1977).[12] Five years later, Prudential entered into an agreement with the EEOC, designed to increase women's representation in its sales force. Allan Kent (1977:6), a twenty-year insurance veteran, interpreted the agreement "as a warning to all companies that their practices of hiring women are about to come under scrutiny."

Sex discrimination against women had long excluded most women from insurance sales, but not until 1979 did women file charges against a major insurance company. In that year three female California State Farm employees who sought to be agents sued the company for sex discrimination on their own behalf and that of others similarly situated. Their attorney contended that between 1970 and 1977, 99.6 percent of State Farm agents were male and that the company had increased women's representation to only 3.5 percent by 1981 (*Equal Employment News*, 1982). State Farm had told the women that it required a college degree for its sales agents, even though it hired men without a degree. One plaintiff said State Farm had told her that agents might have to work at night and that the company could not guarantee her safety (Bishop, 1988). The judge ruled that State Farm had excluded women from positions as agents by (1) relying on a virtually all-male "talking network" to locate recruits; (2) failing to post openings for trainee-agent positions; (3) failing to recruit trainees from primarily female candidate pools such as secretaries, office managers, and solicitors; (4) promoting a "male image" in advertising that discouraged women from applying for positions; and (5) actively discouraging women from applying by misrepresenting the availability of positions and their educational and financial requirements (*Kraszewski et al. v. State Farm*, 1985).

The suit was not settled until 1988, when the company agreed to fill at least half of new agent jobs with women for the next decade and to pay some 1,100 women more than $100 million in monetary damages. Even before the settlement, however, the suit had had national repercussions. As early as 1980, one observer concluded, agencies "started realizing women will be involved in the business, whether [the agencies] wanted it or not" (Kocolowski, 1980a). In 1988 State Farm claimed that nationally, over the previous few years, about 40 percent of their new trainee agents had been female (Gaines, 1988:6).

The women's market and the soft sell.   During the 1970s, several factors contributed to the growth of the "women's insurance market." Women remained single longer, more women earned wages on which their families increasingly relied, grandmothers were less available to take over child care and domestic work if a wife died (Wexler, 1980), and courts invalidated discriminatory insurance policies that paid women lower benefits for higher premiums (*National Underwriter*, 1974a, 1974b; U.S. Commission on Civil Rights, 1982). The women's market was so robust that LIMRA predicted that in the 1980s sales to adult females would increase by over 70 percent, compared to only 20 percent for men (King, 1984).

Because male agents tended to ignore female customers—industry analysts Karene and Anderson (1967:93) claimed that women faced little competition in selling to "members of their own sex because not many [male] agents waste their time on women"—and because firms believed women could sell to other women, the growth in the women's market increased the demand for female agents. LIMRA reported in 1976 that firms had previously hired women primarily "as a means of reaching the 'female market' " (U.S. Department of Commerce, 1980:475). Mutual of New York believed so fully in "the importance of *women talking to women*" that they established a women's unit in their Pittsburgh agency (Gerstenberger, 1981:29; original emphasis).

During the same time that the women's market was expanding, a new and less aggressive sales technique gained popularity, one more in tune with the traditional female sex role.[13] Indeed, the two phenomena may be linked. This new approach is consistent with Hochschild's (1983) concept of female emotional labor—work that involves the management of feelings; she contended that traditional sex-role differentiation affects the type of emotional labor that employers assign to male and female workers. Women have been socialized to deal with others' feelings and are more likely than men to be assigned emotional work that involves "mothering," while men tend to do emotional work that involves degradation or, among "sales*men*, creating a sense of a 'hot commodity' " (Hochschild, 1983:11; emphasis added) by using hard-sell techniques. In traditional selling methods, agents tried to generate anxiety or vulnerability in potential customers and then offered them insurance to quiet their fear of financial ruin.

When the industry recognized that soft-sell, nurturing methods could be effective in certain markets, female gender-role socialization made women "naturals" for the technique. Without question, firms have moved toward more soft selling, as evidenced by comments in recent trade journals emphasizing the empathic side of insurance sales. To illustrate the contrasting stereotypical images of aggressive males and mothering females, a training development manager of Nationwide Life asked, "Would you rather discuss your insurance needs with someone who reminds you of your mother or someone who reminds you of Mr. T?" (Myers, 1984:14). Moreover, as one agent explained, "Most life insurance is sold because one person loves another" (Fort, 1974:138). The president of Canada Life, speaking at the Women Leaders Round Table during the National Association of Life Underwriters meeting, expanded on this sentiment in his contention that women can excel in insurance sales because insurance is designed to protect women and their children:

> You [women] can have a deeper knowledge of the life insurance need than most men. You can *communicate* to both husband and wife the importance of sound financial planning to offset hazards of dying too soon, living too long, or suffering financial loss through disability and illness. (*National Underwriter*, 1978:26; emphasis added)

Similarly, a manager at Combined Life considered the new "interactive" approach of the firm's life and health divisions better suited for women because it requires not a domineering style but greater perceptiveness about a family's needs.[14] He concluded that as a result, his company will have a growing number of successful women agents (Leidner, 1989b). Clearly, the greater acceptance of women in insurance sales occupations reflects less change in sex stereotypes than in presumptions about the most effective way to sell insurance and to whom.

Special recruiting programs.   The combination of pressure from regulatory agencies, a shortage of male agents, and the growing women's market led some insurance companies to target women as possible recruits in the 1970s. Efforts included leaving brochures at job placement centers and participating in "career days" and recruiting seminars (*Kraszewski et al. v. State Farm*, 1985). By the late 1970s twenty-two top companies had established departments with the dual goals of selling life insurance to women and recruiting female agents (Underhill, 1979). For example, Metropolitan Life began actively recruiting women for sales in the mid-1970s, and within five years women's representation in its sales force doubled (*Insurance Salesman*, 1979). In the 1960s the Equitable Life Assurance Society of the United States also started a program to recruit female agents (Riley, 1989). Then, in 1974, a month after Coy Eklund became CEO of the Equitable, he convened the first of several Women's Summit Meetings, at which about fifty female agents and fifty salaried women from the home office offered suggestions for promoting equality for women (Eklund, 1975). Toward this end, he emphasized the need for top management to formulate and disseminate a clear policy concerning the treatment and advancement of women (Eklund, 1976). The Equitable's program showed immediate results.

As these various factors prompted insurance companies to hire more women for sales during the 1970s, women proved their ability, thus eliminating one basis for sex discrimination. At the Equitable, during the first half of 1976, female trainees' commissions exceeded those of males (Ballew, 1978b:57). Bill Zimmerman (1983), an independent general agent, admitted misgivings upon acquiring four saleswomen when his agency bought out another agency. They surprised him by ranking among his top producers, and he now has eight women on a sales staff of thirty agents.

The Attractions of Insurance Sales for Women

A variety of factors have attracted women to insurance sales, primarily the increasing availability of well-paying jobs that require limited training and provide flexible schedules. Although we cannot determine how much a softer sales approach inclined firms toward female agents and how much the growing number of saleswomen reshaped the traditional aggressive sales approach, the softer sales image has broadened the occupation's appeal to women, enticing them to enter the occupation and take advantage of its other benefits.

Income advantage.   Through both its training-salary plan ("financing") and commissions, insurance sales can offer women higher earning potential than many other occupations open to them. In 1979 women employed year round in insurance sales occupations averaged $1,615 more than the average female worker, and the average State Farm agent grossed over $80,000 in 1981 (*Equal Employment News*, 1981; U.S. Bureau of the Census, 1984c). Although a growing proportion of female recruits have graduated from college—up from 30 percent in 1969–72 to 46 percent in 1975 (Boynton et al., 1977)—many women drawn to insurance sales have few equally lucrative employment opportunities. Alternative options mentioned by several of the women I interviewed were other sales jobs or clerical work; both pay less than insurance sales.

In the past, companies discriminated against women in both financing and commissions, but a 1981 U.S. district court decision helped to eliminate the discrepancy between male and female recruits. The judge ruled in favor of a female Allstate trainee whose monthly salary was 82 percent of that of her male counterparts. Although Allstate contended that the difference was based on prior earnings rather than the trainees' sex, the court ruled that basing current pay on prior earnings "reflect[s] a market value which tends to be less for women, and . . . perpetuate[s] past discrimination" (*Equal Employment News*, 1981:8). Three years later, Allstate settled a $5 million equal-pay suit that the EEOC had brought on behalf of Allstate's female agents, and the company agreed to stop basing monthly draws on prior pay. Since October 1984, Allstate has paid the same salary to all new agents in the same market area. Gradually,

Table 9.3
Mean Annual Earnings of Full-Time Female Workers, by Education Level, 1979

Education	Experienced Civilian Labor Force	Secretaries	Insurance Salespersons
Elementary			
0 to 8 years	$8,353	$10,133	$11,041
High school			
1 to 3 years	9,208	10,000	11,130
4 years	10,374	10,514	11,939
College			
1 to 3 years	11,688	10,790	13,045
4 years	13,833	11,234	14,524
5 or more years	16,958	11,648	15,660

Source: U.S. Bureau of the Census (1984c: Table 1).

the entire industry has moved toward equity in financing and commissions. For example, the percentage of female recruits in forty-four companies that offered financing increased from 36 percent for the years 1970–72 to 43 percent for the next three years. The median annual financing that companies provided for women rose from $6,960 in 1972 to $8,052 in 1975, thereby approaching more closely the amount male recruits received ($8,220 in 1972 and $9,432 in 1975). Since most women agents had previously worked in low-paying, traditionally female jobs—secretary was the modal prior occupation of female recruits, according to a LIMRA study (*National Underwriter*, 1982)—those who received financing usually did not suffer a pay loss compared to their former jobs (Boynton et al., 1977; *Insurance Salesman*, 1977; *Kouba aka Hogan v. Allstate Insurance*, 1981).

As trainees gain experience, their compensation usually changes from salary plans to commissions. Since a portion of each commission is deferred to future earnings, higher income is a long-term reward. Now that the average young woman expects to spend almost thirty years in the labor force, women stand to gain more from a career in insurance sales than they did a generation ago. Women also benefit from commission pay, which allows agents to control their own income, and those earnings are not depressed by their sex—a fact that the president of the Women Life Underwriters Conference credited as insurance sales' primary attraction for women (Langevin, 1984). Insurance saleswomen outearn the average secretary at every educational level, as well as the average woman worker with less than postgraduate education (see Table 9.3). Two women I interviewed brought these statistics to life. One had kept her job as a bookkeeper when she started selling insurance on a part-time basis. She reported that after five years she earned more selling insurance part time than she had made full time as a bookkeeper after fourteen years. The other woman, a college graduate in health science, said she could earn more in insurance than she could anywhere in her field.

Availability of training.   The on-the-job training that some companies provide for new recruits (Schuster, 1981), paired with an immediate though initially modest income, was an important attraction to prospective agents, particularly to those changing careers. Figures from insurance training programs indicate that women's enrollment in insurance courses has been increasing.[15] Women's representation among those earning the Chartered Property and Casualty Underwriters designation—which the American Institute of Property and Liability Underwriters confers on those who pass a course and a series of examinations (Davids, 1977)—rose from 5 percent in 1970 to 30 percent in 1980 (*National Underwriter*, 1983). Increases also occurred in life and health programs. In 1980 women accounted for 17 percent of the 28,161 students enrolled in the Life Underwriting Training Council's courses in life and health insurance. Almost four times as many women held the Chartered Life Underwriters (CLU) designation in 1980 as 1970. Since some are not yet agents, companies recruit female agents through their local CLU chapters (Brown, 1981). Thus, training has created a sex-neutral path into the occupation. As the president of the Insurance Information Institute pointed out, women's enrollment "is bringing them into the pipeline," creating a pool of talent for insurance companies (Kocolowski, 1980b).

Flexibility of schedule.   The need to combine work and domestic duties makes occupations with flexible work hours attractive to women with families. Inga Cragg, who started selling insurance in 1926, called her job "a natural for women. . . . It allows more flexibility than most jobs, an important consideration for working mothers" (quoted in Shaw, 1980:7). Industry analysts agree that flexibility is an attractive benefit for female recruits (Schuster, 1981):

> Actually for [a married women with small children] selling life insurance might be far better than working at a nine-to-five office job. As an agent, she can set her own hours, and this means she can take time to get the children's breakfast and send them off to school or . . . stay home when a little one is ill. (Ballew, 1978c:53–54)

However, flexibility is not an immediate privilege: the early years are marked by a rigid training schedule and work weeks of more than 40 hours. Generally, two to three years pass before an agent can enjoy a flexible work schedule.

Opportunities for part-time work may attract women who must combine paid and domestic work or who do not wish to give up their previous jobs. One general agent explained, "A lot of the gals that come into the business work with us on a part-time basis to start off with to see first of all if they like it, . . . if they can make a living at it." Some companies even catered their recruiting programs to potential part-time agents. However, the difference between women and men in the likelihood of working part time is trivial. In 1980 only 13 percent of women sales agents and 9 percent of men worked fewer than 35 hours per week (U.S. Bureau of the Census, 1983a).

| | | | Conclusion

The Equitable's president Coy Eklund (1978:4) acknowledged more than a decade ago that "40 years of employment and promotion practices, during which time women were not accorded genuinely fair and equal opportunity," had produced his company's workforce. By "employment and promotion practices," he meant a variety of long-standing obstacles that had barred women's entry into insurance sales—both managers' prejudicial attitudes against women and the structure of insurance companies. Eklund (1975:6) noted that achieving equal opportunity necessitates more than merely modifying attitudes: "It requires changing the very structure of the organization." Governmental and legal action pressed insurance companies to make these changes. A transformed image of insurance sales and the implementation of special recruiting programs that highlight potentially high earnings and flexible work schedules provide companies with a supply of women from which to draw. Because these developments are quite recent, women's representation has grown during the 1980s and should continue to do so through the 1990s.

Women's growing share of insurance sales jobs may alter the segregation that persists within the occupation. During the 1970s too few women worked as agents to dominate a market. As their experience increases, so too should their chance to move into more lucrative markets—though they will probably not gain equal representation in these markets in the near future. One general agent predicted that insurance sales may follow the same segregation of male and female agents that exists in real estate, with women concentrating on the family market while men dominate the business market. It is true that in many integrating occupations women have moved from being largely excluded to being segregated within the less desirable specialties. The future will show whether insurance sales repeats this familiar pattern.

| | | | Notes

Acknowledgments: I am grateful for the comments and suggestions of Barbara F. Reskin, Patricia A. Roos, and John W. Riley, Jr. I would also like to thank the insurance agents, brokers, general agents, and executives who graciously consented to interviews. Without their cooperation, this study would not have been possible.

1. Agents and brokers accounted for over 70 percent of all workers in insurance sales occupations in 1970 (U.S. Bureau of Labor Statistics, 1972). Other jobs include estate-planning counselor, field representative, home-office representative, pension adviser, and solicitor (U.S. Bureau of the Census, 1982a). From 1970 to 1980 the classification scheme of the occupation remained virtually the same—94.7 percent consistency (U.S. Bureau of the Census, 1986a). Agents concentrating on certain markets often have job titles that reflect their specialization, such as life underwriter, group-insurance specialist, or "debit man" (a job in industrial life).

2. General agents are independent contractors who represent a company in a territory by supervising its business and appointing agents (U.S. Department of Labor, Employment and Training Administration, 1977).

3. For example, women are underrepresented as car and boat salespersons—7.8 percent in 1980 (U.S. Bureau of the Census, 1984b).

4. Aggressiveness is the only personality trait in which sex differences are scientifically well established (Maccoby and Jacklin, 1974).

5. However, he added, an exceptional woman could handle the job—a woman with "a kind of bitchy attitude . . . a biker woman . . . someone hard-core" (Leidner, 1989a:16).

6. This respondent was one of twelve insurance agents, brokers, general agents, and executives whom I interviewed for this study. A public-opinion survey conducted in the 1960s placed insurance agents just above traveling salesmen and auto repairmen. Used car salesmen were not rated (Hodge et al., 1964).

7. Managers' attitudes also hurt women's retention. One agent indicated that the biggest problem women agents face is managers who try to intimidate them.

8. Many night calls can be avoided. One female agent indicated, "In my first year of selling . . . I didn't possess enough skill to pin people down to a [daytime] appointment. This year . . . I've had exactly one evening appointment" (Ballew, 1978c:54).

9. In 1979, "accountants" included accountants and auditors.

10. For women, the average policy size and premium per policy were $47,220 and $394, respectively. Comparable figures for men were $55,330 and $465 (King, 1984).

11. The disparity between this 9,254 increase and the loss of 1,000 male insurance agents, brokers, and underwriters between 1970 and 1980 implied in Table 9.2 stems from differences in their data sources. The former comes from 1980 census data for the civilian labor force (including unemployed persons). Its value is increased by the 1980 census reclassification that added collection agents employed at insurance firms to the insurance sales occupational title. The data in Table 9.2 (which are for employed persons) are based on Current Population Surveys that used the 1970 occupational classification through 1982 and hence exclude collection agents.

12. Some states also regulate sex discrimination in the insurance industry. For example, the Pennsylvania Insurance Department can refuse to issue or renew licenses and can revoke or suspend licenses of companies that discriminate in employment policies (U.S. Commission on Civil Rights, 1982).

13. James D. Reisinger (1977), who sells to women, stressed the importance of "low pressure" sales to succeed in the women's market.

14. Furthermore, he expected the new sales system to make it easier for women with families to succeed as agents because it requires less travel than the old system (Leidner, 1989b).

15. The growth of two-year colleges has made training more available. Such institutions offer prelicensing and continuing-education workshops in both life and health and property and casualty insurance.

Barbara J. Thomas
Barbara F. Reskin

10

A Woman's Place Is Selling Homes: Occupational Change and the Feminization of Real Estate Sales

Between 1960 and 1980 the real estate industry experienced nearly continuous growth. As Table 10.1 shows, the number of jobs increased steadily after 1960 until employment peaked in 1980 with 1,384,000 jobs. In the recession years of 1981 and 1982, the industry lost jobs (U.S. Bureau of Labor Statistics, 1984a).

A similar pattern of growth occurred among real estate sales occupations, those of real estate salespersons and brokers, appraisers, sales superintendents, building consultants, and leasing agents (U.S. Department of Commerce, Office of Federal Statistical Policy and Standards, 1980). Between 1972 and 1979 the employment of real estate salespersons and brokers increased by 76 percent, from 349,000 to 616,000 (see Table 10.2). The 1981 decline in employment in the real estate industry began among salespersons and brokers a year earlier; in fact, their number dropped by almost 100,000 between 1979 and 1982 (U.S. Bureau of Labor Statistics, 1979a, 1983). But the heavy growth of the 1970s left in its wake a marked change in the sex composition of real estate salespersons. In 1950, one in seven brokers and salespersons was female; in 1970, 32 percent were women—about the same proportion as women's share of the labor force overall; in 1980 women made up half of all agents. The number of women in real estate sales occupations began to decline in 1979, however, and the percentage who were female dropped slightly after 1980 (U.S. Bureau of the Census, 1973c, 1980, 1981b; U.S. Bureau of Labor Statistics, 1989).[1]

Table 10.1
Total Employment in the Real Estate Industry and Employment of Brokers and
Salespersons, 1960–1982

	Total Employment (in 1000s)	Percent Change	Brokers and Salespersons (in 1000s)	Percent Change
1960	750	—	—	—
1965	795	6.0	—	—
1970	881	10.8	262	—
1975	1,054	19.6	422	61.1
1980	1,384	31.3	582	37.9
1982	1,336	−3.5	534	−8.2

Sources: U.S. Bureau of Labor Statistics (1982d: Table B-20; 1984a: Table D-2); U.S. Bureau of the Census (1973b: Table 223; 1981b: Table 675; 1983c: Table 696).

Table 10.2
Employment in Real Estate Sales, by Sex, 1970–1981

	Males (1000s)	Change (1000s)	Females (1000s)	Change (1000s)	Percent Female
1970	179	—	84	—	31.9
1972	221	42	128	44	36.7
1977	282	61	220	92	43.8
1978	305	23	250	30	45.0
1979	312	7	304	54	49.4
1980	287	−25	295	−9	50.7
1981	282	−5	280	−15	49.8

Sources: U.S. Bureau of the Census (1973b: Table 223; 1978: Table 681; 1979: Table 686; 1980: Table 697; 1981b: Table 675; 1982c: Table 651).

The purpose of this chapter is to discover why women's representation in real estate sales increased so sharply during the 1970s. To answer this question we examine changes in the occupation, industry, and society, beginning in 1950.

| | | | The Nature of the Occupation

Real estate agents can be brokers or salespersons, and the latter can be associated with brokerage firms as either employees or independent contractors. Employees work regular hours under a broker's supervision, whereas independent contractors work autonomously, if and when they please (Sirota, 1981:14–15). The independent status imposes responsibilities not imposed by the employee status. As independent contractors, salespersons must assume the costs of showing property, pay their own withholding and social security taxes, and arrange their own health insurance and retirement plans (Evans, 1983).

Most real estate sales professionals begin in residential sales, and many remain in that specialty. Salespersons in residential real estate spend most of their time obtaining listings and showing property. In listing a property, they recommend a reasonable price. To do so, they must be familiar not only with the house's amenities but also with the location of schools, shopping facilities, and public transportation (U.S. Bureau of Labor Statistics, 1978c, 1984b). Because good listings are the lifeblood of a real estate firm, the person obtaining the listing receives a share of the commission when the property is sold.

Real estate salespersons spend a good deal of their time on the telephone, exploring leads for possible listings and responding to inquiries about property. Since a customer's first contact with a firm is usually over the phone, the telephone can play a major role in a salesperson's success or failure. Trade journal articles offer instruction on telephone etiquette (see Lester, 1985), admonishing agents to convey expressiveness and courtesy (Pifalo, 1985).

Unlike salespersons, brokers may operate their own businesses, although those who hold a broker's license but do not own or supervise offices ("broker-associates") must work under a broker who does. Brokers who own or manage an office have additional responsibilities (Evans, 1983).[2] In most states, they are legally responsible for the actions of the salespersons in their office. Furthermore, the broker must handle functions such as closings, which salespersons are not legally allowed to perform. These supervisory duties can reduce a broker's sales activity. That most salespersons are independent contractors complicates the broker's role as supervisor. Brokers cannot require that independent contractors take part in training sessions, work specific hours, or handle specific properties. Yet the broker must still make sure that a salesperson is on duty at all times and that each listing gets sufficient attention (Evans, 1983).

The majority of brokers and salespersons (69 and 82 percent, respectively) sell residential real estate (National Association of Realtors, 1984). Other areas of specialization are commercial and industrial brokerage, property management, farm and land brokerage, appraisal, counseling, and syndication. Nonresidential specialties require different knowledge than residential real estate does. Since commercial brokerage deals with income-producing property, commercial buyers want to know the potential return on their investment. Thus, commercial salespeople spend time not only listing and selling property but conducting research on expenses and taxes (Evans, 1983). A major attraction of commercial over residential real estate sales is income: commercial brokers have the second-highest median income among the specialties (see Table 10.3). In addition, because commercial agents deal with businesses, they are less likely to work evenings and weekends (Rejnis, 1977).

Table 10.3

Median Income of Brokers by Primary Business Specialty and Percent Decline, 1974–1983

Specialty	1974	1980[a]	1974–80 Decline	1983[a]	1974–83 Decline
Residential	$20,000	$15,135	24.3%	$12,370	38.2%
Commercial	30,000	23,740	20.9	23,460	21.8
Industrial	25,000	22,365	10.5	—b	—b
Farm and land	22,000	19,854	9.8	13,860	37.0
Property management	25,000	20,631	17.5	21,380	14.5
Appraising	25,000	20,930	16.3	14,850	40.6
Building and development	33,500	24,279	27.5	24,750	26.1
Other	28,000	20,452	27.0	—b	—b
All brokers	24,000	17,282	28.0	14,850	38.1
N =	—b	—b		1,154	

[a] In 1974 dollars.
b Not available.

Source: National Association of Realtors (1984:29).

In the 1970s the real estate industry underwent major changes. A continuing controversy over the employment status of salespersons emerged, economic fluctuation brought uncertainties that affected competitive conditions, and government activities produced additional changes.

The residential brokerage industry has always been vulnerable to economic fluctuations. The downturn in the business cycle that occurred in the late 1970s made operating profitably difficult for most brokerage firms. Some of the largest firms responded by trying to forecast housing booms and slumps. Most brokers lacked this ability, however, so they had to be able to adapt quickly to changing economic conditions by reducing operating costs and using part-time personnel (Miller, 1978).

In the 1970s government increased its scrutiny and regulation of brokerages. For example, states increased the educational requirements for licensing. Federal agencies, especially the Internal Revenue Service, questioned the status of real estate salespersons as independent contractors. The "safe harbor" provision of the Revenue Act of 1978 was a step toward ensuring the independent status of salespersons. Then in 1982 the Tax Equity and Fiscal Responsibility Act (TEFRA) imposed three requirements for independent-contractor status: (1) salespersons must be licensed real estate agents; (2) substantially all of the real estate agent's compensation must be directly related to sales or other output rather than to the number of hours worked; (3) salespersons and their brokers must have a written agreement stating that the former will not be treated as employees for federal tax purposes (*Real Estate Today*, 1983). These regulations influenced the status of salespersons. After TEFRA went into effect, many brokers who had operated under the employer–employee model required employees to become independent contractors (Lipman, 1983), and the vast majority of brokerages now use them exclusively (92.3 percent in 1981; National Association of Realtors, 1984). The independent-contractor status of salespersons saves firms money—social security, unemployment insurance, pension plans, and fringe benefits for sales employees can add 6 to 13 percent to the company's payroll costs (Lipman, 1983)—and simplifies their accounting.

Changing competitive conditions have exerted pressure on the residential brokerage system to which residential brokers have responded in several ways, including advertising and "narrowcasting" on cable television (Block, 1985). Hardest hit in the competitive struggle were small, flexible, and highly specialized local firms comprising several part- or full-time associates.

A solution to uncertain economic conditions is association with nationally affiliated firms or giant diversified conglomerates. Most moderate-to-large offices are franchises of firms with national affiliations. Franchising has made it possible for smaller firms to enjoy many of the advantages of large firms without giving up their autonomy as independent businesses. Real estate franchise agreements resemble those in fast-food chains. In exchange for fees, the parent company provides the local broker with a national name, reputation, advertising, and management services. In 1977 the initial fee ranged from $1,000 to $10,000, and additional annual charges included 4 to 8 percent of their gross income. Franchising is increasing: between 1978 and 1985 the fraction of brokerages in franchise agreements grew from one-fifth to one-third (U.S. Bureau of Labor Statistics, 1978c, 1984b). Century 21 is the leading franchise firm; with more than 75,000 brokers and sales associates in the mid-1980s, it claimed over 11 percent of the residential market (Roulac, 1985).

Diversified conglomerates that also provide such comprehensive financial services as banking, credit cards, loans, mortgages, savings, investment securities services, and financial management include Coldwell Banker, the real estate division of the Sears Financial Network. Coldwell Banker was the highest grossing real estate broker in 1983. In 1985 its closest competitor, Merrill Lynch, employed more brokers licensed to sell real estate than corporate securities (Roulac, 1985).

|||| Women in Real Estate

Women have a long history in real estate sales (Smedley and Robinson, 1945; Brede, 1959). According to Rejnis (1977), the occupation has been receptive to women ever since the first real estate licenses were issued to women in this century. As early as the 1950s the rate at which women entered real estate sales outpaced their growth in the labor force, and during the 1970s their representation among brokers and salespersons increased more than four times as rapidly as their overall representation in the labor force.

In this section we examine explanations for women's post-1960 gains in real estate sales. Because the sexes are concentrated in different specialties, we begin by describing this segregation and examining its causes. Then we consider factors that affect the supply of and demand for women in nonresidential and residential real estate sales. Our analyses are based on lengthy interviews with fifteen Illinois real estate salespersons,[3] data from surveys carried out by the National Association of Realtors (1984) and the Illinois Association of Realtors (IAR; Follain et al., 1986), U.S. Department of Labor publications, and various other published and unpublished documentary sources.

Sex Segregation of Real Estate Specialties

Within real estate sales occupations the sexes are segregated in two ways. First, they are concentrated into different occupational specialties, with women crowded into residential sales and men overrepresented in the more highly rewarded nonresidential specialties. Second, women work disproportionately as salespersons, while men dominate managerial (broker–manager) positions.

Results from a survey of Illinois real estate sales people illustrate the segregation of women and men across different specialties (see Table 10.4). Of the female respondents, fewer than 4 percent worked in nonresidential specialties, compared to 21 percent of the men.[4] Most of the salespersons we interviewed confirmed the prevalence of sex segregation in real estate specialties in their firms.

The second form of segregation occurs with respect to positions. Of the

Table 10.4
Distribution of Illinois Real Estate Salespersons by Specialty and Sex, 1985

	Males (%)	Females (%)	Percent Female
Residential	78.3	96.3	57.0
Commercial	9.0	.9	9.4
Residential–commercial combined	6.8	1.4	18.5
Other	5.9	1.4	10.8
Total	100.0	100.0	51.9
N =	324	350	

Source: Follain et al. (1985).

respondents to the IAR survey, women were 62 percent of the salespersons but only one-third of the brokers. Any salesperson can take the additional instruction and examination required for the broker's license, and more women are acquiring it, but women may have less incentive to get a broker's license because they have fewer opportunities actually to be broker–managers (National Association of Realtors, 1984). A survey of Illinois brokers and salespersons indicated that men who hold broker's licenses were half again as likely to be associate brokers as were women (Follain et al., 1986). The fact that the number of female managers grew in the early 1980s may be related to the depressed real estate market and thus may not reflect unequivocal progress for the new managers. One male broker told us he resigned his management position during the recession because he could earn more by selling than he could as a broker–manager, when his income depended on his staff's performance. A woman filled his position.

Sex segregation also affects earnings. In 1980 women working across all occupations earned 61 cents for every dollar a man made hourly, in part because the sexes were segregated in different and unequally paying occupations and paid unequally in the same occupation. In a single occupation in which earnings are based largely on commission, both these factors should be minimized. However, in 1980 women in real estate sales did only a few cents better than all employed women, averaging 65 percent of what men in real estate sales earned hourly (U.S. Bureau of the Census, 1984c).

One possible explanation for this earnings gap is that men outsell their female counterparts, but the limited evidence available does not support this possibility (Rejnis, 1977). Even if performance differences exist, their contribution to the wage gap is small compared to that of segregation within real estate sales. Residential selling, in which women are concentrated, yields the lowest earnings of all the specialties (see Table 10.3).[5] Some evidence suggests that the earnings gap has narrowed: although full-time saleswomen made 60 cents for every dollar salesmen made in 1974, by 1983 saleswomen were earning 90 percent of salesmen's earnings (see Table 10.5).

Several factors could produce sex differences in brokers' earnings. Between 1974 and 1977, women raised the ratio from 60 to 65 cents per dollar, but since then it has fallen to 56 cents per dollar (National Association of Realtors, 1984). The widened gap is probably due in part to female brokers' disproportionate location in more marginal positions than those their male counterparts hold. Brokers' duties are quite heterogeneous. Brokers who function as salespersons may resemble persons with only the sales license more than they resemble brokers who are managers. The decline in both the absolute and relative income of female brokers in 1977 is consistent with a growing number of women licensed but not working as brokers. Interestingly, since 1980 female *brokers'* earnings have equaled those for male *salespersons*. The fact that 61 percent of female brokers have no ownership interest in their firms adds to their overall economic disadvantage.

Table 10.5
Median Income of Brokers and Full-Time Salespersons by Sex, 1974–1983

	Brokers			Full-Time Salespersons		
	Males	Females	Percent of Male Income	Males	Females	Percent of Male Income
1974	$25,000	$15,000	60.0	$15,000	$9,000	60.0
1977	30,000	19,500	65.0	17,000	12,000	70.6
1980	33,500	18,900	56.4	18,900	12,300	65.1
1983	36,200	20,000	55.2	20,000	18,000	90.0
N =	769	385		315	424	

Source: National Association of Realtors (1984:13, 42).

Explaining Women's Underrepresentation in Nonresidential Real Estate Sales

The vast majority of new agents begin in residential sales: there are fewer requirements, more "jobs," and faster sales to give newcomers a financial and psychological boost (U.S. Bureau of Labor Statistics, 1978c; Evans, 1983). Although most women remain in residential work, men tend to move into nonresidential sales and management. Women's lower likelihood of entering commercial sales occurs partly because the commercial sector is more difficult to enter. Other factors that contribute to the sex imbalance include sex differences in occupational preferences and experience stemming from sex-role socialization and barriers to entry.

Cultural attitudes and sex-role socialization.   Valerie Oppenheimer (1970) has pointed out that over time many occupations have come to be labeled as appropriate for one sex or the other. This "sex labeling" influences the employment decisions of both workers and employers (Reskin and Hartmann, 1986:43). Some of our respondents implied that commercial selling is labeled as male. For example, one interviewee remarked, "I think a good number of men would feel that [commercial] is a man's field and that they can do a better job."

Sex-role socialization probably plays a part in women's underrepresentation in nonresidential specialties and men's preference for them. Several sales people we interviewed believed that women are attracted to residential sales because they are "people oriented," while men dominate commercial sales because they are more "business oriented." Commercial real estate has the reputation of a tough, risky business where deals are made in smoke-filled rooms. Some view commercial salesmen as "high rollers" who are attracted by the risk that commercial sales involve. Commercial selling also requires more mathematics, and the aversion toward mathematics that sex-role socialization allegedly induces in some women (Fox et al., 1979) may deter some from commercial sales. Explaining women's underrepresentation in nonresidential sales and their growing dominance in residential real estate in terms of sex-role socialization is appealing because it fits popular notions of how people behave. Not everyone accepts this explanation, however: "Talking about gender relations in terms of roles, internalized expectations, attitudes, and traits directs attention away from larger structures and focuses explanations of inequality on what is going on inside the heads of the subordinated group. It is a classic case of blaming the victim" (Kessler et al., 1985:35). Therefore, we now consider how structural aspects of the occupation explain segregation in real estate sales.

Occupational information and experience.   People's occupational outcomes are limited by their knowledge of occupational opportunities. To enter an occupation, they must be aware that it exists and can be performed by persons with their experience and background (Reskin and Hartmann, 1986). We argue below that some women learned about opportunities in residential real estate through purchasing and selling their own houses. In fact, the commercial salespersons we interviewed learned about their occupation in a similar way: through buying and selling investment property or working in property management. However, the latter are not typically female activities, and women's underrepresentation in business management reduces their chance to learn of opportunities in commercial real estate sales.

Resistance among employers, coworkers, clients.   Female practitioners agree that sex discrimination exists in the commercial side of the industry. In 1975 a panelist at a Canadian Real Estate Association conference stated: "During the past twenty years women have gradually been accepted in residential real estate. However, in industrial, commercial investment, appraisal, property management, and sales management the doors are almost closed" (Gray, 1975:3).

Some observers believe that the resistance would-be commercial saleswomen may have to surmount comes primarily from employers rather than customers (Gray, 1975; Rejnis, 1977; Crispen, 1978). Practitioners in the 1970s alleged that some brokers and managers refused to hire women, and others would allow only a small percentage of women in their branches (Gray, 1975:3). Some saleswomen told us that brokers did not want women on their staffs because they did not think women could handle commercial selling. Similarly, House (1977:32) found that male managers thought women could do well in residential sales "because they can talk to housewives about their kitchens and bedrooms, but they do not have the business sense and experience required to work with the sharp operators who deal in investment, commercial and industrial property." Crispen (1978:4) claimed that some offices still observed the "commandment" for a woman entering real estate that "thou shalt engage solely in the sale of residential property, and shalt not covet the prerogative of man to engage in whatsoever area he damn well pleaseth." For example, Pat Levy encountered opposition when she tried to move from residential to commercial work after she succeeded in a chance opportunity to handle a commercial sale: "The men in the office didn't let me do it. My boss said, 'If you want to do that, go someplace else, because [commercial selling is] no place for a woman'" (quoted in Rejnis, 1977:44). Another saleswoman recalled that the firm's executive committee had to approve her before she was hired in 1973: "All the men went in [easily] . . . with me it was a matter of five months" (Rejnis, 1977:30).

Several brokers we interviewed agreed that sex discrimination persists in commercial real estate. Indeed, according to one male broker, many commercial firms that appear open to women are just paying lip service to equal opportunity. Most agents we interviewed believed that commercial customers—who are predominantly male—are indifferent to a salesperson's sex as long as she or he is competent; a few claimed that customers still prefer to deal with males and that women in commercial sales must prove themselves by being more professional than their male counterparts.

We interviewed several women who contended that female agents must act differently from male agents—they cannot be "buddy-buddy" with their customers, conducting business on the golf course or at the bar. Women's underrepresentation among office holders on realty boards and professional associations was another professional disadvantage.[6] Women continue to be grossly underrepresented on real estate boards both in the United States and in Canada (Gray, 1975; *Real Estate Today*, 1981). An interviewee told us of a local board that until 1982 adhered to its rule that there could not be a woman president more often than once every seven years.

Lack of power in the professional associations—in the mid-1970s the Society of Real Estate Appraisers and the American Institute of Real Estate Appraisers together had only 60 female members with professional designations out of more than 4,600 members—virtually closed appraising to women. Jean Felts (quoted in Rejnis, 1977:141) explained women's underrepresentation: "[local chapters] had a lot to say about who got in. . . . They could say 'we don't want women.' That no longer exists, but catching up takes time."

Factors Enhancing the Demand for Women in Residential Real Estate Sales

Economic theories of supply and demand provide a framework for examining women's growing dominance in residential real estate sales. Changes in the demand for personnel and in the supply of women interested in the occupation explain women's increased representation.

Several changes in real estate sales, the industry, and society during the 1970s enhanced the demand for sales personnel in general and women in particular. Among these are the growth of the occupation, occupational changes that made residential sales less attractive to men, a change in the occupation's "sex label," and changing attitudes of brokers and customers toward female salespersons.

The long period of growth noted above created a demand for sales staff. Labor shortages during World War II first brought large numbers of women into real estate sales (Crispen, 1978). After the war, returning servicemen ready for home ownership and eligible for Federal Housing Administration and Veterans Administration mortgages created a boom in the housing market. The growing market depleted the primary labor supply—men. Thus, firms turned to women as an alternative.

During the 1970s at least four major changes in real estate sales rendered it both less attractive to men and more attractive to women. First, legislation in the late 1970s and early 1980s that prompted firms to shift salespersons from employee to independent-contractor status lowered firms' "sunk costs"—salaries, social security, worker's and unemployment compensation—and thus reduced the economic disincentives tied to hiring potentially marginal workers. An eleven-year sales veteran who began selling residential real estate when no other industry would hire a woman with a baby commented, "Real estate people didn't inquire into my personal life or question my ability to put in enough time because [I didn't] get a salary" (Herman, 1982:23). At the same time, the disadvantages of independent-contractor status—no salary or benefits—made residential sales less attractive to married men who are usually primary wage earners. In fact, men are three-quarters of the small number of nonowner–nonbrokers who still have employee status (National Association of Realtors, 1984). Since women in the social classes from which real estate salespersons are drawn are less likely to be prime wage earners, and married women usually benefit from their husbands' health insurance and earnings, independent-contractor status deters women less than men.

Second, the economic fluctuations of the late 1970s made commission-based earnings unpopular with primary wage earners. Downturns in the economy make it harder for agents to make a living, and after 1979 both male and female salespersons and brokers declined in number. But men's numbers dropped more sharply than women's, probably because women in residential sales who were contributing a secondary income for their families could wait out the temporary downturn in the market.

Third, the growth of national franchise firms such as Century 21 and national conglomerates such as Coldwell Banker and Merrill Lynch contributed to the feminization of residential sales by creating a large number of new jobs. These chains have both an economic incentive to attract a large sales force and the corporate staff to develop effective recruitment efforts.

Fourth, new real estate specialties, such as condominiums, cooperative management, and syndication, drew men out of residential sales (U.S. Bureau of Labor Statistics, 1978c). For example, Rejnis (1977) reported that the demand for workers in property management exhausted the supply of qualified personnel. These more highly rewarded specialties rendered residential sales less attractive to men and thus created opportunities that brokers filled with women.

Although residential selling was characterized as "an appropriate occupation for women" as early as 1933 (Virginia State Board of Education, 1933), for years many firms refused to hire women (Rejnis, 1977; Crispen, 1978), and some customers preferred male salespersons. Until the 1950s or 1960s it was not acceptable for middle-class wives or mothers to work, and firms discriminated against women on this basis. One interviewee told us, "If they had a grade school kid, even a high school kid, we wouldn't let them in real estate in those days." The women's liberation movement challenged such attitudes and, together with the economic downturn of the 1970s, prompted greater acceptance of the employment of married women with or without children. Those forces and the pressure they engendered for equal opportunity led firms that had previously barred women to hire one or two in residential sales. According to agents we interviewed, their success weakened any remaining resistance. Two brokers we interviewed in 1986 described the ideal residential salesperson as a young married woman with a couple of children and a successful husband: "Because she is young, she will have energy. Because she has children, she will know how to get things done and handle responsibility. Because she has a successful husband, she will be used to having nice things, money, and will be familiar with success." In sum, the reduction in discrimination by employers and customers and the relabeling of residential sales as female opened the doors to women in the 1970s.

Factors Affecting the Supply of Women for Residential Real Estate Sales

The number of women in the labor force grew dramatically during the late 1960s and early 1970s, creating a large supply of new workers on which occupations could draw. A variety of occupational characteristics attract women to real estate sales.

Knowledge of the occupation.   Women learn of jobs in residential sales in several ways—from participating in the purchase or sale of a home; from nonsales employment in a real estate firm; from seeing women realtors in television commercials and magazine and newspaper advertisements; through firms' recruitment efforts, junior college and university real estate courses, and friends and relatives—often involving the opportunity to observe role models. As women's numbers increased in residential sales in the 1950s and 1960s, more female role models demonstrated that selling houses is something women can do. Among the millions of American women who participate in buying or selling homes every year, many see real estate sales as an occupation that can generate considerable income without requiring specialized training. After 1971 even women who had never bought or sold a house saw television commercials that featured women selling houses for national franchises or noticed photographs of real estate sales people of both sexes in newspaper home-buyer guides. Franchises held newspaper-advertised "career nights" to recruit sales people. Clerical workers in real estate offices were ideally situated to learn the occupation's duties and rewards (McMichael, 1967; Evans, 1983). Other women were introduced to the real estate business through their husbands or fathers (McMichael, 1967; *Real Estate Today*, 1980; Mescon and Stevens, 1982).

Ease of entry.   All states require real estate professionals to be licensed, and all but Texas issue both salespersons' and brokers' licenses (Sirota, 1981). To qualify for a license, applicants must be high school graduates and must pass a written examination (U.S. Bureau of Labor Statistics, 1979b). Since most states require additional education in real estate, high schools, vocational schools, colleges and universities, and real estate firms offer courses; many colleges and universities offer degrees in real estate. Thirty hours of classroom instruction on the fundamentals and legal aspects of real estate transactions is the modal requirement for the salesperson's license; typical requirements for brokers are ninety hours of classroom instruction and one to three years of real estate sales experience (U.S. Bureau of Labor Statistics, 1979b). Most states require prospective licensees to name the broker with whom they will be associated (Evans, 1983).

The "credential inflation" that has raised occupational entry requirements since the 1960s (Collins, 1979) did not affect real estate sales until the middle to late 1970s. Until 1978, editions of the *Occupational Outlook Handbook* reported that employers preferred applicants with at least a high school education, though the 1976–77 edition noted that as real estate transactions became more complex, many large firms chose college graduates for sales positions (U.S. Bureau of Labor Statistics, 1976:233). Most states still require only a high school diploma for a license (U.S. Bureau of Labor Statistics, 1979b). And even though some have raised educational requirements for licensing, and many large firms have begun to seek college graduates, most firms consider personal qualities—maturity, tact, sales ability—fully as important as academic background (U.S. Bureau of Labor Statistics, 1978c:241). In addition, in most states a person still needs only thirty hours of classroom

instruction to take the licensing examination. These generally low entry requirements make real estate attractive to older persons who lack a college
degree and do not want to spend an extended period of time in training (Evans,
1983; see also Arthur, 1947), as was the case for many older women who
entered or reentered the labor force during the 1970s.

The increased educational requirements for the license in the early
1970s and high visibility of advertising campaigns helped improve the image
of real estate sales, and its more professional image had attracted several of
the women we interviewed. The increased educational requirements may
also have helped bring women into the occupation because community college catalogs advertised real estate courses, and the courses provided an entry
path into the business. Before they were available, prospective salespersons
either had to know someone in the field who could direct their studies for
the licensing exam or do it entirely on their own. To the extent that brokers
discriminated against women, the need for brokers' sponsorship disadvantaged
women. The development of courses created a formal channel into the occupation. As one male broker we interviewed put it, "We set up a mechanism for
people to get into this business that worked for men and women, and maybe
there were a lot more women out there at the time who wanted to get in."

Perhaps because real estate sales occupations have few entry requirements, the attrition rate is believed to be quite high. Although no accurate
data exist, "industry lore estimates that half of the women entering real estate
drop out in the first year, and that 90 percent are out in five years" (Crispen,
1978:15). These figures seem high in the light of women's increased representation in the occupation during the 1970s. John Lumbleau, head of the real
estate school system in California, estimated a more plausible turnover rate
for his state: about 40 percent in the first year and another 20 percent after two
years (Rejnis, 1977). If attrition has declined with women's more continuous
labor force participation (Blau and Ferber, 1986), women's greater representation in real estate sales would result from both more women entering and
fewer leaving.

Flexible working hours.   As independent contractors, salespersons are
free to make their own schedules and do not need permission to take time
off. A job that does not require a nine-to-five workday fifty weeks a year is
attractive to some women who are raising families (Murray, 1960; Rejnis,
1977; Herman, 1982). For example, in 1960 a commentator characterized
residential real estate as a "natural field for women" because it provides the
flexibility many occupations lack to schedule appointments to accommodate
family responsibilities (Murray, 1960:35). When asked what attracted them
to the field, more women we interviewed mentioned flexibility and independence than any other factor. A former teacher said she wanted to return to

work when her youngest child began kindergarten, "and real estate had more flexible hours than teaching."

Another respondent said that women with children typically reasoned: "I'll go out and sell houses while Susie and Johnny are in school. I can be home when they get home, so it won't disrupt my family life." But women entering real estate, she added, "soon learn that that's not true. . . . We don't have much freedom." She acknowledged that she could still attend school plays, and that driving on class field trips provided an opportunity to "prospect" for listings; nevertheless, newcomers who are attracted by the belief that real estate sales will accommodate their family roles find that this is not always the case. For example, agents who do not respond to customers' evenings and weekend calls risk losing sales (Lindeman, 1981), and some spoke of long work weeks spilling over into weekends. Yet even if residential sales is less flexible work than many newcomers believe, independent-contractor status does allow women to take off blocks of time to meet domestic demands. Interviewees told of taking time off to be with their children during spring vacation or to accompany their husbands on business trips. Thus, both perceived and actual flexibility contribute to the occupation's attraction for women with families.

The opportunity to work part time.   A part-time schedule may attract people who wish to combine market and domestic work and those who do not wish to give up their regular jobs. A significant minority of real estate salespersons work on a part-time basis, and women are more than twice as likely as men to do so—16 percent of men and 39 percent of women, according to the U.S. Bureau of the Census (1984d). If the opportunity for part-time selling increased in the 1970s, this could help explain the influx of women. However, the percentage of women selling part time declined slightly (43 percent in 1970), while the percentage of men who sold on a part-time basis remained stable (16 percent in both 1970 and 1980; U.S. Bureau of the Census, 1973a). Moreover, interviewees suggested that because selling real estate is more time consuming than novices expect, those who begin working part time often increase their hours, and several felt that the increased complexity of the job has made it hard for part-timers to succeed. Many offices will not house salespersons who do not earn enough ($7,000 to $10,000 a year in the late 1970s) to cover costs (Rejnis, 1977). In short, although the perception that the possibility of selling part time may explain the occupation's attraction for women, we found no evidence of a trend toward increasing opportunities for part-time work that would contribute to women's disproportionate movement into real estate sales during the 1970s.

Income advantages.   Real estate selling offers three potential income advantages to women. First, as independent contractors, agents work on a commission basis, receiving a percentage of the sale price of their listings and sales; thus, only time and energy restrict their earnings (Crispen, 1978; Evans, 1983). Several saleswomen indicated that their overall earnings are higher than what they would have been in their previous jobs: "If I had stayed in elementary teaching, I probably wouldn't make 50 percent of what I do."

Second, many women mentioned the attraction of a field where earnings are not depressed by their sex. As Helen Hirt, past president of the Women's Council of Realtors and a vice-president of a large midwestern firm, pointed out, "Real estate is one field where women always have received equal pay for equal work," and a young college graduate echoed this point: "We don't have to battle for equal pay for equal work in this business. . . . There's no rule, thank God, that if a sale is made by a man the commission will be 6 percent, if by a woman, 3 percent" (quoted in Crispen, 1978:3).

Although commission-based earnings preclude wage discrimination, they do mean an irregular monthly income and a lag between making the sale and receiving the commission.[7] However, these problems are less serious for persons who are not the sole support of their households. Thus, real estate may be particularly attractive to married women whose husbands earn enough to sustain their families. Census data for 1980 are consistent with this interpretation: although women in real estate sales, 73 percent of whom are married, averaged only half of what their male counterparts earned, their family incomes exceeded those of men by $1,300 a year (U.S. Bureau of the Census, 1983a).

Third, there is the popular belief that real estate sales is a lucrative occupation for women. Books such as *How Any Woman Can Get Rich Fast in Real Estate* (Crispen, 1978) foster this impression, and most women we interviewed did report earning more in real estate than they thought they could earn in other fields open to them. They are probably right: in 1980 the mean hourly earnings of women in real estate sales was $7.19, while experienced female members of the civilian labor force overall averaged $5.22 an hour. The potential gain is even greater for secretaries and bookkeepers, the most common occupational origin for real estate saleswomen (National Association of Realtors, 1984): in 1980 female secretaries and bookkeepers averaged $5.07 and $5.01 an hour, respectively (U.S. Bureau of the Census, 1984c). One broker targets female recruits with no or little college training because real estate offers them much more than they could earn elsewhere.

Opportunities for self-employment.   Owning one's own business is part of the American dream, and real estate has been a route to achieve it. Compared to retailing and manufacturing, opening a real estate firm requires relatively little capital, so the entrepreneurial opportunity of real estate sales may attract both men and women. According to the National Association of Realtors (1984), 45 percent of brokers own their firms. Though female brokers are less likely than males to have an ownership interest—24 percent versus 42 percent (U.S. Bureau of the Census, 1983a)—real estate does offer women a relatively good opportunity to own a business.[8] Indeed, 7 percent of the 402,025 women-owned U.S. businesses in 1972 were real estate firms (U.S. Department of Commerce, 1976).

Sex stereotypes and sex-role socialization.   Personality traits believed to be related to success in residential sales are consistent with traditional female sex roles. Under real estate sales, in its 1933 edition of *Vocations for Women*, the Virginia State Board of Education listed as qualifications tact, a pleasing personality, confidence, initiative, good judgment, and the ability to approach people, make friends, and work harmoniously with various classes of people— all characteristics stereotypically attributed to women. McMichael (1967:313) claimed that women know how to sell houses because they understand the "feminine psychology" better than men and can point out a listing's advantages from a woman's point of view. He contended that this is important because ultimately most wives decide which house to buy. Other stereotypically female traits that are useful in residential sales include patience, skill, and diplomacy ("useful in persuading husbands whose wives are convinced"), a desire to please, and nurturance (one female broker described residential agents as "mother figures" to their clients). Salespersons we interviewed echoed these views: women are "willing to wait while someone discusses their ambivalence about a yellow bathroom."

An occupation that involves finding houses for people is consistent also with women's relegation to occupations that are "extensions of the home," such as dealing with children, preparing food, and nursing the sick. Moreover, the traditional sexual division of labor that assigns to women the primary responsibility for home care gives women expertise, legitimacy, and interest in houses. As one successful woman broker stated: "Women come into real estate knowing how many cupboards a kitchen should have in order to store a respectable number of pots, pans, and staples. . . . They know a lot about houses—more than most men. That's why they do so well" (Crispen, 1978: 103–4).

Still, caution is in order in drawing conclusions from arguments linking sex-role socialization to women's increased representation in residential sales. If women's stereotyped characteristics suit them so well to real estate sales and are the traits brokers seek in sales staff, why didn't brokers turn to women forty or fifty years earlier? Given the cultural power of such stereotypes, we suspect that the industry offers them as a convenient explanation for a change spurred by other factors.

| | | | **Conclusion**

The increase in women's representation in real estate sales during the 1970s was part of a trend that started decades earlier. Residential selling has long attracted women because of the perceived flexibility of the working schedule, the autonomy that independent-contractor status offers women who wish to take time off to meet family expectations, the higher potential income relative to other occupations open to non-college-educated women, low educational requirements, easy entry, and opportunities for self-employment. The 1970s boom in residential real estate coincided with the entry into the general labor force of a large number of women. The development of real estate college courses during that period provided a means for would-be salespersons to acquire training. In addition, the increased educational requirements along with the image created by new advertising campaigns enhanced the occupation's image, making it more attractive to women. The shift to independent-contractor status during this period deterred men, creating a demand for women. As firms hired women who subsequently performed well, employers' resistance to women in residential sales eroded. The existence of a growing number of women in sales became visible signs to other women of career opportunities in residential real estate, and gradually the occupation has become labeled as a woman's occupation.

Women's gains have been largely confined to residential sales, but women are challenging this sex segregation. As more women learn of opportunities in nonresidential sales and enter other specialties, resistance from employers and clients has declined. However, the effects of sex segregation and discrimination cannot be eliminated overnight. In specialties where women's representation has been extremely low, their numbers must increase for years before male dominance is threatened. Although more women are expected to enter nonresidential specialties, saleswomen we interviewed thought that the residential sector would also continue to feminize.

Women's concentration in lower-level sales is another aspect of segregation in the occupation. A lag exists between women's increased representation in the occupation and the percentage of female brokers. Although the number of brokers nearly doubled from 1975 to 1984, only one-third are women (National Association of Realtors, 1984). Women are not prevented from taking the broker's exam; the reason more do not may be the barriers that prevent female license holders from managing firms. Eliminating such barriers would offer women a greater incentive to obtain a broker's license. However, given the extent of the segregation between specialties and work functions, real estate sales occupations are likely to remain internally segregated for at least the near future.

I I I I **Notes**

Acknowledgments: We thank the University of Illinois Office for Real Estate Research for their support of this study. We are indebted too to the realtors who graciously consented to interviews. Without their assistance, this study would not have been possible. Patricia Roos provided helpful comments.

1. In 1970 the percentages of female brokers and salespersons were nearly identical to those for all real estate sales occupations (31.9 and 31.2 percent, respectively). During the decade, women's representation among brokers and salespersons grew faster than it did for all real estate sales occupations. While women accounted for over half of all brokers and salespersons in 1980, real estate sales occupations overall were only 45 percent female (U.S. Bureau of the Census, 1973b, 1981b, 1984a).

2. Nevertheless, according to the *Dictionary of Occupational Titles* (U.S. Department of Labor, Employment and Training Administration, 1977), salespersons' and brokers' duties are equally complex. The *DOT* describes real estate salespersons as "compiling" data, "persuading" people, and "handling" things (scores 3, 5, and 7, respectively). These ratings reflect moderate degrees of complexity for data and people and the lowest level of complexity for things.

3. We conducted in-person and telephone interviews with salespersons and brokers from a cross section of settings, in both small towns and major metropolitan areas, in residential and commercial sales, and in independent and franchised firms.

4. In the mid-1970s, of 3,188 certified property managers only 3.6 percent were women. Likewise, the majority of the 2 percent of salespersons and 5 percent of brokers who deal with syndication are men. Male brokers are also more likely than females to hold any of the securities licenses (National Association of Realtors, 1984).

5. The income advantage that nonresidential brokers enjoy has persisted at least through the mid-1980s, except for a dip in building and development from 1977 to 1980 and the recent decline in farm and land brokerage (National Association of Realtors, 1984).

6. In 1939 it prompted the formation of the Women's Council of Realtors.

7. Commercial and industrial real estate selling is even more vulnerable than residential, since completing a sale may take months or years; in the long run, however, higher income compensates sales personnel for its irregularity.

8. Women are not likely to make rapid strides in closing the ownership gap. Interviewed brokers explained that the cost of opening one's own office has become financially prohibitive. Mescon and Stevens (1982) reported that the Reagan administration's decision to allow interest rates to rise sharply contributed to a drop in the number of women-owned real estate firms.

Polly A. Phipps

11

Occupational Resegregation among Insurance Adjusters and Examiners

Women's participation in the insurance industry increased during the 1970s. However, women's headway in such male-dominated specialties as under-writing and sales was far outstripped by their gains in the historically male-dominated clerical occupation of adjusters, examiners, and investigators. When the census first classified adjusters, examiners, and investigators as a detailed occupational category in 1960, 6,845 women made up 12 percent of the more than 55,000 occupational incumbents (see Table 11.1). By 1970 the occupation had added some 40,000 new jobs, almost half of which were filled by women. As a result, the number of women quadrupled, and they constituted almost 26 percent of employees in the occupational category. The 1970s witnessed even greater growth, with more than 67,000 new jobs added; moreover, the number of women increased by almost 74,000, to a total of 98,407, while the number of men declined by some 6,000. Thus, by 1980, 60 percent of all insurance adjusters, examiners, and investigators were women.

This chapter investigates women's disproportionate gains, first among adjusters and then among examiners;[1] it then assesses the consequences of these occupations' shift from a male- to a female-dominated one. I suggest that the routinization of the insurance-claims process, partially driven by tech-nological advances in electronic data processing, changed the character of this occupation and—along with social and legal changes—transformed adjust-ing and examining so that both more closely resembled stereotypically female clerical occupations. As a result, the occupation declined in attractiveness,

Table 11.1
Employed Insurance Adjusters, Examiners, and Investigators, by Sex, 1960–1980

	Women	Men	Total	Percent Female
1960	6,845	48,631	55,476	12.3
1970	24,663	71,626	96,289	25.6
1980	98,407	65,179	163,586	60.2

Note: The 1970–80 differences stem in part from classification change. However, the change was very small: in 1980, insurance adjusters, examiners, and investigators lost approximately 4 percent to and gained 3 percent from other categories (U.S. Bureau of the Census, 1989).

Sources: U.S. Bureau of the Census (1963b: Table 2; 1972: Table 8; 1984b: Table 4).

mitigating the advantages generally believed to accrue to women who enter male occupations.[2]

| | | | The Insurance Industry

The two primary segments of the insurance industry are property/liability, which includes automobile, fire, marine, and casualty insurance and employs approximately 37 percent of the insurance workforce; and health/life, which includes medical and life insurance and employs 56 percent of workers (Helfand et al., 1984). Adjusters, who outnumbered examiners four to one in 1970 (U.S. Bureau of Labor Statistics, 1974b), are concentrated in property/liability. The majority work for insurance companies; others work for adjustment bureaus (groups of adjusters formed by several insurance companies) or independent bureaus, or they are self-employed (U.S. Bureau of Labor Statistics, 1972, 1978c, 1982a). Examiners are employed by insurance companies primarily in health/life (U.S. Bureau of Labor Statistics, 1972, 1978c, 1982a). The differences between adjusters and examiners require discussing them separately.

| | | | Insurance Adjusters

Occupational Content

Until 1970 most insurance adjusters were men (U.S. Bureau of Labor Statistics, 1972): hence the common title, "claims men" (Hinkle, 1970a; Ross, 1970). They represented either the insurance company or the insured, and their services were required after a claim was initiated to recover accident damages. Adjusters investigated all kinds of property/liability claims, but the bulk of their cases dealt with bodily injury and property damage resulting from automobile accidents (Rosenbloom, 1968:58). They checked the facts surrounding a claim, took statements from involved parties and witnesses, viewed the scene of the mishap, and accumulated all accident and medical reports. After obtaining sufficient data, they decided any contributory negligence, whether the insured's policy covered the accident, and the possibility of fraud; and they ultimately determined the company's responsibility for paying damages (Rosenbloom, 1968; Ross, 1970; U.S. Bureau of Labor Statistics, 1972). Depending on their experience, in the mid-1960s adjusters could negotiate and settle small to medium-sized claims (usually $150 to $300 for new adjusters and $1,000 to $5,000 for those more experienced); larger claims were referred to supervisors.[3] Some adjusters had limited authority to set the "case reserve"—the money that companies put away for unpaid claims (Rosenbloom, 1968).[4] Thus, the job involved investigation, analysis, evaluation, and negotiation.

In general, adjusters had a great deal of autonomy. They were accountable to supervisors but spent considerable time investigating and negotiating in the field (hence the term "outside adjuster") out of direct supervisory control. Moreover, because adjusters had charge of all the materials in the files on which supervisors could evaluate them, they had a great deal of control over their own evaluation (Ross, 1970). Pressures to close claims quickly often propelled an effort to make quick settlements and omit contradictory materials from the files.

Occupational Qualifications, Entry, and Training

Despite their discretionary power and limited freedom from supervision, claims men were normally midlevel employees, and the claims department was viewed as a "junior partner" in the insurance company because it disbursed rather than received money (Ross, 1970).[5] Claims work was an entry-level job that could lead to underwriting, sales, or management. There were no specific qualifications; companies preferred college graduates but accepted individuals with only high school diplomas (U.S. Bureau of Labor Statistics, 1972). In 1970 the median education level of men in adjusting and examining was 15.2 years (U.S. Bureau of the Census, 1973a), though some adjusters had relevant expertise such as automobile repair or legal training. Given the financial discretion the work involved, companies did generally require comprehensive applications, and they checked work and credit records (Rosenbloom, 1968). A survey of insurance adjusters (Ross, 1970) found that many got their jobs by answering newspaper advertisements or through friends in claims work; others just drifted into adjusting. An individual rarely planned a career in adjusting; it was an available job in a growing bureaucracy.

State licensing requirements for adjusters varied in the late 1960s and early 1970s; many included a written examination on adjusting, proof of completing a course in insurance or loss adjusting, minimum age and state residence, and character affidavits or surety bonding (U.S. Bureau of Labor Statistics, 1972). However, states exempted insurance company employees from state licensing requirements (U.S. Bureau of Labor Statistics, 1974b).

Although some companies, insurance institutes, and colleges offered courses in claims adjusting, most training took place on the job under the supervision of an experienced adjuster. Most companies provided a beginning adjuster with a two- to six-week orientation seminar, after which some combined on-the-job training with home study (U.S. Bureau of Labor Statistics, 1972). In general, supervisors and more experienced colleagues tended to pass on claims procedures informally to new adjusters (Ross, 1970).

High turnover in this low-paying entry-level position frequently resulted in a shortage of experienced personnel; informal hiring practices and casual instruction on procedures meant that adjusters were often poorly selected and undertrained (Rosenbloom, 1968). In consequence, relatively high losses were common—a problem that may have accelerated changes in the occupation during the 1970s.

Despite pay and status comparable to those of ordinary white-collar jobs, many adjusters saw themselves as professionals and their jobs as careers (Ross, 1970). They had more autonomy than many persons in similar positions, such as the freedom to schedule their work; benefits included a company car and, for supervisory positions, expense accounts. They had little status or organizational power, but theirs was a respectable, middle-range job with the chance for upward mobility. It involved little direct supervision from others and a limited range of decision-making power. However, changes beginning in the 1960s eventually revolutionized the work environment, job content, and position of insurance adjusters.

Industrial and Occupational Change

Events that began to unfold in the late 1960s ultimately transformed the work of adjusters, particularly those in automobile adjusting.

The changing relationship between insurer and insured. In the 1960s, a time of increased social consciousness, critics challenged the traditional adversarial relationship between insurance companies and claimants as inimical to the needs of the injured victim (Keeton and O'Connell, 1965; Caddy, 1986). The critics cited problems with recovery on difficult-to-measure damages such as pain and suffering, the requirement that the claim be settled in one sum in exchange for a final release, and the contingency-fee arrangement that gave attorneys a financial interest in the outcome (Hodosh, 1980).

As state legislatures implemented alternatives, they slowly eroded the legal doctrine of contributory negligence, which allowed no payment if the claimant had any responsibility for an accident. For some time, the insurance industry and juries had informally ignored this strict view (Ross, 1970; Magarick, 1978), but the enactment of "comparative negligence" laws formalized partial recovery when the claimant was only partly negligent.

No-fault insurance, which required an insurer to pay regardless of liability, was the second step in weakening the adversarial system. No-fault threatened the profits of the insurance industry and trial lawyers—who received approximately one-third of settlements in personal-injury suits—both of whom lobbied heavily against it. Nevertheless, by 1984 twenty-three states had some form of no-fault insurance (*Consumer Reports*, 1984). State legislatures set the terms, standardized required and optional coverage of the insurance product, set time limits on claims payments, and required companies to develop procedures to accommodate policyholders (Cissley, 1977; U.S. Bureau of Labor Statistics, 1979c:44). No-fault laws had a tremendous impact on the insurance industry, claims departments, and insurance adjusters. They limited the need for investigating and determining liability and thus reduced the work of insurance adjusters.

Extracontractual liability. In general, the "consumer era" accelerated change in insurance products and claims procedures.[6] For example, many states adopted fair-claims acts, requiring insurance companies to investigate and settle claims promptly and fairly (*National Underwriter*, 1970; Hodosh, 1980). Change in other tort laws affected insurance companies and consumers. The weakening of traditional defenses exposed individuals and establishments to additional liabilities (Hodosh, 1980). Extracontractual liability emerged as a legal doctrine, subjecting the insured and the insurance company to new liabilities beyond the formal contract. As a result, the number of insurance policies increased, and existing policies were expanded.

Routinization. Several factors led to routinizing claims procedures. First, no-fault insurance and fair-claims laws required standardized products and put time constraints on claims settlements. Second, complex legalities and expanded liability increased business volume, as did rising income and population growth; one consequence for insurance companies was overwhelming paperwork. Third, insurance companies faced increased financial pressure from low profits, losses, high inflation, and increasingly competitive conditions (Phipps, 1989). The expanded volume of business, in tandem with pressure to increase profits, meant settling more claims with less available capital (*National Underwriter*, 1970). Thus, standardized products, coverage expansion, and time and financial pressure dictated that companies alter claims procedures. They responded by routinizing the claims process.

Insurance firms first transferred property-loss adjusting (particularly in automobile accident or theft cases) from field adjusters to claims workers in insurance offices or claims centers. Next, they shifted simple bodily injury claims from field to office adjusters, who investigated claims by telephone and mail. Finally, they automated claims forms and procedures and transformed office adjusting from manual to electronic processing.

No-fault laws reduced the importance of determining liability in automobile claims, leaving only the extent of damage to be determined. Companies adopted new estimating procedures that involved less fieldwork. Illustrative was the drive-in claim center, where claimants with minor automobile damage could come for an inspection and often receive a check within twenty minutes (*Best's Review, Property/Casualty*, 1975, 1976). Increasing use of these centers reduced the demand for outside adjusters (U.S. Bureau of Labor Statistics, 1974b, 1978c, 1982a).

A second important change was the shift to "inside adjusters" who handled straightforward claims by telephone. Although inside adjusters had to learn the basics of insurance lines and applicable laws and how to take statements, verify damages, and settle cases by phone (Casey, 1970:38), the job was more routine than outside work and lacked the latter's autonomy. Further, with the adoption of standardized procedures, manuals, and contracts, even outside jobs involved less fieldwork and more office time. Several interviewees pointed out that insurance companies, wanting to cut the high costs associated with independent adjusters, hired more staff adjusters to handle claims.

In consequence, the number of outside adjusters declined during the 1970s, while the number of inside company adjusters increased. More closely supervised, inside work involved less discretion and more clerical skill. The work resembled that of lower-status insurance examiners in the life/health sector (discussed below). In fact, the 1974–75 *Occupational Outlook Handbook* (U.S. Bureau of Labor Statistics, 1974b) classified inside adjusters under "examiners" rather than "adjusters."

Decision-making for outside adjusters, especially in automobile insurance, also became routinized, reducing their discretionary activity. Companies began to reserve outside adjusters for unusual circumstances when specialized services were needed (Hinkle, 1970b). Following these changes, articles appeared in trade journals counseling male adjusters about other jobs that would use their skills (Casey, 1970; Hinkle, 1970b).

During the same period, trade publications featured articles on the processing of claims by telephone, particularly its implications for employing women. One, for example, characterized telephone or inside adjusting as "an ideal job for a woman with a college background" (Casey, 1970). Because a telephone adjuster was "only a voice to many people," according to a commentator, she or he had to project empathy, sincerity, and integrity. Apparently, companies assumed that a woman's voice could project those attributes better than a man's, and a growing number of companies began employing women to handle bodily injury claims by phone (Hinkle, 1970b). Industry leaders' linking of women and the telephone was not without precedent: 95 percent of telephone operators were women by 1930 (Rotella, 1981:35). But to whatever extent a demand for clerical and telephone skills may have prompted the hiring of women, from the perspective of insurance companies, telephone adjusting had several advantages. As well as improving customer services, modernizing investigative and adjustment practices, and controlling "claim severity" with lower settlements, it was cheaper and it improved productivity (Casey, 1970).

Computerization. Telephone adjusting was only the beginning of the transformation of the work of adjusters. Another important change was the computerization of claims. The insurance industry, a leader in office automation in the United States (Werneke, 1982; Cornfield et al., 1988), had initially used computers in accounting and billing, ostensibly to improve its loss record rather than to cut clerical hours (U.S. Bureau of Labor Statistics, 1966). In the late 1960s the industry began to hire computer scientists and systems analysts (U.S. Bureau of Labor Statistics, 1979c), who developed sophisticated software with built-in calculating and decision-making functions (Baran, 1985). Soon whole departments—particularly claims, underwriting, and actuarial services—were automated.

The property/liability sector was the last in the industry to automate, because of the complexity of developing software that could handle the decision-making process. The most standardized property/liability products—automobile and homeowner's insurance—were accommodated into computer software first (Rodda, 1969; U.S. Bureau of Labor Statistics, 1979c). Personal automobile insurance, characterized by high-volume, low-dollar, repetitive transactions and a highly formalized rating method, constituted the largest computerized line in property/liability insurance (Cissley, 1977:191). Because no-fault laws often included time limits for settling claims, it also fostered the use of electronic processing (U.S. Bureau of Labor Statistics, 1978c). By the late 1970s, many adjusters were handling claims interactively through on-line terminals. For example, at the United States Automobile Association, claims handlers took claims over the phone, instantly called up clients' records, and entered the new data directly (McDowell, 1982). This on-line investigation and the authorization of computer-printed checks incorporated clerical functions into the work of adjusters (Baran, 1985).

Computerized processing increased productivity dramatically. It also made individual adjusters' productivity easier to measure, and quotas and incentive pay became more common. In view of those changes, the emphasis on productivity in the property/liability trade journals was not surprising

(Smith, 1977; Duncan, 1978; McDowell, 1982). Before tracing the consequences of these changes on the sex composition of adjusters, I describe the
second occupational specialty.

| | | | Insurance Examiners

Occupational Content

Insurance examiners investigated and reviewed claims, primarily in the life/
health sector of the industry.[7] They checked claims for completeness and
accuracy, verified information in policy files, and calculated benefit payments
(U.S. Bureau of Labor Statistics, 1972). Examiners also maintained records
of settled claims and prepared reports to be submitted to data-processing units
(U.S. Bureau of Labor Statistics, 1978c).

In life insurance, examiners determined liability by comparing data on
the application and death certificate or physician's statement with the policy
file and records, after which they approved or disapproved claims. Examiners
in life/health could generally approve payment up to a certain level, above
which they consulted a senior examiner. In 1976, junior examiners (a position
called claims examiner B) reviewed clear-cut claims not exceeding $50,000; a
senior examiner (a position called claims examiner A) handled larger claims,
though generally less than $100,000 (U.S. Bureau of Labor Statistics, 1978a).

The *Dictionary of Occupational Titles* (U.S. Department of Labor, Employment and Training Administration, 1977)—which assesses job complexity
with regard to people, data, and things—rated adjusters' and examiners' work
as equally complex with regard to data and things: both "analyze" data (fairly
complex on the data scale) and "handle" things (a low-complexity task). But
on the people dimension, the *DOT* rates examiners far below adjusters: examiners "speak or signal" (low-complexity tasks); adjusters "negotiate" (a high-
complexity task). Examiners rarely worked in the field and always did more
clerical work and earned less than adjusters. Probably for these reasons, the
occupation has always employed more women: in 1970 half of examiners were
women (U.S. Bureau of Labor Statistics, 1972), while most adjusters were
men (U.S. Bureau of Labor Statistics, 1974b).

Occupational Qualifications, Entry, and Training

In 1970, claims examiners resembled adjusters with respect to the qualifications required. While preferring college graduates, companies accepted
applicants with high school degrees, particularly if they had clerical training
or experience. Sometimes clerical workers moved up to examiner positions,
although advancement to the senior positions usually required some college

background. Traditionally, examiners had to learn their company's settlement procedures and policy provisions, as well as medical and legal terminology; and they needed writing, speaking, and mathematics skills (U.S. Bureau of Labor Statistics, 1974b). Examiners were trained on the job, under the direction of a claims manager, although the Life Office Management Association (LOMA) did offer educational programs for claims examiners (U.S. Bureau of Labor Statistics, 1974b).

Industrial and Occupational Change

The industrial events that affected the adjuster occupation similarly affected examiners. Complex legalities and increased liabilities led to tightened procedures and heightened coverage, as did population growth and rising personal income. In addition, employers were increasingly offering life/health insurance as an employee benefit, thus expanding coverage (Phipps, 1989).

Because the life insurance industry, where examiners are concentrated, was the first to use computers in business procedures, the computerization of claims affected examiners much earlier than adjusters (U.S. Bureau of Labor Statistics, 1966). The already relatively standardized procedures in life/health were readily accommodated in computer software. For example, in processing death-benefit claims, examiners had only to verify eligibility and issue checks (U.S. Bureau of Labor Statistics, 1979c). By the early 1970s integrated electronic systems had the capacity to identify all a claimant's policies, examine the current status of each, compute the amount payable, issue a check, and post the amount to the appropriate ledger (U.S. Bureau of Labor Statistics, 1979c). Health and disability claims were more complex because policies paid for services as well as for protection and indemnity (U.S. Bureau of Labor Statistics, 1979c); as a result, their processing took longer to become fully automated.

Computerization of group-health claims developed phenomenally from 1970 to 1980. Consider Braden's (1979) description of Prudential Insurance Company's conversion from manual to computerized claim processing. In 1976 Prudential began converting to a computerized payment system to eliminate duplication of effort and calculation errors. One-time entry by data clerks made files available on-line to examiners. Most examiners completed an average claim in fewer than thirty screen displays with a response time of about two seconds each. The computerized system automatically reviewed claims, calculated payments, and produced checks that explained benefits. This computerized accounting improved accuracy, saved time, and reduced personnel costs. Computerization also facilitated the monitoring of examiners' performance. When an examiner began work, she keyed in her identification number and time, and an off-line printer displayed any attempt to do unauthorized work. Even early in its use, the system increased productivity by 15 percent.

Summary

With the routinization of claims, the work of many outside adjusters was lost, while the number of inside staff jobs increased. The clerical component of the work grew; decision-making declined. Automated systems built both adjuster and examiner decision-making into the software, eliminating the need for operator reviews and bookkeeping. Thus, these systems enabled insurance companies to improve productivity and cost effectiveness; reduce errors and personnel; cut turnaround time on claims and improve customer service; build in flexibility to accommodate change; and facilitate control, security, and management reporting (Dubinsky, 1982; Sampson, 1983).

While senior examiners and specialized adjusters who handled difficult claims retained most of their original duties, the standardized procedures and computerized systems clericalized the work of most examiners and adjusters.[8] Claims processing on computer-assisted terminals no longer involved analysis and calculation. Work content was simplified and the work process more readily controlled. This change gave rise to a new job within examining and adjusting—"claims processor," a routine data-processing job. Essentially, these changes downgraded the occupation, as the 1980 census job titles reflect. Whereas the original titles denoted the investigative aspect of the occupation (adjuster, investigator, examiner), the 1980 titles for claims workers are "processor," "representative," and "taker" (U.S. Bureau of the Census, 1960a:49; 1971:O-37; 1982b:O-44).

I I I I Women's Entry into Insurance Adjusting and Examining

The changes described above prompted women's disproportionate entry into the adjuster and examiner occupation during the 1970s. There is little doubt that the increased employment of women as insurance adjusters, examiners, and investigators directly resulted from the move of adjusters into the office and from technologically based changes in job content. In her excellent analysis of the insurance industry, Baran (1985) found that as companies computerized both claims and underwriting, departments that had been over 60 percent male became disproportionately female. Both employers and workers see low-autonomy clerical work and data processing as women's work, so the clericalization and automation of claims processing led the occupation's sex label to shift, orienting employers to women workers and driving men out.

Routinization of the claims process clearly transformed the work of adjusters and examiners, making it less attractive to men. Reliance on electronic data processing eliminated much of the discretion in health and life examiner jobs. It also increased supervision and brought about electronic monitoring of employees' output to meet production quotas. A drop in the median age

Table 11.2
Median and Mean Real Earnings of Employed Insurance Adjusters and Examiners, by Sex, 1959–1979

	Women	Men	Female/Male Ratio
Median earnings (in 1967 $)			
1959	$4,145	$6,630	62.5
1969	4,766	8,379	56.9
1979	4,533	7,427	61.0
Mean earnings for full-time employees (in 1967 $)			
1969	$5,302	$9,017	58.8
1979	5,089	8,545	59.6

Sources: U.S. Bureau of the Census (1963a: Table 25; 1973a: Table 1; 1981a: Table 281; 1984c: Table 1).

of female adjusters and examiners—from 35.3 years in 1960 to 29 years in 1980—suggests that insurance companies hired younger women workers with limited experience to fill less desirable positions. In contrast, in 1980 the median age of male adjusters and examiners was 36.6, almost two years older than it had been in 1960 (U.S. Bureau of the Census, 1963a: Table 4; 1981a: Table 280). This indicates that older men, probably concentrated in the most desirable positions, continued in the occupation, while few young men entered it (Phipps, 1989). Further, an increase in the number of job titles for the adjuster and examiners occupation—from eighteen in 1960 to thirty in 1980 (U.S. Bureau of the Census, 1960a:49; 1971:O-37; 1982b:P-44)—is consistent tent with job fragmentation and a demarcation of "women's" and "men's" work (Baron and Bielby, 1986).

Thus, automation-based deskilling and erosion of decision-making and discretionary power in claims adjusting stimulated men's departure.[9] Moreover, the real earnings of male adjusters and examiners dropped substantially during the 1970s. As a result, insurance adjusting and examining became less lucrative and hence less attractive to men. Table 11.1 traces this trend, showing a loss between 1970 and 1980 of more than 6,000 male adjusters and examiners. Occupational growth during the 1970s exacerbated the shortage of adjusters and examiners. The occupation added some 67,000 new jobs in the 1970s.

Companies took advantage of men's departure—and sometimes hastened it—by replacing men with women at lower wages. Table 11.2 shows that female adjusters and examiners have always earned about 60 percent of what their male counterparts make, so substituting men for women reduced insurance companies' total wage bill. Moreover, adjusters' and examiners' real earnings dropped during the 1970s for both sexes, but men's real earnings dropped over four times as much as women's. In addition, male and female adjusters' and examiners' average earnings declined, compared with all male and female workers in the labor force (U.S. Bureau of the Census, 1973a, 1981a), but in 1979 full-time women adjusters and examiners earned 106 percent of the women's labor force average, while full-time claims men earned only 99 percent of the average for all men.

Despite its declining wages for women, insurance adjusting and examining took advantage of the large supply of women entering the labor force during the 1970s. The projected growth of the occupation, reported in the *Occupational Outlook Handbook* since the early 1970s (U.S. Bureau of Labor Statistics, 1972, 1974b, 1978c), could have stimulated women's entry, but the unevenness of male and female employment implicates other variables.

In 1972 the Equal Employment Opportunity Commission (EEOC) put insurance on its list of industries to be watched for noncompliance with federal antidiscrimination regulations (Dunetz, 1977). Six years later the Office of Federal Contract Compliance Programs (OFCCP), charged with enforcing the antidiscrimination and affirmative-action regulations of Presidential Executive Order 11246 (amended 11375), targeted the insurance, banking, and mining industries for special scrutiny. It is difficult to ascertain whether the attention of these federal agencies contributed to women's increased representation in the adjuster and examiner occupations. However, insurance examining, already 50 percent female in 1971 (U.S. Bureau of Labor Statistics, 1972), does not offer evidence of EEOC or OFCCP action. Limited statistical evidence shows the highest proportion of female entry into life insurance examining occurring between 1966 and 1976 (Phipps, 1989:106),[10] long before the OFCCP targeting and limited EEOC action.[11]

Insurance adjusting, a heavily male-dominated occupation in 1970 (U.S. Bureau of Labor Statistics, 1972), seems more likely than examining to have attracted enforcement agents' efforts. Charges filed with the EEOC, leading to a 1974 lawsuit, did account for some women's entry into insurance adjusting. In *Wetzel v. Liberty Mutual Insurance Company* (1974, 1978) a U.S. district court ruled that Liberty Mutual had discriminated against women claims representatives by not hiring and promoting them into claims adjuster positions. This case against one of the ten largest U.S. property/liability companies presumably had influence beyond the company as well, but neither trade magazines nor government agencies' reports provide any evidence that federal intervention precipitated women's entry into adjusting or examining. In fact, the trade journal articles on women as "inside adjusters" were published before 1972, the year the EEOC targeted the industry, and even as of 1978 federal compliance activities were not of a scope to affect the occupational distribution of women (U.S. Commission on Civil Rights, 1982; Reskin and Hartmann, 1986). In 1980 the OFCCP subjected the insurance industry to special scrutiny, allocating 11 percent of its resources for compliance reviews and investigation of employment practices. These investigations revealed that women and minorities continued to be placed in low-paying clerical jobs (U.S. Commission on Civil Rights, 1982). So while the EEOC played a part in increasing the number of women in insurance adjusting, government enforcement of antidiscrimination laws probably had only a minimal role in prompting women's overall employment as adjusters and examiners.

In summary, then, women's disproportionate entry into insurance adjusting and examining was primarily due to routinized procedural and technological changes that altered the work content and rewards and, ultimately, the cultural sex label placed upon the occupation, making it less attractive to men. The inability to attract men and the transformed nature of the work made adjusting and examining jobs more accessible to women. Substantial occupational growth and high turnover allowed feminization to occur rapidly.

Consequences for Earnings of the Changing Labor Process

Since changes in job content, including technological changes in claims processing, coincided with and hastened the feminization of adjusters, examiners, and investigators, it is difficult to assign unique causal responsibility to technological change or to feminization for subsequent changes in the occupation's status and rewards. Nevertheless, the feminization of formerly predominantly male occupations may be accompanied by declining rewards (Carter and Carter, 1981). Predominantly male outside adjusters have always outearned predominantly female inside adjusters (U.S. Bureau of Labor Statistics, 1972, 1974b), and partly for that reason male adjusters and examiners have always earned more than women (see Table 11.2). Time-series data show that life insurance occupations with the greatest increased percentage of female employees are those in which real wages declined most (Cornfield et al., 1988). Likewise, Baran (1985) found that the size of the increase in percent female was related to declines in real wages in each sector: between 1968 and 1978, real wages in the life insurance segment of the industry, which had the largest percentage of increase in female labor, declined 6 percent; wages in property/liability, with a small percentage of new female entrants, dropped 3 percent; and wages in medical/health, where little substitution of female labor occurred, actually increased.

Table 11.3 presents real weekly wage changes for examiners in the life insurance industry from 1971 to 1980. Women's representation in claims examiner A positions increased 13.2 percent between 1971 and 1976, while real wages dropped $16.12 a week. Another large decline in real wages, $24.09 weekly, occurred between 1976 and 1980, following a small increase in the percentage of female incumbents. These declines were among the largest in the thirty-seven life insurance occupations surveyed.

Among claims examiner B positions, wages declined by $14 per week

Table 11.3

Change in Percent Female and Real Weekly Wages of Life Insurance Claims Examiners, 1971-1980

	Percentage-Point Increase in Female Representation	Weekly Wage Change (in 1967 $)
Examiner A positions		
1971-76	13.2	-16.12
1976-80	1.1	-24.09
Examiner B positions		
1971-76	16.5	-23.23
1976-80	5.4	-14.38

Note: The sample for the Life-Insurance Industry Wage Survey comprises establishments with 50 or more workers. Examiner A workers handled claims whose dollar value was approximately double those of examiner B.

Sources: Industry Wage Surveys, U.S. Bureau of Labor Statistics (1973a: Table 1; 1978a: Table 67; 1981: Table 1; unpublished tabulations from the U.S. Bureau of Labor Statistics).

after the five years during which women's representation increased most. Given the role of automation in both changes, feminization and wage declines probably occurred concomitantly: firms automated offices, hired women, and reduced wages or failed to raise them to keep pace with inflation. Automation probably affected the more highly skilled claims examiner A later than examiner B jobs, prompting the large real wage declines for examiner A between 1976 and 1980.

Resegregation

Although a fair amount of nominal sex integration occurred in adjusting and examining between 1970 and 1980, it was never genuine integration in which men and women were employed in the same jobs. Internal segregation was the norm, with men retaining the remaining outside-adjuster jobs and monopolizing higher-level examiner specialties, and women concentrated in examining and in inside-adjuster specialties. Thus, a sexual division of labor continued to characterize adjusting and examining.

At some time between 1970 and 1980 equal numbers of women and men worked in this occupation; following this brief period of nominal occupational-level integration, women replaced men as the predominant sex. The absolute loss of over 6,000 male insurance adjusters and examiners between 1970 and 1980 and the increase in the percentage of females from 26 to 60 percent in the same time span mark this formerly male occupation's resegregation as female. Nor did the process end in 1980. U.S. Bureau of Labor Statistics (1989) data indicate that insurance adjusting and examining has continued to feminize, reaching 72 percent female in 1988.

Summary

In sum, women's disproportionate movement into insurance adjusting and examining resulted largely from the routinization and automation of the work process. As claims work moved from outside to inside positions, men abandoned the posts, and firms turned to women to fill them. In automating claims processing, firms made the work exclusively clerical and then hired women in large numbers and at lower wages.

The consequences of technological change and feminization have been vivid. Women adjusters and examiners rarely receive the rewards traditionally associated with entering a male-dominated occupation—not surprisingly, since by the end of the 1970s this was no longer the male occupation it had been, in either its job content or its sex composition. The real wages of the increasingly female workforce—including those of the men who remained in adjusting and examining—declined steadily. This study suggests that what appeared to be occupational sex desegregation, occurring when the work became less attractive to men, at first masked within-occupation segregation and then gradually led to resegregation. This is not to say that women's numerical inroads into insurance adjusting and examining are without value, but they are a small step in a much larger journey.

I I I I **Notes**

Acknowledgments: Special thanks go to Barbara F. Reskin, Katharine M. Donato, H. Laurence Ross, and all the adjusters and examiners I interviewed for their assistance on this chapter. I presented an earlier version at the 1986 annual meeting of the American Sociological Association, New York City. The conclusions offered here are my own and do not necessarily represent the views of the U.S. Bureau of Labor Statistics.

1. Although the detailed census occupational category of insurance adjuster, examiner, and investigator includes many job titles, the primary division is between adjusters and examiners (U.S. Bureau of Labor Statistics, 1972, 1974b, 1978c; also see generally *Best's Review; National Underwriter*), and most job titles can be classified as one or the other. The adjuster category has included investigators since 1939 (U.S. Department of Labor, 1939, 1949, 1965; U.S. Department of Labor, Employment and Training Administration, 1977).

2. I used government documents (including data from the U.S. Census Bureau and the Bureau of Labor Statistics), insurance trade journals, and social science literature in this analysis, supplemented by interviews with ten employed insurance adjusters and examiners.

3. In automobile accidents involving injury, 95 percent of the claims were settled by adjusters through negotiation (Ross, 1970).

4. Required by law in all states, reserves protect the public against claim defaults. If a company consistently sets reserves low, it can be in financial jeopardy; in fact, "underreserving" has been a major cause of insurance company insolvency (Tarangelo, 1977).

5. One woman I interviewed, noting the low regard for claims departments, suggested that many adjusters felt "sour about how they were treated"; she added that "departments such as underwriting were held in high respect because of the emphasis on money coming in the door."

6. President John F. Kennedy ushered in the consumer era in 1962, formulating the rights of consumers to be safe and informed, to have meaningful choices, and to be heard (Hodosh, 1980:40).

7. The small number of examiners working in property/liability primarily supervise claims adjusters and handling.

8. Independent adjusters still perform many of their traditional duties, although the number of such jobs has declined (*Insurance Almanac*, 1961, 1971, 1981). Outside adjusters in company field offices have also retained much of their traditional work. Interviewees suggested that in the 1980s women were slowly entering these positions, with some companies reporting one woman to every four men.

9. Whether the skills necessary to carry out the occupational duties have declined dramatically is questionable. Clerical skills have traditionally been undervalued and underrated, because they are skills used in "women's" work. Computer-mediated work, as Baran (1985:39) pointed out, demands much of the worker, including mental alertness, flexibility in learning new procedures, and more responsibility for data quality (Helfgott, 1960; Baran, 1985). It also demands the ability to conceptualize an entire operation and use abstract symbols. However, with monitoring and routinization, much autonomy has been lost, and autonomy, considered a skill indicator, is often used to justify income inequality (Form, 1987).

10. The Bureau of Labor Statistics applies the general occupational title of "approver" to the diverse job titles (including examiner) used by life insurance companies for the occupational category in question. I use "examiner" to avoid confusion.

11. The EEOC did not become a serious threat to most employers until the appointment of Eleanor Holmes Norton as director in 1977.

Linda A. Detman

12

Women behind Bars: The Feminization of Bartending

Historically, men have dominated bartending. Ethnographic accounts from as recently as 1975 characterized bartenders as authoritarian, tough, strong, and male. Bartenders were thought to "represent a stronghold of masculinity and authority" (Spradley and Mann, 1975:71). Novels and motion pictures have long depicted bars as dark, smoky rooms that are loud and dangerous, sometimes fronts for drug dealing, prostitution, and other illicit activities. "Bars in America are not as much deviant settings as they are places of potential deviant activity" (Cavan, 1966:37)—in short, not the kind of place a "self-respecting lady" would seek employment. Nonetheless, women have long worked in bars as waitresses and barmaids, serving food and drinks; the movement of large numbers of women to the other side of the bar, however, has been relatively recent. In 1890 women held 146 of the 55,806 bartending jobs in the country (Hooks, 1947), and their job share crept up to only 2.5 percent by 1940. In 1970 women constituted 21.2 percent of employed bartenders, but by 1980 that percentage had more than doubled to 44.3 percent (see Table 12.1), and in 1988 women were nearly half (49.6 percent) of all bartenders (U.S. Bureau of Labor Statistics, 1989). This chapter identifies the factors that permitted and then hastened women's acceptance behind the bar.[1]

Table 12.1
Number of Employed Bartenders, by Sex, 1970, 1980

	Total	Female	Male	Percent Female
1970	215,788	45,662	170,126	21.2
1980	318,425	141,142	177,283	44.3
Net increase	102,637	95,480	7,157	23.1

Source: U.S. Bureau of the Census (1984a).

| | | | A History of Women and Bartending

Women worked as brewers, innkeepers, and wine and ale merchants as early as 1750 in England (Pinchbeck, 1977). In the United States, however, census data extending back to 1890 indicate that through 1930 women never attained more than five of every thousand bartending jobs. Customs that excluded women from settings where liquor was served kept women out of bartending jobs and affected waitresses as well. To understand women's recent advance in bartending, we must look at the difficulties they had getting work in related jobs. Finding employment in the food-service industry was difficult, partly because of widespread reluctance to hire women to do any kind of work in establishments that sold liquor. Waitresses fought with their union to gain the right to compete for jobs in places that sold liquor, but in winning their fight, they simultaneously encouraged a system that kept women out of bartending jobs for the next thirty years (Cobble, 1989b).

Constitutionally conferred police power let states control who could own, work in, and patronize bars. In the late nineteenth and early twentieth centuries many enacted laws that prohibited women from working in places where liquor was sold, much less working behind the bar (Baker, 1969; Baer, 1978; Cobble, 1988). Selling liquor was among those occupations from which states prohibited women "to protect their morals and their health" (Baker, 1969:251). Some women's organizations such as the Consumers' League of the City of New York, the New York State Bureau of Women in Industry, and the Women's Trade Union League had a hand in instituting these restrictions, partly through their efforts to secure maximum-hours laws.[2] But proposed legislation meant to exclude women from serving liquor met stiff opposition from waitress unionists, and proponents of such statutes abandoned the pursuit when the labor shortage sparked by World War I extended to waiters and bartenders—requiring women to fill some of their positions—and a few years later when Prohibition rendered the effort superfluous.

With the repeal of Prohibition, proposals for laws prohibiting women from serving liquor reappeared. While these laws no doubt reflected the sentiment of the time that any involvement with liquor was corrupting, their end result was to keep the more lucrative waiting jobs off limits to women. At the 1933 Hotel and Restaurant Employees and Bartenders International union (HREBI) convention, resolutions called for blanket restrictions on women serving liquor because it would morally corrupt them. Again, waitresses resisted, blocking the resolution. Their active lobbying prevented several state legislatures from passing proposed statutes (Cobble 1988:16). An analysis by Dorothy Sue Cobble (1989b), on which this section draws heavily, discussed in detail the waitresses' struggle for jobs in liquor service. Some waitresses thought that men had a legitimate claim to certain types of work related to liquor, and many believed that women should not serve cocktails unless they were also serving food. It must be kept in mind that waitresses were striving for the right to work as waitresses in such establishments; the right to *mix* liquor was less important to them. Such a sentiment can be understood when we consider that waitresses who were union members recognized the territorial rights of the practitioners of other crafts. Many union waitresses did not "feel right" encroaching on another craft's territory in serving drinks, much less mixing them, unless they also served food. By 1936 most union locals had granted waitresses the right to work in establishments that sold liquor, but they accepted a provision in these agreements that denied bartending jobs to women. Cobble (1988) pointed out that waitresses, concerned about their own economic security—as working-class women, their position was precarious—feared that insisting on women's right to work *behind* the bar would jeopardize their opportunity to work in establishments that served liquor.

Before the 1940s, cultural attitudes labeled any work involving liquor as eminently corruptible to women. Society frowned on women's presence in bars, and employers and patrons of such establishments, being exclusively male, strove to preserve bars as a refuge for men. Because of this, it's no wonder that women's representation in bartending was small and that waitresses who needed and sought jobs in establishments selling liquor encountered such resistance.

After allowing women to work as waitresses in places serving liquor, it was the male-dominated HREBI, that played a crucial role in keeping women out of bartending. Until 1942 the union's stance was that "bartenders' work [is] a cloister for the male gender" (Babcock et al., 1975:280). But when World War II recreated the shortage of male bartenders that had occurred during World War I, barmaids often replaced them (Josephson, 1956:297). The union, not wanting to risk a takeover by nonunion workers, allowed this influx of women in order to maintain union control over the craft of bartending and its work standards. By admitting women into bartending during the war the union actually increased its membership (Josephson, 1956). However, when veteran male bartenders returned after the war, female bartenders "constitute[d] a knotty problem for [the] International Union," according to

HREBI's acting president Hugo Ernst. In the April 1946 issue of the union's trade journal, the *Catering Industry Employee*, he reported on a resolution that the union's General Executive Board approved:

> Few, indeed, are the number of women physically and temperamentally qualified to endure the hardships connected with tending bar, quite apart from the fact that *our International Union has held, during its entire history, that tending bar is a man's job.* . . . Since the emergency which occasioned the employment of barmaids [as bartenders] has ceased to exist, the work of tending bar must revert to men in accordance with the traditions of our International Union, and . . . barmaids must be replaced wherever and whenever feasible with men. . . . Let's all cooperate in an effort to put into effect again the *traditional principle of our International Union that bartending is a man's job!* (Ernst, 1946:4–5; emphasis added)

Citing the union's tradition of bartending as male work and the G.I. Bill that ensured veterans' claims on their former jobs, the union effectively shut women out of unionized bartending.

Legitimation for segregating the sexes and excluding women from typically male jobs is cloaked in stereotypical thinking about differences between the sexes in strength and ability required to do various jobs (Ferree, 1987). Male bartenders—afraid that female bartenders would work for less—claimed that women could not be "'proficient mixologists,' and were not 'emotionally or temperamentally suited for the job'" (Cobble, 1988:19). Endorsing the cultural sentiment of the time that liquor was inherently corrupting, they held that women would be unable to control patrons who imbibed too much. The view that alcohol was corrupting also justified the claim that women should be protected from liquor. Protective legislation reflecting such paternalistic concerns reinforced stereotypes of women's inability to tend bar. These so-called protective laws—particularly maximum-hours laws and weight-lifting restrictions—hindered the few women who did manage to find jobs in bartending by characterizing them as unfit for the work. In some states specific statutes ensured females' exclusion from bartending.[3]

In addition to the union's renewed opposition, various exclusionary statutes, for which the union also lobbied, prevented most women from bartending before the 1970s. The union's success at crafting legislation effectively excluded women from *all* bartending jobs, union or not. In 1945 a host of states passed laws, in part as a result of efforts by HREBI, forbidding women to tend bar unless their fathers or husbands owned the bar. A state exclusionary law was first challenged in 1948, when two women bar owners and two of their women employees challenged Michigan's law on the grounds that the statute hurt them economically. When their suit, accompanied by twenty-four affidavits from similarly situated women, reached the Supreme Court (*Goesaert v.*

Cleary, 1948), a six-judge majority upheld the exclusionary legislation, citing moral and social problems associated with women tending bar and women's need for male protection in such establishments:

> Michigan could, beyond question, forbid all women from working behind a bar. . . . The fact that women may now achieve the virtues that men have long claimed as their prerogative and now indulge in vices that men have long practiced, does not preclude the States from drawing a sharp line between the sexes, certainly, in such matters as the regulation of the liquor traffic. . . . Since the line they have drawn is not without basis in reason, we cannot give ear to the suggestion that the real impulse behind this legislation was an unchivalrous desire of male bartenders to try to monopolize the calling. (Quoted in Babcock et al., 1975:94–95)

In response to this historic Supreme Court ruling, bartender locals of the Hotel and Restaurant Employees and Bartenders' International launched a campaign to help preserve bartending as an all-male occupation (Cobble, 1988), and HREBI published pamphlets showcasing their successful efforts. Buried in the 1949 HREBI convention proceedings was a pledge to "initiate work throughout the country to gain adoption of local ordinances and state laws which will help raise the standards of the liquor industry . . . like . . . the anti-barmaid laws being sought in many states" (*Officers Report and Daily Convention Proceedings*, 1949). The June issue of the *Catering Industry Employee* (1949:15) reported the union's support for a proposed Ohio law that would forbid women's employment as bartenders. In an effort to justify this stance, the article stated that the union's objective was "clearly not discrimination since 45% of our employees are women." It went on to insist that waitresses considered tending bar a man's job and that "employers prefer male bartenders because they wield greater authority on the job."

In sum, women's struggle to work behind the bar was hampered by social conventions regarding women's proper role in liquor dispensing, by union opposition from both male bartenders interested in protecting their turf and waitresses who condoned the idea of preserving craft spheres, and by state exclusionary laws that kept the door to bartending virtually shut to women until the 1970s.

In 1971 these barriers began to crumble with a major assault on state exclusionary laws. That year, would-be female bartenders successfully used Title VII of the 1964 Civil Rights Act to challenge statutes prohibiting women from tending bar in *Sail'er Inn, Inc. v. Kirby, McCriminon v. Daley, Krause v. Sacramento Inn* (see Babcock et al., 1975). In the same year, at its thirty-seventh general convention, the HREBI passed a pro-women resolution that called for expanded efforts to organize women workers, more government- and union-run twenty-four-hour day-care centers, liberalized tax deductions for child care, equal pay and opportunity, maternity leaves, and education and training programs to help women upgrade their qualifications. This resolution purported to improve women's chance for employment in the eating-and-drinking-places industry, but the question of women tending bar had fueled the debate,[4] so this resolution may have sought in part to soothe women's growing dissatisfaction with their exclusion from bartending jobs.

Also probably contributing to the passage of the resolution was the HREBI's opposition to the Equal Rights Amendment. At the same convention, the HREBI had thrown its support behind the AFL-CIO's effort to stop the ERA (*Officers Report and Daily Convention Proceedings*, 1971), which the HREBI membership seemed to fear would further erode protective legislation already weakened by Title VII and leave working women vulnerable. The struggle for passage of the Equal Rights Amendment engendered passionate protest because bartenders perceived it as potentially opening bartending to women. By tossing a bone to women in the form of this resolution, the union hoped to prevent its female members from getting on the ERA bandwagon. A major coup for the union was having its women members endorse its position on protective legislation and the ERA. Vice-president Myra Wolfgang framed the problem as a *class* issue, contending that other unions had been co-opted to do the work of white, middle-class feminists. Testifying in 1970 before the Senate Judiciary Committee concerning Title VII, Wolfgang had said, "We, who want equal opportunity, equal pay for equal work and equal status for women, know that frequently we obtain real equality through a difference in treatment rather than identity in treatment" (quoted in Babcock et al., 1975: 279).

Despite the defeat of the ERA, the invalidation of state statutes against female bartenders opened bartending to women, and subsequently, union opposition to women's presence behind the bar declined. The HREBI, which enjoyed control over more than a quarter of all employees in the food-and-beverage industry at its peak in the 1950s, had declined in strength by the 1970s, particularly among bartenders (Cobble, 1989b). In 1980 only about one in nine bartenders belonged to the union, now named the Hotel Employees and Restaurant Employees International Union (Filer, 1988), and by 1989, HERE International's director of research and education estimated bartenders' membership at 7.5 percent (Grogan, 1989). Although this analysis emphasizes the role of the union in segregating bartending jobs by excluding women from union jobs and lobbying for legislation, the social and historical context in which the liquor-service struggle arose had a pronounced effect, particularly for nonunionized bars and restaurants. Because the union had played such an important role in galvanizing male bartenders against females, however, the decline in union strength probably contributed to the feminization of bartending by weakening another barrier to women's entry.[5] In support of this possibility, Cobble (1989b) has speculated that women probably initially obtained bartending jobs in nonunion establishments. A former vice-president of the union supported Cobble's hunch, saying that nonunion establishments were especially quick to hire women, because they did not demand the union's standard asking wage. As their numbers in these settings increased, public opposition to women in bartending weakened, and union resistance became futile.

After Congress passed the 1964 Civil Rights Act barring sex discrimination in employment, then, it was only a matter of time until the courts struck down state laws deterring women from tending bar. These early 1970s court cases eliminated a major obstacle to women's access to bartending jobs.

I I I I The 1970s: A Decade of Change

The 1970s brought other changes that contributed to women's gains in bartending. During the struggle the occupation itself was changing. Consider how the Department of Labor reworded its description of this occupation in its *Occupational Outlook Handbook* between 1972 and 1980.[6] The 1972–73 edition advised that "bar *boys*" and "bus *boys*" who wanted to become bartenders should "watch the bartender at work, and when *he* has time to give instruction they can learn how to mix drinks and do other tasks" (U.S. Bureau of Labor Statistics, 1972:342; emphasis added). This description assumed that women did not and should not hope to tend bar. However, the next edition of the *OOH* extended the same advice to "bus girls" and mentioned women bartenders, who, it noted, constituted about one-fourth of the bartenders who were employed full time (U.S. Bureau of Labor Statistics, 1974b). The 1976–77 edition of the *OOH* marked a turn toward sex-neutral language. It replaced the term "bar boy" with "bartender helper," made all its references to bartenders sex-neutral, and remarked that women were a growing proportion of bartenders in the industry (U.S. Bureau of Labor Statistics, 1976). Since the entire volume was purged of sexist language at this time, however, it is not clear to what extent the changes in the bartender entry were a reflection of change in the cultural conception of bartenders, a recognition of women's increasing numbers in the occupation, or part of an effort to placate feminists.

According to a vocational-guidance publication, the bartender's main job is to prepare and serve drinks made from beers, wines, and distilled liquors (*Brief 544*, 1986:1). Yet bartenders do much more than serve drinks; they also serve snacks, prepare garnishes and appetizers, take orders and charge customers, inventory and order supplies, and stock the bar. Bartenders are also responsible for creating attractive displays behind the bar, washing glassware, keeping the premises neat, and cleaning up at closing time. In large establishments a bartender's helper assists with these tasks. Interacting with customers is also a big part of the job; a rich cultural lore surrounds bartenders' ability to listen to patrons' troubles (*Time*, 1972; *Newsweek*, 1975). As one bartender I interviewed put it, "You need to be an Ann Landers, psychiatrist, babysitter, divorce lawyer, and bouncer." The vocational-guidance publication reinforced the need for good interpersonal skills, including friendliness, good listening skills, patience, tact, and the ability to please guests and handle stress (*Brief 544*, 1986).[7]

Many of these desired qualities for bartenders—especially the ability to provide fast, efficient service, to be a good listener, and to work well with people—are stereotypically female traits. Indeed, many of the female bartenders I interviewed felt that they were better able than men to manage unruly patrons, to cut off people's drinking, and to interact with customers.[8] Ironically, while Spradley and Mann (1975:4) characterized women's supporting roles in bars as "serving wenches, hostesses, bunnies, barmaids, or cocktail waitresses, [as] extension[s] of the traditional female role in the home," these aspects of bartending—which have not changed from the decades when the occupation was overwhelmingly male—were not sufficient for its feminization as long as male bartenders were able to exclude women. Although bartending involves stereotypically female characteristics, they have not become more important in bartending during its period of feminization, so they do not explain women's growing representation. Indeed, they demonstrate the irrelevance of gender-role stereotypes for governing an occupation's sex composition: if these stereotyped characteristics influenced bartending's sex composition, we would have to wonder why men dominated the job for so long.

The work that bartenders perform did not significantly change over the decade in which it feminized, although the 1974–75 issue of the *Occupational Outlook Handbook* did indicate a change in how some bartenders worked. It described an automatic mixing device that could "increase bartender efficiency and also reduce skill requirements" (U.S. Bureau of Labor Statistics, 1974b:342). The "Electra-Bar" hooks a cash register up to a computer so that when the bartender pushes a register button, the device mixes the drink automatically. By also monitoring receipts and inventory and minimizing waste, it can cut down on bartenders' work (*Business Week*, 1970). However, in contrast to some feminizing occupations in which dramatic changes in technology precipitated an influx of women, bartending is still done today pretty much as it always has been done. The industry, at least in the United States, has largely ignored the Electra-Bar.[9] Around 1970 the industry introduced a device known as a liquor gun, which hooks up a standard liquor bottle to a hose and nozzle that dispense a single shot. Liquor guns control costs by regulating the quantity of liquor dispensed, and they are quite common today. However, most bartenders I interviewed denied that the guns have deskilled the job; bartenders still must know how to mix drinks, which is the real skill involved.[10] An exception was a woman who began bartending before such devices were in use and who felt that the purpose of the liquor gun was partly to decrease the job's skill.

Changes within bartenders' primary work setting—eating and drinking places—have had an impact, albeit limited, on how they do their job. The introduction of new technologies and increased productivity in food-and-drink service has spurred growth throughout the industry and increased the number of available bartending jobs. Between 1967 and 1982, 48,691 new establishments opened for business, an increase of almost 18 percent. These new establishments contributed to the creation of over 100,000 new jobs for bartenders in the 1970s. Economists for the Bureau of Labor Statistics attributed the rise in the industry's productivity to the simplification of menus; improvements in architectural layout that reduced employees' walking time; the introduction of new cooking technologies; the decline of single-unit, non-chain drinking establishments; and Americans' increased spending on meals away from home (Carnes and Brand, 1977). As a result, employment in the industry category of eating and drinking places doubled between 1958 and 1976. However, while the number of establishments has increased overall, the number of places strictly for drinking actually declined by over 80,000 between 1967 and 1982, to 61,289. This indicates that more establishments are serving both food and alcohol, and it is these that have always been most likely to employ women. Also, the numbers of individual proprietorships and partnerships have declined for both drinking places and eating and drinking places, while the number of those under corporate ownership has expanded, indicating the proliferation of chain establishments. Significantly, an increase in chain establishments has meant a tendency toward standardized work (Carnes and Brand, 1977).

Although the growing number of eating and drinking establishments created thousands of jobs, they have increasingly relied on a part-time labor force. Over an eighteen-year period industry employees' median weekly hours declined by more than 20 percent: from 35.6 hours in 1958 to 28.0 hours in 1976. By 1975, half of all workers employed in eating and drinking places worked part time, compared with just under one-third in 1962. Among bartenders, however, the trend was more complex. Of the 102,637 new bartending jobs, almost one-quarter were part time. Thus, although bartenders of each sex were more likely to work full time in 1980 than in 1970, about 32,000 more women worked part time in 1980 than had done so a decade earlier (see Table 12.2). All of 31,995 new part-time jobs went to women, and 7,864 of those new part-time female bartenders replaced men, whose representation in part-time jobs had declined by that number.

Jobs in eating and drinking places are characterized by rapid turnover, which is partly why the U.S. Department of Labor expects jobs in the industry to continue to be plentiful (U.S. Department of Labor, 1986a; *Bartender,*

Table 12.2
Full- and Part-time Employment in Bartending, by Sex, 1970, 1980

	Women			Men		
	Number Full Time	Number Part Time	Percent Full Time	Number Full Time	Number Part Time	Percent Full Time
1970	25,434	20,228	55.7	112,623	57,503	66.2
1980	88,919	52,223	63.0	127,644	49,639	72.0

Sources: U.S. Bureau of the Census (1984a); 1980 data estimated from U.S. Bureau of the Census (1983a).

1988). Bartending is an occupation that people drift into and out of. The national director of the American Bartenders' Association alluded to this tendency as "dressing-up to play bartender" (Ferguson, 1988). Recent data suggest that few bartenders remain in any one job for more than four years; only a quarter of all bartenders have worked more than nine years for their current employers (Carey, 1988). This high turnover facilitated women's rapid entry into the occupation, since rapid change in personnel, combined with lower skill levels and the lack of job ladders, generates greater "permeability" in occupations' sex composition (Snyder, Hayward, and Hudis, 1978:710). Also because industry expansion made such a large number of bartending positions available in the 1970s, high turnover meant that employers had to fill some of the 200,000-plus bartending jobs a number of times.

Because bartending was traditionally structured as a craft, access to the occupation had been through an informal apprenticeship in which a would-be bartender worked under a professional bartender, typically as a bar boy. Although this apprenticeship structure still exists, the more frequent route to bartending is through on-the-job training. A few bartenders entered through bartending school, and limited evidence suggests that more women than men may have entered the occupation this way. In 1978 the executive vice-president of the American Bartenders School estimated that women made up 60 percent of its 1978 graduates (Butrick, 1978). However, ten years later, 70 percent of the schools on the American Bartenders' Association's list were out of business. The schools lost favor in the industry because many did not train their students consistently and because most establishments offer in-house training (Ferguson, 1988).[11]

During the 1970s the total number of bartenders increased from 215,788 to 318,425, and women's representation increased from 45,662 to 141,142; thus, they filled 93 percent of the 102,637 new jobs (see Table 12.1). By contrast, despite men's traditional monopoly on bartending, they claimed only 7,157 of the new jobs. Clearly, something had made bartending less attractive to men. One significant factor was purely economic—there was simply less

Table 12.3
Median and Mean Earnings of All Employed Bartenders, by Sex, 1969, 1979

	Median			Mean		
	1969	1979[a]	Percent decline	1969	1979[a]	Percent decline
Men	$5,338	$2,659	−50.2	$6,787	$3,364	−50.4
Women	2,848	1,932	−32.2	4,122	2,258	−45.2
Female/male earnings ratio	.534	.727		.607	.671	

[a] In 1969 dollars.

Sources: U.S. Bureau of the Census (1972: Tables 19, 24); 1979 data estimated from U.S. Bureau of the Census (1983a).

money to be made bartending than there had been in 1970. A comparison of 1969 and 1979 average earnings tells the story. Table 12.3, which adjusts 1979 earnings for inflation, shows that bartenders, especially men, experienced a substantial decline in real earnings over the 1970s. This drop did not result from a decline in hours worked, because a greater proportion of bartenders worked full time in 1980 than 1970. It probably reflected real-wage decline resulting in part from a 1966 federal law. In that year Congress amended the Fair Labor Standards Act to allow employers to classify employees in the eating-and-drinking-places industry as "tipped employees" and to pay them 50 percent of the minimum wage (U.S. Bureau of Labor Statistics, 1968).[12] This enforced reliance on tips and decline in wages made bartending less attractive for men. Another factor was the increasing tendency to hire less skilled, nonunionized labor throughout the industry (Carnes and Brand, 1977).

Women's wages also declined, but not so severely. Moreover, to women already employed in other capacities in eating and drinking establishments, bartending may have seemed a more challenging, prestigious, and lucrative alternative, despite real-wage decline. A Chicago columnist wrote in 1934 that for women, bartending was "one step away from the lowest form of livelihood" (cited in Cobble, 1989b:25). However, one woman bartender I interviewed claimed that the chance to make fairly decent money seemed to attract women to the job, and others echoed this sentiment. All the women I interviewed believed that they could make a decent living as bartenders—certainly more than they could earn as waitresses, and without the hassles that waitressing involves. An ethnography of a college-town bar (Spradley and Mann, 1975) unveiled an informal status hierarchy in such establishments that placed bartenders second to managers and owners in terms of prestige. For women, traditionally confined to food or cocktail waitressing with its low wages, low prestige, and sexualization, bartending represents a step up. Bartenders I interviewed confirmed this. Every woman I talked with remarked on the element of control that came with the job. Bartenders control the bar and may dictate the behavior of other workers, and of customers as well. It is a position of strength and power unusual in traditionally female service occupations.

As cocktail waitresses and even as customers, women were in a good position to learn of job opportunities in bartending and to see what the work involved. Cocktail waitresses in particular must have recognized that they could easily acquire the necessary skills to do the job, and many did just that. Yet even as more women entered the world of bartending, discrimination remained. One interviewee told of having to threaten a lawsuit in the early 1970s to get her position. She had previously worked as a cocktail waitress in an upscale hotel bar, where her duties included training newly hired male bartenders. Although she asked to be considered for the job, she was repeatedly denied it in favor of men hired from outside the establishment. It was not until she threatened a lawsuit that she got the bartending job.

Combined with the elimination of formal barriers and ease of entry are two additional factors favoring women's rapid move to positions behind the bar: changing social attitudes about the acceptability of bartending for women, and the growth of a sex-specific demand for female bartenders. When I first asked the national director of the American Bartenders' Association why he thought women have made dramatic inroads into bartending, he claimed that women decided they could get the jobs, partly because the women's liberation movement had given them the confidence to apply (Ferguson, 1988). When I later repeated the question, he attributed part of the reason to the industry's having cleaned itself up: "[bars] aren't dark and sleazy any more." In reference to women's presence in and behind bars forty years ago, Baer (1978:117) asserted, "The bars of the 1940's were not, after all, the saloons of the Wild West, those scenes of frequent brawls and shootouts. Indeed, some of the evidence in the [*Goesaert v. Cleary*] brief suggest[ed], and it is entirely plausible to conclude, that bars are less violent places in recent years *precisely because women patronize and work in them* [emphasis added]." In fact, eating and drinking places, which employed four out of five bartenders in 1980, have undergone a face-lift since then.[13] Chain and franchise establishments are replacing the single-unit enterprises of the past; their share of all drinking establishments increased from 36.6 percent in 1977 to 44.6 percent in 1982 (U.S. Bureau of the Census, 1985b). Also, in an effort to capture some of the increasing food and drink dollars spent away from home, many establishments are catering to the family (Carnes and Brand, 1977). Because of this, they have become more "respectable." The 1970s were a time of changing cultural values prompted by the sexual revolution and the women's liberation movement. These changes undermined the cultural taboos against female bartenders that had been based on bars' image as morally corrupting to women. The erosion of such taboos presumably enhanced both bar owners' propensity to hire women and women's interest in tending bar.

Once the legal and cultural barriers had fallen, the primary mechanism to exclude women from tending bar was employers' hiring practices. By the mid-1970s, perhaps as a result of waning taboos, there was the appearance of an absence of discrimination against women; in fact, some bar owners and managers sought women for the job. Bernard Grogan (1989), director of research and education for the HERE International Union, attributed women's influx into bartending to their appeal to bar owners, who believe that women enhance their trade, do not steal, are better equipped than men to respond to an increased female clientele, and will work for less money. The bartenders I talked with reinforced this view. They indicated that they saw many more women coming into bars than in the past and that female customers "feel safer with women behind the bar." In fact, one woman bartender commented that her employer cited more single women customers as one of the reasons he hired her. Another told me, "A lot of places switched to females because males' pants have pockets in them," alluding to the ease with which bartenders can dip into the till.

Cultural barriers to bartending jobs have not crumbled easily. One woman who has been bartending for ten years told me that when she first started, she felt "like I was on stage back there." She recounted that at first men were sexually suggestive, questioning her motives for working behind the bar. This is not surprising, considering that men have long considered women in bars—whether cocktail waitresses or customers—as fair game for sexual comment and harassment. This bartender added, "Now I'm like one of the guys." Another woman began bartending twenty years ago when women were referred to as "bartendresses," and "customers used to say, 'Isn't that cute: she's playing bartender.'" Respect was a long time coming for her, but over time customers' attitudes have changed. She said, "I figured after twenty years I *earned* the title bartender!"

While women are garnering a greater share of bartender jobs, they still earn less than their male counterparts. In 1980 the average male bartender earned approximately $7,960 per year, and his female counterpart averaged $4,900. If we look only at those employed full time, year round, men averaged $11,391 and women $7,464, about 66 percent of the men's wages. If women are employed disproportionately as bartenders' helpers, this could explain part of the wage gap. Such information is not available from census data, but none of my interviews supported this possibility. Still, although women and men are similarly distributed across the spectrum of bartender-employing establishments, it is likely that women bartenders work in less prestigious establishments than men, where wages and tips are lower. HERE International's Bernard Grogan confirmed that women bartenders tend to be concentrated in smaller establishments and in smaller towns. He said that in large cities such as Los Angeles, Chicago, and New York, where the union has organized more of the larger clubs, very few women tend bar (Grogan, 1989). Also contributing to men's higher earnings is the fact that male bartenders are twice as likely to be self-employed (10 percent versus 5 percent), meaning that they own or manage the establishment as well (U.S. Bureau of the Census, 1984b).

| | | | Conclusions

Although women have long dominated service occupations—including serving food and beverages and preparing food—they are relative newcomers to bartending. Yet they are newcomers who have in fewer than twenty years come to make up half of this traditionally male occupation. The data I examined suggest that women's increasing presence behind the bar has resulted primarily from the elimination of the legal and cultural barriers that kept women out of bartending jobs and the rapid expansion of the eating-and-drinking-places industry. Legal barriers, erected primarily through union efforts, were knocked down with the passage of the 1964 Civil Rights Act and the court cases it spawned. A decline in HREBI's strength shifted control over the bartending workforce from a male-controlled union, which had an incentive to exclude women, to bar owners, who could profit from women's need to work by paying them lower wages. As the union lost its legal fiat and declined in power, women flooded into bartending jobs.

Hastening the feminization of bartending was the growth of the eating-and-drinking-places industry, which created over 100,000 new jobs for bartenders in a single decade. The labor shortage resulting from the industry's expansion was exacerbated by a drop in the supply of male labor as the increased reliance on tips and the failure of wages to keep up with inflation induced men to look for greener pastures. Faced with a shortage of bartenders, employers sought out women.

Adding to women's attractiveness to some bar owners and managers was the potential that they would reduce an establishment's wage bill, serve its growing female clientele, and perhaps upgrade its image. Additionally, societal reservations concerning women as bar patrons and as workers declined over the 1970s. Noting the general changes in the atmosphere of bars, perceptive bar owners found it profitable to employ women. Women, for their part, found bartending more lucrative than waitressing; it offered them more control than other jobs in the industry; and they could discover the availability of jobs and could learn the work easily.

At the end of the 1980s bartending was divided fifty-fifty between women and men. The doors to bars and bartending, once a haven for men, have swung wide open to admit women. Yet although women have won the right to work behind some bars, the earnings disparity among full-time, year-round bartenders tells us that women bartenders still face barriers to equality with their male counterparts. In the hope of hurdling those barriers, I propose a toast to women bartenders: May the future bring you the economic equality you so richly deserve. Cheers!

I I I I **Notes**

Acknowledgments: I am indebted to Laurel Graham and Barbara F. Reskin for extensive editorial assistance and helpful comments; David Bott, Dorothy Sue Cobble, Virginia Husting, Patricia A. Roos, and Georganne Rundblad also provided useful suggestions. Bob Dixon of Union Local 24 in Southfield, Michigan, provided interview contacts and his own views, for which I am most grateful. I also thank Clifford Christians and John Masiunas for temporarily releasing me from other responsibilities. And finally, I thank my interviewees for sharing their experiences and insights.

1. This analysis focuses on the primary employing industry of bartenders: eating and drinking places.

2. They did so with good reason; many women, particularly in the restaurant industry, worked long hours with few or no breaks.

3. The effects of protective legislation depended on whether women were the majority or the minority in an occupation. Protective laws may have created a better work environment for women in female-dominated occupations but often excluded women from occupations in which they had been the minority. In essence, if men dominated the occupation, protective laws relieved men of competition from women for their jobs and thus served to maintain segregated jobs.

4. Indeed, at the time of the convention a case concerning women as bartenders, pending in the California court system, had led California to revoke its protective law.

5. However, this argument runs both ways: women may have contributed to the decline of the union because they are concentrated in part-time positions and are less likely than men to belong to the union.

6. Prior to 1972 the *OOH* did not list bartending as a separate job category.

7. The list also included a good memory, honesty, neatness, punctuality, a businesslike approach, and physical fitness.

8. I interviewed five bartenders, four union officials, and three industry representatives.

9. In Canada by 1980, sixty large drinking establishments had converted to computerized bars, where bartenders (referred to as "operators") pushed buttons to mix drinks (Tausz, 1979), but computerization of bars is still more a novelty than a common practice in the United States.

10. The tendency to use prepared mixers has further simplified the job.

11. Only one of the five female bartenders I interviewed had attended a bartending school; the rest learned on the job.

12. The act applied to persons employed in establishments with annual sales of $250,000 or more.

13. Other bartenders worked for hotels (6.9 percent), entertainment establishments (4.6 percent), and membership organizations (3.5 percent) and in such unexpected settings as construction sites, hospitals, and government facilities; see U.S. Bureau of the Census (1983a).

Thomas Steiger
Barbara F. Reskin

13

Baking and Baking Off: Deskilling and the Changing Sex Makeup of Bakers

Picture a baker. Do you see the nursery-rhyme baker—a portly man in a chef's hat, crowded in a tub with his cronies the butcher and the candlestick maker— or the media cliché of the apron-clad wife and mother, pulling home-baked cookies and bread from the oven? When by "baker" we mean people who *earn* their bread by baking it, Mother Goose is closer to the mark than Madison Avenue. Over the centuries in which baking has been an occupation, men have dominated it (Laslett, 1965). Indeed, as in most guild-organized crafts, women were often formally barred (Thrupp, 1933; Clark, 1968). Men continued to monopolize baking into this century, and as recently as 1950 seven of every eight bakers were male. However, since 1950 women's share of baking jobs has climbed steadily: to 29.8 percent in 1970, 40.7 percent in 1980; and in 1988—when women made up 45 percent of the labor force— they claimed 47.8 percent of all baking jobs (see Table 13.1).[1]

In this chapter we examine the factors that have given rise to the statistical sex integration of baking. Our data come from government documents; trade publications such as *Baker's Digest, Progressive Grocer,* and *Bakery Magazine*; California State Employment Service staffing schedules from the late 1960s and early 1970s for fifteen bakeries that employed more than 3,000 workers; and interviews.[2] After describing the work bakers do, we show how changes in the occupation and the industry account for women's statistical advances in baking.

Table 13.1
Bakers in the Experienced Civilian Labor Force, by Sex, 1950–1980

	Women	Men	Total	Percent Female
1950	13,920	106,170	120,090	11.6
1960	17,662	93,625	111,287	15.9
1970	32,558	76,634	109,192	29.8
1980	44,821	65,326	110,147	40.7

Sources: U.S. Bureau of the Census (1956: Table 1; 1963a: Table 1; 1972:244; 1984b:301.

I I I I The Job of Baking

In 1949, according to the *Dictionary of Occupational Titles,* or *DOT* (U.S. Department of Labor, 1949), bakers measured and mixed ingredients to produce bread, cakes, cookies, and pastries; they formed dough, prepared fillings, baked, and decorated. Today they accomplish the same tasks, though more bakers rely on machines. In contrast to the stereotype of the all-round baker who turns out finished baked goods, contemporary baking involves an elaborate division of labor. Baking includes several specific occupations for those who help prepare baked goods from scratch: *mixers* weigh and combine ingredients in blending machines; *dough molders* and *molding-machine operators* form dough; *bench hands* shape the dough into fancy bread and rolls; *ovenmen* adjust oven temperature and timers; *helpers* grease pans, depan bread, and push racks; *icing mixers* and *icers* decorate products; and *slicing- and wrapping-machine operators* feed products onto conveyors and supply machines with bags and labels (U.S. Bureau of Labor Statistics, 1972:640–41). Joining the ranks of these "scratch" bakers in the last twenty years are *bake-off bakers,* who finish preparing and then "bake off" products that have been partially prepared by wholesale manufacturing bakeries.

Baking is hard physical labor that can involve lifting 50- to 100-pound sacks as well as stooping, kneeling, and crawling (U.S. Department of Labor, Manpower Administration, 1968:A-2; U.S. Department of Labor, Employment and Training Administration, 1981). Most of the bakers we interviewed mentioned the physical effort their jobs require, and several reported injuries such as a bad back or pulled shoulder from unloading heavy trays of baked goods. Baking can also be hot work: oven temperatures are high, and the temperature in wholesale bakeries can range from 85 to 100 degrees. Burns are common, and when pastries are deep-fried, a "grease mist" settles on workers' clothes and hair.

Although the *DOT* (U.S. Department of Labor, Employment and

Training Administration, 1981) asserted that bakers need two to four years of specific vocational training to learn their trade,[3] the extent of training depends on skill level. Traditional bakers who combine ingredients to make a baked product from scratch sometimes still serve long apprenticeships, whereas bake-off bakers can easily learn the work on the job. According to our interviews and California State Employment Service staffing schedules, most contemporary bakers learned on the job. For example, the staffing schedule for the pretzel division of a baking firm specified that entry-level jobs such as mixer-extruder and ovenman required no prior training. Only two bakers we interviewed had had any pre-employment training: one had taken a hobbyist-oriented cake-decorating class, and a second had begun but did not finish a formal apprenticeship. None of their employers demanded any qualifications other than a high school diploma, the ability to speak English, or passing a math test.

Most bakers work in retail trade or wholesale manufacturing (see Table 13.2). In 1980, 53 percent of the 110,147 bakers worked in retail stores (either grocery stores or retail bakeries); an additional 4 percent were in wholesale trade. Wholesale manufacturing accounted for another 26 percent of bakers. Food-service settings such as restaurants and school, hospital, and company cafeterias employed most of the remainder to prepare baked goods for employees or clients.

The distribution of bakers across industries in 1980 represented a dramatic change from thirty years earlier. In 1950, the manufacturing of baked goods employed 55 percent of all bakers, while retail food stores—mostly bakeries—accounted for just one-third. By 1970, wholesale manufacturing employment had dropped to 27 percent, and retail had increased to 40 percent. Ten years later, the proliferation of bakeries within grocery stores had created 10,499 new jobs. This job growth partly compensated for the loss of 9,212 baking jobs in food-service settings, including 4,662 baking jobs in restaurants and 4,538 in schools. As we will see, these changes in where bakers work and what they do figure prominently in women's influx into baking.

| | | | Women's and Men's Employment across Industrial Settings

In medieval times, baking—like other crafts—was organized in guilds that restricted competition by limiting access to the trade. This strategy included an almost blanket ban on women (Laslett, 1965:3). For example, the London Worshipful Company of Bakers forbade bakers to employ women to "sett, season or carry any bread" (Thrupp, 1933:313). Of the few women who baked commercially, most did so as bakers' wives or widows, not in their own right.[4]

Table 13.2

Employment of Bakers by Sex and Industrial Distribution , 1950–1980

	Men	Women	Total	Percent Female	Industrial Distribution (Percent)	
					All Bakers	Women Bakers
1950						
Wholesale manufacturing	57,390	6,150	63,540	10	55	45
Wholesale trade	150	30	180	17	0	0
Retail bakeries	34,590	3,600	38,190	9	33	27
Food service	9,750	3,750	13,500	28	12	28
Total	101,880	13,530	115,410	12	100	100
1960						
Wholesale manufacturing[a]	65,787	6,516	72,303	9	68	39
Wholesale trade	203	20	223	9	0	0
Retail bakeries[a]	13,192	2,581	15,773	16	15	15
Food service	10,512	7,624	18,136	42	17	46
Total	89,694	16,741	106,435	16	100	100
1970						
Wholesale manufacturing	24,789	4,552	29,341	16	27	14
Wholesale trade	6,533	1,152	7,685	15	7	4
Retail bakeries[b]	30,434	7,910	38,344	21	35	24
Grocery bakeries[c]	3,908	1,805	5,713	32	5	6
Food service	10,970	17,139	28,109	61	26	53
Total	76,634	32,558	109,192	30	100	101[d]
1980						
Wholesale manufacturing	21,765	6,976	28,741	24	26	16
Wholesale trade	3,312	1,223	4,535	27	4	3
Retail bakeries	28,048	13,714	41,762	33	38	31
Grocery bakeries[c]	5,646	10,566	16,212	65	15	24
Food service	6,555	12,342	18,897	25	17	28
Total	65,326	44,821	110,147	41	100	102[d]

[a] Data apparently incorrect (Priebe, 1988).

[b] In 1970 the Census Bureau disaggregated retail bakeries into two categories: retail bakeries and grocery-store bakeries.

[c] Outside firms sometimes operate in-store bakeries, so these data underestimate the number of bakers who work in grocery stores.

[d] Error due to rounding.

Sources: U.S. Bureau of the Census (1954: Table 2; 1963b: Table 2; 1972: Table 8; 1984b: Table 4).

A permissible activity for bakers' wives and women servants was selling bread in the marketplace (Thrupp, 1933:41). The current division of labor in which men produce bread and women sell it preserves this pattern. In 1980 only a small fraction of women bakers worked in manufacturing baked goods. In contrast, they were overrepresented in grocery-store bakeries (see Table 13.2). In addition, men in retail settings are more likely than women to bake products from scratch rather than "baking off" partially made products, and women bakers in wholesale manufacturing settings are concentrated in packaging, near the retail end of the process.

Although women's share of baking jobs in the wholesale manufacture of baked goods has grown, it has done so more slowly than their increasing representation in the occupation as a whole. Women's share of retail bakery jobs more closely approximates their overall representation in baking (see Table 13.2). However, the proliferation of bakeries within grocery stores during the 1960s has preserved sex segregation in the retail sector. Though regular (independent or stand-alone) bakeries increasingly employed female bakers, these bakeries have remained predominantly male.[5] Meanwhile, grocery-store bakeries quickly became female dominated, and food-service settings (school cafeterias, restaurants, and the like)—a smaller sector of the industry that was disproportionately female as early as 1950—has increasingly feminized over time.

Wholesale Manufacturing Bakeries

Wholesale manufacturing bakeries—establishments that do not sell directly to the public—have always produced most of the commercially prepared baked goods, and at least through 1950, they employed over half of the nation's bakers.[6] Then the development of continuing-processing equipment in the 1940s and 1950s revolutionized wholesale baking (LePage, 1973:13). According to a history of the Bakery, Confectionery and Tobacco Workers Union (BC&T), automation meant that a single person could run a mixing or molding machine, replacing six to ten skilled male handworkers (Kaufman, 1987:51). Between 1950 and 1970 the dissemination of this technology halved the wholesale workforce. Continuous mixing shortened the conventional process and facilitated cleanup so that one or two continuous-mix operators could produce as much as six or seven bakers using conventional methods (U.S. Bureau of Labor Statistics, 1979c:2–3). High-speed mixing cut labor further by reducing fermentation time, and liquid fermentation had the same effect by permitting more flexible scheduling (Burth, 1971:48; U.S. Bureau of Labor Statistics, 1979c:3). Pneumatic bulk-handling systems transferred ingredients automatically, eliminating up to one production worker per shift (*Food Processing*, 1971b), and automatic pan handling (Anderson, 1974:55) and microwave proofing eliminated the jobs of two to three more workers

(*Food Processing*, 1971a:37; Schiffman et al., 1971:57). This trend—which is still under way—toward what one supervisor termed "superautomation" transformed bakers' work from manually producing baked goods to regulating specialized machines and transfer equipment. Lifetime bakers saw continuous-flow operations and modern assembly lines replace handwork in most whole-sale bakeries (Kaufman, 1987:165), a change we can see by comparing the Department of Labor's changing descriptions of baking (U.S. Department of Labor, 1949; U.S. Bureau of Labor Statistics, 1972:640): in 1949 it depicted bakers as mixers, measurers, and decorators; in 1972 it highlighted machines that "production workers load and unload, watch, . . . and inspect."

Industrial concentration accompanied automation (Huffstutler and Riche, 1972), and between 1972 and 1982 the number of wholesale bakeries declined by 27 percent (U.S. Department of Commerce, 1972a:SR3–8, 9; 1982:5–9).[7] Abetted by improved preservation techniques and the national highway system, concentration meant that large regional and national whole-salers could penetrate local markets. Local wholesale bakeries lacked the scale to afford to automate (U.S. Bureau of Labor Statistics, 1979c). Moreover, increased costs of ingredients and energy[8] and new government standards in food processing that banned some traditional baking practices impaired their ability to compete with large companies. Thus, by driving smaller bakeries out of business and by decreasing the labor needs of large companies, automation cost wholesale manufacturing 34,199 baking jobs between 1950 and 1970 (see Table 13.2).

Men absorbed 95 percent of the jobs lost in the manufacturing sec-tor during the 1960s; in the 1970s they lost another 3,033, while women gained almost 2,500 manufacturing jobs. Over a thirty-year period, while men lost 35,625 manufacturing jobs, women bakers gained 826. In consequence, despite women's small numerical gain, their job share increased from 9.7 to 24.3 percent.

That men sustained most of the job losses was due almost entirely to overwhelming sex segregation in the manufacture of baked goods. In whole-sale bakeries women and men rarely do the same jobs. According to late 1960s data for fifteen California baking companies, men monopolized high-paying production jobs—mixing, blending, and baking goods—and women worked at the end of the line in the lower-paying, often monotonous jobs of loading and unloading the machines that package the goods.[9] For example, in 1967 a California baking company that employed 62 workers explicitly acknowledged that it assigned "inexperienced *workers*" to jobs as panners, toppers, or rackers but employed "inexperienced *women*" as depanners, wrapping-machine feed-ers, or hand packers. Our interviews indicated that the pattern persisted in the late 1980s. A woman described her typical job in bakery manufacturing as standing at her "cake-line" wrapping machine for an entire shift, placing cupcakes on pieces of cardboard on a conveyor; a female coworker puts the finished packages on trays as they come out of the machine.

Companies often cite a job's physical demands to justify a male sex label (Milkman, 1987). Although doing so is no longer legal, some employers continue to hire men for jobs that require heavy lifting, and many still see such jobs as "men's" work.[10] For example, a female wholesale baker we interviewed classified working in the mixing room, operating the oven, and "catching bread" as men's jobs for this reason.[11]

Sex segregation within manufacturing jobs shapes the sector's sex makeup. Plants in which most baking jobs are labeled men's work obviously employ mostly men. Thus, because a relatively larger share of jobs in cookie and cracker manufacturing, compared with bread and cake production, are finishing jobs (operating slicing and wrapping machines) that the industry defines as women's work, women are overrepresented in cookie and cracker manufacturing.

Because men monopolized production jobs, when automation eliminated many of these jobs, men bore the brunt of the loss. Sometimes employers have used automation to justify replacing men with women in production jobs—at lower wages. As early as the turn of the century, after employers mechanized baking, they hired women and even children to do the deskilled jobs (Kaufman, 1987:51). A similar pattern of mechanization and deskilling occurred recently with the same effect at the firm of a woman we interviewed. Previously, skilled men had decorated cakes, each doing an entire cake at a time. Then, to increase production, management introduced a detailed division of labor in which one person fills the icing bags, and six others stand around a table with a revolving disk on which spindles hold twenty-four cakes. As the disk revolves, each decorator performs a specialized task: making roses, stems, leaves, or borders. The seven-person team decorates twenty-four cakes every four minutes to produce nearly 3,000 cakes a day.[12] Under the new assembly-line pacing, the company began replacing men with women.

Changing physical demands have helped bring women into traditionally male production jobs. Vaughn Ball (1986), education and research director for the BC&T, attributed women's increased employment in wholesale manufacturing bakeries to automated bulk-handling systems that reduced the physical demands on bakers.[13] However, other BC&T members and staff we interviewed insisted that although the work may be less physically demanding than in the past, it is still demanding enough to continue to limit women's jobs in wholesale baking (Castillo, 1988).

Apart from the physical effort that production jobs require, other reasons more women have not obtained such well-paid jobs include men's desire to retain them, women's reluctance to transfer into them, and employment practices in the manufacturing sector. Among the 6,300 bakers in a 5 percent sample of the 1980 census, men employed full time, year round in manufacturing averaged $13,197 in 1979—and 88 percent worked full time (U.S. Bureau of the Census, 1983a). These wages exceed those of bakers in retail nongrocery bakeries or food service, and they compare favorably with the earnings of unskilled production workers in the labor force as a whole. Moreover, wholesale baking is heavily unionized (Ball, 1986), in contrast to other settings, so most bakers enjoy good benefits.[14] Hence, the male bakers working in this sector have no incentive to leave these jobs.

Sex discrimination in job assignment has kept some women out of traditionally male production jobs. A west coast union representative told us that in the 1960s, when bakeries called the union for workers, they often specified "men only" except for packing jobs (Castillo, 1988). An interviewee explained that a large bread plant in her midwestern town had no female employees because the male workers had served notice that they would not work with women. A few women have challenged sex segregation and discrimination in wholesale baking. The trade journal *Bakery* (Kimbrell, 1986:48) reported a wrapping-machine operator's fight to win the right to bid on an all-male higher-paying production baking job which, she said, "at that time, women couldn't bid on. . . . I more or less insisted." Although management and coworkers tried to intimidate her—"they wanted women to stay where they were"—she persisted and won the job. Nevertheless, male opposition or an all-male environment deters some women from seeking production jobs, particularly in union settings where women's wages in female-dominated jobs are high, and the extra dollar or two an hour for production jobs is not worth the physical stress the work may involve or the possible personal costs of integrating male work settings (Castillo, 1988).

Unionization of wholesale manufacturing bakeries can contribute to women's low representation when contracts specify bidding procedures that permit posting job openings in home departments before plantwide posting. One woman who succeeded in circumventing this system in her plant described the methods that kept women from bidding on "men's" higher-paid mixing-room jobs: departments were sex segregated, and same-sex workers had first crack at openings (Kimbrell, 1986:48).

In 1973 two women employees charged a Nabisco plant with sex discrimination in promotion, bidding, training, and other conditions of employment (*Federal Rules Decisions*, 1978:395). Although the women won a favorable out-of-court settlement (*Federal Rules Decisions*, 1978:405–6), the chief negotiator for the eastern region of the BC&T doubted that these cases had any repercussions in the bakery manufacturing industry as a whole (D'Angelo, 1987). However, a west coast observer disagreed; she said that by the late 1970s, if a woman wanted to train for a production job, the union would assist her. She added that by that time large companies were cognizant of affirmative-action regulations (Castillo, 1988).

Retail Bakeries

Until well into this century, retail bakeries resembled their historical precursors, preparing goods from scratch to sell on the premises (Thrupp, 1933:98–99). Then, in the 1950s, technical advances in preserving baked goods, which permitted shipping them long distances without noticeable loss of freshness, fueled the growth of shops that "bake off" premixed or frozen goods that have been prepared elsewhere. This led to the emergence of regional and national bakery chains and doughnut, cookie, and pretzel franchises, now fixtures at most shopping malls.[15]

The spread of bakeries within other retail stores further challenged the traditional independent retail bakery. Grocery stores began opening in-store bakeries in the 1950s as part of an effort to attract customers by offering non-grocery items and services, including liquor, flowers, and pharmaceuticals. By 1975 three-fourths of new supermarkets contained bakeries (*Progressive Grocer*, 1975:68) that tempted customers with the smell of fresh baked goods. In-store bakeries' competitive advantage over independents (they tended to be more mechanized and better capitalized and had lower overhead) helped them to supplant the independents.

The proliferation of bake-off and chain-store bakeries transformed retail baking. The period between 1954 and 1977 saw the number of retail bakeries increase by almost 900 (U.S. Department of Commerce, 1954:1–5, 1963:1–7, 1967:1–6, 1972b:7, 1977a:12). This growth created 5,867 new retail baking jobs between 1950 and 1970, and another 13,917 in the 1970s (see Table 13.2). In 1950 nine of every ten retail bakers were male; in 1970 men still claimed almost eight of each ten jobs. During the 1970s, however, retail baking added 14,565 women to its ranks, and the number of men declined slightly. The result was a retail workforce (for retail bakeries and grocery bakeries combined) that was 42 percent female (computed from Table 13.2). Implicated in women's numerical gains are both the development of a new kind of baking in the retail sector and the persistence of sex segregation within retail baking that assigned men to scratch baking in the back and relegated women to "finishing"—slicing and wrapping goods, icing cakes and doughnuts, filling display cases, and waiting on customers. The changes played out differently in independent bakeries, on the one hand, and supermarket and chain bakeries, on the other.

Regular retail bakeries. Women gained 5,804 new jobs in regular (nongrocery) bakeries during the 1970s, while male bakers lost 2,386 jobs. As a result, women's representation increased, but only slightly faster than it did in the entire occupation (12.2 versus 10.9 percentage points). Several factors helped to keep a lid on women's gains in this sector. First, the sector enjoyed only moderate growth—3,418 new jobs. Second, among retail bakeries the independents were probably most likely to continue baking goods from scratch and hence to preserve the historical sexual division of labor. Though we lack direct evidence on this point (because census data do not distinguish independent bakeries from bakery chains), the sex difference in the percentage of retail bakers who worked full time, year round (59 percent of the men compared to 34 percent of the women in 1980) and the 62-cents-to-the-dollar wage disparity between female and male full-time, year-round bakers both point to continued sex segregation in duties.

Presumably, this sex segregation persisted because scratch baking requires traditional skills that women have had less opportunity to learn and because employers assume that men are better able to sustain the physical effort involved. Independent bakeries that either cannot afford to automate or that specialize in fancy scratch-baked items depend on skilled labor. This entails physical effort, because without sophisticated transfer equipment bakers must lift heavy bags of flour and wheel racks of filled pans into proofing rooms.[16] The male head baker in a scratch bakery claimed that the need to be able "to handle a three-gallon dough" (made of seventy pounds of ingredients) disqualified women: "Out of all my years in the plant, 80 percent of the women can't handle the work; it is too physical." He added, "Women balk at lifting 50 to 100 pounds, [and the few who] can do it . . . look like gorillas."

That the number of women in regular retail bakeries grew as much as it did probably reflects the inclusion within this category of nongrocery bakery chains, which are more likely than independent bakeries to bake off products. Our informants uniformly assured us that the retail sector views baking off as women's work; hence, the larger the bake-off bakers' share of all retail baking, the greater the women's share of all jobs.

Grocery and chain-store bakeries.   In 1970 men outnumbered women by more than two to one in supermarket bakeries (see Table 13.2). However, women captured 83 percent of the 10,499 new jobs this sector created during the 1970s, and by 1980 its sex ratio had flipped, with women constituting 65 percent of grocery-store bakers. Why did most of the thousands of new jobs for in-store bakeries and, we suspect, bakery chains go to women? Here too the answer lies primarily in sex segregation within retail bakeries in which men do the scratch baking and women are assigned to baking off.[17] Most in-store and chain-store bakeries are primarily bake-off shops (*Progressive Grocer*, 1975), so they provide few scratch baking jobs. Most hire a head baker or manager (usually male) with technical skills to supervise baking done on the premises, and most of the remaining jobs are defined as women's work.

Several factors have led employers to label most in-store baking jobs as "women's work." First, baking off requires fewer skills and less training than scratch baking. For example, one supermarket bakery manager told us that his chain had made the job "so easy that anyone could quickly learn it." The absence of entry barriers makes baking off an attractive option for inexperienced workers. For some, the possibility that it might serve as an entry to scratch baking is an additional attraction.

Second, baking off is lighter work than scratch baking, so employers are less likely to rule women out as too weak. Although some heavy work remains, one strong worker can usually manage all of it. Indeed, one manager said that every bakery should have one man to do the heavy work because men can do it faster; a supermarket baker told us that her store has a firm policy against women doing any heavy lifting; and two female in-store bakers said that their male manager always lifted the 50-pound sacks of ingredients. However, some women we interviewed said they did the heavy work themselves.

Third, the fact that grocery stores are a female space enhances the likelihood that women will work there. Because some aspects of bake-off baking resemble the work of other grocery clerks—themselves disproportionately female—a female sex label for bake-off bakers seems natural. We talked to one manager who said his store wants women bakers to wait on its bakery customers. Its male bakers stay in the back, while the primary job of the women, who may also work in back, is serving customers. (Interestingly, bakers see working up front as the least desirable work. According to one, "No one wants to be on the counter," where they must deal with customers.) That most other nonbakery grocery employees are female contributes to the hiring of women as in-store bakers because sex-segregated friendship networks make it likely that women employees will mention job openings to other women. Several female grocery bakers we interviewed learned of their jobs from female friends or relatives. Women also learn of job opportunities as customers.[18] Further, in female settings employers may be predisposed to hire women for new non-sex-labeled jobs, and such settings may attract female job applicants.[19]

The changing sex makeup of grocery bakeries also reflects workers' preferences and their access to more desirable alternatives. Men are underrepresented in retail groceries partly because bake-off baking does not pay well; it is often part time; and hours may vary from week to week, making earnings uncertain.[20] In a midwestern in-store bake-off bakery, bakers who belonged to the United Food Workers earned $3.95 to $5.95 an hour in the mid-1980s. Among the bakers in the 5 percent sample from the 1980 census, 44 percent of the women and 17 percent of the men employed in grocery-store bakeries worked fewer than thirty-five hours per week (U.S. Bureau of the Census, 1983a). Many part-time women we interviewed wished to work more hours. A male baker in the Midwest said that after the large grocery chains broke the unions in that region, wages dropped sharply, and men left baking. He added, "Men are not going to work at such a hard job for five dollars an hour when they can work in an office for the same money," a point that a California male manager reiterated. In fact, an Illinois bakery manager reported that no men have applied in the eight years he has managed the bakery. In 1980, food-service and regular retail bakers averaged the lowest annual incomes for both sexes. Grocery-store bakers fared better, but even the top incomes were well below the national medians: $8,154 for men and $3,905 for women. Hence, given men's wider array of occupational options, few must settle for such low wages.

Women, in contrast, especially those who lack vocational training or education, are in a different boat. Among the growing number of women who work to support themselves and their households, supermarket bake-off baking may be the best of a limited set of options. Three women we interviewed applied to grocery bakeries because they had heard "they paid well." Obviously, they meant "well" relative to the alternatives open to women with limited experience. For example, in 1979 women employed full time, year round as bakers in groceries earned 27 percent more than the average woman employed full time in food service and 14 percent more than the average service worker (computed from data in U.S. Bureau of the Census, 1984c: Table 1). A manager with twenty years of experience attributed women's increased representation in grocery baking to the economic necessity that has forced a large number of single mothers with limited vocational training into the labor market. Another manager admitted exploiting this situation by hiring inexperienced women with children who are "working to make ends meet, [because they] are not going to call in and beg out of work for a Friday night date." The difficulty of obtaining adequate child care (not to mention finding time for domestic work) makes part-time retail bakery jobs attractive to women with limited economic needs. However, the economic situation of many women precludes their voluntarily choosing less than full-time employment.

Food-Service Settings

A final sector where bakers work comprises establishments that provide meals —restaurants, hotels, school and employee cafeterias. At least since 1950 women bakers have been overrepresented in these settings. At that time, although food service employed only 12 percent of all bakers, it accounted for 28 percent of women bakers (see Table 13.2). In 1970 educational institutions alone accounted for 29 percent of female bakers, and restaurants and other food-serving settings accounted for another 23 percent.

During the 1970s the number of bakers employed in food service declined by 9,212. More women than men lost jobs in schools and restaurants, but across all food-service settings a total of 4,415 male jobs disappeared, compared to 4,797 female jobs. Improvements in preserving and shipping baked goods meant that food-serving establishments could serve fresh baked goods without hiring bakers.[21] As in the retail sector, the surviving baking jobs increasingly involved baking off rather than scratch baking. Thus, the reasons for women's growing prominence in this sector are the same as the reasons they dominate bake-off baking: (1) the pay is low and the work often part time (in 1980, only 26 percent of the women and 61 percent of the men worked full time, year round), so it does not attract men; (2) easy entry attracts inexperienced women entering or reentering the labor force; and (3) the work settings—schools, restaurants—are predominantly female and hence tend to be hospitable to women.

| | | | Discussion and Conclusion

The occupation of baker has been feminizing since 1950. Between 1950 and 1980 men lost 40,844 baking jobs, while women's numbers more than tripled, giving rise to a net gain of almost 31,000 women bakers. In 1988 women constituted almost 48 percent of this traditionally male occupation. At first glance, these numbers suggest that women took jobs away from men. In fact, almost no direct replacement occurred. Nor has the occupation undergone much genuine sex integration. Instead, sex segregation persists within industry sectors: men still dominate production baking (although their numbers have declined as a result of automation), and women continue to finish and package baked goods.

What has changed is not the traditional sexual division of labor in baking but the baking process and, in consequence, the contours of the baking industry. Technological innovations that permitted freezing and preserving dough so it could be shipped long distances ushered in bake-off bakeries and allowed schools, hospitals, and restaurants to purchase ready-made or ready-to-bake products instead of baking them from scratch. Bake-off bakeries—both in groceries and in chains—increasingly dominate the retail market. Baking off differs from scratch baking in that it requires less skill and is often less physically demanding; it is more likely to be part time and pays less.[22]

Our evidence regarding the sex composition of traditional and bake-off bakers suggests a scenario in which some men in small traditional bakeries lost their jobs, while modern bake-off bakeries—usually located in supermarkets or retail chain stores—increasingly employed a female workforce to do less skilled work. The bake-off, in-store bakery phenomenon almost wholly explains women's gains in baking during the 1970s. The 14,565 women who entered the ranks of retail baking in the 1970s (60 percent of whom work in grocery stores) more than account for the total increase of 12,263 female bakers between 1970 and 1980 (see Table 13.2). Thus, technical improvements in the baking process laid the groundwork for women's increased role in commercial baking. Rather than significantly altering the entrenched social roles of men and women in the baking industry, technical innovations gave rise to a less skilled variant, bake-off baking, that was quickly defined as women's work.

Technological change also affected employment in the manufacturing sector. Automation meant that bakers were increasingly operating machines rather than "baking," that some work became less physically demanding, and that companies needed fewer production workers. However, automation affected the sex composition of bakers primarily through eliminating formerly male production jobs and thereby leaving women with a larger share of the remaining jobs, rather than by substantially enhancing women's access to the more mechanized but traditionally male production jobs.

What about women workers' preferences? According to Tienda et al. (1987:263), supply-side factors in the labor market "push" women into traditional "women's" jobs, and demand-side factors "pull" them into nontraditional jobs. Most of the explanation for women's increased representation among bakers lies with the demand side of the labor market—changes in the industrial composition of employment and growth of retail and in-store bake-off bakeries. An important supply-side factor is women's increased need to contribute to or assume the support of their families. In reducing the skill that bakers need, technological change may have made baking more accessible to women with limited experience and the need to juggle their schedules to care for their children. Such women often turn to low-paying service-sector jobs. For them, in-store baking with its chance to learn skills may represent an attractive option. For many women the familiar environment, a female-dominated setting, competitive pay (at least relative to other female unskilled and service jobs), and employers' apparent preference for untrained women clinch the matter.

Men's work preferences also contributed to bake-off baking's becoming women's work. Wages in bake-off bakeries are too low to attract enough men to meet the labor demand. In fact, comparing all bakers' 1969 *median* earnings to their *mean* 1979 earnings *in 1969 dollars* reveals that while women's real income rose by 8 percent ($225 in 1969 dollars), men's declined by 12 percent ($843 in 1969 dollars).[23] For men, baking became less lucrative. Thus, employers of bakers turned to women after a new, less skilled specialty emerged. Women's share of all baking jobs grew as they held on to traditionally female jobs in production and in the food-service sectors and garnered the lion's share of the new bake-off jobs in retail settings.

Has women's increasing representation in baking brought greater economic equity for female bakers? Although the different statistical measures the census published in 1970 and 1980 preclude exact comparison,[24] the data suggest that women bakers' economic disadvantage declined somewhat during the 1970s. In 1969 women bakers averaged 41 cents for each dollar a man made (see Table 13.3). By 1979 the disparity between male and female bakers in annual wages had dropped so that women made 50 cents to the men's dollar, although men still outearned women by almost $2 an hour. Because women

Table 13.3

Earnings of Bakers in the Experienced Civilian Labor Force, by Sex and 1979
Employment Status, 1969, 1979

	Worked in 1969		Worked in 1979			Worked Full Time 1979	
	Median		*Mean*		*Real*[a]	*Mean*	*Real*[a]
	Annual Wages	*Weeks Worked*	*Hourly Wage*	*Annual Wages*	*Annual Wages*	*Annual Wages*	*Annual Wages*
Men	$6,895	50+	$5.98	$11,985	$6,052	$14,094	$7,117
Women	2,798	47.7	4.00	5,987	3,023	8,604	4,345
Female/male wage ratio	.41	—[b]	.67	.50	.50	.61	.61

[a] Adjusted to 1969 dollars.
[b] Value lies between .917 and .954.

Sources: For 1969, U.S. Bureau of the Census (1973d: Table 19); for 1979, U.S. Bureau of the Census (1984c: Table 1).

bakers were more likely than men to work part time (43 and 14 percent, respectively), though often not by choice, the wage gap among full-time bakers was smaller: women averaged 61 cents to each male dollar.

The sexual division of labor within both wholesale manufacturing and retail baking continues to translate into a wage disparity between female and male bakers. In 1979 male full-time, year-round bakers in wholesale manufacturing averaged $13,197, half again as much as their female coworkers earned (U.S. Bureau of the Census, 1983a). Moreover, only 65 percent of the women wholesale bakers had full-time jobs, compared to 88 percent of the men. Among bakers who did not work full time, year round, women averaged just slightly over half of what men earned. Most of the thousands of women who entered baking in the 1970s were relegated to its lowest-paying sectors and the least lucrative jobs within sectors, while men retained a near-monopoly on the better-paying jobs. The primary reason for the wage gap is the segregation of men and women bakers in (a) different industrial sectors that have different wage structures, rates of unionization, and chances for full-time work, and (b) different jobs within sectors.

Thus, for the most part, women bakers do different work from male bakers, in different settings, for fewer hours, and at lower wages. The harsh reality is that while the number of women bakers has increased, women bakers have moved only a little closer to economic parity, and the occupation remains highly sex segregated.

| | | | **Notes**

Acknowledgments: We gratefully acknowledge the assistance of Vaughn Ball, education and research director for the Bakery, Confectionery & Tobacco Workers International Union; Felisa Castillo of the BC&T, Local 5; and the bakers who described their work to us. We thank Patricia A. Roos for her useful comments on this chapter and James N. Baron and William T. Bielby for giving us access to their data on California baking establishments.

1. The large increase in percentage female during the 1970s is not an artifact of the 1980 change in the census occupational classification. Assuming that the 160 persons classified as bakers in the double-coded sample from the 1970 census are representative, had the census used the 1980 scheme in 1970, women would have accounted for only 25.4 percent of bakers (Bianchi and Rytina, 1984: App. 1) rather than the 29.8 percent the 1970 census reported, so the 1970–80 increase would have been even greater.

2. We interviewed seventeen bakers employed in wholesale bakeries, retail bake shops, and grocery bakeries, as well as representatives of the Bakery, Confectionery and Tobacco Workers International Union (BC&T), the American Institute of Baking, and two school superintendents.

3. Vocational schools teach baking, as does the American Institute of Baking (AIB), which trains about 200 students a year in four- to five-month classes. Many students, most of whom are male, come from large wholesale firms that pay their tuition and help shape the curriculum (which increasingly focuses on management). Most of the few women in AIB classes are self-sponsored (Embers, 1987).

4. For example, the by-laws in one English town decreed that "noe Persons . . . shall brew or bayk to sell but only freemen and thare wifes" (Clark, 1968:211). A baker's widow who remained unmarried might be permitted to take over her late husband's business (Thrupp, 1933:66, 69; Laslett, 1965:7–8; Kaplan, 1984:357).

5. Independent bakeries are single-unit establishments that are not part of another retail enterprise such as a grocery or department store.

6. We say "*at least* through 1950" because the 1960 industrial data for wholesale and retail settings appear unreliable (Priebe, 1988).

7. Between 1967 and 1982 about 40 percent of all bakeries and baking companies folded (U.S. Department of Commerce, 1977a, 1982).

8. The costs of sugar, shortening, and paper products had increased sharply, and Soviet wheat sales led flour prices to skyrocket (Kaufman, 1987:165). To make matters worse, the oil crisis raised energy prices.

9. The Census Bureau classifies depanners, but not wrapping-machine feeders or hand packers, as bakers (U.S. Bureau of the Census, 1971:O-45; 1982b:O-91). Whether or not women who are concentrated in packaging are classified as bakers depends on the job title they reported in their census returns. Our point is that within the wholesale companies that manufacture baked goods, women typically hold finishing rather than production jobs.

10. Before 1964, protective labor laws in many states barred employers from letting women lift more than 15 to 30 pounds, so employers did not hire women for jobs that might involve lifting—including some baking jobs. Supreme Court decisions

under Title VII of the 1964 Civil Rights Act invalidated these state laws, in theory rendering jobs that involved heavy lifting more accessible to women. However, as late as the 1970s, long after the courts struck the protective statutes from the books, many employers continued to exclude women from jobs solely because of the work's physical demands (Bielby and Baron, 1986).

11. Not all male production jobs are physically demanding: a woman we interviewed in a manufacturing bakery named the mostly male task of operating the mixing machine as the best job: "You push a button at regular intervals and watch that nothing goes wrong."

12. Our informant told us that by the day's end the decorator's hand "would be a claw" and "pain would shoot up her arm."

13. To the extent that employers comply with Occupational Safety and Health Administration (1985:562) regulations requiring devices for moving bowls that weigh more than 80 pounds, the rules would give women access to physically demanding jobs. However, evidence suggests that OSHA enforcement—and thus compliance—has been limited (Nelkin and Brown, 1984).

14. Filer (1988) has estimated that 35 percent of all bakers are unionized. The percentage for wholesale manufacturing is much higher and that for the retail and food-service sectors correspondingly lower.

15. Some of these chains bake products from scratch but according to such detailed guidelines from the franchiser that the baking requires limited skills. For example, Dunkin' Donuts provides detailed instructions for preparing each type of doughnut; the company gives franchisees a chart describing common problems and sets quality-control standards that leave baking employees with little need for judgment (Luxenberg, 1985:78–79).

16. A scratch baker in an all-female doughnut shop told of having injured her back several times in lifting heavy sacks of ingredients and mixing bowls. However, injuries are hardly unique to women. A male scratch baker told us that every baker he knows has a bad back.

17. A male in-store bakery manager told us that his union still classifies him as "pastry hostess," a holdover term from the time when wholesale bakeries produced all the store's baked goods and when a woman (hence, "hostess") displayed them in retail stores.

18. We saw signs advertising part-time bakery jobs on the doors of several groceries where their customers would see them.

19. At least on the west coast, affirmative action may have played a part in women's growing numbers in supermarket bakeries during the 1970s, as large chains felt the need to implement affirmative-action programs (Castillo, 1988). In order to avoid sanctions, and with the BC&T's cooperation, they responded by hiring women and enrolling interested women in apprenticeship programs.

20. Interviewees at midwestern and west coast grocery chains told us of employers who limited bakers to 24 hours per week to prevent their being entitled to union benefits.

21. Jobs in schools also dropped because enrollments declined after 1975 (U.S. Bureau of the Census, 1980: Table 254) and because federal school-lunch subsidy policies changed. Previously, when the federal government provided surplus commodities

(flour, sugar, milk) to local schools, hiring skilled bakers to bake from scratch was cost effective. However, the federal government reduced this program in the 1970s; in addition, federal subsidies under Title I of the Elementary and Secondary Education Act favored prepackaged lunches for which school districts contracted out, so fewer schools hired bakers.

22. However, adding baking off to selling duties would "enskill" the work of the retail clerical worker. Indeed, the third edition of the *DOT* (U.S. Department of Labor, Manpower Administration, 1965), listed "bakery girl" as a low-skill job, but the fourth edition (U.S. Department of Labor, Employment and Training Administration, 1977) replaced "bakery girl" with "grocery clerk," a job rated higher in complexity in dealing with people and data. This possibility reminds us of the need, when discussing deskilling, to specify what jobs are involved (also see Walsh, 1989).

23. The increase for women at least partly reflects their greater likelihood in 1979 than in 1969 of working full time and year round; were the data available to adjust for hours worked, we might find that women's real hourly earnings also declined.

24. Comparing means and medians is undesirable because extreme values influence the former. Men were more likely than women to have earned very high salaries in 1979, so using the mean for 1979 could inflate the 1969–79 difference for men.

Patricia A. Roos

14

Hot-Metal to Electronic Composition: Gender, Technology, and Social Change

Printers were once the quintessential craft workers, the aristocracy of the blue-collar workforce, according to Lipset et al. (1956). They were better educated than the average production worker, and the International Typographical Union (ITU) assured them high income, job autonomy, and occupational community. These printers were also invariably men. Women were singularly unsuccessful in integrating the hot-metal composing room, where the operators typeset and composed the final printed layout, or the apprenticeship programs leading to these well-paid jobs.

Since 1970, however, the print production process and its workforce have changed dramatically. Extraordinary technological advances revolutionized typesetting, and as a consequence print shops switched to electronic composition.[1] Printers lost their educational edge, along with their high relative income and job autonomy. A major shift in sex composition attended these changes: between 1970 and 1980 the percentage of typesetters and compositors who were female increased from 17 to 56 percent. By 1988, 74 percent of typesetters and compositors were women (U.S. Bureau of Labor Statistics, 1989:187).

The main purpose of this chapter is to explain the feminization of typesetting and composition, especially during the 1970s. Employment data show that the substantial influx of women into this occupation was the result of women replacing men in a dying occupation. Overall, the number of persons working in typesetting declined 18 percent in the 1970s; in fact, the number

Table 14.1

Employment in Typesetting and Composition, by Sex, in the Experienced Civilian Labor Force, 1970, 1980

	Total	Men	Women	Percent Female
1970	86,571	72,040	14,531	16.8
1980	70,515	31,205	39,310	55.7
Percent change	−18.5	−56.7	171	38.9

Sources: Data based on samples from 1970 and 1980 censuses; see U.S. Bureau of the Census (1984a).

of men declined 57 percent, but the number of women actually increased by 171 percent (see Table 14.1). Thus, a full exploration of the feminization of typesetting requires an understanding of why women are entering and men exiting this occupation.[2]

I focus on the 1970s because that is when the dramatic change in typesetting's sex composition first occurred. There are two additional reasons to highlight this period. First, only during this decade were electronic technologies widely disseminated. In 1970 there were 23 video display terminals in use in American Newspaper Publishers Association (ANPA) newspapers; by 1982 there were 46,217 (Dertouzos and Quinn, 1985:7). A U.S. Bureau of Labor Statistics (1982c) report concurs: between the mid-1960s and 1978 the number of phototypesetting machines increased from 1,000 to 40,000. Second, while some print workplaces did use some form of computerization before 1970, it was during this decade that the newest generation of electronic composition techniques made hot-metal Linotypes obsolete. Between 1970 and 1982 the number of Linotypes and similar machines in ANPA newspapers decreased from 10,290 to 194 (Dertouzos and Quinn, 1985:7). Large newspapers such as the *Los Angeles Times,* the *San Francisco Chronicle,* the *New York Times,* and the *Washington Post* switched from Linotypes to electronic composition in the middle to late 1970s, somewhat later than smaller newspapers.

| | | | Industrial Context

Employment Overview

In 1986, printing employed almost 1.5 million people, 33 percent more than in 1972. The Bureau of Labor Statistics (BLS) projected that print employment would increase an additional 17 percent by the year 2000 (Personick, 1987: Table 6). However, the proportion of print *production* workers declined between 1967 and 1982: from 50 to 37 percent among newspaper workers, 26 to 23 percent in book publishing, and 82 to 77 percent in book printing (U.S. Bureau of the Census, 1985a: Table 1b). The BLS projected that between 1982 and 1995 the number of typesetters and compositors in manufacturing would drop an additional 12 percent and the number of newspaper compositors by 31 percent (U.S. Bureau of Labor Statistics, 1984a:138, 148).

The printing industry comprises the largest collection of small businesses in domestic manufacturing: 80 percent of the industry's plants employ fewer than twenty people (U.S. Bureau of Labor Statistics, 1982c:5). Some run "Mom and Pop" print firms from their homes as cottage industries. Daily newspapers are the exception: in 1982, only 6 percent of daily newspapers employed fewer than twenty persons, compared to 84 percent of weekly and other newspapers (U.S. Bureau of the Census, 1985a).[3]

Newspaper publishing/printing and commercial printing are the two major sectors of the printing industry, each accounting for approximately one-third of its total employment (U.S. Bureau of Labor Statistics, 1982c:11). The remaining employees work in other print sectors such as periodicals and books or for corporations with in-house print shops. In this chapter I collapse all nonnewspaper workers in the printing industry into one category labeled "commercial sector."[4] I classify typesetters and compositors working outside the printing industry as part of the "in-house" sector. I thus consider three sectors: newspapers, the commercial sector, and corporate in-house print shops. Typesetters and compositors are not distributed evenly across the three: in 1980, 32 percent worked in newspapers, 54 percent in commercial printing, and 14 percent in corporate in-house shops (see Table 14.2).[5]

Table 14.2
Industrial Distribution of Typesetters and Compositors, by Sex and Percent Female, 1980

Sector	Percent	Percent Female	Men (%)	Women (%)
Newspapers	31.8	61.9	27.3	35.4
Commercial	53.9	48.7	62.3	47.2
In-house	14.3	67.8	10.4	17.4
Total	100.0	55.7	100.0	100.0
N =	3,886		1,723	2,163

Note: Sample includes only those members of the experienced civilian labor force who worked in 1979. Census and SIC codes associated with these sectors: newspaper publishing and printing—census code 171, SIC code 271; printing, publishing, and allied industries, except newspapers—census code 172, SIC codes 272–279; all other industries—all other census and SIC codes for printing.

Source: 1980 public use microdata (U.S. Bureau of the Census, 1983a).

Women in Printing

Women have always worked in printing in the U.S. (Abbott, 1909; Barnett, 1909; Baker, 1964). In 1776 the founding fathers commissioned Mary Katherine Goddard, publisher of the *Baltimore Advertiser* and the *Maryland Gazette*, to print the Declaration of Independence (Bonham, 1977). Goddard was not unusual; typesetting and bookbinding were two of the seven occupations most accessible to women in the early nineteenth century (Baker, 1964:38). But the number of women in typesetting declined with the increasing adoption of the Linotype in the early twentieth century and did not increase again until the 1970s. In the interim, women continued to work in bookbinding and paper manufacture, more traditionally women's work. The few women who remained in composition found jobs with rural newspapers or in commercial ("book and job") printing.

Printing remains a "male" industry today,[6] but signs of women's entry abound. Women now constitute approximately 40 percent of all printing employees (U.S. Bureau of Labor Statistics, 1982c:11), and industry leaders and trade publications acknowledge their presence. Currently a woman edits the *American Printer*, one of the industry's major trade publications, and several top managers of a leading employers' association, the Printing Industries of America, are women. Articles have appeared featuring women print workers (e.g., Rupp, 1980; Caskey, 1983; *Tradeswomen*, 1984; Loftus, 1985; *Printing Impressions*, 1986) and describing how women in the graphic arts are faring (National Association of Printers and Lithographers, 1978, 1982, 1985; Chazin and Berglund, 1979; Wallace, 1986). Women constitute an increasing proportion of the composing room workers whom the Master Printers of America (1986) have recognized for excellent service.

Women are not, however, equally represented across print occupations. They remain concentrated in such sex-traditional fields as secretarial work, binding, proofreading, and accounting. According to surveys conducted by the *American Printer* and the National Association of Printers and Lithographers (NAPL), women have made progress toward integrating management: 25 percent of the firms surveyed in 1984 had a woman president or owner, up from 17 percent in 1982 (National Association of Printers and Lithographers, 1985:1).[7] For the most part, women co-own small family businesses (National Association of Printers and Lithographers, 1978:1–2; Chazin and Berglund, 1979:46): women owned or managed one-third of the firms with 1 to 25 employees; comparable figures for firms with 51 to 75 employees and with more than 100 were 13 and 5 percent, respectively. Women also made progress in sales (which increased from 17 to 42 percent female between 1976 and 1984); presswork (from 7 to 24 percent); and art and composition (from 47 to 61 percent), according to the NAPL (1985:2). Managers are increasingly seeking saleswomen because they see them as skilled, aggressive, and particularly adept at working with people. They also recognize that the growing number of women buyers may prefer female sales personnel (National Association of Printers and Lithographers, 1978:3).

| | | | Explaining Women's Entry: The Social Context of Technology

During the 1970s the technology of print production moved closer to what society generally perceives as "women's work." As a consequence the occupation's gender type switched from male to female. I use the term "gender type" in this context to articulate how gender ideology shaped managers' recruitment choices as well as the choices of job entrants or switchers.[8] In fostering a change in typesetting's gender type, technology thus helped to pave the way for a shift in its sex composition. Ultimately, however, technology is adopted within social settings in which workers and employers exert a force of their own. Automating typesetting need not have led inexorably to management's substituting women for men; indeed, the history of composition offers evidence to the contrary. When print employers introduced the Linotype to workplaces in the early twentieth century, they intended to hire women to do simple typesetting and even described the job as appropriate for women (Baron, 1981). However, the ITU thwarted their scheme by restricting women's entry and thus secured the occupation for unionized male workers.[9]

To explain the feminization of composition during the 1970s, therefore, one must identify other social processes that operated—in conjunction with but also independently from technology—to facilitate women's entry and encourage male flight.[10] Though technology is important (Hartmann et al., 1986), relying solely on this determinant is too simplistic. Rather, it is useful to think of technology as having set the context for and helped to generate other forms of social change that may (or may not) have affected occupational sex composition. I thus focus in this section on both technological and social determinants of the changing sex composition of typesetting and composition.[11]

Technological Change in the 1970s

Effects on job duties and work organization. The dramatic changes in the technology of typesetting significantly transformed the duties of typesetters and compositors. Regardless of industrial sector, the production process in the hot-metal composing room, more common prior to 1970, involved composition, platemaking, printing-press operations, and various finishing activities (U.S. Bureau of Labor Statistics, 1973b:39–40). At newspapers, for

example, reporters and editors prepared and copyedited articles, which Linotype operators set in type. Composing-room workers then laid out, proofed,
and corrected the pages; other craft workers made plates; pressroom workers
attached these plates to presses and supervised the printing; and mailroom
workers prepared the papers for distribution.

Ottmar Mergenthaler, an electrical machinist in Baltimore, Maryland,
invented the commercial Linotype in 1886 (Dreier, 1936; Romano, 1986).
Although the Linotype was subsequently modified—during the 1950s with
the introduction of the Teletypesetter, operators used standard keyboards to
punch a tape that automatically operated a Linotype (Baker, 1964)—Mergenthaler's machine remained in workplaces for nearly a century. Linotype
operators worked on a large, bulky machine with a special 90-key keyboard;
the standard typewriter's "QWERTY" keyboard has 44. The letters were positioned differently, and the keys were larger and spaced farther apart (Cockburn,
1983). As the linotypist selected letters, the machine assembled them into
"lines of type" and cast them in molten metal (hence the "hot-metal" designation) into strips called "slugs." Compositors gathered these into type frames to
make printing plates. Linotype operators hyphenated words and justified lines
as they worked. Highly skilled operators could set 5 lines of type per minute.
In the 1960s automatically driven Linotypes increased productivity to 6 lines
per minute, and computer-driven Linotypes eventually boosted output to 14
lines per minute (Compaine, 1980:114).

The shift in the 1970s from hot-metal to electronic ("cold") typesetting dramatically altered the technical nature of typesetters' duties (for additional information, see U.S. Department of Labor, Employment and Training
Administration, 1977; U.S. Bureau of Labor Statistics, 1984b). The major
change in typesetting technology was the replacement of Linotype machines
and other hot-metal equipment with computerized typesetters, high-speed
electronic phototypesetters, and electronic scanners (U.S. Bureau of Labor
Statistics, 1982c). Today, phototypesetter operators use video display terminals (VDTs) with QWERTY keyboards. They code the size and style of type,
specify column width and paging instructions, and type the text. The phototypesetting machine produces a film of the article, which is then processed
and composed into final layout for proofing (U.S. Bureau of Labor Statistics,
1984b:317). Compaine (1980:118) estimated that phototypesetter machines
made typesetting 4 to 123 times faster and more accurate than Linotypes, even
those driven by punched paper tape.

Electronic composition is rapidly rendering the composing room obsolete. Major newspapers no longer require traditional typesetting. To "capture
the original keystrokes electronically," reporters, staff writers, editors, and advertisement takers enter copy at what insiders refer to as the "front end" of
the business (Compaine, 1980; Smith, 1980; U.S. Bureau of Labor Statistics,
1982c), thus eliminating redundancy in typing. Newspapers retrained some

hot-metal composing-room employees on the new machines and others as pasteup assemblers, who paste phototypeset stories on page layouts according to preset specifications.[12]

This shift of traditional composing-room tasks to the originators of information is not restricted to newspapers. Book publishers also find it economical to have clerical workers enter the text into a computer or to ask authors to input their own manuscripts. These practices eliminate or substantially reduce the need for commercial typesetting (Doebler, 1973, 1975). Similarly, commercial typesetting firms often request that their clients input their own copy, using optical character recognition (OCR) or word processing. Relocating typesetting responsibilities with the authors of texts gives clients more control over the copy preparation and cuts typesetting firms' labor costs (Romano, 1977, 1978b).

Electronic-pagination (automatic page makeup) and facsimile-transmission technologies may well complete the elimination of the traditional composing room. Some newspapers and many commercial shops are already using electronic pagination, especially for advertisements, thereby eliminating even the pasteup and makeup jobs (Gottschall, 1977a, 1977b; Romano, 1978a; Shotwell, 1981; U.S. Bureau of Labor Statistics, 1982c:6, 1984b:316). Newspapers are also using satellite networks and facsimile technology to serve a "national" readership (*Printing Production*, 1968; Chazin, 1978; *American Printer and Lithographer*, 1979:47–48). For example, because the *Wall Street Journal* sends its Florida edition from Massachusetts by satellite, just nineteen people can run the entire Florida plant (Udell, 1978:6). Metropolitan newspapers such as the *Los Angeles Times* and the *Washington Post* use facsimile technology to transmit copy for printing at other locations, eliminating the need for compositors and other prepress workers outside the main office.

Effects on sex composition.   The technological transformation of typesetting converted a stereotypically male, blue-collar job to a female, white-collar one. Two factors emerge as paramount in the change of sex makeup among typesetters and compositors that accompanied *technological* innovation: the switch to the QWERTY keyboard, and the obsolescence of the traditional composing room.

First, the introduction of the standard QWERTY keyboard opened the occupation to those with typing skills—mostly women—and thus allowed employers especially in nonunion shops to recruit from a different and cheaper labor pool. Several interviewees mentioned that the number of women first began to increase with the introduction of Teletypesetter (TTS) terminals, which had the standard keyboard. As one put it, "A lot of the men did not want to use the typewriter . . . because women had those skills" (see also Hill, 1984). However, the number of women remained small at first, thanks to the efforts of journeyman printers who lobbied to ensure that women did not have access to the full range of hot-metal print jobs. It was not until Linotypes were eliminated in the 1970s that printers' claims of unique expertise collapsed, and in consequence, their ability to restrict women's access waned.

Manufacturers and employers could have chosen a "Linotype lay," a keyboard that superimposed the Linotype layout on the QWERTY keyboard (Cockburn, 1983). But the switch to a standard keyboard better served the political and economic interests of employers, because it effectively curtailed the male compositors' status and power and opened up the job to women, whom employers saw as a cheaper and more compliant workforce. My interviews provide anecdotal evidence of such employer motives. One industry analyst commented:

> I still think, deep in my heart, that most employers think they can pay women less and therefore that's what they tend to do. . . . Also they make less trouble than a guy would make. It used to be in New York City that you never wanted to hire a male operator because there was the possibility he would be in with the union, and you didn't want to bring the union into your plant.

A male newspaper compositor concurred: employers hire women, he said, because "they just want a workforce that really doesn't say much. . . . They would like young ladies that pretty well *have* to have that job. . . . Women are seen as malleable by management: they will do as they are told."

Existing gender ideology reinforced the view that women were the appropriate labor pool for the new technology. As one industry commentator put it:

> We do have a certain chauvinism in our society that if you're a typist, you're a woman; if you're a woman, you're a typist. . . . [Because of differences in training] there was this base of people who were available now who could type, and most of them were women. [Women] saw an ad that said "typesetting person, must have typing skills," and they said "I can type," and they called up and there they were.

Second, the new electronic technologies enabled employers to bypass the composing room. This meant that newspaper publishers had achieved a long-sought goal: a technological fix to what they described as the composing room "bottleneck" (Compaine, 1980:122).[13] Once the well-paid, unionized male printers became nonessential, employers were free to eliminate the composing room entirely, or at least to reduce substantially the number of people working there. Every newspaper I visited, large or small, had significantly cut its production workforce, either by attrition or by outright layoffs. Remaining workers were understandably wary about their job security as they contemplated the coming of electronic pagination. One male newspaper compositor perceptively commented on his publishers' intentions: getting rid of the composing room "would tickle them pink because they don't want any production workers, especially any workers with any past history of having any say-so. . . . You want to erase that memory, and I think they're working to erase that memory." With the elimination of the composing room, that memory will be permanently "block-deleted."

Employers have been variably successful in their attempts to eliminate composing rooms or to replace composing-room men with women. Their success has depended on shop size, whether it was unionized, and the union's power. In union workplaces the ITU was often able to guarantee union members first choice of the transformed jobs (e.g., see Baron, 1982). Cornfield (1988) has documented the success of the Chicago Typographical Union (Local 16) in maintaining job control and jurisdiction over the new technology as the composing room shifted to cold type. In the large newspapers I visited, the employees staffing the new composing rooms were retrained Linotype operators and compositors. As they retired or were "bought out" (given financial incentives to take early retirement) by management, no replacements were being hired. Few female compositors work in such newspapers.

Some union printers negotiated pacts with publishers to protect their job rights at the expense of women workers. Hill (1984) found that unionized printers at New Zealand's *Star* newspaper frustrated employer attempts to hire female TTS operators for phototypesetting. Because of its remaining strength and the perishable nature of newspapers, the printing union there was able to secure management's agreement to retrain only linotypists and compositors— typically men—on the new VDT equipment. This meant that even though the female TTS operators knew the QWERTY keyboard and the men did not, the latter won out in the competition for the technologically transformed jobs, while the women remained on the obsolete TTS technology, where their numbers declined through attrition.

In smaller newspapers that lack a strong union tradition and in most commercial shops, the situation differed dramatically. There employers used electronic composition to bypass the composing room entirely. A prominent example occurred in 1971 in Richmond, Virginia (Compaine, 1980: 182; Dertouzos and Quinn, 1985:1). After Media General introduced computerized technology to its two newspapers, the ITU local struck. But Media General continued to publish both papers by using secretarial and unskilled employees, and the new equipment paid for itself within a year. The Richmond case recurred in many other locations, and the once powerful ITU found that its jurisdictional claims went unheard.

At a small midwestern newspaper a similar transformation occurred when the publisher replaced several compositors with lower-paid "trainees"— mostly women—to operate new electronic typesetters. In this case the union survived, but it was substantially weakened. According to my informant, a male union member, trainees work alongside retrained male union members and do identical work. The newspaper maintains this two-tiered system by requiring trainees to relinquish their jobs within four years. Negotiated between management and the union, this tenure bar (Cohn, 1985) ensures that the trainees remain secondary and lower-paid workers.[14] In the Chicago local that Cornfield (1988) studied, in 1985 the newspaper replaced male strikers with women, who were paid half the union wage. The newspaper retained some of these replacement workers, after the strike was settled, as nonunion employees at reduced wages.

A similar shift to a more "clerical" and female workforce occurred at a small commercial print shop in New York when it adopted electronic composition in the late 1970s. This firm's management replaced three male Linotype operators with two female typesetters. As the owners described it, one man left immediately upon introduction of the new system, a second "could not adjust and was fired," and a third "tried to get used to the computer, could not, and quit."[15] Given the large numbers of women moving into typesetting, this scenario is probably fairly typical of what occurred in other small print shops as well.

Changed Working Conditions

The technological changes that transformed typesetting also spurred other changes in the print workplace—in the nature of the work, its educational requirements, and its rewards. All these, in turn, produced a change in gender type that led to the feminization of composition.

The transformation of the composing room was perhaps the most striking of the changes accompanying the switch to electronic composition. The old hot-metal composing room was "a combination of a dungeon and a blacksmith shop, with added discomforts of ink mists and loud noise" (Udell, 1978:10). The hot-metal Linotypes were noisy and required that operators work with lead. Compositors worked on their feet for long hours and carried heavy type frames (U.S. Bureau of Labor Statistics, 1984b). In contrast, the working conditions of today's typesetters and compositors resemble those of white-collar workers. Well-lit, air-conditioned offices have replaced the hot and noisy composing room with its ink and lead. Composing-room jobs now require only average physical strength. Production workers in today's newspaper and commercial printing firms also dress more like clerical and professional workers. One result is that newspaper firms have saved substantial sums in insurance premiums by arguing that their composing rooms are clerical rather than mechanical operations. Louis Franconeri, vice-president for operations for the *Baltimore Sun*, reported that the *Sun* papers have saved $12,000 a year in insurance costs since 1971 by reclassifying composing rooms as clerical (Newsom, 1984:15). The National Council on Compensation Insurance classifies photocomposition workers in the same category as artists, designers, and clerical employees, thus lowering workers' compensation insurance rates.

The new work, then, was more in line with what existing gender ideology considered appropriate for women. As one commentator I interviewed noted:

> No longer did you have to work at a machine that required you to lift a magazine [set of trays of type] that could weigh 50 or 60 pounds, so it was not something a woman could do easily. Linotype rooms were a noisy place, with cursing. There were sweaty men, the machines were hot, there were always problems with metal squirting. That's why it was male dominated. With phototypesetting, you could actually put it in an office.

The shift to a white-collar environment facilitated employers' efforts to hire women and discouraged them from retaining male linotypists. More women were likely to view the occupation as appropriate. As one woman I interviewed remarked, "It's now possible for women to handle the job." But male linotypists were less pleased about the job's changing technology and working conditions. Text input on a standard keyboard is reminiscent of traditional "women's work," a fact that the remaining typesetters recognized and deplored. The retrained men whom Cockburn (1983:103) interviewed complained that everything about their new work reminded them of "women's work": the keyboard layout, the plastic machine, the operator's posture, and the association of typing with women. They described the conditions as not masculine enough and less virile than the hot-metal composing room. As one newspaper printer commented, "Now it's work that any high school girl could do" (Rogers and Friedman, 1980:6). Thus, the restyling of the composing room reinforced the conversion of the printer's job from male, blue-collar employment to female, white-collar work.

Changed Skill Requirements

One explanation generally proposed for the feminization of composition is that the occupation deskilled. Those who study the printing industry generally concede that the technological and workplace changes I have documented do represent deskilling (e.g., Zimbalist, 1979; Compaine, 1980; Rogers and Friedman, 1980; Smith, 1980; Wallace and Kalleberg, 1982; Kalleberg et al., 1987). The Census Bureau itself recognized this in 1980 when it changed the classification of typesetters and compositors from skilled "craftsmen and kindred workers" to "machine operators, assemblers, and inspectors," a semiskilled category (U.S. Bureau of the Census, 1982b). However, these analysts have paid insufficient attention to the sectoral composition of the industry. Conclusions about deskilling rely primarily on reports about the effects of electronic composition on *newspaper* composing rooms; little information about the *commercial* or *corporate in-house* sectors has found its way into the debate. These sectors experienced different rates of feminization: by 1980, 62 percent of newspaper typesetters and compositors were women, compared with 49 and 68 percent of those in the commercial and in-house sectors, respectively (see Table 14.2). Treating them separately enables us to disentangle the connection between deskilling and feminization.

Newspapers.   In 1964 Blauner portrayed printing occupations as a classic case of skilled, nonalienated labor. He argued that relative to the average blue-collar job, printing was a craft occupation that demanded more educated intelligence (in order to hyphenate, justify the typed lines, and proofread the type), knowledge of the craft's specialized tools (such as the Linotype keyboard), and the eye-and-hand dexterity necessary to manipulate nonstandardized material. Workers learned these latter skills during a lengthy apprenticeship.

Blauner's (1964) description of printing no longer accurately portrays newspaper typesetters and compositors. As literacy increased, the general public was less likely to view print workers as more intelligent than the average production worker, a change leading to a decline in their prestige. In addition, electronic composition subsumed some of the printer's traditional skills (hyphenation, justification), and the QWERTY keyboard made the Linotype operators' special keyboard skills obsolete. Finally, even strength was not needed in the electronic composing room, since printers no longer had to carry heavy type frames.

My interviews confirmed that retrained printers see their work as deskilled. As one male commented:

> I think the skills are less, so I think there's a degradation of work. These young ladies coming in now, they don't have the work ethic that we had. . . . They're much less dedicated to the job. . . . For instance, most of us would go to our work sick. You see, they would not do that. I don't blame them; they're coming now and they're told in four years you won't have a job. How committed would you be to your job if they told you that?
>
> I see it as no achievement for women to become printers under the present circumstances. Employers hire women to abuse them. They are given unequal pay. A weak union allows women to be ordered around or chided by management without much grievance procedure. A woman can be made to stand in one place all day, for example, with no recourse. Women and trainees are given no job security or future with the company, since they are told that in four years they will go. So a woman has to constantly perform in this repressive atmosphere.

Yet although the skills required of those remaining in the newspaper composing room are clearly not the same as they once were, deskilling may not be the best description of what took place in the 1970s. First, Cornfield (1988) found that the real deskilling of print work occurred in the transition from hand composition to the Linotype (at the turn of the century) rather than with the shift to photocomposition technology in the 1970s. Using measures of skill from the *Dictionary of Occupational Titles* (complexity of the occupation with respect to data and things, specific vocational preparation, mathematical development, and language development), he found that occupations associated with Linotype and computerized photocomposition technologies differ little in terms of skill. Hand composition occupations were more skilled, according to these criteria, than either Linotype or photocomposition occupations.

Second, while technology has rendered many of the typesetters' skills obsolete, these tasks have shifted to other parts of the organization. Reporters, editors, and advertisement takers now input the original text electronically, eliminating the need for rekeyboarding by typesetters.

Third, pockets of skilled work remain in what is left of the transformed composing room. Some compositors focus on the design aspects of newspaper layout. Others work on color separation, a more skilled job than straight typing or pasteup work. At one newspaper I visited, the production staff retained much of the responsibility for designing the printed newspaper page, deciding height, width, and type of display. One printer was developing fonts for newspaper ads, in essence teaching the computer to print company logos.

Finally, even new entrants are skilled, albeit less so than their predecessors. In addition to knowing how to type, many also have training in typography, computer editing, and specialized printing packages. These skills differ from earlier print training primarily in that they are often learned *prior* to job entry rather than on the job, a change made possible by the switch from a specialized to a standard keyboard.

Whether or not one regards the changes as deskilling or skill obsolescence,[16] there is no doubt that newspaper typesetters and compositors did lose much of their job autonomy and that newspaper composition declined in status and earnings. Employers, not male union members, now control the transformed print jobs, and employers are increasingly turning to women to staff the new typesetting jobs. By 1980 only 27 percent of male typesetters and compositors worked for newspapers, compared with 35 percent of comparable women (Table 14.2). In a dramatic change from the 1970s, women now represent 62 percent of typesetters in this declining sector.[17] Of course, the significant decrease in the number of production jobs helps to ensure that fewer workers, male or female, can get composition jobs in newspapers. It is notable that women made their greatest strides in newspapers, the sector hit hardest by technological displacement. This finding is reminiscent of Hacker's (1979) results for women's job gains at AT&T.

Commercial sector. Deskilling is an even less apt description of changes in the commercial sector. The characterization of printing as "graphic arts" is particularly appropriate for this sector, since the term reflects the role of design in typesetting and composition work. Within commercial printing a skill hierarchy emerged in the 1970s among those doing keyboard entry (Romano, 1981). The least skilled are "typists" who keyboard text on typewriters or word-processing machines. Somewhat more skilled are "typists who set type," entering copy and a few simple printing formats on a direct-input typesetting machine such as a VariTyper. Because both these jobs are primarily clerical, the census occupational classification scheme codes them as clerical workers. A composing-room manager I interviewed reported that she recruited varitype operators by advertising for "typists, book publishing," and then trained them on the VariTyper.

More skilled and autonomous than either of these jobs are "typesetters," who differ from typists who set type because they exercise judgment about how the finished product should look and know the printing codes to achieve the desired outcome. Because skilled typesetters are scarce and in high demand, many firms reserve them to "mark up" manuscripts with command codes. Clerical employees then do the less-skilled task of inputting the text.

At the top of the skill hierarchy are "typographers," who have the greatest latitude in decision making and the highest level of professionalism and skill (Romano, 1979). Skilled typography is more than knowing how to type and code. It also involves making aesthetic judgments, such as choosing the typeface, type size, and spacing. Industry observers' description of typography as a "servant art" or the "interface between technology and art" indicates that it is a means to a desired artistic product (Gottschall, 1977a:46–47). Computer-assisted typography enables typographers to apply design principles to setting type better than hot-metal machines could. Some of the improvements over the Linotype include an inexhaustible number of characters; the ability to mix different styles of type without stopping to change fonts; easy modification of intercharacter spacing for better fitting of letters; fewer errors; and built-in hyphenation (Gottschall, 1977a:42–46). Allman (1985:14) described the advent of photographic typesetting as "freeing the type producer from the limitations of hot metal . . . [and] opening a new world of typographic creativity with typefaces to evoke just about any emotion or feeling." With the development of page makeup and digitized typesetting (the technology of creating characters from thousands of tiny dots), typographers' ability to design images and layouts has been enhanced (Romano, 1978a).[18]

In view of the diversity of machinery available for typesetting, the different printing codes used, and the lack of standardization and training in the industry, one can understand why skilled typographers are in great demand and earn high salaries (Romano, 1981). Unlike newspaper compositors, commercial printers can claim a unique expertise. While men still predominate in commercial firms, the continued demand for workers is prompting employers to turn increasingly to women to staff graphic-arts production departments

(Carruthers, 1987). By 1980, 62 percent of male compositors were working in the commercial sector; the comparable figure for women was 47 percent (see Table 14.2).

Corporate in-house print shops. One manifestation of the trend to move production back to the originators of information is that many firms are establishing their own printing departments. These in-house shops use computerized technology on the premises to accomplish much of their business composition (Green, 1977:13; Ris, 1979; Romano, 1979; *American Printer and Lithographer*, 1980:106A; *American Printer*, 1983:35). The U.S. Bureau of Labor Statistics (1980b) estimated that the number of in-house shops increased from 25,000 in 1967 to well over 70,000 by 1978. As of 1977, 450 of the Fortune 500 companies had in-plant printing operations, as did most companies with 100 or more employees (Gottschall, 1977a:2). This trend is displacing the traditional production functions of the typesetter and will probably accelerate as word processing increasingly merges with typesetting technology (Gottschall, 1977a, 1977b; National Association of Printers and Lithographers, 1978:3; Borum, 1980:19).

In 1980, two-thirds of typesetters and compositors working in the in-house sector were women (see Table 14.2). Industry observers speculate that the growth of this sector has provided more opportunities for women than for men, a conclusion that census data support: in 1980, approximately 17 percent of women typesetters and compositors staffed in-house shops, compared with 10 percent of the men (Table 14.2). One reason for women's predominance is the very nature of in-house operations, which combine word processing with reproduction and copying services (Chazin and Berglund, 1979:48). Women's greater representation may also be attributable in part to the greater security and better benefits these larger firms offer, compared with small commercial printing shops (Wallace, 1986:37).[19]

One consequence of this shift to the corporate "front end," as opposed to subcontracting to commercial typesetters, is that typesetters and typographers must interact more with clients in designing the printed product. In the past, design was left largely to the professionals' discretion (Nikcevich, 1983:47). While this change may represent a decrease in their autonomy, it requires a new skill—communicating effectively with laypersons about typefaces and page layouts: "At the top of [the] list of requirements for graphic communications graduates [are] vastly improved communications skills, a working knowledge of human relations, and high levels of competence in practicing interpersonal skills—working with people" (Carruthers, 1987:58). This shift in skills provides yet another reason for the occupation's shift in gender type: the dominant ideology has long attributed to women greater communication skills. The gender ideology that sees women and men as exhibiting distinct traits thus reinforces the effect of technological change.

Unionization and Declining Job Autonomy

One change in the nature of typesetting and composition that bears directly on the shift from a predominantly male to a majority female workforce is deteriorating union power and the concomitant decline in job autonomy. In its heyday the ITU's power was reflected in excellent benefits, typically including maximum hours of work per week and day, a closed shop, and worker control in the composing room (Lipset et al., 1956:24–25). Workers had the right to designate their own substitutes; only union members were allowed on the shop floor; and foremen had to belong to the union and thus were subject to union sanctions. The ITU also controlled hiring and firing and ran the apprenticeship programs that recruited and trained new employees.

Prior to the 1970s, the ITU successfully claimed newly introduced technologies—including computerized equipment—as the sole province of its members. In 1955, the ITU asserted jurisdiction over the photocomposition machine (Kelber and Schlesinger, 1967:48), and in 1970 it claimed control over the cathode ray tube, or CRT (*Editor and Publisher*, 1970a). These claims represented the ITU's acceptance of new technology as long as its members ran the equipment. With the advent of electronic type, however, newspaper publishers could more readily bypass the composing room. Fighting a losing battle to protect job control, ITU locals sought agreements that protected their members' job security (Raskin, 1978; see also Cornfield, 1988). In a 1974 agreement with New York publishers, ITU's Local 6 won lifetime job guarantees for all its members. Some ITU members retired early, with lump-sum "buyouts"; others were retrained for less skilled tasks in the electronic composing room (Rogers and Friedman, 1980; Newsom, 1982; Dertouzos and Quinn, 1985; Kalleberg et al., 1987). In 1978 the *New York Times* eliminated its Linotypes altogether, switching completely to electronic composition (Raskin, 1978).

The most visible illustration of the ITU's loss of power is the dramatic decline in its membership, even relative to other unions (Loftus, 1984; Farber, 1987). Between 1970 and 1982, while the total employment in the industry increased 13 percent, active ITU membership declined 40 percent; the union shut its training schools (Salgado, 1984:17; Kalleberg et al., 1987); and the number of apprentices dropped 74 percent (Dertouzos and Quinn, 1985:12). Moreover, since 1970 the ITU has lost 45 percent of its representation and 85 percent of its decertifying elections—a far cry from 1944, when major printing unions won 83 percent of their representation elections (Loftus, 1984:18).

A final indication of the print unions' weakness is the growing number of union mergers, a strategy designed to better their bargaining position. Recent examples include the Graphic Communications International Union (GCIU), formed in 1983 from a merger of the Graphic Arts International Union and the International Printing and Graphic Communications

Union. After discussing consolidation with several others, the International Typographical Union merged in December 1986 with the Communications Workers of America (Noble, 1986; Warren, 1986). The once powerful ITU had ceased to exist.

The collapse of the ITU's jurisdictional claims gave women greater access to the composing room. While historically the union had successfully argued that women could not do composition work (Baron, 1981; Cockburn, 1983), employers' ability to bypass the composing room rendered the ITU's arguments moot. The power to control the job, and with it the ability to hire women, shifted to employers. Printers are well aware of this shift in power. As one compositor in a midsized newspaper commented:

> Business used to have to contend with workers as people. The craft has ended up with segments that perhaps don't require as much skill. The employer does not want to pay skilled people. . . . In general, women are hired to fill printing jobs while men lose prestige, pride in their work, and so on, which has nothing to do with women per se. If a woman quits, the employer can always hire another one to replace her, perhaps at even less cost.

A residual negative effect of unions remains today, as shown by the fact that women have made their greatest gains in nonunion shops, regardless of sector. In 1982, for example, among those responding to the NAPL surveys, union firms reported that women made up 39 percent of their art and composition force, compared to 70 percent in nonunion firms. Similar differences exist for presswork (4 versus 16 percent) and sales (18 versus 34 percent) (National Association of Printers and Lithographers, 1982:4). This negative correlation between unionization and women's representation is well known. The predominance of men in unionized newspaper shops, noted one industry analyst,

> is a vestige of an older period. It was all male oriented, male dominated, and undoubtedly the most chauvinistic group you'd ever find. And it was only when the de-unionization of the industry occurred . . . that women started to enter it in large numbers. So I think that proves my point. Wherever you find a union installation, you will still find a preponderance of men.

Education and Training

Just as electronic composition changed job duties and other aspects of composition, so has it changed the amount and kind of education and training required. When Lipset and his colleagues (1956:33) studied the ITU, they found that compositors were slightly better educated than other skilled workers, a fact reflected in their status as the aristocracy of the blue-collar workforce. But by 1980, compositors had lost their educational edge: the average typesetter had completed 12.4 years of schooling, slightly less than the average U.S. worker (U.S. Bureau of the Census, 1986b:121).

The most important training that compositors formerly received was a six-year apprenticeship certifying them as "journeymen." The union ran these programs, the only entry into a unionized shop. Even nonunionized firms often required an apprenticeship for employment in their composing rooms (U.S. Bureau of Labor Statistics, 1970:501). After the introduction of the Linotype, this six-year requirement reflected the union's power more than the job's requirements (Lipset et al., 1956:33), as the ITU belatedly recognized in 1968 when they reduced the required apprenticeship to four years (*Editor and Publisher*, 1968). Today, prospective print workers can be partly trained by vocational or manual-arts high schools or through high school industrial arts courses (Gottschall, 1977b:54; Crouch, 1985). Others learn informally on the job.

Unions are no longer charged with producing qualified compositors, and no adequate training programs have emerged to fill the vacuum (Palmer, 1979; Carruthers, 1987). With the change in technology, computer and engineering skills have become important assets for applicants to commercial printing firms (Beckett, 1986). Industry observers are calling for a better educated labor pool, and for management to refocus interest away from technology and toward upgrading print personnel (Carruthers, 1987). Frank Romano (1983:34), a longtime industry observer, described the current training dilemma as "everyone [learning] from scratch." He revealed (Romano, 1988) that because they can afford the cost, corporations are taking the lead in training typesetters, many of whom come from the secretarial ranks. The only way other employers get qualified personnel is to train them themselves or "steal" them from the larger companies (Eldred and Orr, 1980:50).

My interviews reflected this haphazard training pattern. One male typesetter learned composition while working in a leftist print shop and was subsequently able to get a job in a typographical shop being organized by the ITU. With union privileges, he finally moved into a composition job at a daily newspaper. Another moved into his current ad makeup job after starting as a TTS operator for a unionized newspaper. Two women I interviewed broke into the business through a family-owned firm.

One consequence of the disappearance of apprenticeships as a recruitment channel is that women have greater access to the print labor pool. In turning to a better-educated labor force, employers are increasingly turning to women. These new female recruits average 0.4 year more education than the average male, probably in part because they are approximately ten years younger than the male compositors (see Table 14.3).

Table 14.3
Average Age and Earnings of Typesetters and Compositors, by Industry and
Sex, 1980

	Total	Men	Women
Mean Age			
Newspapers	37.7	45.0	33.3
Commercial	37.3	42.3	32.1
In-house	34.8	40.0	32.3
Total (all industries)	37.1	42.8	32.5
Mean Earnings			
Newspapers	$9,304	$14,168	$6,316
Commercial	12,019	15,682	8,166
In-house	10,474	14,713	8,461
Total (all industries)	10,935	15,168	7,563

Note: Sample includes only those members of the experienced civilian labor force who worked in 1979.
N = 3,886.

Source: 1980 public use microdata (U.S. Bureau of the Census, 1983a).

Occupational Rewards

Finally, occupational rewards for composition workers have declined. Lipset et al. (1956:33) found that even though the overall social status of printing had declined somewhat with the switch to the Linotype (see also Cornfield, 1988), workers still believed they commanded substantial respect from the general population. Twenty-five years later, when Rogers and Friedman (1980:6) interviewed members of the same local, the ITU compositors expressed lowered estimates of their own prestige.

Typesetters and compositors' relative earnings have also apparently declined, at least in the newspaper sector (Compaine, 1980; Wallace and Kalleberg, 1982). Historically, an influx of women into an occupation has been associated with declining relative earnings, and printing appears to be no exception. Wallace and Kalleberg (1982:318) found that while hand compositors and Linotype operators traditionally enjoyed a wage advantage over the average manufacturing worker, this gap declined considerably between 1910 and 1978. They observed the same pattern of decreasing relative earnings when they compared hand compositors and Linotype operators with all unionized print workers, suggesting that the traditional earnings advantage of the former had eroded as well.

Composing personnel in newspapers suffered the sharpest decline in their relative earnings (Wallace and Kalleberg, 1982:318), probably because this sector experienced technological change earlier than the less unionized commercial sector. Published BLS data (U.S. Bureau of Labor Statistics, 1985, 1987a) confirmed Wallace and Kalleberg's findings: between 1950 and 1986 the average weekly earnings of newspaper production workers, expressed as a percentage of the weekly earnings of all printing production workers, fell from 106 to 89 percent. Three-quarters of this drop occurred between 1970 and 1986, the period of greatest dissemination of electronic technologies. This period also coincides with the rapid influx of women into newspaper composing. These data suggest that the shift to a greater percentage of females in the workforce exacerbated a long-term decline in the relative earnings of print craft workers.

By 1980, newspaper typesetters were averaging $9,304, notably less than the average of $12,019 that typesetters in the commercial sector earned (see Table 14.3). Some of this gap is attributable to women's overrepresentation in the newspaper sector and women's lower average earnings. However, even controlling for sex, women and men in commercial printing outearn their counterparts in newspapers. In-house shops offer women compositors their highest salaries, which may reflect the higher salaries and better benefits of establishments large enough to maintain in-house printing facilities (Wallace, 1986:37).

The higher earnings of commercial-sector compositors are consistent with the greater skill retention in that sector. In addition, they outearn their newspaper peers because of the shortage of qualified personnel to meet the heavy demand for their skills. According to the New York State Department of Labor, in 1986 Long Island printing production workers averaged $12.40 an hour, second only to production workers in the transportation–equipment manufacturing industry. As an industry observer noted, "If you're a technician and you know how to handle this equipment, you can almost write your own ticket. . . . The electronic revolution is still going on inside the printing industry" (Beckett, 1986).

| | | | Discussion

The social changes that occurred in typesetting and composition in the 1970s provide an excellent opportunity to view the *dynamics* of occupational segregation by sex. Typesetting represents an occupation that underwent an extraordinary change in its technology of production and an equally dramatic feminization (from 17 to 56 percent between 1970 and 1980). Investigating the relationship between these two social changes reveals that technological innovation is socially embedded.

To be sure, technological change in typesetting and composition is a major explanation for the occupation's feminization: the introduction of the QWERTY keyboard opened the occupation to women. Whereas the Linotype had required occupation-specific knowledge, generally provided through lengthy apprenticeships, the VDT with its standard keyboard was accessible to anyone who could type. In addition, the shift of the production function to the front end of the print operation meant that employers could more easily bypass composing-room employees, typically well-paid, male union members. Electronic pagination, when fully implemented, threatens to eliminate the composing room altogether, at least in newspapers.

But technological change per se is only part of the overall picture; how technology is adopted is also consequential. The adoption of electronic composition has had disparate effects on different print sectors: while newspaper typesetters and compositors are threatened with redundancy, those in the commercial sector are in demand and earn relatively high salaries. Investigating the reasons for these differences is instructive for our ultimate task of understanding why women made inroads into composition, especially newspaper composition.

Newspaper publishers had a strong incentive to adopt technology that would bypass the composing room. In the past the ITU used strikes effectively to win wage- and job-control concessions precisely because news is highly perishable and composing-room employees were critical to the production process. The union also used its power to restrict women's entry to the craft. To contain costs and break the power of the union, publishers sought a technology fix that would bypass the composing room (Compaine, 1980). As one newspaper official commented, "Technology is useless without eliminating people" (Dertouzos and Quinn, 1985:v). With electronic composition, the ITU's claims of unique expertise collapsed, and employers increasingly drew on women to staff remaining composing jobs.

In the commercial sector, less unionization and smaller shops reduced employers' incentive (and even ability) to bypass the traditional production process. Even though this sector also transferred text entry to the front end, the focus on design and artistic skills fueled a demand for skilled typesetters and typographers capable of operating the newest technological equipment. This strong demand for workers, which employers claim men cannot meet (Carruthers, 1987), helps to ensure women's continued access.

One major reorganization that occurred in print workplaces was the physical modification of the composing room. Employers replaced the noisy, dirty hot-metal composing room with a clean, well-lit, air-conditioned office. Such restyling reinforced the technological recasting of the occupation's gender type from male to female. It was no wonder, then, that employers saw women as more suitable than men for the transformed composing rooms.

Other occupational changes also hastened women's entry. As the education, skill, status, and earnings of (especially newspaper) typesetters and compositors eroded relative to those of other craft workers, employers had greater incentive to hire women, and men were less motivated to train for or remain in these jobs. Furthermore, the declining number of composition jobs, especially in newspapers, meant fewer opportunities for either men or women to enter the craft.

In sum, technological change was an important factor in promoting the rapid decline in the number of men in typesetting and encouraging the increase in the number of women. But as I have shown, one must view technological change in its social context. Although typesetters and compositors in electronic production departments may be producing the same products as did their predecessors in hot-metal composing rooms (newspapers, periodicals, books, and other print services), the occupation has otherwise changed radically. Job incumbents labor in markedly different environments and with vastly different technologies. They obtain different skills and acquire them differently. They are less likely to be represented by a union. And, most important for our purposes, they are also more likely to be women. The sex composition of this occupation, like its gender type, has become female. With three-quarters of occupational incumbents now women, the gender switch of typesetting and composition is nearly complete.

| | | | Notes

Acknowledgments: A previous version of this paper was presented at the annual meeting of the American Sociological Association, New York, August 1986. I thank Lee Clarke, Barbara F. Reskin, Andrew Abbott, Robert Althauser, Paul Attewell, Daniel Cornfield, Ruth Cowan, Katharine M. Donato, James Rule, Steven Vallas, and Michael Wallace for helpful comments. I also thank Elizabeth Chute, Elizabeth Hein, and Valerie Hilicus for valuable research assistance, and my interviewees, who shared their insights. This research was supported by grants from the National Science Foundation (SES-85-12586) and the Rockefeller Foundation (RF 84036, Allocation No. 26), Barbara F. Reskin and Patricia A. Roos, Principal Investigators.

1. I use the terms "typesetting" and "composition" interchangeably for ease of presentation. While these are distinct jobs, the census places both in the same detailed occupation code (736—"typesetters and compositors"). Historically, printers who completed the lengthy apprenticeship program were certified as equally skilled in both jobs.

2. Feminization could also be attributable to women's outnumbering male entrants in a growing occupation. This is clearly not the case for typesetting and composition.

3. As Kalleberg et al. (1987) have documented, since the late 1940s, the American newspaper industry has experienced a concentration of newspaper interests, a rapid growth in the number of chains following mergers and consolidations, declining competition in metropolitan areas, and a shift from primarily family ownership to corporation ownership (see also Dertouzos and Quinn, 1985).

4. My definition of the commercial sector is thus broader than that of the SIC (Standard Industrial Classification). In its narrower sense, commercial printing refers

to the actual printing (as opposed to the publishing) of newspapers, books, magazines, and the like, or to the performing of services for the printing trade, such as bookbinding or platemaking (U.S. Office of Management and Budget, 1987).

5. These and subsequent statistics, unless otherwise specified, are from the 1980 public use microdata, A sample (U.S. Bureau of the Census, 1983a).

6. For example, an announcement in the *PIA Communicator* (1985) requested nominations for the "1985 Graphic Arts Man-Of-The-Year Award," despite the disclaimer that "the nominee is not limited by age, sex, race or geographic location."

7. These figures should be interpreted with caution, since they represent responses to surveys published in the *American Printer*. The number of firms responding for 1978, 1982, and 1984 were 420, 453, and 678, respectively (NAPL special reports, 1978, 1982, 1985).

8. "Gender type" is distinct from "sex composition," which I use to refer to the percentage of females in the occupation's workforce. While these two concepts are empirically related (e.g., most people view secretary as a "female" job, and women predominate as secretaries), they need not be synonymous. In fact, typesetting illustrates how an occupation's gender type can change more rapidly than its sex composition. During the 1970s, typesetting's gender type switched rapidly to female. The occupation's sex composition altered more slowly. By 1980, 56 percent of incumbents were women, making this a mixed-sex occupation. By 1988, with 74 percent of typesetters and compositors female, the occupation's sex composition had all but caught up with its gender label.

9. This story is fascinating in its own right. In contrast to the dramatic *increase* in the number of women compositors that occurred with the switch to electronic composition in the 1970s is the actual *reduction* in the number of women compositors that followed the introduction of the Linotype at the turn of the century. For a more detailed comparison of these two historical periods, see Roos (1986).

10. We can quickly reject one commonsense explanation for composition's changing percentage female—that the census misclassified female clerical workers as typesetters and compositors. The specific job titles, or Standard Occupational Classification (SOC) codes, included in the census detailed code indicate that the 1980 classification retained a skill distinction (U.S. Department of Commerce, 1980; U.S. Bureau of the Census, 1983b: Appendix I). The more skilled precision typesetters and typesetting and composing machine operators remain in the appropriate census title (736—"typesetters and compositors"), while those who perform less skilled tasks, such as the typesetting of advertisement copy from phone orders or typing text onto computer terminals according to preset instructions (varitypists, photocomposition keyboard operators, typesetter-perforator operators), are appropriately coded as clerical personnel (325—"classified-ad clerks," or 385—"data-entry keyers").

11. For evidence, I relied on government documents, trade publications, social science literature, and interviews with occupational incumbents.

12. At one newspaper I visited, some of the former linotypists spend at least part of their time demonstrating their obsolete skills for the newspaper tours that public relations representatives regularly bring through what they call the "composing room museum." Like the machinery on which they worked, these skilled craft workers have become museum pieces.

13. A compositor I talked with argued that these "bottlenecks" were fiction: "In

24 years in the composing rooms where I worked, ads or copy were never turned away. I can remember no failure to complete work by a set time. The employer may have had to hire overtime or extras, but the only bottleneck was a failure of management to correctly perceive needs and gauge the amount of people needed. . . . employers have chosen to see the composing room as a bottleneck because that makes technology more acceptable to investors, other departments, etc. Employers always have a rationale for introducing technology."

14. One of France's biggest daily newspapers instituted a similar two-tiered system (Maruani and Nicole, 1987). With the advent of the computer in 1969, the newspaper's publisher hired female compositors, whom they classified as unskilled employees. While the men and women did almost identical work (both typed copy and corrected their own work), the women earned substantially less, were paid according to output as opposed to a salary, and were entitled to a break of twenty minutes per day, compared to the men's ten minutes per hour. In addition, the women's hours were set; the men could leave when they finished their work. When a curtain that had physically separated the sexes was removed in 1983, revealing for the first time the glaring sex inequities, the women compositors went on strike. The strike was partially successful: the publisher created a small number of better-paid jobs for which the women could compete. And, at the request of both the women and the men, the curtain was installed once again.

15. Kevin Delaney conducted this interview with the owner of a small print shop specializing in business cards, brochures, and small journals in September, 1985. I thank him and Paul Attewell for access to the interview transcript.

16. Burris (1989:170) suggests that to the extent that shifts to a female workforce are an intentional outcome of employers' adoption of new technology, "skill restructuring" (Cockburn, 1987, quoted in Burris, 1989) might be a better description of the resulting social change.

17. There is some evidence—albeit questionable, since the Census Bureau changed its occupational classification system between 1970 and 1980—for assuming that women have indeed integrated more rapidly into the newspaper sector. Data from the 1970 census show that 15 percent of newspaper "compositors and typesetters" (as they were titled in 1970) were women, compared with 11 percent of those in other printing sectors (U.S. Bureau of the Census, 1972). The comparable figures in Table 14.2 suggest that though women increased their representation in all sectors over the decade, their growth was most dramatic in newspaper establishments.

18. There are claims that "desktop publishing" computer programs will make the design skills of typesetters and typographers obsolete. Others assert to the contrary that the design aspects of type format are still better done by graphic-arts professionals, regardless of how much power one's computer system has (Machrone, 1986:62). Several people I interviewed expressed irritation at manufacturers' claims that anyone could operate their machines and software. These respondents claimed that using the new technology requires programming skills, a good head for math, and a good sense of design.

19. Large organizations may also be more vulnerable to affirmative-action regulations and hence be looking for suitable sex-atypical jobs in which they can place women.

Part III
Conclusion

15

Summary, Implications, and Prospects

Although researchers disagree over the causes of sex segregation in the workplace, they agree on its pervasiveness and persistence. Between 1900 and 1970 the extent of occupational-level sex segregation fluctuated only slightly (Gross, 1968; Jacobs, 1989b). Of course, aggregate-level stability in the extent of segregation can conceal infrequent shifts in the sex makeup of particular occupations, but as Chapter 1 showed, such changes have been rare. Indeed, it was the historical stability in occupations' sex composition that drew our attention to women's marked inroads during the 1970s into such diverse male occupations as pharmacist, typesetter, and bus driver.

The statistical desegregation of those and several other customarily male occupations raised three questions for us. First and foremost, what accounted for women's disproportionate movement into an assortment of traditionally male occupations during a decade in which women made modest headway at best into most such occupations? The 1970s witnessed several large-scale changes that could be implicated in occupations' changing sex composition: the continued shift from a goods- to a service-producing economy and the creation of thousands of new jobs; women's unprecedented levels of participation in paid work; declining family earnings, a growing divorce rate, and the feminization of poverty; a computer revolution that transformed both white- and blue-collar jobs; a rebirth of feminism that challenged traditional sex roles and male privilege; and increased governmental regulation of employment practices. We sought to learn whether and how each contributed to the post-1970 desegregation of several traditionally male occupations.

Because we recognize that women's entry into male *occupations* does not necessarily integrate men's *jobs*, our second question was the extent to which women and men held the same jobs *within* desegregating occupations. The same occupation can include jobs in different industries and establishments, jobs that entail different working conditions and offer different rewards. Thus, occupations undergoing desegregation may include jobs that remain segregated. We sought to determine whether and how much genuine job-level integration accompanied the occupational-level desegregation that occurred in the occupations we studied.

Our third question was the extent to which women entered male occupations on an equal footing with male incumbents. Did entering customarily male occupations bring women career opportunities and economic rewards equivalent to those they conferred on male workers?

We assembled data to answer these questions through fourteen case studies of occupations that had become disproportionately more female during the 1970s, eleven of which are described in Chapters 4 through 14. In this final chapter we summarize our answers to the three questions that guided our study, then probe the theoretical implications of our findings, and appraise women's prospects for entering other sex-atypical occupations during the 1990s.

| | | | Summary of Findings

Explaining Women's Inroads into Male Occupations

Labor shortages, occupational growth, and declining occupational attractiveness.   The fundamental reason for women's disproportionate entry into the occupations we studied was a shortage of male workers. In a few occupations, shortages resulted from the dramatic growth that accompanied the expansion of the service sector. All the feminizing occupations we studied except baking and typesetting produce services,[1] and all contributed to the growth of the service economy during the 1970s by creating thousands of new service-providing jobs or by transforming existing jobs so that they increasingly provided services. However, growth does not inevitably smooth the way for women to enter male occupations. Among those we studied, it did so only when it depleted the supply of suitable men. In growing male occupations with plentiful qualified male prospects, or those for which men could easily become qualified, employers continued to hire men. It is when job growth outstrips the number of qualified prospective workers from the normal labor supply that employers resort to nontraditional workers. During the 1970s, employers were especially likely to turn to women to fill jobs in accounting and systems analysis in which the need for specialized skills limited the number of qualified male prospects.

More important than sheer growth for women's disproportionate entry into most of the occupations we studied was a change in the work process or rewards that rendered jobs less attractive to men than competing opportunities.[2] Some occupations such as insurance adjusting/examining and typesetting/composing deteriorated after employers reorganized the work process or introduced new technologies that robbed jobs of their skill, diversity, and autonomy. Technological change figured also in the feminization of baking, *both* by creating new retail jobs that men did not want *and* by disproportionately eliminating male production jobs. Other occupations such as book editing and pharmacy deteriorated in men's eyes as their prestige, job security, promotion prospects, and real earnings declined. When these deteriorating occupations were simultaneously undergoing growth—as did residential real estate sales, insurance adjusting and examining, and bartending—they feminized especially rapidly. In a nutshell, employers turned to women to fill jobs that men, for various reasons, eschewed.

Sex-specific demand for women.   Fostering desegregation in a few of our occupations was the emergence of a sex-specific demand for women. Four phenomena produced such a demand: antidiscrimination regulations and litigation that raised the potential cost of giving men preference; the growth within an occupation of tasks already labeled as women's work; the growth of a female clientele; and economic exigencies that spurred employers to take advantage of women's lower labor price.

We see the effect of the first of these factors in women's gains as bank managers, which stemmed partly from enforcement activities by the Office of Federal Contract Compliance Programs. The requirement by regulatory agencies that employers report employees' sex across broad occupational classifications fostered women's gains in bank management and public relations and probably in personnel and labor relations. Reinforcing the effect of regulatory agencies was litigation by individual women or women's organizations. Highly visible lawsuits and those that challenged major barriers such as state laws opened jobs to women in bartending, broadcast reporting, and book editing. The risk to employers of losing federal contracts, broadcast licenses, discrimination suits, or their reputations generated a sex-specific demand for women by raising the potential cost of male preference.

A second economic incentive for hiring women for jobs in male occupations was job changes that employers thought would make women more productive workers than men. Chapter 2 recounted how the clericalization of newspaper typesetting and insurance adjusting allowed firms to recast them as women's work. To a lesser extent, women's headway in public relations, systems analysis, and personal banking resulted from a growing emphasis on communicating with or serving clients—skills at which women stereotypically excel. Third, a growing number of female customers, clients, or role partners addressed by public relations specialists, book editors, insurance salespersons, and perhaps real estate salespersons contributed to what Baron and Bielby (1985) have called "gender-based" integration in these occupations.

Fourth, changed economic environments in some occupations, requiring employers to cut labor costs, made women more attractive employees. For instance, unstable interest rates and high inflation led insurance companies to cut costs by routinizing the work of insurance adjusters and examiners. Deregulation prompted banks to compete with savings and loans by creating thousands of service-oriented management jobs in personal banking. The proliferation of retail drugstore chains and of pharmacies in discount stores, supermarkets, and health-maintenance organizations fueled the demand for less expensive pharmacists who did not aspire to be entrepreneurs.

Changing social attitudes and declining discrimination. Until the 1960s, sex discrimination was widely accepted as a fact of life that played a major role in excluding women from men's jobs (Blau, 1984). But challenges by the civil rights and feminist movements to white men's birthright to the first place in the labor queue transformed public attitudes about the propriety of excluding people from jobs simply because of their color or sex. Liberalized public sentiment—backed by antidiscrimination regulations—encouraged employers to espouse equal-employment practices; and a publicly endorsed notion of entitlement to equal opportunity, combined with media attention to women pioneers in men's jobs, gave women permission to aspire to occupations formerly off limits to them. As a result, growing numbers of women, anticipating equal treatment, trained for traditionally male jobs.[3]

Despite the prevailing wisdom that liberalized attitudes have opened male jobs to women, we could document an effect only in bartending, where women's exclusion had been reinforced by public fears that tending bar would corrupt them. In the other feminizing occupations we studied, changing attitudes were unimportant compared with labor shortages or economic pressures. Most of these occupations were no exception to Rotella's (1981) assertion that changes in occupations' sex labels follow rather than precede occupations' feminization.

Declining resistance by male workers. Facilitating the desegregation of typesetting/composing and bartending was men's declining ability to exclude women as union membership dropped and unions' clout waned. Of course, in occupations that experienced sharp growth, women's entry did not threaten men's ability to retain desirable jobs. But men failed to resist women's entry into many feminizing occupations because the latter were no longer worth preserving as male territory. Here, as elsewhere (Hartmann et al., 1986:60), most of women's increased numbers in feminizing occupations did not result from their taking jobs away from men.

Women's labor supply and preferences. Women's increasing share of the labor force and the pools from which employers recruit workers (such as M.B.A.'s) contributed to their movement into some male occupations, but unless circumstances impelled employers to hire women, the increased supply of women would not have been sufficient to feminize these male occupations. We must remember that women's growing representation in the specific labor pools was largely a *response* to employers' need for workers in occupations that were more attractive than those to which the gender queue customarily relegated women. Opportunities beckoned, and women responded. Important in persuading women to study pharmacy, systems analysis, accounting, journalism, and financial management was their confidence that antidiscrimination and affirmative-action regulations and public opposition to discrimination ensured that jobs would await them when they had finished their education. Moreover, as larger numbers of women pursued sex-atypical jobs, their presence stimulated "natural" forces that fostered the employment of even more women: jobs' sex labels and employers' preferences changed; women recruited more women through their informal networks; and some men fled or avoided feminizing jobs, increasing employers' reliance on women—and potentially leading to resegregation.

The importance of demand does not mean that supply-side factors had no effect on women's occupational outcomes.[4] The relationship between supply and demand runs two ways: although a supply of qualified and cheap workers may enhance demand, demand invariably generates supply. In the occupations we studied, this process was often simply a matter of employers transferring women from sex-typical to sex-atypical jobs. In banking, publishing, insurance, real estate, and the labor force as a whole, women in sex-typical jobs were queued up—ready to respond to a demand for their labor in better jobs. Those last two words, "better jobs," explain women's readiness to move into customarily male occupations. As we showed in Chapters 2 and 3, these formerly male occupations were better than the kinds of jobs usually available to women. Although women's increasing need to support themselves and their dependents heightened their interest in sex-atypical jobs (Padavic, 1989), women might have been just as responsive to higher wages a generation earlier—when fewer women supported themselves and their dependents— had the opportunities existed.

In most of the desegregating occupations we studied, then, a dearth of qualified men led employers to seek another source of labor—women. The exception to this generalization occurred in occupations in which economic or regulatory pressures increased women's attractiveness to employers.

Segregation within Desegregating Occupations

As Chapter 3 and the case studies show, within desegregating *occupations* female and male workers were concentrated in different *jobs*. In none of the occupations we studied were the sexes so genuinely integrated that men and women performed the same jobs, in the same settings, and at the same level in the organizational hierarchy. Within some occupations such as baking and bus driving, integration was wholly nominal: women and men worked in different industries that were probably almost as segregated in 1980 as they had been in 1970. In others the sexes worked in the same industry, but the division of labor relegated women and men to different specialties (as in real estate sales) or different tasks (as in systems analysis, public relations, and bank management) or different firms (as in accounting). In most, men and women were vertically segregated as well. For instance, men monopolized the top posts in retail and hospital pharmacy, bank management, book editing, and accounting. In short, despite reduction in women's underrepresentation in or an end to their near-exclusion from the occupations we studied, sex-based job differentiation has remained robust. Indeed, two formerly male occupations, insurance adjusting/examining and typesetting/composing, have become re-segregated as predominantly female, and a few occupational specialties have been relabeled as women's work. As was true a century ago, women and men still rarely work side by side on the same jobs.

These nominally desegregating occupations remained internally segre-gated for the same reasons that the labor force as a whole has done so: white men's favored position ensures them the most desirable and most highly re-warded jobs and allows most of them to dodge less attractive jobs for which women must settle. This pattern occurs *within* as well as *across* occupations. Because occupational sex integration will appreciably reduce the earnings gap between the sexes only if desegregating occupations become and remain genuinely integrated, the substantial segregation we discovered within desegre-gating occupations has bleak implications for women's prospects of achieving economic equity with men.

Movement toward Earnings Equity
within Desegregating Occupations

Chapter 3 also addressed the question of whether moving into customary male occupations has brought women the economic rewards those occupations offer male incumbents. The case study data point to only limited progress toward economic equity within desegregating occupations. Women failed to narrow the earnings gap substantially. In occupations in which the gap between female and male coworkers did decline, it did so mostly through an erosion of men's real earnings during the 1970s. These findings call for skepticism in interpreting women's large-scale movement into the traditionally male occupations we studied as denoting more than token progress toward sex equity. One bright note is that women who migrated into desegregating occupations raised their earnings relative to the overall average for women. Although real earnings declined in most of the desegregating occupations, women who entered feminizing male occupations outearned, on average, the women they left behind in traditionally female occupations. Any rise in women's earnings reduces their economic dependency and concomitant risk of poverty, and we applaud progress wherever it occurs. However, researchers do women a disservice if they let some women's progress *relative to other women* overshadow the distance women of all backgrounds have to travel to achieve an equitable return on their labor. By way of illustration, while some women bake-off bakers outearn domestic workers, they earn far less than unionized (predominantly male) wholesale bakers. Society's self-congratulations on women's advances into male occupational titles are premature and must await women's entry into the jobs men still dominate.

| | | | **Theoretical Implications**

A Queueing Approach to Occupational Feminization

A single perspective—queueing—encompasses the widely different factors that precipitated the feminization of the fourteen occupations we studied. As we explained in Chapter 2, the queueing perspective views labor markets as comprising labor queues (employers' ranking of possible workers) and job queues (workers' ranking of jobs); it sees occupational composition as the result of a matching process in which the top-ranked workers get the most attractive jobs and so forth, so that the lowest workers end up in jobs that others have rejected. By identifying the structural properties of queues, we can pinpoint the conditions that lead occupations' composition to change. They do so when (1) the relative distributions of elements—workers across labor queues, jobs across job queues—change, (2) employers rerank workers or workers rerank jobs, or (3) the intensity of workers' or employers' preferences for or against particular elements decline or grow.

Does the queueing perspective go beyond simply saying that workers' and employers' preferences affect their labor market decisions? What does it add to the neoclassical economic approach to occupational segregation? According to the traditional neoclassical economic account, employers' and workers' preferences (or "tastes") influence the employment decisions of individual actors in the labor market. In emphasizing individuals' preferences to explain occupational outcomes, economists assume (1) that in deciding how to invest their human capital and in selecting jobs, individual workers act rationally to maximize their lifetime earnings; (2) that differences in the sexes' distribution across jobs stem primarily from limits that women's domestic responsibilities impose on their participation in market work; and (3) that employers strive to maximize earnings by hiring the most productive workers, although they are occasionally sidetracked from their economic best interests by discriminatory impulses. Thus, traditional economic analysis treats segregation as the *aggregate* outcome of the mostly rational choices of *individuals*. It implies that the sexes' distribution across occupations will change when (1) occupations' potential economic payoffs change, (2) women increasingly pursue wage work as their primary, lifetime occupation, or (3) economic conditions change to reduce or eliminate the disparity in the sexes' expected productivity. The superficial similarity between these conditions and the structural bases for change that the queueing perspective implies should not obscure the basic differences between the two perspectives. Empirically, the human-capital account of sex segregation (and sex discrimination) has been shown to be fundamentally flawed and at odds with the empirical evidence (England, 1982; Corcoran et al., 1984).

The queueing perspective improves on the traditional economic approach to changing sex composition in the factors it emphasizes. First, queueing stresses the *collective* nature of sex segregation. It sees segregation as not merely the sum of individual decisions but the result of *socially structured rankings* by *groups in conflict*. Thus, queueing highlights the roles of power and of conflict between groups with contradictory interests in shaping occupations' composition. (Below we examine further how the queueing perspective elucidates the role of group power in shaping occupational access.)

Second, it takes seriously the effects of noneconomic factors on workers' rankings of occupations and employers' rankings of prospective workers. It reminds us that working conditions, autonomy, social standing, career opportunities, and sex composition influence workers' appraisals of jobs; and that prejudices, stereotypes, custom, ideology, peer pressure, and the desire to preserve their own and other men's advantages influence employers' rankings of workers.

Third, because the queueing perspective assumes that the sexes respond to similar occupational characteristics in ranking occupations, occupational feminization is no puzzle. Queueing theory predicts that the superior rewards of male occupations will spur female entry. To explain occupations' feminization, it directs our attention to changes in employers' demand for women and to declining barriers to women's access to traditionally male jobs. In other words, the queueing perspective redirects us from the characteristics of female workers to the structural properties of labor markets, which in turn are shaped by the preferences of employers and male workers.

Finally, the queueing metaphor serves as a heuristic device that formalizes the role of explanatory variables and elucidates why they fostered women's entry into formerly male occupations and ghettoized them into certain jobs. In queueing terms, the occupations we studied feminized because (1) occupational growth changed the shape of job queues; (2) workers reordered jobs in some queues in response to changing relative rewards; (3) employers reranked the sexes with the emergence of a sex-specific demand for women or declining inclination or ability on the part of male workers to exclude women; (4) employers' gender preferences became weaker with growing public opposition to discrimination and firsthand evidence that women were as able as men; and (5) women's share of labor queues for male occupations expanded.

Gender Queues: Power and Coalitions in Ordering the Labor Queue

Our case studies confirmed the conclusion implicit in a vast body of research on the sexes' labor market outcomes: most labor queues are so overwhelmingly ordered by sex that they are essentially gender queues.[5] Thus, in examining how power and conflict affect occupations' composition, we must bear in mind that three groups have a stake in which sex predominates in an occupation. These three groups—employers (who are overwhelmingly male), male workers, and female workers—are motivated at least partly by what members see to be the group interest of their own sex. Importantly, they differ greatly in the power to pursue those interests successfully. Nonetheless, the operation of the labor market necessitates that various pairs enter into a coalition explicitly or implicitly in opposition to the third group. Occupations' sex compositions result from these coalitions.

Coalitions between employers and male workers. Male workers' monopoly over the most desirable occupations stems from a tacit coalition with male employers: male workers have often resisted women's entry with their male bosses' active contrivance (Baker, 1964; Cockburn, 1988). Gender solidarity that prompts employers to forgo profits out of loyalty to less favored members of their sex may explain why employers help male workers to exclude women (Baker, 1964; Hartmann, 1976; Cockburn, 1988).[6] This kind of loyalty, we suspect, is most likely among bosses who share a similar background with their male workers, who previously held those male jobs at risk of integration, and who currently work alongside their former coworkers (blue-collar supervisors and sales managers are two examples). In addition, employers and managers have a personal stake in excluding women from jobs that are labeled as male because sex differentiation maintains sex stratification (Reskin, 1988), or because women in lower-level male jobs might eventually threaten their own.

As long as male preference is universal among a group of competitors (Strober, 1988) and employers can operate in the black, hiring practices that shore up the sex–gender hierarchy are just one of many amenities that their profits can purchase (Stolzenberg, 1982). Employers may prefer such practices to the penalties for desegregation imposed by male workers, customers, or other men (Bergmann and Darity, 1981; Strober, 1988), or to the uncertainties attendant on modifying employment practices (Cohn, 1985; Strom, 1987; Figart and Bergmann, 1989:36). Male workers' ability to penalize employers who desegregate jobs deters bosses from placing significant numbers of women in "men's" jobs. So too do jobs' sex labels, inertia, and the fact that modern organizations confront a multitude of other, often pressing, problems. In downranking women, then, employers take the course of least resistance by following standard operating procedures, while perhaps appeasing male workers who could make hiring women costly and indulging a shared sex bias. The resulting de facto coalition explains why, in feminizing occupations, employers confine women to the least desirable jobs and provide male incumbents the chance to move to still-male jobs as a safe haven (Cockburn, 1988).[7]

Male workers' disadvantaged economic position vis-à-vis employers means that they would stand to gain from acting collectively with women workers. However, their advantaged sex status means that integration would expose them to job and wage competition from women who must settle for lower wages—and render them vulnerable to losing the domestic benefits they derive from sex differentiation (Hartmann, 1976; Reskin, 1988). For these reasons, male workers maximize their short-run situation by monopolizing male jobs rather than by welcoming female coworkers with whom they might collectively fight for better pay. Indeed, in the short run they have a greater incentive than do employers to exclude women from their jobs. As a result, Hartmann (1976:167) has pointed out, under normal conditions male workers are more important than employers in maintaining sex-segregated jobs. As we showed in Chapter 2, male workers withdrew from coalitions with their male bosses primarily when their jobs no longer provided better economic and noneconomic rewards than available alternatives.

Coalitions between male employers and female workers.   Given male workers' incentives to maintain segregation and employers' deference to custom, feelings of male solidarity, reluctance to pay the costs associated with backing out of coalitions with male workers, and their willingness to use segregation to prevent working-class unity, why does segregation ever break down? Why don't patriarchal employers raise wages or improve jobs to attract more men when too few seek jobs? In occupations that employers transformed in order to cut labor costs, raising wages would have defeated their purpose. Even in occupations that became less attractive to men for reasons largely beyond employers' control, when external events provided the occasion to feminize, employers' preference for their own sex took a back seat to their economic interests.

Employers have flouted custom, set aside their biases, and ignored possible adverse reactions of male workers when their firms' survival was at stake. Employers may gladly exploit segregation to win men's allegiance, but "if they can supersede experienced men with cheaper women, so much the better" (Hartmann, 1976:166). In the occupations we studied, threats to survival came from heightened competition, regulatory-agency pressure, and unions that frequently disrupted work. For instance, competition prompted the insurance industry to reorganize adjusting and examining to cut labor costs. Similarly, competition prompted banks to provide more services as well as increase productivity. Regulatory agencies and the courts intervened in only a few occupations but did so with dramatic effect. Vulnerability to union control of the work process spurred newspaper publishers to develop a printing technology that the overwhelmingly male International Typographical Union could not control and that cost men their monopoly on typesetting and composing jobs. In such periods of economic flux, firms' willingness to donate profits to the support of white male privilege went by the wayside, and they struck a bargain with women workers that led occupations to feminize.

Why women enter into de facto coalitions with male employers is hardly a mystery. Women's disadvantaged position relative to male workers and male employers means that they stand to gain from forming coalitions with either group. When women's numbers are large, they are most likely to succeed in forging an alliance with employers. Cobble's (1989b) comparison of women's struggle to serve drinks with women's efforts to tend bar demonstrates this point: waitresses' considerable representation in union locals gave them the clout to block proposed restrictions against women's serving alcoholic drinks, whereas women bartenders' small numbers doomed their efforts to prepare drinks until they had Title VII of the Civil Rights Act on their side. Large numbers mean that women can better spot their sex's relegation to the least desirable jobs and more effectively protest it. In the 1970s, women capitalized on their numbers in the book publishing, newspaper, broadcasting, and banking industries to challenge their exclusion from male jobs. For this reason, women's increased share in the labor queues for male occupations has contributed to their gains not only by increasing the odds that employers would get down to women in the hiring queue but also by making women more powerful adversaries. Ultimately, however, women's major bargaining chip in inducing male employers to enter into a coalition is their ability to levy costs on employers. In none of the occupations we studied did women impose sufficient costs to prompt employers to hire them for male jobs without the threat of governmental penalties. For example, although women reporters filed dozens of suits against newspapers that discriminated in job assignments and wages, their representation in journalism during the 1970s increased more slowly than it did in the entire labor force.

The resistance of male workers.   Male workers' stake in retaining the best jobs encourages them to oppose employers' efforts to hire women. In the extreme case, men hold an effective veto over employers' efforts to integrate women through their ability to reduce women's productivity. Whether men win their battle to preserve some jobs, specialties, and entire occupations as male depends on their power base. Early in the industrial revolution, when fledgling unions had little power, employers feminized jobs easily (Kessler-Harris, 1982:266; Cohn, 1985; Milkman, 1987; Cockburn, 1988). Employers' ability to replace resisting men, especially "in times of overwhelming social or economic necessity occasioned by vast increases in the demand for labor" (Cockburn, 1988), thwarted men's campaigns to exclude women. Once well established, however, unions could exclude women. They did so for years in the three craft occupations we studied (bartending, baking, and typesetting and composing).

Because we focused on occupations that thousands of women entered, obviously men did not ultimately prevent their entry. In the unionized occupations we studied, their ability to do so was hampered by declining union membership. Thus, the ITU forestalled feminization during its heyday at the turn of the century but was unable to prevail in the 1970s against the well-funded American Association of Newspaper Publishers. Similarly, the bartenders' union relied heavily on state laws to bar women; once the courts overturned those laws, the union had no effective mechanism to press its cause. However, even in the case study occupations, men have not suffered total defeat: at least through the 1970s they limited women's numbers in some specialties within feminizing occupations, such as production baking, commercial real estate, and unionized typesetting and composition for large metropolitan dailies.

In rapidly growing occupations, men did not resist women's entry because women constituted no threat: growth ensured that good jobs were plentiful, and within-occupation segregation preserved men's access to the best jobs or at least an escape route. During the feminization of insurance adjusting, for instance, the insurance industry press offered tips on job opportunities for men who had worked as outside adjusters.

Male incumbents in high-turnover occupations (book editing, bartending, insurance adjusting, residential real estate sales) have little stake in what happens in the long run, and workers are unlikely to be sufficiently organized to resist integration. When federal regulatory agencies intervened, male workers bowed to the inevitable.[8] Cobble (1989b) argued that male union-ists' response to women's entry depends partly on the number of women in their trade. Although an exclusionary policy is feasible when the number of women is small, once women achieve a critical mass, unions usually try to organize them and advocate equal pay to keep employers from using women to undercut wages. To defuse male opposition, employers have an effective tool: recasting restructured jobs as women's work. For instance, after insur-ance companies transformed the work of adjusters, industry trade journals depicted the ideal insurance adjuster as a woman. Employers are ideally situ-ated to define appropriate workers because they presumably know best their labor needs, what a job involves, and so forth. Finally, of course, in scorn-ing available jobs in most of the feminizing occupations, male workers gave employers the go-ahead to hire women.

In summary, the sometimes divided, sometimes overlapping interests of female workers, male workers, and mostly male employers play themselves out within the queues that structure the labor market.

| | | | Prospects and Policy Implications

How much progress have women made in integrating male occupations? And what are the prospects for genuine integration in the future? Before hazarding answers to these two questions, we must note the limitations in our findings' generalizability. We selected for study occupations that were exceptional in the magnitude of women's gains: in each, during the 1970s, women's rep-resentation increased at least twice as much as it did in the labor force as a whole. Most of them included specialties or work settings that had feminized at varying rates, so we also learned about conditions in specialties in which women's progress had been slower or nonexistent. Nonetheless, the occupa-tions we studied do not represent the much larger number of male occupations in which women posted only modest gains or even slight losses. Possibly, then, more genuine gains occurred within occupations in which women's inroads were less pronounced. Our statistical analyses of all 503 detailed occu-pations, under way at the time of this writing, will permit us to assess the generalizability of the case study findings. Meanwhile, however, the queueing perspective we have developed leads us to hypothesize similar processes across the full range of occupations.

Turning to the question of women's progress in integrating male occu-pations, we can say this much with confidence. First, the sex compositions of several census occupational titles became more balanced after 1970 (although some segregated occupations that we did not study became even more seg-regated). Women's movement into predominantly male occupations that did not subsequently become female dominated contributed to a drop in the index of occupational sex segregation after 1970 (Jacobs, 1989b). However, at least within the occupations we studied, we must be cautious in inferring "progress" from women's disproportionate entry. When we see data that show a big jump in women's representation in some occupation, it is natural to conclude that they reflect a new, *permanent* state of affairs.[9] Given how little the sex composition of most occupations has varied, we tend to assume that these data represent a stable attribute of the occupation in question, with the new percentage female as an *end point* in a now complete process of integration. However, scholarship on *residential racial and ethnic segregation*, from which sex-segregation researchers borrowed their conceptual approach, warns us that this assumption may be fallacious. As Duncan and Duncan (1957) recognized in their classic analysis of residential segregation, changing patterns of racial dominance in neighborhoods reflect a *process* of racial succession. What follows the entry of a few minority group members into a neighborhood that formerly excluded them is an influx of those outsiders along with an exodus of some of the formerly dominant group. During this period of "consolidation," which may last for years, the neighborhood is technically integrated. But as still more outsiders arrive and more former insiders flee, the neighborhood "tips" and becomes resegregated. Similarly, what appears to be movement toward occupational integration may thus represent an ongoing process of resegregation. This process can be seen in Table 1.6 and in Blau's (1989) analysis showing that of 16 male occupations that became predominantly female between 1970 and 1983, 8 continued to feminize after 1983.

Perhaps readers might ask what is wrong with resegregation. After all, it means jobs for large numbers of women in occupations that offer rewards superior to those of traditionally female-dominated occupations. In response, we point out that predominantly female occupations pay less at least partly *because* women are the majority (Treiman and Hartmann, 1981). Resegregation is problematic because it is accompanied by reduced earnings.[10] Although the case studies presented here cannot fully disentangle the bases for the links between occupational change, declining rewards, and feminization, it is likely that earnings declined in part because occupations feminized (see, e.g., Strober and Arnold, 1987a). Because resegregation occurs when a limited number of male occupations become open to the millions of women seeking better jobs, the only way to prevent it is to eliminate barriers to women's access to all male occupations.[11] If women have access to the full range of jobs, they will not crowd into a few, and men need not fear women's entry as a harbinger of wage and status loss.

Prospects for Sex Desegregation in the 1990s

If a queueing approach eludicates the factors that facilitate feminization and affect its form within occupations, what does it tell us about women's prospects for moving into customarily male occupations in the 1990s? Sources of future feminization arise from the structural properties of queues: their shape, their ordering, and the intensity of raters' preferences. Changes in the shape of the job queue are not likely to bring much additional desegregation in the 1990s. As the economy slows down and more jobs are exported, economists predict less job growth in the 1990s than in the 1970s, when the occupations we studied desegregated (Personick, 1987). Moreover, half of the ten occupations predicted to produce the largest job growth through the year 2000 are already predominantly female occupations: retail salespersons, registered nurses, cashiers, general office clerks, and waiters and waitresses. The predominantly male occupations slated to add the most jobs are general managers, engineers, truck drivers, janitors and cleaners, and guards (Silvestri and Lukasiewicz, 1987). Of these, women's prospects appear brightest for jobs in management, in janitorial work, and as crossing guards.

Yet experts anticipate continued growth in women's labor force participation (Brand, 1988:32): women are projected to account for 64 percent of net growth through the year 2000, when equal numbers of women and men are expected to be in the labor force (Kutscher, 1987; U.S. Department of Labor, Women's Bureau, 1989), whereas white men will contribute less than 10 percent. Moreover, women will continue to increase their average levels of education and work experience (Brand, 1988:32). As labor queues for specific occupations (such as managerial jobs) move toward greater balance across the sexes, the probability that employers will have to hire women will rise, especially in growing occupations. Moreover, women's increasing numbers should enhance their ability to enforce their claims to male jobs. Of course, employers faced with labor shortages have other alternatives besides hiring American women: in particular, mechanizing jobs, exporting them abroad, or seeking lower-priced labor—nondocumented workers or youth. Already, for example, satellite technology has permitted insurance companies to export claims-processing jobs to the Caribbean and Ireland, and the dean of the Pharmacy College at the University of California at San Francisco has predicted substantial mechanization of retail pharmacy jobs in the years ahead (Goyan, 1988).

For changes in the shape of the labor queue to bring substantial desegregation, employers must reorder the labor queue. Through the 1980s labor queues have functioned as gender queues, with men ranked ahead of women for preferred occupations. Are employers likely to abandon workers' sex as a ranking principle? Heightened societal repugnance toward discrimination in the 1970s eroded the intensity of employers' preferences for men, even if their ordering of the gender queue remained fixed. In other words, discrimination persisted, its manifestations sometimes remarkably similar to those of the distant past.[12] Counteracting the negative effects on the prospects for integration of any renewed public tolerance of discrimination are the beneficial effects on employers of observing women successfully perform customarily male jobs. The scattered and anecdotal evidence reviewed in Chapter 2 suggests that women newcomers may try harder and be better qualified than the average male worker. Discovering that women can competently perform sex-atypical work could assuage employers' anxieties about women's ability—if they do not dismiss the success of individual women as exceptions (Cooper and Fazio, 1979)—and thus destroy one basis for discrimination (Reskin and Padavic, 1988). Certainly, in occupations and industries in which domestic or international competition becomes more intense, employers will face economic pressure to subordinate gender considerations to productivity and to insist that their employees follow suit.

Women's movement into decision-making posts may also lead to the suppression of gender queueing, or at least to a drop in the intensity of gatekeepers' preference for men for the best jobs. However, women in such positions may be subject to subtle or overt pressure to preserve the status quo. Thus it is difficult to predict how much women's increasing role in hiring for customarily male jobs will reduce the impact of prospective workers' sex on job assignments.

We doubt that either regulatory agencies or women's collective action will greatly undermine gender queues in the near future. The presidential administrations of the 1980s weakened federal regulatory agencies: the limited but occasionally important effect of affirmative action in the late 1970s on desegregating some male occupations disappeared after the Reagan administration derailed enforcement efforts (Burbridge, 1984; Leonard, 1988), and recent Supreme Court affirmative-action decisions (especially *Martin v. Wilks*, 1989)[13] have undermined employers' incentive to desegregate jobs.[14] Given the breadth of concerns to which employers must respond, even the most fair-minded are unlikely to assign high priority to integrating jobs without pressure to do so, especially given continued pressure from male workers to preserve attractive jobs for them. Indeed, decisions such as *Martin v. Wilks* may encourage men to resist integration more vigorously. Politicians are not likely to champion the policies that helped open a few male occupations to women during the 1970s and early 1980s without broad public support for enforcing antidiscrimination and affirmative-action regulations (Hirsch, 1986:45).[15]

Of course, women can pressure employers directly, but without the threat of the government's big stick, their efforts are likely to be in vain. Although women's collective action has led few employers to modify discriminatory personnel policies, women's collective tactics have prompted the government and some unions to enact and sometimes enforce regulations banning discrimination, and employers are more likely to listen to federal regulators and unions than to women's groups. Thus, some occupational desegregation since 1970 resulted indirectly from women's collective action. Moreover, throughout the 1980s, women's pressure on regulatory agencies had a broader payoff than suits by individual women against single employers. The latter exact a high personal price from plaintiffs, proceed at a snail's pace, have been only moderately successful even under fairly liberal standards for proving discrimination, and, when they have succeeded, tended to benefit individual women rather than women as a class (Burstein, 1989). Moreover, at the time of this writing, challenges to women's right to legal abortions (and, to a lesser degree, the need for affordable child care) have diverted the energies of the women's movement from employment issues. Finally, the popular notion that women have come a long way is likely to lead women to attribute their failure to advance in the workplace to idiosyncratic circumstances rather than structural barriers, and women's scattered inroads into traditionally male lines of work are likely to divert their attention from their continued exclusion from some blue-collar occupations and their restricted opportunities for mobility in many white-collar male occupations. Thus, we do not anticipate a quick repetition of the widespread protest against sex discrimination in the workplace that helped women's cause in the 1970s.[16]

Ironically, women's successes in the 1970s and 1980s, because they benefited the most privileged women, may inhibit broad-based collective action in the 1990s. The progress of the beneficiaries of desegregation has created a rift between women in professional and managerial jobs and those who remain employed in the home or in traditionally female jobs, reducing the possibility for effective coalitions. One challenge the 1990s bring women is to create political bases for demanding genuine sex equity, bases that transcend these differences between more and less favored women.

We leave for last the structural change in queues that contributed most to women's inroads into the case study occupations: men's reordering of the job queue. By downranking jobs in customarily male occupations, men abandoned them to women. It is this source of occupational feminization that seems most likely to contribute to *nominal* desegregation in the future. Behind most occupational depreciation was occupational change. In some occupations, employers totally transformed the work process so that its primary resemblance to earlier work was its product (a newspaper, an insurance claim). In others, the work process changed only slightly, but workers performed it in altered settings. In still others, both the work process and the work setting remained unchanged, but workers' rewards (autonomy, task diversity, career prospects, and so forth) deteriorated. Experts expect continued, often technologically based, occupational change. Although technological innovations can enrich work, they have often created jobs for women in male occupations when they reduced rather than raised skill requirements (Hacker, 1979; Hartmann et al., 1986; Figart and Bergmann, 1989:35).[17] As Hartmann (1976:160) observed, "In several cases [an occupation's] shift to women was accompanied by technical innovations which allowed increased output and sometimes reduced the skill required by the worker." Scott (1982) echoed this sentiment:

"Machinery that extended the division of labor, simplified and routinized tasks and called for unskilled workers rather than skilled craftsmen was usually associated with [a shift to the] employment of women."[18] Technologically based deskilling leads to feminization because employers automate or computerize in order to justify low wages, which limited occupational alternatives force women to accept.[19]

This analysis does not offer a very rosy prognosis for desegregation, much less for genuine integration, during the 1990s. Jobs in male occupations that deteriorate will continue to draw some women away from typically female occupations; further, we do expect some traditionally male professions that did not feminize disproportionately during the 1970s to do so in the 1990s. These include medicine, veterinary medicine, and the clergy, all of which have disproportionately feminized since 1980 (U.S. Bureau of Labor Statistics, 1989). In medicine, for example, bureaucratization has combined with declining profitability, social status, and entrepreneurial potential to weaken men's interest in becoming physicians (Luxenberg, 1985; Leslie, 1987:39–40). Between 1975 and 1985 the number of male medical students dropped by more than one-third, and women have been making up an increasing share of medical students. The clergy, 97.1 percent male in 1970 and 94.2 percent in 1980, have lost stature, and since 1984 white male divinity-school enrollments have plummeted, leaving a female majority in some of these schools (Kenkelen, 1988). We do not wish to imply that access to these high-status professional occupations does not denote success for women. Of course it does. However, within them women are once again being ghettoized into a few specialties (see Nesbitt, 1989), and it is troubling that women's large gains appear to be confined primarily to occupations and jobs that men are devaluing. Moreover, we suspect that these women's disproportionate movement into medicine, veterinary medicine, and the clergy will still represent the exception rather than the rule.

Prospects for Equal Pay in the 1990s

Nominal occupational desegregation in the 1970s economically benefited women entrants primarily in comparison with other women. What factors can help women significantly reduce the earnings gap with men? The resilience of sex segregation points to the need to develop a broad range of remedies to redress the economic imbalance between the sexes. Foremost is achieving women's access to the full range of male occupations. To do this, we need sex equity in educational institutions and job training programs to ensure that women are well represented in the labor queues for nontraditional jobs. Sex equity means more than eliminating entrance restrictions. It requires overcoming the effects of previous barriers, which in turn requires committed leadership for equal opportunity in private establishments as well as public agencies. We cannot overemphasize the importance of affirmative-action programs, whose goals and timetables can open the doors of desirable male jobs. Essential also is a national commitment—expressed in the mandate and budgets of enforcement agencies—to keep those doors open. We remind readers that in the late 1980s the wage gap between the sexes differed only slightly from its level in 1955 and that a substantial proportion of the gap results from the sexes' segregation into different and unequally paying jobs. Barring significant job integration, proponents of wage equity have proposed regulations to ensure that workers are paid according to the value of their work not their jobs' sex composition. We endorse the use of pay equity (comparable worth) to eliminate sex bias from wages, but we do not expect comparable-worth pay policies to improve women's economic status substantially, relative to that of men. In the United States, comparable worth has been limited to the public sector, and even there implementation has usually watered down its effectiveness (Steinberg, 1984–85; Blum, 1987; Ames, 1989; Evans and Nelson, 1989). This is not to disparage pay equity as a strategy for reducing the wage disparity between the sexes but rather to point out that bureaucratic and political limits on its implementation mean that pay equity is not likely to eliminate economic inequity between the sexes.

| | | | Conclusion

In 1986 Bielby and Baron, in pointing out that greater balance in the sex composition of occupations does not necessarily imply decreased segregation of jobs in specific work settings, warned that "occupational-level studies obscure the sexual division of labor by overlooking segregation within and across organizations, even within occupations that appear integrated" (p. 753). Our findings confirm their insight as to the impropriety of drawing conclusions about trends toward sex integration from census occupational data. Yet social analysts cannot ignore them, because it is precisely these data that policymakers and the media use to assess change. As sociologist W. I. Thomas taught us, situations that people define as real *are* real in their consequences (Merton 1957:421). And consequences surely followed from misleading comparisons of 1970 and 1980 census data, subsequently promulgated in newspaper stories touting women's rapid progress in male occupations. The most obvious—and, in our view, false—conclusion is that the government need no longer regulate employers to ensure that they treat the sexes equally. Misleading reports of women's gains have fueled efforts to eliminate affirmative-action programs. Steinberg (1989) noted another implication of exaggerating women's progress: doing so reinforces the ideology that members of all disadvantaged groups can advance through their own efforts, so that the country does not need structural solutions to redress the continued unequal distribution of economic opportunity.

Readers should not conclude from this critique that analyzing data at the occupational level is a pointless exercise. The very deceptiveness of such statistics necessitates that researchers continue to use them as we have done in this study—not as social facts but as social constructions, whose validity we must assess in order to determine whether the trends they imply are genuine.

More than twenty years ago, Gross (1968) summed up his review of occupational sex segregation from 1900 through 1960 by quoting, "The more things change, the more they stay the same." In 1990 his conclusion remains apt: the occupations in which women made the greatest numerical headway remained internally segregated. This does not deny the more modest gains that women have made in other traditionally male occupations, but we must remember that in speaking of "modest gains" we are by definition talking about relatively few women entering an occupation. Despite the economic progress some women have achieved relative to their sisters, the structure of white, male advantage remains largely intact (Steinberg, 1989). Although employers now construe as "women's work" different jobs from those so labeled twenty years ago, jobs remain sex and race segregated, thereby perpetuating economic and social inequality. The continuing entry of modest numbers of women into male occupations in the 1990s notwithstanding, without renewed pressure on policymakers to ensure the access of all women and all people of color to all jobs, we risk ending the twentieth century with a labor force only slightly less segregated by race and sex than it was when the century began.

|||| Notes

1. Moreover, retail food stores in the service sector were home to the feminizing jobs within baking.

2. Labor shortages occurred when a new or growing specialty in a male occupation failed to attract men, given their other options. Bake-off baking and school-bus driving exemplify this pattern.

3. Of course, many employers persist in discriminating against women, sometimes on the grounds that women are more expensive to employ or less productive than men in traditionally male jobs (Bielby and Baron, 1986).

4. Supply factors also operate through queueing processes by influencing *which* of the close to 50 million women in the labor force end up in the more desirable, sometimes male jobs.

5. This is not to say that other characteristics do not also appreciably influence the order of labor queues, the most obvious being race and ethnicity.

6. For example, Hirsch (1986:32) recounted that the Pullman Company transferred women clerical workers out of the central office because, in the words of a

Pullman representative, "they were standing in the way of young men, whom we wished to educate and promote."

7. For example, when a large publishing firm was forced to promote women to jobs as editorial assistants, it created a new, higher rank into which it promoted men who had been editorial assistants (Osterman, 1979).

8. Exploiting this propensity, employers have sometimes blamed affirmative action for their not hiring white men whom they would not have hired anyway. This and other benefits of affirmative action (such as its use as a defense against discrimination charges) probably fueled the National Manufacturers Association's opposition to the Reagan administration's attempts to weaken affirmation-action requirements.

9. The wish to believe that we are progressing toward a desirable social goal probably reinforces this tendency.

10. Indeed, consistent with our findings in Chapter 3, Blau and Beller (1988) found that during the 1970s women's payoff for working in a male occupation declined, relative to men's.

11. There is no way to prevent male flight, but as Cockburn (1988) pointed out, employers committed to workplace integration can refuse to provide men with escape routes out of feminizing jobs.

12. In 1911 Aetna Life Insurance segregated female clerical workers on the top floor so that their presence would not offend Aetna's president (Murolo, 1987:38). Seventy-six years later a women bank manager said that when she asked why her career had apparently derailed, the personnel manager explained, "The chairman and president want . . . people that they are comfortable with, and they are not . . . comfortable with women" (see Chapter 7).

13. This decision allowed white firefighters in Birmingham, Alabama to make a reverse-discrimination case against the hiring and promotion of black firefighters that had resulted in part from affirmative-action provisions in a consent decree put into effect in 1981.

14. Also, according to Thierry Noyelle (1987, cited in Burris, 1989:176), equal-employment regulations involved the assumption that getting minorities and white women into internal labor markets would reduce discrimination. But just as large numbers were positioned to take advantage of internal labor markets, other forces weakened those markets, making it difficult for women and minority men to advance.

15. The elimination of official pressure on employers to rectify past discrimination may undermine some affirmative-action–based desegregation of the 1970s and 1980s—especially in the event of economic reversals. Early in the 1980s, Collins (1983) warned that minorities' occupational gains resulting from affirmative-action pressure, and the demand for women and minorities in protected niches (such as personnel and labor relations), were precarious. Her warning has been borne out; for examples, see journalistic accounts of the vulnerability of minorities to corporate belt tightening (Monroe and Friday, 1988), and evidence that fewer women held blue-collar steel-industry jobs in 1982 than before the 1974 consent decree that prompted firms to hire women (O'Farrell, 1988:269).

16. A rare but heartening exception occurred in the early 1950s when black women bartenders in Chicago successfully fought union and city policies that sought to prevent them from tending bar (Cobble, 1989b).

17. Given the social propensity to devalue women's work (Phillips and Taylor,

1980; Reskin, 1988), we must be cautious in concluding that clerical work is less skilled than the nonclerical methods male workers formerly used to produce the same products.

18. Even when employers deskill jobs in order to feminize them, men do not necessarily yield their jobs to women. Whether or not they do so depends on their access to more desirable alternatives and their power to resist.

19. Technological change can also foster feminization by providing employers with the opportunity to relabel male jobs as appropriate for women. As Davies (1975: 282) and Rotella (1981:162, 165) have pointed out, changes in the work process can circumvent the stereotypes of appropriate workers so that employers do not seem to be giving men's jobs to women.

Appendix,
References,
Index, and
About the Authors

Appendix

Guidelines Used for Occupational Case Studies

A. Statistical Summary
   1. How has the representation of each sex changed within the census occupation during this century and particularly since 1970? Present table showing breakdown by sex and percent female. Check most recent January issue of *Employment and Earnings* for recent data on sex composition.
B. Occupational Description and Characteristics
   1. Describe occupational duties in 1970 and 1980 based on the *Occupational Outlook Handbook* (*OOH*) and the *Dictionary of Occupational Titles* (*DOT*), vocational guides, other published sources, and interviews.
   2. Census classification: describe whether and how 1970–80 changes in the census occupational classification affect how this occupation is classified.
   3. Include as much detail as possible regarding the nature of work and the conditions under which it is carried out (any outdoor work, physical work, lifting, dirty work, etc.), elaborating on the *DOT* ratings of working conditions (*Selected Characteristics of Occupations Defined in the Dictionary of Occupational Titles*).
   4. Indicate industries in which work is done (from *Occupation by Industry* census subject reports), noting changes in industrial distribution since 1950 and especially since 1970.
C. Within-Occupation Segregation
   1. To what extent have the sexes historically done different jobs within this occupation?
   2. To what extent are the sexes currently distributed over subspecialties (i.e., is there internal segregation)? Are the sexes concentrated in different settings? Do they tend to work for different kinds of employers? Do they tend to be physically

segregated or work with coworkers of the other sex in the same occupation? Are there any data on how the percentage female in various subspecialties or employment contexts has changed (e.g., hospital pharmacies, research jobs, private pharmacies, chain stores)? In other words, are women segregated into certain specialties? If so, are the specialties in which women are concentrated lower-status, lower-paid, less autonomous jobs, or undergoing deskilling as a result of technological or organizational change? (For example, are female systems analysts more likely to work in banks and insurance than in the productive sector?)

3. Is there any evidence of sex differences in rank and career opportunities? Do men disproportionately hold supervisory or managerial rank? Is there any evidence of sex differences regarding typical length of time before promotion?

D. Changing Nature of Occupation

1. How has the occupation changed? Include long-term and historical changes as well as changes that may have affected sex composition or work content since 1970. How have the duties of incumbents changed, especially since 1970 (e.g., shift of adjusters inside offices, use of video display terminals, shift to more telephone work)?

2. Have new clients, coworkers, or role partners emerged? Have the characteristics (especially sex, age) of clients, coworkers, or role partners changed?

3. Has specialization increased or declined? Do specialties vary in skill level, rewards? Are new or growing specialties located in different industries or work settings? Do they involve different duties than the occupation formerly involved?

4. Have the duties changed relative to related occupations (e.g., pharmacists taking on some clinical tasks of nurses and doctors; insurance agents taking over clerical tasks)?

5. What technological changes have occurred in the work process or in the industry(ies) in which occupational incumbents are employed? How did changes affect the nature of work? Have the machines or equipment used changed? Does the occupation now require different skills? What are they?

6. Setting: note any changes in work setting or contexts in which incumbents work. Are workers concentrated in different settings as a result of organizational growth or change (e.g., the proliferation of small branch banks or chain-store pharmacies; the growth of the traditionally female subsidiary-rights specialty in publishing)? Has the location of work become more or less flexible (e.g., emergence of suburban employment settings, possibility of home work—perhaps via computer terminals)? Have the industries in which occupation is practiced changed (e.g., the increasing employment of pharmacists in hospitals rather than in retail stores)? Have state or local governments become more or less important as employers? Is there any evidence of change in the geographic locations (region: urban, rural, or suburban) in which the occupation is typically practiced?

7. Working conditions: has the proportion of part-time, part-year, or flex-time jobs changed? Is shift work more or less frequent?

8. Demand: has the occupation become larger or smaller? What level of growth was projected for this occupation in the late 1960s and early 1970s? Did the projected trends occur? According to the *Occupational Outlook Handbook*, what

are the projections over the next 5, 10, 20 years? Have shortages or oversupply of workers been widely publicized? Have there been concerted attempts to train or recruit additional workers? Have the populations, occupations, or industries that the occupation serves grown or declined or are they expected to do so? What is the unemployment rate and what was it during the 1960s and 1970s?

9. Economy: did changes in the economy (e.g., recession in building trades, high inflation) during the 1970s or 1980s affect the occupation's size, status, health?

E. Training and Education

1. How do workers prepare to enter the occupation? How long do training programs typically last? Who controls entry into training programs? What kinds of restrictions apply to applicants (e.g., age)? Have training programs grown or declined in size, number, or location since 1970? Have they changed in length, requirements, setting, cost, or the availability of financial assistance? Did federal loans or grants become available or disappear? Have new training programs (e.g., community-college classes) become available?

2. What are the occupation's educational requirements, if any? Is an undergraduate degree required? Sufficient? Are advanced degrees increasingly expected (e.g., the M.B.A. for management jobs)? Has the median education of male and female incumbents changed since 1960 or 1970? Does the typical educational attainment of incumbents differ by sex (when age is controlled)?

3. Has the number of persons in training and educational programs varied since the 1960s? Why? How has women's representation in such programs changed over time? Have both sexes been equally likely to complete training? Has the extent of any sex differences changed over the period of interest? Why? Have the sexes differed in the past in access to training or relevant education? Have any sex differences in training or educational programs disappeared?

4. Has the federal government been involved in relevant training or educational programs, either in providing funding, encouraging growth (e.g., pharmacist), or enforcing Title IX to eliminate barriers to women's entry to training programs?

F. Certification and Licensure

1. Do states license or certify persons who wish to practice the occupation? Are there trends toward increasing or decreasing state control over practitioners?

G. Labor Market Processes

1. How do incumbents typically obtain their positions? Do training programs offer placement services?

2. Unionization: must workers belong to unions? Has the proportion of workers who are unionized changed, and if so, how and why? Have the unions representing incumbents changed? Historically, what has been the union's position on women? Did it change during the 1960s or 1970s? If so, why? Were there major strikes in the period? Have major employers acted to reduce union influence (e.g., move location, restructure work as in typesetting)?

3. Professional and occupational associations: do incumbents typically belong to professional or occupational associations? If so, what has been the association's position on women, and did it change during the 1960s or 1970s?

4. Have government regulatory agencies intervened in the occupation's labor market to enforce antidiscrimination regulations and laws (Title VII, Title IX, Ex-

ecutive Order 11375, state equal-employment laws). Describe any litigation or enforcement activities for relevant employers or industries (the AT&T case, the steel industry consent decrees, etc.) since 1960. Who brought the action? Was a settlement negotiated? What were its terms? Has anyone evaluated its consequences? Have major employers or industries implemented affirmative-action programs?

5. Have women's organizations (caucuses) acted collectively to improve women's occupational prospects?

H. Characteristics of Incumbents

1. Does the occupation draw on particular population groups? Have the race, ethnicity, age, marital status, and educational distributions of incumbents changed over the decade? Why?

I. Occupational Rewards

1. Include all available information on earnings of incumbents (by sex, specialty, setting, industry, experience, rank, etc.) in 1969 and 1979.

2. 1970 census publishes income data for detailed occupations in Subject Report, *Occupational Characteristics*, vol. 2, Part 7A, 1973. Table 1 provides earnings percentage distribution for experienced civilian labor force across income categories by sex with medians. Table 16 provides earnings percentage distribution across income categories by sex for workers *16 years and older*. For several traditionally male occupations data are provided only for men. Table 19 of the same volume provides *mean* earnings by sex for persons who worked 50–52 weeks (but not necessarily full time). Table 24 provides wage and salary data with *median* earnings for *all* workers, regardless of how much they worked. See also Subject Report PC(2)-7C, pp. 246–49.

3. 1980 Census has income data in Subject Report, *Earnings by Occupation and Education*, vol. 2, PC80-2-8B, 1984. Table 1 provide *means* for all workers *18 years and older* and for the subset who worked full time, year round. For a somewhat more aggregated set of census occupations, more data are available (e.g., editors and reporters are aggregated with writers and artists). Table 281, *Detailed Population Characteristics, U.S. Summary*, Section A (PC80-1-D1-A; 1984) provides means for all workers aged 16+ and medians for full-time workers, pp. 1-269-273, but aggregates some occupations. See also Tables 2, 4 in Subject Report, *Occupation by Industry*, vol. 2, Pt. 7C, 1984. Additional 1979 income data are available in the public use microdata (A sample) (U.S. Bureau of the Census, 1983a).

4. Convert income data to constant dollars to adjust for inflation. For example, to compare 1980 income data (in 1979 dollars) with 1970 data (in 1969 dollars), multiply 1979 dollars by the deflation coefficient .505. This translates 1979 dollars into 1969 dollars and allows you to assess increases or declines in *real* (inflation-free) earnings.

5. Did the real earnings of incumbents decline or grow during the 1970s? Have they changed relative to the entire labor force? To specific comparable occupations? Is there any evidence that decreasing or increasing wages are related to the changing sex composition of the occupation?

6. Tabulate earnings by sex and full-time versus part-time status (or experience,

if available). Sources: 1970 and 1980 census subject reports on Earnings by Occupation and Education for Full- and Part-time Employment; also Bureau of Labor Statistics Industry Wage Surveys.

  7. Is there any evidence of changing occupational prestige?
  8. Is there any evidence that opportunities for mobility have changed?
  9. Is there any evidence that opportunities for autonomy have changed?
  10. Is there any evidence that opportunities for entrepreneurship have changed? Compare percentage self-employed in 1960, 1970, 1980.

J. Position of Women in Occupation

  1. Provide basic statistics on how men's and women's positions in the occupation have changed.
  2. Include data on the percentage female for as many years between 1970 and 1980 as possible, so that we can determine whether the rate of change has been constant and identify the effects of any particular precipitating events, such as litigation.
  3. What is position of women in the occupation in other Western societies? Include information about the occupation's sex composition in other countries where possible and whether it has changed or is changing (e.g., pharmacy and dentistry are considered female occupations in certain European countries).

K. Explanations for Changing Sex Composition

  1. Explore all possible explanations that might be implicated in the occupation's changing sex composition. In pursuing this question, note whether occupation became more female because number of both women and men grew but number of women did so more rapidly, or whether number of women grew while number of men stayed constant or declined. Also look at whether women's increasing representation was concentrated in some specialty (e.g., women in retail baking) on which you should focus special attention.
  2. Specifically address whether the occupation grew or declined in size and whether the supply of qualified workers of each sex grew or declined.
  3. Look for instances of technological change—especially new technologies that altered the nature of work, job deskilling, routinization, organizational changes, any federal intervention in the training or employment of persons in occupation, changes in earnings and in other occupational rewards, and men's responses to women's entry (where applicable).
  4. Document evidence of past discrimination (which may have declined or ceased, thus opening doors to women).
  5. What about efforts by organizations or female incumbents (caucuses, clubs, guilds, unions, or other special-interest groups that have encouraged the employment of more women or addressed sex discrimination in the occupation (or a major relevant employer or industry)? Be sure to locate and interview active members in such organizations, especially any task forces concerned with the status of women. Look for any reports, publications, newspaper stories, etc. Also look for evidence of legal or organizational activity by women within an organization (e.g., sit-ins, suits by female reporters at major newspapers and magazines).
  6. Is there changing resistance to women's entry by male workers?

7. Do you see any evidence of resegregation?

L. Documentary Data Sources

1. *Occupational Outlook Handbook,* U.S. Bureau of Labor Statistics, published biennially.

2. *Dictionary of Occupational Titles,* U.S. Department of Labor (check all four editions for changes in description of occupation).

3. *Selected Characteristics of Occupations Defined in the Dictionary of Occupational Titles,* U.S. Department of Labor (accompanies fourth edition of *Dictionary of Occupational Titles*).

4. *Detailed Population Characteristics, 1980 Census of Population,* U.S. Bureau of the Census.

5. *Detailed Occupations of Experienced Civilian Labor Force by Sex for the U.S. and Regions: 1980 and 1970, 1980 Census of Population,* U.S. Bureau of the Census.

6. *Occupation by Industry,* 1960, 1970, 1980 Census of Population, U.S. Bureau of the Census.

7. *Earnings by Occupation and Education, 1980 Census of Population,* U.S. Bureau of the Census.

8. *Classified Index of Occupations and Industries,* 1970, 1980 Census of Population, U.S. Bureau of the Census.

9. *Occupational Characteristics,* 1950, 1960, 1970 Census of Population, U.S. Bureau of the Census.

10. U.S. Bureau of Labor Statistics bulletins and special reports. Bulletins include industry wage surveys, technology and labor in major and selected industries, time-series data for input–output industries, etc.

11. U.S. National Center for Education Statistics reports and *Educational Digest,* U.S. Department of Education.

12. Office of Federal Contract Compliance Programs compliance reports by industry.

13. Professional association reports or journals; e.g., *National Association of Insurance Commission Reports; American Journal of Pharmaceutical Education.*

14. Relevant trade publications; e.g., *Bests Review, National Underwriter, Editor and Publisher.*

15. Indexes for *Business Week, Wall Street Journal, New York Times.*

16. *Readers' Guide to Periodical Literature.*

17. *Social Science Citation Index.*

18. *Dissertation Abstracts.*

19. *Sociological Abstracts.*

20. *Lexis* (legal index for finding legal cases).

References

ABA Banking Journal. 1982. "Bright Forecast for Women and Minority Bank Officials." Vol. 74 (2): 18.

Abbott, Edith. 1909. Women in Industry: A Study in American Economic History. New York: Appleton.

Abrahamson, Mark, and Lee Sigelman. 1987. "Occupational Sex Segregation in Metropolitan Areas." American Sociological Review 52 (October): 588–97.

Ackerman, Marilyn. 1975. "The Shrinking Commission Dollar." Spectator 183 (December): 22–23, 26.

Acosta, R. Vivian, and Linda Jean Carpenter. 1988. "Women in Intercollegiate Sport: A Longitudinal Study—Eleven-Year Update, 1977–1988." Unpublished manuscript, Department of Physical Education, Brooklyn College.

Allen, Woody. 1975. Love and Death. Jack Rollins and Charles H. Jaffe Productions. MGM/United Artists.

Allman, Tina. 1985. "You've Come a Long Way, Maybe." Southern Graphics, June, pp. 14, 16, 18, 29.

Altbach, Philip G. 1975. "Publishing and the Intellectual System." Annals of the American Academy of Political and Social Science 421 (September): 1–13.

American Council on Education. 1979. The American Freshman: National Norms for Fall 1979. Los Angeles: University of California.

American Druggist. 1968a. "Rise in Number of Women Students Tops Men 3 to 1." Vol. 157 (February 12): 17–21.

———. 1968b. "Assistant's Case Will be Appealed." Vol. 158 (October 21): 30.

———. 1968c. "Are Co-ops Essential to Survival?" Vol. 158 (November 18): 17–18.

————. 1969a. "Technicians Alleviate Shortage of RX Men, MDs." Vol. 159 (January 13): 65–66.

————. 1969b. "What's Happening with Drug Store Rents?" Vol. 159 (January 27): 21–22.

————. 1969c. "Pharmacy Is a Women's World." Vol. 160 (July 14): 51–52.

————. 1970. "Study Seeks to Revamp Hospital RX Man's Role." Vol. 162 (November 16): 16.

————. 1971a. "A Pharmacy School Geared for Women?" Vol. 163 (May 3): 30.

————. 1971b. "Bringing the Pharmacy to the Patients' Bedside." Vol. 163 (May 31): 31–33.

————. 1972a. "Apple Assails Hospitals That Vie with Community Pharmacists." Vol. 165 (January 10): 26.

————. 1972b. "Michigan College Gets HEW $ to Start Hospital Pharmacy Technician Program." Vol. 165 (January 10): 36.

————. 1973a. "Administration's Budget-Cuts Hurt Pharmacy Schools." Vol. 169 (March 1): 16–20.

————. 1973b. "Independents vs. Chains." Vol. 168 (September 15): 31–36.

————. 1974. "How Supreme Court Ruling May Affect Drug Retailing in U.S." Vol. 169 (January 1): 16.

————. 1976a. "Unions Tighten Their Grip on Pharmacy." Vol. 173 (January): 74–77.

————. 1976b. "Dr. Gosselin Defends Rx College against Manpower Critics." Vol. 173 (January): 71.

————. 1976c. "Pharmacy's Class of '76 Faces a Tough Job Market." Vol. 173 (June): 22–26.

————. 1977. "Women Say Stereotypes Block Them from Pharmacy's Best Careers." Vol. 175 (June): 60–61.

————. 1978. "Hospitals' Appeal to Pharmacy Grads Increases." Vol. 177 (June): 62–70.

————. 1979. "Pharmaceutical Technicians Make Inroads despite Roadblocks." Vol. 178 (August): 41–51.

————. 1987. "Over 4 of 10 Grads Head for Chain Jobs." Vol. 196 (August): 19–26.

American Journal of Hospital Pharmacy. 1973. "Pharmacy Manpower: Numbers Game?" Vol. 30:299.

American Pharmaceutical Association Task Force. 1981. *Women in Pharmacy: Final Report.* Washington, D.C.: American Pharmaceutical Association.

American Pharmacy. 1980. "Pharmacy System Features and Functions." N.s., vol. 20:23.

American Printer. 1983. "Forecast '84. Graphic Arts Rebound: Mirage or Reality?" Vol. 192 (December): 33–43.

American Printer and Lithographer. 1979. "Forecast 1980: Zeroing In on the Future." Vol. 184 (December): 39–54.

————. 1980. "New IPMA Survey Provides the Latest Profile of In-Plant Shops." Vol. 184 (March): 106A.

Ames, Linda J. 1989. "Pay Equity—What Works?" Paper presented at Women's Policy Research Conference, Washington, D.C.

Anderson, Karen Tucker. 1982. "Last Hired, First Fired: Black Women Workers during World War II." *Journal of American History* 69 (June): 82–97.

Anderson, Robert C. 1974. "Automatic Pan Handling." *Bakers Digest*, April, pp. 55–56.

Arrow, Kenneth. 1972. "Models of Job Discrimination." In Anthony H. Pascal, ed., *Racial Discrimination in Economic Life*, 83–102. Lexington, Mass.: Heath.

Arthur, Julietta K. 1947. *Jobs for Women over Thirty-Five*. New York: Prentice-Hall.

Ashenfelter, Orley, and Timothy Hannan. 1986. "Sex Discrimination and Product Market Competition: The Case of the Banking Industry." *Quarterly Journal of Economics* 101 (February): 149–73.

Association of American Publishers, Education for Publishing Committee. 1977. *The Accidental Profession: Education, Training, and the People of Publishing*. New York: Association of American Publishers.

Attewell, Paul, and James Rule. 1984. "Computing and Organizations: What We Know and What We Don't Know." *Communications of the ACM* 27:1184–91.

Austin, Jo Ellen, and Mickey C. Smith. 1971. "Women in Hospital Pharmacy—A Study in Eight States." *American Journal of Hospital Pharmacy* 28:26–35.

Babcock, Barbara Allen, Ann E. Freedman, Eleanor Holmes Norton, and Susan C. Ross. 1975. *Sex Discrimination and the Law: Causes and Remedies*. Boston: Little, Brown.

Baer, Judith A. 1978. *The Chains of Protection*. Westport, Conn.: Greenwood Press.

Baker, Elizabeth Faulkner. 1964. *Technology and Woman's Work*. New York: Columbia University Press.

———. 1969. *Protective Labor Legislation*. New York: AMS Press.

Baker, Ross K. 1977. "Entry of Women into Federal Job World—At A Price." *Smithsonian* 8 (July): 82–91.

Baldwin, Herbert E., Jr. 1979. "Where Have All the Agents Gone?" *Life Association News* 74 (April): 115–20.

Baldwin, Leona B. 1986. "Face to Face with Opportunity." *Best's Review, Life/Health* 86 (March): 51–52.

Ball, Vaughn. 1986. Personal communication.

Ballew, James A. 1978a. "A Man's Preserve." *Insurance Salesman*, July, pp. 45–48.

———. 1978b. "Look Who the New Recruit Is!" *Insurance Salesman*, August, pp. 55–57.

———. 1978c. "Some Disadvantages of Being a Woman Agent." *Insurance Salesman*, September, pp. 53–54, 56.

Bannon, Barbara A. 1972. "Writers and Editors, the Publishing Lifeline." *Publishers Weekly* 201 (April 10): 100–106.

Baran, Barbara. 1985. "The Technological Transformation of White-Collar Work: A Case Study of the Insurance Industry." Roundtable on the International Economy, Berkeley, Calif.

Barnett, George E. 1909. *The Printers: A Study in American Trade Unionism*. Cambridge, Mass.: American Economic Association.

Baron, Ava. 1981. "Women's 'Place' in Capitalist Production: A Study of Class Relations in the Nineteenth-Century Newspaper Printing Industry." Ph.D. diss., New York University.

————. 1982. "Women and the Making of the American Working Class: A Study of the Proletarianization of Printers." *Review of Radical Political Economics* 14: 23–42.

Baron, James N., and William T. Bielby. 1985. "Organizational Barriers to Gender Equality: Sex Segregation of Jobs and Opportunities." In Alice S. Rossi, ed., *Gender and the Life Course*, 233–51. New York: Aldine.

————. 1986. "The Proliferation of Job Titles in Organizations." *Administrative Science Quarterly* 31:561–86.

Baron, James N., Brian S. Mittman, and Andrew E. Newman. 1988. "Targets of Opportunity: Organizational and Environmental Determinants of Gender Integration within the California Civil Service, 1979–85." Revised version of paper presented at meeting of the American Sociological Association, Atlanta, December.

Baron, James N., and Andrew E. Newman. 1989. "Pay the Man: Effects of Demographic Composition on Wage Rates in the California Civil Service." In Robert T. Michael, Heidi I. Hartmann, and Brigid O'Farrell, eds., *Pay Equity: Empirical Inquiries*, 107–30. Washington, D.C.: National Academy Press.

————. 1990. "For What It's Worth: Organizations, Occupations, and the Value of Work Done by Women and Nonwhites." *American Sociological Review* 55 (April): 155–75.

Bartender. 1988. "Happy Hour." Vol. 14 (2): 6.

Bassi, Robert A. 1980. "Your Year If You Want It Badly Enough." *NABW Journal*, July–August, p. 5.

Bates, Don. 1983. "A Concern: Will Women Inherit the Profession?" *Public Relations Journal* 39 (7): 6–7.

Beasley, Maurine H., and Sheila Gibbons. 1977. *Women in Media: A Documentary Source Book*. Washington, D.C.: Institute for the Freedom of the Press.

Beasley, Maurine H., and Kathyrn T. Theus. 1985. "The New Majority: A Look at What the Preponderance of Women in Journalism Education Means to the Schools and the Profession." College Park: College of Journalism, University of Maryland.

————. 1988. *The New Majority*. Lanham, Md.: University Presses of America.

Bechtold, Grace. 1946. *Book Publishing*. Vocational and Professional Monographs. Boston: Bellman.

Becker, Gary. 1957. *The Economics of Discrimination*. Chicago: University of Chicago Press.

————. 1975. *Human Capital*. New York: National Bureau of Economic Research.

Beckett, Jamie. 1986. "High Technology's Imprint on Printing." *Newsday*, August 18.

Beechey, Veronica, and Tessa Perkins. 1987. *A Matter of Hours: Women, Part-time Work, and the Labor Market*. Cambridge, U.K.: Polity Press.

Beller, Andrea H. 1984. "Trends in Occupational Segregation by Sex and Race, 1960–1981." In Barbara F. Reskin, ed., *Sex Segregation in the Workplace: Trends, Explanations, Remedies*, 11–26. Washington, D.C.: National Academy Press.

Bem, Sandra L. 1983. "Gender Schema Theory and Its Implications for Child Development: Raising Gender-Aschematic Children in a Gender-Schematic Society." *Signs* 8 (Summer):598–616.

Benjamin, Curtis G. 1981. "The Weaving of a Tangled Economic Web." *Publishers Weekly* 219 (April 24): 41–45.

Bennett, Robert A. 1986. "Now, the Age of Fast-Buck Banking." *New York Times*, December 14, pp. 1F+.

Benton, Lyda. 1981. "Personal Conviction Helps Build a Clientele." *Life Association News* 76 (February): 37–40.

Berg, A. Scott. 1978. *Max Perkins*. New York: Dutton.

Bergmann, Barbara R., and William Darity. 1981. "Social Relations, Productivity, and Employer Discrimination." *Monthly Labor Review* 104 (April): 47–49.

Bernays, Edward L. 1945. *Public Relations*. Vocational and Professional Monographs. Boston: Bellman Publishing Company.

———. 1952. *Public Relations*. Norman: University of Oklahoma Press.

Bernstein, Peter W. 1982. "Women: The New Stars in Banking." *Fortune* 106 (1): 84–95.

Berry, Leonard L. 1979. "Service Strategies in the 1980s." *Journal of Retail Banking* 1 (2): 1–10.

Berry, Leonard, and Thomas Thompson. 1982. "Relationship Banking: The Art of Turning Customers into Clients." *Journal of Retail Banking* 4 (2): 63–73.

Berryman, Susan E. 1983. *Who Will Do Science? A Special Report*. New York: Rockefeller Foundation.

Berryman, Sue E., and Linda J. Waite. 1987. "Young Women's Choice of Nontraditional Occupations." In Christine Bose and Glenna Spitze, eds., *Ingredients for Women's Employment Policy*, 115–36. Albany: State University of New York Press.

Best's Review, Property/Casualty. 1975. "Telecommunication Speeds Settlement of Auto Accident Claims." Vol. 77 (November): 102.

———. 1976. "The Big Payoff in Productivity." Vol. 77 (September): 111–13.

Bianchi, Suzanne M., and Nancy F. Rytina. 1984. "Occupational Change, 1970–1980." Paper prepared for the annual meeting of the Population Association of America, Minneapolis, May.

Bielby, Denise D., and William T. Bielby. 1987. "Writing for the Screen: Gender, Jobs, and Stereotypes in the Entertainment Industry." Paper presented at the meeting of the American Sociological Association, Chicago, August.

———. 1988. "She Works Hard for the Money." *American Journal of Sociology* 93 (March): 1031–59.

Bielby, William T., and James N. Baron. 1984. "A Woman's Place Is with Other Women: Sex Segregation within Organizations." In Barbara F. Reskin, ed., *Sex Segregation in the Workplace: Trends, Explanations, Remedies*, 27–55. Washington, D.C.: National Academy Press.

———. 1986. "Men and Women at Work: Sex Segregation and Statistical Discrimination." *American Journal of Sociology* 91 (January): 759–99.

———. 1987. "Undoing Job Discrimination: Job Integration and Comparable Worth." In Christine Bose and Glenna Spitze, eds., *Ingredients for Women's Employment Policy*, 211–29. Albany: State University of New York Press.

Bingley, Clive. 1972. *The Business of Book Publishing*. Oxford: Pergamon Press.

Binkin, Martin, and Shirley J. Bach. 1977. *Women and the Military*. Washington, D.C.: Brookings Institution.

Bishop, Katherine. 1988. "California Women Receiving Millions to Settle Bias Case." *New York Times,* January 20, pp. A1, B7.

Blau, Francine D. 1977. *Equal Pay in the Office.* Lexington, Mass.: Lexington Books.

———. 1984. "Occupational Segregation and Labor Market Discrimination." In Barbara F. Reskin, ed., *Sex Segregation in the Workplace: Trends, Explanations, Remedies,* 117–43. Washington, D.C.: National Academy Press.

———. 1989. "Occupational Segregation by Gender: A Look at the 1980s." Revised version of a paper presented at the 1988 meeting of the American Economics Association, New York.

Blau, Francine D., and Andrea H. Beller. 1988. "Trends in Earnings Differentials by Gender." *Industrial and Labor Relations Review* 41 (July): 513–29.

Blau, Francine D., and Marianne A. Ferber. 1986. *The Economics of Women, Men, and Work.* Englewood Cliffs, N.J.: Prentice-Hall.

Blau, Francine D., and Wallace E. Hendricks. 1979. "Occupational Segregation by Sex: Trends and Prospects." *Journal of Human Resources* 14:197–210.

Blau, Peter M., John W. Gustad, Richard Jessor, Herbert S. Parnes, and Richard C. Wilcock. 1956. "Occupational Choice: A Conceptual Framework." *Industrial and Labor Relations Review* 9:531–43.

Blauner, Robert. 1964. *Alienation and Freedom: The Factory Worker and His Industry.* Chicago: University of Chicago Press.

Block, H. I. 1985. "Narrowcasting: Affordable Television Marketing." *Real Estate Today* 18:42.

Blum, Linda. 1987. "Possibilities and Limitations of the Comparable Worth Movement." *Gender & Society* 4 (December): 380–99.

Bolger, Robert J. 1971. "The Professional Woman as Employee." *American Journal of Hospital Pharmacy* 143:136–40.

Bolton, Francis M. 1976. "Women as Insurance Agents—Let's Separate the Fact from Fiction." *Life Insurance Selling,* December, pp. 28, 30.

Bonham, Barbara. 1977. "Remember the Ladies." *Graphic Arts Monthly,* June, p. 62.

Borum, Rodney L. 1980. "The Printing Industry—A Ten-Year Prediction." *PIA Communicator* 24 (January–February): 19–21.

Bose, Christine E., and Peter H. Rossi. 1983. "Gender and Jobs: Prestige Standings of Occupations as Affected by Gender." *American Sociological Review* 48 (June): 316–30.

Bowden, Elbert. 1980. *Revolution in Banking.* Richmond, Va.: Robert F. Dame.

Boylan, Ross. 1988. "A Model of the Matching Process of Persons and Entry-Level Jobs." Paper presented at the annual meeting of the American Sociological Association, Atlanta.

Boynton, Nancy D., Barbara L. Donovan, and Archer L. Edgar. 1977. "The New Female Agent." *Best's Review, Life/Health* 78 (December): 22–28.

Braden, Richard T. 1979. "Computerized Processing of Group Health Insurance Claims." *Best's Review, Life/Health* 79 (April): 92–96.

Brand, Horst. 1988. "Productivity and Employment: The 1988 International Symposium." *Monthly Labor Review* 111 (August): 32–33.

Brand, Horst, and John Duke. 1982. "Productivity in Commercial Banking: Computers Spur the Advance." *Monthly Labor Review* 105 (December): 19–27.

Braverman, Harry. 1974. *Labor and Monopoly Capital.* New York: Monthly Review Press.

Brede, William J. 1959. *Creative Thinking in Real Estate.* New York: Harper.

Brewer, Willis R. 1969. "Report of the Committee of Future Enrollment Problems of the American Association of Colleges of Pharmacy." *American Journal of Pharmaceutical Education* 33:591–92.

Brief 544. 1986. *Bartenders.* 4th ed. Moravia, N.Y.: Chronicle Guidance.

Broadcasting. 1973. "Post-Newsweek TV's in Jacksonville and Miami Are the First Targets of License-Renewal Challenges." January 8, pp. 16–19.

Broom, Glen M. 1982. "A Comparison of Sex Roles in Public Relations." *Public Relations Review* 8 (3): 17–22.

Broom, Glen M., and David M. Dozier. 1985. "Determinants and Consequences of Public Relations Roles." Paper presented at the annual convention of the Association for Education in Journalism and Mass Communication, Memphis.

Brown, Robert B. 1981. "Women Sales Reps Can Boost Life Income." *Rough Notes* 124 (11): 45.

Bryant, Anne L. 1980. "Women in Banking: Changes of the Decade." *Journal of Retail Banking* 11 (4): 21–26.

Burbridge, Lynn. 1984. *The Impact of Changes in Policy on the Federal Equal Employment Opportunity Effort.* Washington, D.C.: Urban Institute.

Burris, Beverly H. 1989. "Technocracy and Gender in the Workplace." *Social Problems* 36 (April): 165–80.

Burstein, Paul. 1989. "Attacking Sex Discrimination in the Labor Market: A Study of Law and Politics." *Social Forces* 67 (March): 641–65.

Burth, Norman. 1971. "Dough Development by Ultra-High Speeding Mixing." *Bakers Digest,* pp. 46–48.

Business Week. 1970. "A Computer That Tends the Bar." September 26, p. 46.

———. 1978. "PR: The Velvet Ghetto of Affirmative Action." May 8, p. 122.

Butrick, Ann. 1978. "The Making of a Lady Bartender." *Cosmopolitan* 185:170–82.

Caddy, Douglas. 1986. *Legislative Trends in Insurance Regulation.* College Station: Texas A and M Press.

Campbell, Dorcas. 1947. "Are Women 'a Natural' in Public Relations?" *Public Relations Journal* 3 (3): 21–24.

Canfield, Cass. 1969. "The Real and the Ideal Editor." *Publishers Weekly* 195 (March 31): 24–27.

Caplette, Michele. 1979. "Editorial Career Paths in College Textbook Publishing." Paper presented to the annual meeting of the American Sociological Association, Boston.

———. 1981. "Women in Publishing: A Study of Careers in Organizations." Ph.D. diss., State University of New York at Stony Brook.

———. 1982a. "Women in Book Publishing: A Qualified Success Story." In Lewis Coser, Charles Kadushin, and Walter Powell, eds., *Books: The Culture and Commerce of Publishing,* 148–74. Chicago: University of Chicago Press.

———. 1982b. "Women in Book Publishing: Common Denominators in the Careers of Twelve Successful Women." Presented to the Women's National Book Association.

————. 1987. Personal communication.

Carey, Max. 1988. "Occupational Tenure in 1987: Many Workers Have Remained in Their Fields." *Monthly Labor Review* 111 (October): 3–12.

Carnes, Richard B., and Horst Brand. 1977. "Productivity and New Technology in Eating and Drinking Places." *Monthly Labor Review* 100 (September): 9–15.

Carr-Saunders, A. M. 1966. "Professionalization in Historical Perspective." In Howard V. Vollmer and Donald L. Mills, eds., *Professionalization*, 3–9. Englewood Cliffs, N.J.: Prentice-Hall.

Carruthers, Rod. 1987. "The Manpower Crisis." *Graphic Arts Monthly* 59 (May): 52–58.

Carter, Michael J., and Susan Boslego Carter. 1981. "Women's Recent Progress in the Profession, or, Women Get a Ticket to Ride After the Gravy Train Has Left the Station." *Feminist Studies* 7 (Fall): 477–504.

Carter, Robert A. 1983. "The Human Factor: When Companies Are Sold, Merged, or Conglomerated, What Happens to the People Who Work for Them." *Publishers Weekly* 223 (January 21): 41–46.

————. 1984. "Acquiring Books for Fun and Profit." *Publishers Weekly* 225 (March 23): 24–26.

Caruth, Donald. 1984. *Work Measurement in Banking.* Boston: Bankers Publishing Company.

Casey, Thomas. 1970. "Modern Claim Adjusting Techniques." *Best's Review, Property/Liability* 70 (March): 36–38.

Caskey, Clark. 1983. "Effective Management: The Woman Hater." *Southern Graphics* (October): 34–36, 43–44.

Castillo, Felicia. 1988. Personal communication.

Castro, Janice. 1985. "More and More, She's the Boss." *Time,* December 2, pp. 64–66.

Catanzarite, Lisa M., and Myra H. Strober. 1988. "Occupational Attractiveness and Race-Gender Segregation, 1960–1980." Paper presented at the annual meeting of the American Sociological Association, Atlanta, August.

Catering Industry Employee. 1949. "Barmaid Bill Over First Ohio Hurdle." Vol. 58 (6): 15.

Cavan, Sherri. 1966. *Liquor License.* Chicago: Aldine.

Cerf, Bennett. 1977. *At Random.* New York: Random House.

Chaney, Bev, ed. 1984. *The First Hundred Years: Association of Book Travelers, 1884–1984.* New York: Association of Book Travelers.

Charnizon, Marlene. 1987. "Women at the Top." *Publishers Weekly* 231 (January 23): 27–31.

Chasin, Steven H. 1985. "Report of Fall 1984 Undergraduate Enrollment in Schools and Colleges of Pharmacy." *American Journal of Pharmaceutical Education* 49 (Fall):191.

Chazin, Michael. 1978. "Newspaper Operations: The Future Arrives Sooner Than Expected." *Inland Printer/American Lithographer* 181 (June): 39–45.

Chazin, Michael, and Elizabeth G. Berglund. 1979. "Women in the Graphic Arts . . . How Far Have They Really Come?" *American Printer and Lithographer* 183 (July): 46–51.

Chicago Women in Publishing. 1973. "Survey II: Comparative Status of Women and Men in Chicago Area Book Publishing." Unpublished report, Fall.

Christenberry, Boyd. 1979. "Industry Should Recruit More Women Agents." *National Underwriter, Life/Health* 83 (December 29): 10.

Cissley, Charles H. 1977. *Systems and Data Processing in Insurance Companies.* New York: Life Office Management Association.

Clark, Alice. 1968. *Working Life of Women in the Seventeenth Century.* New York: Augustus M. Kelley.

Clark, Earl. 1976. "Keeping the American Agency System Strong." *Life Association News* 71 (January): 91–94.

Cline, Carolyn Garrett, Elizabeth Lance Toth, Judy Van Slyke Turk, Lynne Masel Walters, Nancy Johnson, and Hank Smith. 1986. *The Velvet Ghetto: The Impact of the Increasing Percentage of Women in Public Relations and Business Communication.* San Francisco: IABC Foundation.

Cobble, Dorothy Sue. 1988. " 'Practical Women': Waitress Unionists and the Controversies over Gender Roles in the Food Service Industry, 1900–1980." *Labor History* 29 (1): 5–31.

———. 1989a. Personal communication.

———. 1989b. " 'Drawing the Line': The Construction of a Gendered Workforce in the Food Industry." Forthcoming in Ava Baron, ed., *Work Engendered.* Ithaca: Cornell University Press.

———. Forthcoming. *Dishing It Out: Waitresses and Their Unions in the Twentieth Century.* Urbana: University of Illinois Press.

Cockburn, Cynthia. 1983. *Brothers: Male Dominance and Technological Change.* London: Pluto Press.

———. 1987. "Restructuring Technology, Restructuring Gender." Paper presented at the annual meeting of the American Sociological Association, Chicago, August.

———. 1988. "The Gendering of Jobs: Workplace Relations and the Reproduction of Sex Segregation." In Sylvia Walby, ed., *Gender Segregation at Work,* 29–42. Milton Keynes, U.K.: Open University Press.

Cohn, Samuel. 1985. *The Process of Occupational Sex-Typing: The Feminization of Clerical Labor in Great Britain.* Philadelphia: Temple University Press.

Cole, Robert. 1982. "Public Relations for Branch Managers." *Journal of Retail Banking* 4 (4): 15–26.

Collins, Randall. 1979. *The Credential Society.* New York: Academic Press.

Collins, Sharon. 1983. "The Making of the Black Middle Class." *Social Problems* 30: 369–82.

Collinson, David, and David Knights. 1983. "The Gendered Labour Process in Life Insurance: Professional and Entrepreneurial Practice and Sex Discrimination." Paper presented at the UMIST/ASTON Conference on Organization and Control of the Labour Process, Owens Park, Manchester, U.K.

Compaine, Benjamin M. 1980. *The Newspaper Industry in the 1980s: An Assessment of Economics and Technology.* White Plains, N.Y.: Knowledge Industry Publications.

Computers and People. 1978. "Bell Labs Fellowship Program Aids Minority and Women Students Pursuing Doctoral Degrees." Vol. 21:25.

Consumer Reports. 1984. "Whatever Happened to No-Fault?" Vol. 49 (9): 511–13, 546.

Cooper, Joel, and Russell H. Fazio. 1979. "The Formation and Persistence of Attitudes That Support Intergroup Conflict." In William G. Austin and Stephen Worchel, eds., *The Social Psychology of Intergroup Relations*, 149–59. Monterey, Calif.: Brooks/Cole.

Corcoran, Mary, Greg Duncan, and Michael Ponza. 1984. "Work Experience, Job Segregation, and Wages. In Barbara F. Reskin, ed., *Sex Segregation in the Workplace: Trends, Explanations, Remedies*, 171–91. Washington, D.C.: National Academy Press.

Cornelius, James. 1983. "Staying Alive—Young People in Publishing." *Publishers Weekly* 25 (November): 32–35.

Cornfield, Daniel B. 1988. "Technological Change and Labor Relations in U.S. Newspaper Composing Rooms." Report prepared for the International Labour Office, Geneva, Switzerland.

Cornfield, Daniel, Polly Phipps, Diane Bates, Deborah Carter, Trudie Coker, Kathleen Kitzmiller, and Peter Wood. 1988. "Office Automation, Clerical Workers, and Labor Relations in the Insurance Industry." In Daniel Cornfield, ed., *Workers, Managers, and Technological Change: Emerging Patterns of Labor Relations*, 111–34. New York: Plenum Press.

Coser, Lewis. 1975. "Publishers as Gatekeepers of Ideas." *Annals of the American Academy of Political and Social Science* 421 (September): 14–22.

Coser, Lewis, Charles Kadushin, and Walter Powell. 1982. *Books: The Culture and Commerce of Publishing.* Chicago: University of Chicago Press.

Council on Economic Priorities. 1977. *Women and Minorities in Banking: Short-changed/Update.* New York: Praeger.

Crispen, Margaret. 1978. *How Any Woman Can Get Rich Fast in Real Estate.* Kansas City, Mo.: Sheed Andrews and McNeel.

Crouch, J. Paige. 1985. "Graphic Communication Education: How It's Doing and What YOU Can Do." *Southern Graphics*, September, pp. 22–23, 36, 40.

Cullen, Andrew J. 1964. "Nine Publics That Must Be 'Sold' on Your Company." *Public Relations Journal* 20 (11): 13–16.

Cutlip, Scott M., Allen H. Center, and Glen M. Broom. 1985. *Effective Public Relations.* 6th ed. Englewood Cliffs, N.J.: Prentice-Hall.

D'Angelo, Robert. 1987. Personal communication.

Datamation. 1972. "Getting Out." May, pp. 80–81.

Davids, Lewis E. 1977. *Dictionary of Insurance.* Totowa, N.J.: Littlefield, Adams.

Davies, Margery W. 1975. "Women's Place Is at the Typewriter: The Feminization of the Clerical Labor Force." In Richard Edwards, Michael Reich, and David Gordon, eds., *Labor Market Segmentation*, 279–96. Lexington, Mass.: Heath.

———. 1982. *Woman's Place Is at the Typewriter: Office Work and Office Workers, 1870–1930.* Philadelphia: Temple University Press.

de Haen, Paul. 1971. "The Pharmacists and the Physician." *Journal of the American Pharmaceutical Association*, April, pp. 154–57.

Dertouzos, James N., and Timothy H. Quinn. 1985. *Bargaining Responses to the Technology Revolution: The Case of the Newspaper Industry.* Rand Report R-3144-DOL. Santa Monica, Calif.: Rand Corporation.

Dessauer, John P. 1974. *Book Publishing*. New York: Bowker.
———. 1982. "The Uses of Adversity—A Study of the Book Industry in Recession." *Publishers Weekly* 222 (December 17): 32–38.
Deutsch, Claudia H. 1987a. "The Haves—and Have Nots—in Public Relations." *New York Times*, May 31, p. 12.
———. 1987b. "The Ax Falls on Equal Opportunity." *New York Times*, January 4, pp. 3-1, 27.
DiPrete, Thomas A., and Whitman T. Soule. 1988. "Gender and Promotion in Segmented Job Ladder Systems." *American Sociological Review* 53 (February): 26–40.
Doebler, Paul. 1973. "Electronic Editing via Long Distance." *Publishers Weekly* 204 (October 1): 64–66.
———. 1975. "Video Editing Comes to Book Publishing." *Publishers Weekly* 208 (September 1): 43–48.
———. 1978. "The Statistics of Concentration." *Publishers Weekly* 214 (July 31): 26–30.
Doeringer, Peter B., and Michael J. Piore. 1971. *Internal Labor Markets and Manpower Analysis*. Lexington, Mass.: Heath.
Donato, Katharine M., and Patricia A. Roos. 1987. "Gender and Earnings Inequality among Computer Specialists." In Barbara D. Wright, Myra Marx Ferree, Gail O. Mellow, Linda H. Lewis, Maria-Luz Daza Samper, Robert Asher, and Kathleen Claspell, eds., *Women, Work, and Technology: Transformations*, 291–317. Ann Arbor: University of Michigan Press.
Dong, Stella. 1980. "Publishing's Revolving Door." *Publishers Weekly* 218 (December 18): 20–23.
———. 1984. "What Authors Look For in Editors." *Publishers Weekly* 226 (December 14): 22–27.
Dozier, David M., Sharon Chapo, and Brad Sullivan. 1983. "Sex and the Bottom Line: Income Differences among Women and Men in Public Relations." Paper presented to the Association for Education in Journalism and Mass Communications," Corvallis, Oregon, August.
Dreier, Thomas. 1936. *The Power of Print—and Men*. Brooklyn, N.Y.: Mergenthaler Lintotype.
Dubinsky, Mark J. 1982. "Over the Short Haul: Some Effects of Automating Health Claims." *Best's Review, Health/Life* 83 (8): 68–74, 108.
Duncan, Otis Dudley, and Beverly Duncan. 1955. "A Methodological Analysis of Segregation Indices." *American Sociological Review* 20:200–217.
———. 1957. *The Negro Population of Chicago: A Study of Residential Succession*. Chicago: University of Chicago Press.
Duncan, Walter J. 1978. "A Claims System Profile." *Best's Review, Property/Casualty* 78 (April): 38–46.
Dunetz, Mary Chichester. 1977. "The Next Decade—Womanpower." *Best's Review, Property/Casualty* 78 (July): 77–78.
Editor and Publisher. 1968. "ITU Apprenticeship Trimmed to 4 Years." Vol. 101 (August 10): 16.
———. 1970a. "ITU Embraces CRT for Job Jurisdiction." Vol. 103 (August 15): 36–37.

———. 1970b. "Guild Steps Up Fight for Female Equality." Vol. 103 (November 28): 44.

EDP Analyzer. 1976. "Bringing Women into Computing Management." August 14, pp. 1–14.

Edwards, Richard. 1979. *Contested Terrain: The Transformation of the Workplace in the Twentieth Century*. New York: Basic Books.

Ehrenreich, Barbara, and Deirdre English. 1979. *For Her Own Good: 150 Years of Experts' Advice to Women*. Garden City, N.Y.: Anchor Books.

Eklund, Coy. 1975. "Woman in Insurance." Report presented to the joint board meeting ILI-ALIA, San Diego, September.

———. 1976. "Women in Business." Keynote address at New York University's Women in Management Conference Series, April.

———. 1978. "Widening the Space for Living." Paper presented at the meeting of the National Association of Insurance, New York City, June 19.

Eldred, Nelson R., and David Orr. 1980. "Where Will the Skilled Workers Come From?" *American Printer and Lithographer* 185 (June): 50–51.

Electronic News. 1979. "Computer Jobs Increasing for Women." Vol. 25:12S.

Ellsworth, William W. 1919. *A Golden Age of Authors*. Boston: Houghton Mifflin.

Embers, Ken. 1987. Personal communication.

England, Paula. 1982. "The Failure of Human Capital Theory to Explain Occupational Sex Segregation." *Journal of Human Resources* 17:358–70.

England, Paula, and Lori McCreary. 1987. "Gender Inequality in Paid Employment." In Beth B. Hess and Myra Marx Ferree, eds., *Analyzing Gender*, 286–320. Newbury Park, Calif.: Sage.

Epstein, Cynthia Fuchs. 1983. *Women in Law*. Garden City, N.Y.: Anchor Books.

Equal Employment News. 1981. "News of Special Special Interest: Business and Industry." Vol. 3 (3): 7–8.

———. 1982. "News of Special Special Interest: Business and Industry." Vol. 4 (1): 8.

Equal Employment Opportunity Commission. 1987. Personal communication.

Equinews. 1975. "Eklund Discusses Women's Equality." October, pp. 1–2.

Ernst, Hugo. 1946. "Bartending Must Revert to Bartenders, Says the G.E.B." *Catering Industry Employee* 55 (4): 4–5.

Evans, David W. 1983a. "Lobbying Is a Public Relations Responsibility, but Is It PR's Brainchild or Stepchild? Part I." *Tips and Tactics* 21 (9): 1–2.

———. 1983b. "Lobbying Is a Public Relations Responsibility, but Is It PR's Brainchild or Stepchild? Part II." *Tips and Tactics* 21 (10): 1–2.

Evans, Mariwyn. 1983. *Opportunities in Real Estate*. Skokie, Ill.: VGM Horizons.

Evans, Nancy. 1978. "How Authors Are Affected [by Mergers]." *Publishers Weekly* 214 (July 31): 45–47.

———. 1979. "Line Editors: The Rigorous Pursuit of Perfection." *Publishers Weekly* 216 (October 15): 24–31.

Evans, Sara M., and Barbara J. Nelson. 1989. *Wage Justice: Comparable Worth and the Paradox of Technocratic Reform*. Chicago: University of Chicago Press.

Farber, Henry S. 1987. "The Recent Decline of Unionization in the United States." *Science* 238:915–20.

Federal Rules Decisions. 1978. Vol. 78. St. Paul, Minn.: West Publishing.

Ferguson, Douglas P. 1988. Personal communication.

Ferree, Myra Marx. 1987. "She Works Hard for a Living: Gender and Class on the Job." In Beth B. Hess and Myra Marx Ferree, eds., *Analyzing Gender*, 322–47. Newbury Park, Calif.: Sage.

Fields, Judith, and Edward Wolff. 1989. "The Decline of Sex Segregation and the Wage Gap." Economic Research Report 89–04, C. V. Starr Center for Applied Economics, New York University, March.

Figart, Deborah M., and Barbara Bergmann. 1989. "Facilitating Women's Occupational Integration." Paper prepared for the U.S. Department of Labor, Commission on Workforce Quality and Labor Market Efficiency, American University, May.

Filer, Randall K. 1985. "Male-Female Wage Differences: The Importance of Compensating Differentials." *Industrial and Labor Relations Review* 38:426–37.

———. 1988. Personal communication.

Flanley, Mabel G. 1946. "Women: A Forgotten Public." *Public Relations Journal* 2 (3): 24–26, 40.

Flanley, Mabel G., and Sally Woodward. 1955. "This Business of Women." *Public Relations Journal* 11 (10): 58–61, 128–30.

Fletcher, F. Marion. 1971. *The Negro in the Drug Store Industry*. Report No. 24, The Racial Policies of American Industry, Wharton School of Finance and Commerce. Philadelphia: University of Pennsylvania.

Florida Pharmacy Today. 1989. "The Schering Report: Women Eventually Will Attain Majority Role in Pharmacy." Vol. 53 (April): 7–14.

Folbre, Nancy, and Marjorie Abel. 1988. "Women's Work and Women's Households: Gender Bias in the U.S. Census." Paper presented at the annual meeting of the Population Association of America, New Orleans, April.

Follain, James R., Terry Lutes, and David A. Meier. 1985. Unpublished data from study for Illinois Association of Realtors.

———. 1986. *Why Do Some Real Estate Salespeople Earn More Than Others?* Champaign-Urbana, Ill.: Office of Real Estate Research.

Food Processing. 1971a. "Cuts Proofing 80–90 Percent, Improves Uniformity." December, p. 37.

———. 1971b. "Reduces Work Force by Three: Pneumatic Conveying of Flour More Efficient, More Sanitary." December, p. 38.

Form, William. 1987. "On the Degradation of Skills." *Annual Review of Sociology* 13:29–47.

Fort, Mary E. 1974. "Why Are GAs Afraid to Recruit Women Agents?" *Life Association News* 69 (August): 135–39.

Foster, Anna. 1969. "Executive Potential on the Distaff Side." *Banking* 61 (12): 47.

Fox, Lynne H., Diane E. Tobin, and Linda Brody. 1979. "Sex-Role Socialization and Achievement in Mathematics." In Michele Andrinsin Wittig and Anne C. Peterson, eds., *Sex Related Differences in Cognitive Functioning*, 303–32. New York: Academic Press.

Freeman, Richard B., and Richard L. Medoff. 1984. *What Do Unions Do?* New York: Basic Books.

Friedman, Sam. 1984. "A Case of Equality." *National Underwriter, Life/Health* 88 (August 18): 8.

———. 1985. "Department Stores Want a Larger Role." *National Underwriter, Life/Health* 89 (March 2): 2.

Fullerton, Howard N. 1987. "Labor Force Projections: 1986 to 2000." *Monthly Labor Review* 110 (September): 19–29.

Fry, Maxwell, and Raburn Williams. 1984. *American Money and Banking*. New York: Wiley.

Gabriel, Trip. 1989. "Call My Agent!" *New York Times Magazine*, February 19, pp. 45–80.

Gaines, Sallie, 1988. "State Farm Settles Sex Bias Case." *Chicago Tribune*, January 20, pp. A1, 6.

Galassi, Jonathan W. 1980. "Double Agent: The Literary Editor in the Commercial House." *Publishers Weekly* 217 (March 7): 28–30.

Garland, Charles H. 1901. "Women as Telegraphists." *Economics Journal* 6 (June): 251–61.

Gee, Nancie. 1975. "Banks Tap the Women's Market." *Public Relations Journal* 31 (8): 14–30.

Geracimos, Ann. 1974. "Women in Publishing: Where Do They Feel They're Going?" *Publishers Weekly* 206 (November 11): 22–27.

Gersh, Debra. 1986. "Insight into Journalism Graduates." *Editor and Publisher* 119 (February 22): 14–15.

Gerson, Judith M. 1987. "Home-Based Clerical Work and the Sexual Division of Labor." Paper presented at the annual meeting of the American Sociological Association, Chicago, August.

Gerstenberger, Paula P. 1981. "The Woman's Unit." *Managers Magazine* 56 (10): 29–31.

Ghiloni, Beth W. 1984. "Women, Power, and the Corporation." *Power and Elites* 1 (1): 37–50.

Gilroy, Angele A. 1980. "An Economic Analysis of the U.S. Domestic Book Publishing Industry." *Printing and Publishing* 21 (4): 8–11.

Giroux, Robert. 1982. "The Education of an Editor." *Publishers Weekly* 221 (January 8): 54–60.

Glabberson, William. 1987. "Will Takeovers Be Bad for Books?" *New York Times*, April 5, p. 3.

Glazer, Nona Y. 1984. "Servants to Capital: Unpaid Domestic Labor and Paid Work." *Review of Radical Political Economics* 16:61–87.

———. 1988. "Overlooked, Overworked: Women's Unpaid and Paid Work in the Health Services' 'Cost Crisis.'" *International Journal of Health Services* 18:119–37.

Goldman, Sheril Evans. 1974. "Computers—and Liberated Women?" *Computers and People* 23:8.

Golembe, Carter, and David Holland. 1986. *Federal Regulation of Banking 1986–87*. Washington, D.C.: Golembe Associates.

Gottschall, Edward. 1977a. "Vision '77: Communications, Typographics. Part 1." *International Journal of Typographics* 4 (3): 2–56.

———. 1977b. "Vision '77: Communications, Typographics. Part 2." *International Journal of Typographics* 4 (4): 2–65.

Goyan, Jere E. 1988. "Some Thoughts on the M-Word Needs of the Future." Albertson's Lecture, Idaho State University, Pocatello, October 24.

Grannis, Chandler B. 1985. "The Structure and Function of the Book Business." In

Elizabeth Geiser et al., eds., *The Business of Book Publishing*, 12–20. Boulder, Colo.: Westview Press.

Granovetter, Mark S. 1974. *Getting a Job: A Study of Contacts and Careers*. Cambridge, Mass.: Harvard University Press.

Gray, Robert K. 1986. "In Defense of Lobbyists." *New York Times*, April 24.

Gray, Susan Lynne. 1975. "Women Panelists Charge Sex Bias in Industry." *CREA Reporter*, December, p. 3.

Green, Richard H. 1977. "'Typesetting? . . . Interesting Statistics." *Inland Printer* 180 (October): 13.

Greenbaum, Joan M. 1979. *In the Name of Efficiency*. Philadelphia: Temple University Press.

Greenlawn, Cal W., and Darryl D. Zellers. 1978. "Computerized Drug–Drug Interaction Screening System." *American Journal of Hospital Pharmacy* 350:5670.

Griffin, Albert. 1945. *Banking*. Vocational and Professional Monographs. Boston: Bellman.

Grogan, Bernard. 1989. Personal communication.

Gross, Edward. 1968. "*Plus ça change*. . . . The Sexual Segregation of Occupations over Time." *Social Problems* 16:198–208.

Grossack, Martin. 1970. "Humanized Banking: New Approach to New Markets." *Banking* 63 (3): 52.

Hacker, Sally L. 1979. "Sex Stratification, Technology, and Organizational Change: A Longitudinal Study of AT&T." *Social Problems* 26:539–57.

Hapgood, Fred. 1986. "At 411, It's Simply a Matter of Keeping in Tune with the Numbers." *Smithsonian* 17 (November): 66–78.

Harragan, Betty, v. J. Walter Thompson Advertising. 1971.

Hartmann, Heidi I. 1976. "Capitalism, Patriarchy, and Job Segregation by Sex." *Signs* 1 (3): 137–70.

Hartmann, Heidi I., Robert E. Kraut, and Louise A. Tilly, eds. 1986. *Computer Chips and Paper Clips: Technology and Women's Employment*. Vol. 1. Washington, D.C.: National Academy Press.

Health Insurance Association of America. 1983. *Source Book of Health Data, 1982–83*. Washington, D.C.: Health Insurance Association of America.

Health Insurance Institute. 1961. *Source Book of Health Insurance Data, 1961*. New York: Health Insurance Institute.

———. 1973. *Source Book of Health Insurance Data, 1972–73*. New York: Health Insurance Institute.

Helfand, Sol D., Vito Natrella, and Ann E. Pisarksi. 1984. *Statistics for Transportation, Communication, and Finance and Insurance: Data Availability and Needs*. Staff report for the Committee on National Statistics, National Research Council. Washington, D.C.: National Academy Press.

Helfgott, Roy B. 1960. "EDP and the Office Work Force." *Industrial and Labor Relations Review* 19:503–16.

Herbers, John. 1983. "Women and Blacks Gained in Jobs, U.S. Says." *New York Times*, April 24, pp. 1, 18.

Herman, Eleanor S. 1982. "Women in Real Estate." *Real Estate News*, February, pp. 22–24.

Hicks, Larry. 1988. *San Jose Mercury*, July 11, p. 30C.

Hill, Roberta. 1984. "From Hot Metal to Cold Type: New Technology in the News-paper Industry." *New Zealand Journal of Industrial Relations* 9:161–75.

Hinkle, David B. 1970a. "Claims Men and the Future." *National Underwriter, Fire/Casualty* 74 (October 9): 12–16.

———. 1970b. "The Adjuster in the Seventies." *Best's Review, Property/Casualty* 80: 38–50.

Hirsch, Susan E. 1986. "Rethinking the Sexual Division of Labor: Pullman Repair Shops, 1900–1969." *Radical History Review* 35 (May): 26–48.

Hochschild, Arlie Russell. 1983. *The Managed Heart: Commercialization of Human Feeling.* Berkeley: University of California Press.

Hodge, Robert W. 1973. "Toward a Theory of Racial Differences in Employment." *Social Forces* 52 (September): 16–31.

Hodge, Robert W., Paul Siegel, and Peter Rossi. 1964. "Occupational Prestige in the United States." *American Journal of Sociology* 70:286–302.

Hodges, Parker. 1986. "Salary Survey: Small Change for DP Pros." *Datamation* 32 (18): 72–87.

Hodosh, Frederick R. 1980. "Claims Adjusting in the 1970s." *Best's Review, Property/Casualty* 80:38–50.

Holcomb, Betty. 1988. "The Druggist's Crucial New Role." *New York Times Magazine,* April 17, pp. 39–40, 60–63.

Holubowich, Alexandra. 1977. "Women, Money, and Power: Highlights of the NABW Convention." *Trusts and Estates* 116:41.

Hooks, Janet M. 1947. *Women's Occupations through Seven Decades.* U.S. Department of Labor Women's Bureau Bulletin 218. Washington D.C.: U.S. Government Printing Office.

House, J. D. 1977. *Sociology of Residential Real Estate Agents.* Westport, Conn.: Greenwood Press.

Hout, Michael. 1986. "Opportunity and the Minority Middle Class: A Comparison of Blacks in the U.S. and Catholics in Northern Ireland." *American Sociological Review* 51 (April):214–23.

Huffstutler, Clyde E., and Martha Farnsworth Riche. 1972. "Productivity in the Bakery Products Industry." *Monthly Labor Review* 95 (June): 25–28.

Hugill, Philip R., and Nathan Watzman. 1973. "Comprehensive Health Manpower Training Act of 1971: An Update of Federal Support of Pharmacy Education." *American Journal of Pharmaceutical Education* 37 (May):237–41.

Hunter, Bill. 1983. "Public Relations: 'Velvet Ghetto' for Women, Part I." *Ragan Report,* October 17, p. 1.

Hurlahe, Marianne E., Clemenceau A. Jamail, and Beverly Laughlin Brooks. 1980. "Women on the Debit." *Managers Magazine* 55 (8): 13–17.

Insurance Almanac. 1961. Englewood, N.J.: Underwriter Printing and Publishing.

———. 1971. Englewood, N.J.: Underwriter Printing and Publishing.

———. 1981. Englewood, N.J.: Underwriter Printing and Publishing.

Insurance Information Institute. 1972. *Insurance Facts.* New York: Insurance Information Institute.

Insurance Salesman. 1977. "Female Agents Are Doing Well." October, p. 74.

———. 1979. "Women Agents Find 'Room at the Top.'" April, p. 24.

International Association of Business Communicators. 1988. Personal communication.

Ireton, Barbara. 1967. "Female Practitioner Talks about Her Status." *Public Relations Journal*, September 23, pp. 14–15.

Jackall, Robert. 1978. *Workers in a Labyrinth: Jobs and Survival in Bank Bureaucracy.* Montclair, N.J.: Allanheld, Osmun.

Jacobs, Donald. 1980. "Taking a Look at Banking in the '80s—1." *ABA Banking Journal* 72 (8): 65–66.

Jacobs, Jerry A. 1983. "The Sex Segregation of Occupations and Women's Career Patterns." Ph.D. diss. Harvard University.

———. 1989a. *Revolving Doors: Sex Segregation and Women's Careers.* Stanford, Calif.: Stanford University Press.

———. 1989b. "Long-Term Trends in Occupational Sex Segregation." *American Journal of Sociology* 95 (July): 160–73.

Jacobs, Jerry A., and Theresa Labov. 1989. "Trends in the Racial Composition of Urban Occupations: A Longitudinal Test of Queueing Theory." Presented at the meeting of the Population Association of America, Baltimore, April.

Jacobs, Jerry A., and Ronnie Steinberg. 1991. "Compensating Differentials and the Male-Female Wage Gap." *Social Forces*, forthcoming.

James, Caryn. 1987. "New York's Spinning Literary Circles." *The World of New York*, *New York Times Magazine* supplement, April 26, pp. 40, 50–53.

Jencks, Christopher, Lauri Perman, and Lee Rainwater. 1988. "What Is a Good Job? A New Measure of Labor-Market Success." *American Journal of Sociology* 93 (May): 1322–57.

Johnson, C. Anderson, Richard J. Hammel, and J. Stephen Heinen. 1977. "Levels of Satisfaction among Hospital Pharmacists." *American Journal of Hospital Pharmacy* 34:241–47.

Jones, Jacqueline. 1985. *Labor of Love, Labor of Sorrow.* New York: Basic Books.

Jones, Jo Ann, and Rachel Rosenfeld. 1989. "Women's Occupations and Local Labor Markets." *Social Forces* 67 (March): 666–92.

Josephson, Matthew. 1956. *Union House, Union Bar.* New York: Random House.

Judd, D. F. 1972. "The Need for Systems Analysts." *The Office*, January: 120–21.

Kalleberg, Arne L., Michael Wallace, Karyn A. Loscocco, Kevin T. Leicht, and Hans-Helmut Ehm. 1987. "The Eclipse of Craft: The Changing Face of Labor in the Newspaper Industry." In Daniel B. Cornfield, ed., *Workers, Managers, and Technological Change: Emerging Patterns of Labor Relations*, 47–71. New York: Plenum Press.

Kanter, Rosabeth Moss. 1977. *Men and Women of the Corporation.* New York: Basic Books.

Kaplan, Steven L. 1984. *Provisioning Paris: Merchants and Millers in the Grain and Flour Trade during the Eighteenth Century.* Ithaca, N.Y.: Cornell University Press.

Karene, Ethel B., and Kenneth L. Anderson. 1967. *Women in Our Life—Insurance.* Indianapolis, Ind.: Research and Review Service of America.

Kato, Donna. 1989. "Computer Talk Is Perfect Prescription for Getting Needed Drug Information." *Champaign-Urbana News Gazette*, April 23, p. E-11.

Kaufman, Stuart Bruce. 1987. A *Vision of Unity: A History of the Bakery and Confectionery Workers International Union.* Urbana: University of Illinois Press.

Keeton, Robert F., and Jeffrey O'Connell. 1965. *Basic Protection for the Traffic Victim: A Blueprint for Reforming Automobile Insurance.* Boston: Little, Brown.

Kelber, Harry, and Carl Schlesinger. 1967. *Union Printers and Controlled Automation.* New York: Free Press.

Kenkelen, Bill. 1988. "Fewer White Men in Divinity Schools." *San Jose Mercury,* May 7, p. 11C.

Kent, Allan. 1977. "The Coming Mandate to Hire Women Agents." *Life Insurance Selling,* June, pp. 6, 8.

Kessler, Suzanne, D. J. Ashenden, R. W. Connell, and G. W. Dowsett. 1985. "Gender Relations in Secondary Schooling." *Sociology of Education* 58:34–48.

Kessler-Harris, Alice. 1982. *Out to Work: A History of Wage-Earning Women in the United States.* New York: Oxford University Press.

———. 1986. "Women's History Goes to Trial: EEOC vs. Sears, Roebuck and Co." *Signs* 11 (Summer): 767–79.

Kimble, Mary Ann. 1975. "The Sleeping Women." *Drug Intelligence and Clinical Pharmacy* 9 (March): 153.

Kimbrell, Wendy. 1986. "Women Move In." *Bakery,* September, pp. 44–52.

Kinchen, David M. 1990. "More Men Drawn to Real Estate Sales Careers." *Los Angeles Times,* March 15, p. K15.

King, Carole. 1984. "Female Agents: A Progress Report." *Best's Review, Life/Health* 85 (September): 132–34.

Kirk, Kenneth W. 1976. "Pharmacy Students Revisited as Pharmacists." *American Journal of Pharmaceutical Education* 40 (May):125–28.

Kirk, Kenneth W., and Metta Lou Henderson. 1975. "Expectations of Female Pharmacy Students." *Journal of the American Pharmaceutical Association,* n.s. 15: 622–23, 651.

Kirk, Kenneth W., and Richard A. Ohvall. 1972. "Women Pharmacists in Hospital and Community Practice." *American Journal of Hospital Pharmacy* 29:761–66.

Kleinfield, N. R. 1987. "Pills and Peas—at the Pharmacy." *New York Times,* May 31, p. 3–4.

Knapp, David A., and Deanne E. Knapp. 1968. "An Appraisal of the Contemporary Practice of Pharmacy." *American Journal of Pharmaceutical Education* 32 (December): 747–58.

Knight, James R., and Wayne F. Conrad. 1975. "Review of Computer Applications in Hospital Pharmacy Practice." *American Journal of Hospital Pharmacy* 32: 165–73.

Knowlton, Winthrop. 1974. "How Harper & Row Meets the Demands of Women." *Publishers Weekly* 205 (May 13): 12.

Kocolowski, Linda. 1980a. "Insurance Women Are Starting to Move Up." *National Underwriter, Property/Casualty* 84 (31): 26.

———. 1980b. "Speaker Gives Tips to Insurance Women on How to Advance." *National Underwriter, Property/Casualty* 84 (28): 20–21.

Konrad, Allison M., and Jeffrey Pfeffer. 1991. "Understanding the Hiring of Women and Minorities: How Gender and Ethnic Composition Is Produced and Reproduced in Educational Institutions." In press. *Sociology of Education.*

Kouba, Lola, aka Lola Hogan, v. Allstate Insurance Company. 1981.

Kraft, Philip. 1977. *Programmers and Managers: The Routinization of Computer Programming in the United States.* New York: Springer-Verlag.

———. 1979. "The Industrialization of Computer Programming: From Programming to 'Software Production.'" In Andrew Zimbalist, ed., *Case Studies on the Labor Process,* 1–17. New York: Monthly Review Press.

Kraft, Philip, and Steven Dubnoff. 1983. "Software Workers Survey." *Computerworld,* November 14, pp. 1–17.

Kraszewski, Muriel E., et al. v. State Farm General Insurance Company et al. 1985.

Kulczycky, Maria. 1977. "Women at the Top?" *NABW Journal,* November–December, pp. 7–11.

Kulis, Stephen, and Karen A. Miller. 1989. "The Changing Sex Composition of a Contracting Profession: Academic Sociology in the Early 1980s." Paper presented at annual meeting of the American Sociological Association, San Francisco.

Kutscher, Ronald E. 1987. "Overview and Implications of the Projections to 2000." *Monthly Labor Review* 110 (September): 3–9.

Landon, Dorothy D. 1974. "Adam's Rib—Can Do!" *Life Association News* 69 (August): 59–63.

Lane, Michael. 1975. "Shapers of Culture: The Editor in Book Publishing." *Annals of the American Academy of Political and Social Science* 421 (September): 34–42.

Langevin, Karen. 1984. "Women CLUs Striving toward Professionalism." *National Underwriter, Life/Health* 88:36–37.

Laskey, Burton. 1969. "Who'll Do the Work?" *Publishers Weekly* 196 (December 15): 13–14.

Laslett, Peter. 1965. *The World We Have Lost.* New York: Scribner.

Lee, Alfred McClung. 1947. "Trends in Public Relations Training." *Public Opinion Quarterly,* Spring, pp. 83–91.

Lehman, David. 1987. "The Belles of Letters." *Savvy,* August, pp. 40–44, 84, 89.

Leidner, Robin. 1989a. "Interpreting Gender: Work and Identity in Interactive Service Jobs." Unpublished manuscript, Department of Sociology, University of Pennsylvania, May.

———. 1989b. Personal communication.

Leonard, Jonathan S. 1988. "Women and Affirmative Action in the 1980's." Paper presented at annual meeting of the American Economic Association, New York.

LePage, Regis A. 1973. *Seventy Years of Quality.* New York: Newcomen.

Leslie, Connie. 1987. "Making Doctors Human." *Newsweek on Campus,* September, pp. 39–40.

Lester, William M. 1985. "A Message for You." *Real Estate Today* 18:58.

Lewis, Cherie Sue. 1986. "Television License Renewal Challenges by Women's Groups." Ph.D. diss., University of Minnesota.

Lieberson, Stanley. 1980. *A Piece of the Pie.* Berkeley: University of California Press.

Life Association News. 1986. "Stress and the Woman Underwriter." Vol. 81 (June): 89.

Liggett v. Baldridge. 1928. U.S. Supreme Court.

Lindeman, Bruce. 1981. *Real Estate Brokerage Management.* Reston, Va.: Reston Publishing.

Lipman, Linda. 1983. "ICs, Employees . . . or Both?" *Real Estate Today* 16 (7): 23–25.

Lipset, Seymour Martin, Martin A. Trow, and James S. Coleman. 1956. *Union Democracy: The Internal Politics of the International Typographical Union.* Garden City, N.Y.: Anchor Books.

Literary Marketplace. 1986. New York: Bowker.

Lofquist, William S. 1970. "New Census Data Identifies Book Industry Trends." *Printing and Publishing* 11 (April): 6–9.

Loftus, Dan. 1984. "The Decline of Organized Labor." *PIA Communicator* 28 (Fourth Quarter): 17–19.

———. 1985. "Sexual Harassment in the Workplace." *PIA Communicator* 30 (Second Quarter): 12–14.

Lorence, Jon. 1987. "A Test of 'Gender' and 'Job' Models of Sex Differences in Job Involvement." *Social Forces* 66:121–42.

Louviere, Vernon. 1978. "Women's Growing Role in Lobbying." *Nations Business,* June, pp. 80–84.

Luxenberg, Stan. 1985. *Roadside Empires.* New York: Viking Press.

Lyson, Thomas A. 1985. "Race and Sex Segregation in the Occupational Structures of Southern Employers." *Social Science Quarterly* 66:281–95.

McCall, Alan S., and Manfred O. Peterson. 1980. "Changing Regulation in Retail Banking Services: The Evidence from Maine." *Journal of Retail Banking* 2 (3): 46–55.

McCarthy, Joseph P. 1977. "EEO Compliance—A Process, Not a Program." *Best's Review, Property/Casualty* 78 (August): 69–73.

Maccoby, Eleanor Emmons, and Carol Nagy Jacklin. 1974. *The Psychology of Sex Difference.* Stanford, Calif.: Stanford University Press.

McDowell, Edwin. 1987. "Women Move to Top in Publishing." *New York Times,* October 25, p. E24.

McDowell, Robert. 1982. "Claims Processing in a Paperless Environment." *Best's Review, Property/Casualty* 82 (January): 64–66.

Machrone, Bill. 1986. "Desktop Publishing: Fact or Fiction." *PC Magazine* (July): 61–62.

McLaughlin, Richard A. 1975. "DP Salary Survey." *Datamation* 21:40–46.

McLean, Dora. 1946. "The Click of Her Heels." *Public Relations Journal* 2 (8): 31–34.

McLean, Gilbert. 1978. "Ohio Female Agents' First Program Attracts 200." *National Underwriter, Property/Casualty* 84 (47): 28–29.

McMichael, Stanley L. 1967. *How to Operate a Real Estate Business.* Englewood Cliffs, N.J.: Prentice-Hall.

Magarick, Patrick. 1978. "Claims Handling—Past and Future." *Best's Review, Property/Casualty* 78 (April): 34–36.

Malveaux, Julianne, and Phyllis Wallace. 1987. "Minority Women in the Workplace." In Karen S. Koziara, Michael H. Moskow, and Lucretia D. Tanner, eds., *Working Women: Past, Present, Future,* 265–98. IRRA Series. Washington, D.C.: Bureau of National Affairs.

Markham, William T., Sharon L. Harlan, and Edward J. Hackett. 1987. "Promotion Opportunity in Organizations: Causes and Consequences." *Research in Personnel and Human Resources Management* 5:223–87.

Martin, Marguerite R. 1982. "Women Are No Different from Men Except for . . . ." *Life Association News* 77 (July): 99–103.

Martin, Susan Ehrlich. 1980. *Breaking and Entering*. Berkeley: University of California Press.

Martin v. Wilks. 1989. U.S. Supreme Court.

Maruani, Magaret, and Chantal Nicole. 1987. "Can Computerization Break Down Sexual Barriers?" Paper presented at the annual UMIST/ASTON Conference on Organization and Control of the Labour Process, Manchester, U.K. April.

Maryles, Daisy. 1974. "Macmillan Charged with Sex Bias in Hiring." *Publishers Weekly* 206 (September 30): 19.

Marzolf, Marion. 1977. *Up from the Footnotes*. New York: Hastings House.

Mason, Ida W. 1975. "Psychology and the Systems Analyst." *Data Management* 13: 29–31.

Master Printers of America. 1986. Personal communication.

Mathis, Marylin, and David H. Jones. 1974. "Finding More Women and Minorities for Management-Level Jobs." *Banking* 66:94–100.

Mello, John P., Jr. 1980. "Allyn and Bacon Settles in Sex Discrimination Suit." *Publishers Weekly* 217 (May 23): 23.

Mellor, Earl F. 1984. "Investigating the Differences in Weekly Earnings of Women and Men." *Monthly Labor Review* 107 June: 17–28.

———. 1985. "Weekly Earnings in 1983: A Look at More Than 200 Occupations." *Monthly Labor Review* 108 (January): 54–59.

Merton, Robert. 1957. *Social Theory and Social Structure*. Glencoe, Ill.: Free Press.

Mescon, Timothy, and George E. Stevens. 1982. "Women as Entrepreneurs: A Preliminary Study of Female Realtors in Arizona." *Arizona Business*, November, pp. 9–13.

Mesler, Mark A. 1989. "Negotiated Order and the Clinical Pharmacist: The Ongoing Process of Structure." *Symbolic Interaction* 12:139–57.

Metzger, Robert. 1982. "The Changing Role of Branch Manager." *Journal of Retail Banking* 4 (2): 45–52.

Milkman, Ruth. 1976. "Women's Work and Economic Crisis: Some Lessons of the Great Depression." *Review of Radical Political Economics* 8 (Spring):73–97.

———. 1987. *Gender at Work*. Urbana: University of Illinois Press.

Miller, Ann R., Donald J. Treiman, Pamela S. Cain, and Patricia A. Roos. 1980. *Work, Jobs, and Occupations: A Critical Review of the Dictionary of Occupational Titles*. Washington, D.C.: National Academy Press.

Miller, Annetta, and Todd Barrett, with Elizabeth Bradburn. 1989. "Pitching to Patients." *Newsweek*, May 8, pp. 40–41.

Miller, Floyd. 1977. "Specialization in the Systems Profession." *Journal of Systems Management* 28:14–21.

Miller, N. J. 1977. "Unlimited Opportunities for Female Managers with 'Attuned' Attitudes." *Data Management* 15:14–16.

Miller, Norman G. 1978. "The Changing Structure of Residential Brokerage." *Real Estate Review* 8:46–50.

Mincer, Jacob, and Solomon Polachek. 1974. "Family Investments in Human Capital: Earnings of Women." *Journal of Political Economy* 82 (March–April, Part II): S76–108.

———. 1978. "Women's Earnings Reexamined." *Journal of Human Resources* 13 (Winter): 118–34.

Monroe, Sylvester, and Carolyn Friday. 1988. "Blacks and the Wall St. Purge." *Newsweek*, February 1, pp. 38–39.

Morantz-Sanchez, Regina Markell. 1987. *Sympathy and Science: Women Physicians in American Medicine.* New York: Oxford University Press.

Mosier, Jean. 1949. "Opportunities for Women in Public Relations." *Public Relations Journal* 5 (6): 33–40.

Ms. 1988. "All the President's Women." March, pp. 70–71.

Much, Kathleen. 1988. Personal communication.

Murolo, Priscilla. 1987. "White-Collar Women and the Rationalization of Clerical Work." In Robert E. Kraut, ed., *Technology and the Transformation of White-Collar Work*, 35–51. Hillsdale, N.J.: Lawrence Erlbaum.

Murray, Jean Grissom. 1960. "The Modern Real Estate Office." In Edith J. Friedman, ed., *Real Estate Encyclopedia*, 22–44. Englewood Cliffs, N.J.: Prentice-Hall.

Myers, Ann. 1984. "Real Men Can't Sell Insurance." *Managers Magazine* 59 (2): 12–15.

Nadler, Paul S. 1970. "A Banker's Look at the 1970s." *Banking* 62 (1): 37–38.

———. 1977. "Changing Career Paths in Banking." *Banker's Monthly* 94 (2): 11–14.

National Association of Printers and Lithographers. 1978. *Women Move Forward in the Graphic Arts.* Special Report. New York: National Association of Printers and Lithographers.

———. 1982. *Women Progress in the Graphic Arts.* Special Report. Teaneck, N.J.: National Association of Printers and Lithographers.

———. 1985. *Women in the Graphic Arts: Women Are Progressing Steadily in Managerial and Priority Jobs.* Special Report. Teaneck, N.J.: National Association of Printers and Lithographers.

National Association of Realtors. 1984. *Membership Profile: 1984.* Washington, D.C.: National Association of Realtors.

National Committee on Pay Equity. 1987. *Women Have Made Slow Steady Progress in the Labor Market since 1979, but the Wage Gap Has Not Suddenly Narrowed Significantly.* Washington, D.C.: National Committee on Pay Equity.

National Investor Relations Institute. 1987. Personal communication.

National Underwriter, Fire/Casualty. 1970. "Insurers' Interpersonal Claims Tactics Seen as Threat to Independent Adjuster." Vol. 44 (October 30): 2, 33.

———, *Life/Health.* 1973. "Bettylou Scandling: Too Few Women in Sales." Vol. 77 (September 19):27.

———, *Life/Health.* 1974a. "New York Civil Liberties Union Hit Schenck with 'Sex Bias' Suit." Vol. 78 (February 2): 1, 21.

———, *Life/Health.* 1974b. "Pennsylvania Insurers Accused of Sex Discrimination." Vol. 78 (February 2): 1, 18.

———, *Life/Health.* 1978. "LIMRA Survey Shows Agents Retention Gains." Vol. 82 (June 24): 14.

———, *Property/Casualty.* 1979. "Commission Dollars Lagging: NASCSA." Vol. 83 (October 19): 2, 55.

———, *Life/Health.* 1981. "How It Is, Was, and Could Be for the Woman Agent." Vol. 85 (September 16): 4, 36–37.

———, *Life/Health.* 1982. "Female Agent Recruitment Studied." Vol. 86 (June 5): 2, 12.

————, *Property/Casualty*. 1983. "CPCUs: Better Educated; More Likely Female." Vol. 87 (September 9): 136.

Nation's Business. 1985. "High Tech Power for Small Firms." Vol. 73:72–75a.

Navasky, Victor S. 1973a. "In Cold Print: What Is an Editor Worth?" *New York Times Book Review*, April 15, p. 2.

————. 1973b. "In Cold Print: Selling Out and Buying In." *New York Times Book Review*, May 20, p. 2.

Nelkin, Dorothy, and Michael S. Brown. 1984. *Workers at Risk*. Chicago: University of Chicago Press.

Nesbitt, Paula D. 1986. "Implications of Gender Mobility on Organization Communication: An Occupational Analysis." Unpublished manuscript, Department of Sociology, Harvard University.

————. 1989. "The Feminization of the American Clergy." Unpublished manuscript, Department of Sociology, Harvard University.

Neumann, Karl. 1972. "Physicians' Viewpoint." *American Druggist* 166 (July 10): 10.

Newhouse, Joseph P. 1966. "Technological Change in Banking." In National Commission of Technology, Automation, and Economic Progress, *The Employment Impact of Technological Change*, appendix to vol. 2, *Technology and the American Economy*, 157–71. Washington, D.C.: U.S. Government Printing Office.

Newsday. 1985. "LILCO Hires Press Chief." August 22, p. 33.

Newsom, Clark. 1982. "For Printers, Life Varies after Accepting 'Buyouts.'" *Presstime* 4 (December): 32–33.

————. 1984. "Safety Remains a Major Concern: Modern-Style Newspaper Has Its Own Hazards." *Presstime* 6 (March): 14–19.

Newsweek. 1975. "Bar-Stool Psychiatrists." September 8, pp. 49–50.

Nikcevich, Mark. 1983. "Typesetting as the 'Key Stroke' to Franchising in the Graphic Arts." *American Printer* 191 (April): 46–49.

Noble, Kendrick. 1978. "Assessing the Merger Trend." *Publishers Weekly* 214 (July 31): 35–42.

Noble, Kenneth B. 1986. "Printers' Union Reaches Tentative Merger Pact." *New York Times*, July 8.

North Dakota State Board of Pharmacy v. Snyder's Drug Stores, Inc. 1972.

Noyelle, Thierry J. 1987. *Beyond Industrial Dualism*. Boulder, Colo.: Westview Press.

Occupational Safety and Health Administration. 1985. *Code of Federal Regulations, Parts 1900–1910*. Washington, D.C.: Office of the Federal Register National Archives and Research Services Administration.

O'Farrell, Brigid. 1988. "Women in Blue-Collar Occupations: Traditional and Nontraditional." In Ann Helton Stromberg and Shirley Harkess, eds., *Women Working*, 258–72. 2d ed. Mountain View, Calif.: Mayfield.

O'Farrell, Brigid, and Sharon Harlan. 1982. "Craftworkers and Clerks: The Effect of Male Co-Worker Hostility on Women's Satisfaction with Nontraditional Jobs." *Social Problems* 29:252–65.

————. 1984. "Job Integration Strategies: Today's Programs and Tomorrow's Needs." In Barbara F. Reskin, ed., *Sex Segregation in the Workplace: Trends, Explanations, Remedies*, 267–91. Washington, D.C.: National Academy Press.

Officers Report and Daily Convention Proceedings. 1949. 32nd General Convention,

Hotel and Restaurant Employees' and Bartenders' International Union. Chicago, April 25–29.

————. 1971. 37th General Convention, Hotel and Restaurant Employees' and Bartenders' International Union, AFL-CIO, Chicago, June 14.

Olzak, Susan, Johan Olivier, and Elizabeth West. 1988. "The Changing Job Queue: Causes of Shifts in Ethnic Job Segregation in American Cities, 1870–1880." Paper presented at the annual meeting of the American Sociological Association, Atlanta, August.

Oppenheimer, Valerie. 1968. "The Sex Labeling of Jobs." *Industrial Relations* 7: 219–34.

————. 1970. *The Female Labor Force in the United States: Demographic and Economic Factors Governing Its Growth and Changing Composition.* Westport, Conn.: Greenwood Press.

Orr, Jack. 1970. "Report on Enrollment in Schools and Colleges in Pharmacy, First Semester, Term, or Quarter, 1969–70." *American Journal of Pharmaceutical Education* 34 (February): 98.

O'Shields, Joseph B. 1977. "Banks Are Losing the Battle for Executive Talent." *Banker's Magazine* 160 (3): 51–54.

Osterman, Paul. 1979. "Sex Discrimination in Professional Employment: A Case Study." *Industrial and Labor Relations Review* 32 (4): 451–64.

Padavic, Irene. 1989. "Shiftwork's Effect on Women's Interest in Blue-Collar Jobs." Paper presented at the meeting of the American Sociological Association, San Francisco, August.

Padavic, Irene, and Barbara F. Reskin. 1990. "The Effect of Men's Behavior on Women's Interest in Blue-Collar Work." Unpublished paper.

Palmer, Carl R. 1979. "Who Will Train the Typographers of Tomorrow?" *Graphic Arts Monthly* 51 (January): 108–11.

Pentland, Mary. 1948. "Public Relations as a Career for Women." *Public Relations Journal* 5 (4): 13–17.

Personick, Valerie A. 1987. "Industry Output and Employment through the End of the Century." *Monthly Labor Review* 110 (September): 30–45.

Peterson, Paul V. 1985. *Today's Journalism Students: Who They Are and What They Want to Do—A Survey.* Columbus: Ohio State University.

Pettigrew, Thomas F. 1969. "Racially Separate or Together." *Journal of Social Issues* 25:43–69.

Phalon, Richard. 1981. "Publishing." *Forbes* 5 (January): 253–54.

Pharmacy News. 1970. "What's the Big Attraction?" Vol. 11 (Summer): 8–14.

Phelps, Edmund S. 1972. "The Statistical Theory of Racism and Sexism." *American Economic Review* 62:659–66.

Phillips, Anne, and Barbara Taylor. 1980. "Sex and Skills." *Feminist Review* 6:79–88.

Phipps, Polly A. 1989. *Sex Segregation and the Changing Sex Composition of Insurance Adjusters and Examiners.* Ph.D. diss., University of Michigan.

PIA Communicator. 1985. "1985 Graphic Arts Man-Of-The-Year Award." Vol. 30 (2):15.

Pifalo, Donald M. 1985. "The Telephone: Friend or Foe?" *Real Estate Today* 18: 55–56.

Pinchbeck, Ivy. 1977 (1930). *Women Workers and the Industrial Revolution, 1750–1850.* Totowa, N.J.: Frank Cass.

Povall, Margery. 1986. "Equal Opportunity Developments in Banking: An International Perspective." *Equal Opportunities International* 5 (2): 1–13.

Powell, Walter. 1982. "From Craft to Corporation: The Impact of Outside Ownership on Book Publishing." In J. S. Ettema and D. C. Whitney, eds., *Individuals in Mass Media Organizations*, 33–52. Beverly Hills, Calif.: Sage.

———. 1985. *Getting into Print.* Chicago: University of Chicago Press.

———. 1988. Personal communication.

PR Reporter. 1985. "Twenty-First Annual Survey of the Profession, Part I: Salaries." Vol. 28 (38).

PRSA Education Department. 1987. Personal communication.

Presstime. 1982. "Job Discrimination Cases Continued at Five Newspapers." Vol. 4 (10): 53.

Press Woman. 1975. "Competition Keen in Communications." October, pp. 12–15.

Prial, Frank J. 1982. "More Women Work at Traditional Male Jobs." *New York Times*, November 15, p. 1.

Priebe, John. 1988. Personal communication.

Printing Impressions. 1986. Special issue, *Women in Printing.* Vol. 28 (February).

Printing Production. 1968. "The 1970s: Forecast of Printing's Future: Big Picture of a Changing Industry." Vol. 98 (June): 70–121.

Progressive Grocer. 1975. "How In-Store Bakeries Fight the Profit Battle." Vol. 54 (February):3.

Public Relations Journal. 1951. "Women in Public Relations." Vol. 7 (8): 6–8, 16.

Publishers Weekly. 1969. "Who's Who among the Travelers?" Vol. 195 (March 10): 3.

———. 1970. "McGraw-Hill Picketed by Women in Publishing." Vol. 198 (July 6): 35.

———. 1971. "The Rise of Women in Publishing." Vol. 199 (February 15): 66, 69.

———. 1974. "Some Harsh Words on How Women Fare in Publishing." Vol. 205 (March 25): 25.

———. 1975a. "Women Editors File Suit against HM for Sex Bias." Vol. 208 (November 24): 18.

———. 1975b. "News Brief." Vol. 208 (December 8): 13.

———. 1976a. "Mass. Attorney General Joins Sex Bias Suit against HM." Vol. 209 (March 8): 27.

———. 1976b. "Sex Bias Complaint Settled at Macmillan." Vol. 200 (April 19): 28.

———. 1979. "Why Are Women So Successful in Sub Rights?" Vol. 215 (June 18): 58–62.

———. 1980. "Affirmative Action and Inaction." Vol. 218 (August 8): 25–26.

Quinn, Lawrence R. 1987. "Making a Mess out of a Merger." *Executive Financial Woman* 2 (3): 6–15.

Raskin, A. H. 1978. "The Big Squeeze on Labor Unions." *Atlantic Monthly* 242 (October):41–48.

Rawson, Hugh, and Arnold Dolin. 1985. "The Editorial Process: An Overview." In Elizabeth Geiser et al., eds., *The Business of Book Publishing*, 21–42. Boulder, Colo.: Westview Press.

Real Estate Today. 1980. "Husbands and Wives in Real Estate." Vol. 13:25–28.

————. 1981. "Women in Business—and the Business Is Real Estate." Vol. 14:16–17.

————. 1983. "Legal Briefs." Vol. 16:26, 48.

Reed, W. Robert, and Julie Holleman. 1988. "Do Women Prefer Women's Work?" Working Paper 88–02, Department of Economics, Texas A&M University.

Reisinger, James D. 1977. "No Competition in the Women's Market." *Life Association News* 72 (May): 65–68.

Rejnis, Ruth. 1977. *A Woman's Guide to New Careers in Real Estate.* Chicago: Regnery.

Reskin, Barbara F. 1988. "Bringing the Men Back In: Sex Differentiation and the Devaluation of Women's Work." *Gender & Society* 2 (March): 58–81.

Reskin, Barbara F., and Heidi I. Hartmann. 1986. *Women's Work, Men's Work: Sex Segregation on the Job.* Washington, D.C.: National Academy Press.

Reskin, Barbara F., and Irene Padavic. 1988. "Supervisors as Gatekeepers: Male Supervisors' Response to Women's Integration in Plant Jobs." *Social Problems* 35 (December): 401–15.

Reskin, Barbara F., and Patricia A. Roos. 1989. "The Feminization of Male Occupations: Integration, Ghettoization, or Resegregation?" Paper presented at the first Women's Policy Conference, Institute for Women's Policy Research, Washington, D.C.

Reuter, Madalynne. 1976. "Boston Women in Publishing Hails Job Posting Efforts." *Publishers Weekly* 210 (October 11): 18.

————. 1980. "Addison-Wesley Agrees to $360,000 Sex-Bias Accord." *Publishers Weekly* 217 (April 11): 10.

Riche, Richard W., David E. Hecker, and John U. Burgan. 1983. "High Technology Today and Tomorrow: A Small Slice of the Employment Pie." *Monthly Labor Review* 106 (November): 50–58.

Riday, John. 1966. "Problems in Finding Qualified Employees." *Banking* 59:51–52.

Riechers, Maggie, and Jere Kane. 1979. "Looking into Insurance." *Women's Work* 5 (May–June): 11–14.

Riley, John W., Jr. 1989. Personal communication.

Ris, Howard C. 1979. "The Need to Control Information Has [Led] to More In-Plant Shops." *American Printer and Lithographer* 184 (November): 72A–72B.

Ritzer, George, and David Walczak. 1986. *Working: Conflict and Change.* 3d ed. Englewood Cliffs, N.J.: Prentice-Hall.

Rodda, W. H. 1969. "Conglomerates, Computers, Public Shape Future Homeowners' Insurance Policies." *Weekly Underwriter* 200:28–32.

Rodowskas, Christopher A., Jr. 1988. "Where Have All Our Pharmacy Grads Gone?" *Michigan Pharmacist* 26 (April): 4–9.

Rogers, Theresa F., and Nathalie S. Friedman. 1980. *Printers Face Automation: The Impact of Technology on Work and Retirement among Skilled Craftsmen.* Lexington, Mass.: Lexington Books.

Romano, Frank. 1977. "Capturing Keystrokes. . . . The Best Input Is Really No Input at All . . . Really." *Inland Printer/American Lithographer* 179 (September): 82.

————. 1978a. "Digital Processing Simplifies Page Make-Up Procedures." *Inland Printer/American Lithographer* 181 (June): 54–56.

————. 1978b. "Typesetting Trends Provide Some Insight on Where the Technology May Be Heading." *Inland Printer/American Lithographer* 182 (October): 66.

———. 1979. "RX for Typesetting Service Obsolescence: Good Management plus Contingency Plans." *American Printer and Lithographer* 184 (December): 72.

———. 1981. "Who's on the Keyboard Is an Important Consideration to Purveyors of Fine Type." *American Printer and Lithographer* 186 (January): 58P.

———. 1983. "Automated Composition: The Best of Times or the Worst of Times?" *American Printer* 191 (September): 31–34.

———. 1986. *Machine Writing and Typesetting: The Story of Sholes and Mergenthaler and the Invention of the Typewriter and the Linotype.* Salem, N.H.: GAMA.

———. 1988. Personal communication.

Rooney, J. J. 1975. "The Computer Manpower Evolution." *Occupational Outlook Handbook* 19:25–27.

Roos, Patricia A. 1986. "Women in the Composing Room: Technology and Organization as Determinants of Social Change." Paper presented at the annual meeting of the American Sociological Association, New York, August.

Roos, Patricia A., and Barbara F. Reskin. 1984. "Institutional Factors Contributing to Sex Segregation in the Workplace." In Barbara F. Reskin, ed., *Sex Segregation in the Workplace: Trends, Explanations, Remedies,* 235–60. Washington, D.C.: National Academy Press.

Rose, Clair, and Sally Ann Menninger. 1979. "Women in Computer Sciences." Keynote address at Women's Career Day in Computer Science, University of Southern California, October 7.

Rose, Peter. 1987. *The Changing Structure of American Banking.* New York: Columbia University Press.

Rose, Sonya O. 1988. "Gender Antagonism and Class Conflict." *Social History* 13: 191–208.

Rosenbaum, J. A. 1979. "Organizational Career Mobility: Promotion Chances in a Corporation during Periods of Growth and Contraction." *American Journal of Sociology* 85 (July): 21–48.

Rosenbloom, Jerry S. 1968. *Automobile Liability Claims: Insurance Company Philosophies and Practices.* Homewood, Ill.: Richard D. Irwin.

Rosenthal, Ellen, Carter Smith, Hope Steele, Clifford Crouch, et al. 1986. "My Say." *Publishers Weekly* 230 (August 29): 392.

Rosenthal, Herbert C. 1961. "What Do Female Stockholders Think of Your Annual Report?" *Public Relations Journal* 17 (9): 7–8.

Rosler, Lee. 1966. *Opportunities in Life Insurance.* New York: Vocational Guidance Manuals.

———. 1974. *Opportunities in Life Insurance.* Rev. ed. Louisville, Ky.: Vocational Guidance Manuals.

Ross, H. Laurence. 1970. *Settled out of Court: The Social Process of Insurance Claims Adjustments.* Chicago: Aldine.

Rotella, Elyce. 1981 (1977). *From Home to Office: U.S. Women at Work, 1870–1930.* Ann Arbor, Mich.: UMI Research Press.

———. 1987. "Comments." In Clair Brown and Joseph Pechman, eds., *Gender in the Workplace,* 149–54. Washington, D.C.: Brookings Institution.

Rotella, Elyce J., and Robert A. Margo. 1981. "Sex Differences in the Market for School Personnel: Houston, Texas, 1892–1923." Working paper 45, Department of Economics, Wellesley College.

Roulac, Stephen E. 1985. "Should Real Estate Brokerages Be Supermarkets or Corner Groceries?" *Real Estate Review* 14:78–81.

Rupp, Carla M. 1980. "Women Production Exec at Dow Jones." *Editor and Publisher*, 113 (June 14): 39, 44.

Russell, Diane E. 1980. "The Best Me." *Life Association News* 75 (November): 152–54.

Rytina, Nancy F. 1982. "Earnings of Men and Women: A Look at Specific Occupations." *Monthly Labor Review* 105 (April):25–31.

Rytina, Nancy F., and Suzanne Bianchi. 1984. "Occupational Reclassification and Changes in Distribution by Gender." *Monthly Labor Review* 107 (March): 11–17.

Sabo, Sandra R. 1985. "Winning at the Old Boy's Game." *Association Management* 37 (4): 68–73.

Salgado, Robert J. 1984. "The State of the Printing Labor Union." *Printing Impressions* 26 (October and November): 12, 43–46.

Sampson, Richard. 1983. "Taking Control of Health Care Costs." *Best's Review, Health/Life* 84 (November): 64–66.

Sanders, Marlene, and Marcia Rock. 1988. *Waiting for Prime Time*. Urbana: University of Illinois Press.

Sasseen, Jane. 1986. "The Great National Bank Hold-Up." *Savvy*, March, pp. 34–36.

Schering Laboratories. 1988. *A Profession in Transition: The Changing Face of Pharmacy*. Report X. Kenilworth, N.J.: Schering Laboratories.

Schiffman, K. E., E. W. Stein, and H. B. Kaufman. 1971. "The Microwave Proofing of Yeast-Raised Doughnuts." *Bakers Digest*, February, pp. 55–57.

Schlegel, John F., Christopher A. Rodowaskas, Jr., Carol E. Gill, Caroline S. Ostoff, and Amy F. Katlin. 1975. "Report on Fall Undergraduate Enrollment in Schools and Colleges of Pharmacy." *American Journal of Pharmaceutical Education* 40 (August):279–92.

———. 1980. "Report on Fall 1979 Undergraduate Enrollment in Schools and Colleges of Pharmacy." *American Journal of Pharmaceutical Education* 44 (May): 180.

———. 1981. "In What Pharmacy Sites Are Pharmacists Now Actively Practicing?" *Pharmacy Times*, December, pp. 40–41.

Schmidt, Peggy. 1986. "Legislative Mills Stir Up Lobbying." *New York Times*, October 12, p. 16LI.

Schroedel, Jean Reith. 1985. *Alone in a Crowd*. Philadelphia: Temple University Press.

Schuster, Terry J. 1981. "A Candid View of Women in the Industry." *Managers Magazine* 56 (8): 4–9.

Schwartz, John, with Mary Hager. 1987. "Now, One-Stop Medicine?" *Newsweek*, May 25, pp. 32–33.

Schwirian, Patricia M. 1973. "Occupational Roles of Ohio's Practicing Pharmacists." *Journal of the American Pharmaceutical Association*, n.s. 13:618–21, 637.

Scott, Joan Wallach. 1982. "The Mechanization of Women's Work." *Scientific American* 247 (September): 169–87.

Shaeffer, Ruth Gilbert, and Edith F. Lynton. 1979. *Corporate Experiences in Improving Women's Job Opportunities*. New York: The Conference Board.

Shaw, Nancy. 1980. "In the '20s She Was Known as the Insurance Lady." *Managers Magazine* 55 (8): 7.

Sheperd, Marvin D., and Kenneth W. Kirk. 1981. "Men and Women as Pharmacy Managers." *American Journal of Hospital Pharmacy* 38:1463–66.

———. 1982. "Analysis of Pharmacy Practice Patterns of Men and Women Pharmacy Graduates." *Contemporary Pharmacy Practice* 5:189–97.

Shotwell, Robyn. 1981. "Computerized Page Makeup Just around the Corner." *Publishers Weekly* 219 (April 10): 34.

Shulsky, Sam. 1951. *Opportunities in Finance.* Vocational Guidance Manuals. New York: Grosset & Dunlap.

Sifton, Elisabeth. 1985. "The Editor's Job in Trade Publishing." In Elizabeth Geiser et al., eds., *The Business of Book Publishing,* 43–61. Boulder, Colo.: Westview Press.

Silberman, Charles E. 1978. *Criminal Violence, Criminal Justice.* New York: Random House.

Silvestri, George T., and John M. Lukasiewicz. 1987. "A Look at Occupational Employment Trends to the Year 2000." *Monthly Labor Review* 110 (September): 46–63.

Simpson, Ida Harper, Richard L. Simpson, Mark Evers, and Sharon Sandomirsky Poss. 1982. "Occupational Recruitment, Retention, and Labor Force Cohort Representation." *American Journal of Sociology* 87 (May):1287–1313.

Sirota, David. 1981. *Winning in Real Estate.* Reston, Va.: Reston Publishing.

Smedley, Doree, and Lura Robinson. 1945. *Careers in Business for Women.* New York: Dutton.

Smith, Anthony. 1980. *Goodbye Gutenberg: The Newspaper Revolution of the 1980s.* New York: Oxford University Press.

Smith, Murray. 1977. "Finding and Filling Gaps in Claims Performance." *Best's Review, Property/Casualty* 77 (April): 32–42.

Smith, Rea W. 1968. "Women in Public Relations." *Public Relations Journal* 24: (October): 26, 27, 29.

Smith, Wendy. 1981. "Houghton Reaches Accord in Sex Bias Suit." *Publishers Weekly* 219 (January 16): 19.

Snyder, David, Mark D. Hayward, and Paula M. Hudis. 1978. "The Location of Change in the Sexual Structure of Occupations, 1950–1970: Insights from Labor Market Segmentation Theory." *American Journal of Sociology* 84 (November): 706–17.

Snyder, David R., and Paula M. Hudis. 1976. "Occupational Income and the Effects of Minority Competition and Segregation." *American Sociological Review* 41 (April): 209–34.

Snyder, Richard E. 1977. "Richard E. Snyder, President of Simon & Schuster, on His Firm's Explosive Success and the Present Industry Ferment." *Publishers Weekly* 211 (April 11): 32–38.

Sokoloff, Natalie J. 1987. "Employment for Professional Black Women in the Twentieth Century." In Christine Bose and Glenna Spitze, eds., *Ingredients for Women's Employment Policy,* 53–72. Albany: State University of New York Press.

————. 1989. "Are Professions Becoming Desegregated? An Analysis of Detailed Professional Occupations by Race and Gender." Paper presented at the annual meeting of the American Sociological Association, San Francisco, August.

Sommers, Dixie. 1974. "Occupational Rankings for Men and Women by Earnings." *Monthly Labor Review* 97 (August): 34–51.

Spaeth, Joe L. 1988. "Determinants of Promotions in Different Types of Organizations." Unpublished manuscript, University of Illinois.

Splaver, Sarah. 1973. *Nontraditional Careers for Women*. New York: Julian Messner.

Spradley, James P., and Brenda J. Mann. 1975. *The Cocktail Waitress: Women's Work in a Man's World*. New York: Wiley.

Sprowls, Joseph B. 1940. "Women in Pharmacy." *American Journal of Pharmaceutical Education* 4 (October): 560–62.

————. 1967. "Report on Enrollment in Schools and Colleges of Pharmacy First Semester, Term, or Quarter 1964–1965." *American Journal of Pharmaceutical Education* 31 (February): 40–47.

Srole, Carole. 1987. "A Blessing to Mankind, and Especially to Womankind: The Typewriter and the Feminization of Clerical Work, Boston, 1860–1920." In Barbara D. Wright, Myra Marx Ferree, Gail O. Mellow, Linda H. Lewis, Maria-Luz Daza Samper, Robert Asher, and Kathleen Claspell, eds., *Women, Work, and Technology: Transformations*, 84–100. Ann Arbor: University of Michigan Press.

Starr, Paul. 1982. *The Social Transformation of American Medicine*. New York: Basic Books.

Steinberg, Ronnie J. 1984–85. "Identifying Wage Discrimination and Implementing Pay Equity Adjustments." In *Comparable Worth: Issues for the 80s*, vol. 1. Washington, D.C.: U.S. Commission on Civil Rights.

————. 1989. "Issues in Employment Equity." Paper presented at the first Women's Policy Research Conference, Washington, D.C.

Stolzenberg, Ross. 1982. "Industrial Profits and the Propensity to Employ Women Workers." Paper presented at the Workshop on Job Segregation, Women's Employment and Related Social Issues, National Research Council, Washington, D.C., May.

Stone, Irene. 1978. "Group Sales as a Woman's Career." *Life Insurance of Canada*, January–February, pp. 8–9.

Strainchamps, Ethel. 1974. *Rooms with No View: A Woman's Guide to the Man's World of Publishing*. New York: Harper & Row.

Strazewski, Len. 1982. "Role of Women in Agency System Still Not Up to Par." *Business Insurance*, March 1, p. 26.

Strober, Myra H. 1984. "Toward a General Theory of Occupational Sex Segregation." In Barbara F. Reskin, ed., *Sex Segregation in the Workplace: Trends, Explanations, Remedies*, 144–56. Washington, D.C.: National Academy Press.

————. 1988. "The Processes of Occupational Segregation: Relative Attractiveness and Patriarchy." Paper presented at the meeting of the American Educational Research Association, New Orleans, April.

Strober, Myra H., and Carolyn L. Arnold. 1987a. "The Dynamics of Occupational Segregation among Bank Tellers." In Clair Brown and Joseph Pechman, eds., *Gender in the Workplace*, 107–48. Washington, D.C.: Brookings Institution.

————. 1987b. "Integrated Circuits/Segregated Labor: Women in Computer-Related Occupations and High-Tech Industries." In Heidi I. Hartmann, ed., *Computer Chips and Paper Clips: Technology and Women's Employment*, 2:136–82. Washington, D.C.: National Academy Press.

Strober, Myra H., and Laura Best. 1979. "The Female/Male Salary Differential in Public Schools: Some Lessons from San Francisco, 1879." *Economic Inquiry* 17 (April): 218–36.

Strober, Myra H., and Lisa M. Catanzarite. 1988. "Changes in Black Women's Representation in Occupations and a Measure of the Relative Attractiveness of Occupations, 1960–1980." Paper presented at the meeting of the American Education Research Association, New Orleans, April.

Strom, Sharon Hartman. 1987. "'Machines instead of Clerks': Technology and the Feminization of Bookkeeping, 1910–1950." In Heidi I. Hartmann, ed., *Computer Chips and Paper Clips: Technology and Women's Employment*, 2:63–97. Washington, D.C.: National Academy Press.

Sussman, Leila A. 1948. "The Personnel and Ideology of Public Relations." *Public Opinion Quarterly* 12(Winter): 697–708.

Szafran, Robert F. 1984. "Female and Minority Employment Patterns in Banks." *Work and Occupations* 11 (1): 55–76.

Talbert, Joan, and Christine Bose. 1977. "Wage Attainment Processes: The Retail Clerk Case." *American Journal of Sociology* 81 (September):403–24.

Tarangelo, Richard M. 1977. "Proper Claims Procedures Help Control Insurance Company Insolvencies." *Best's Review, Property/Casualty* 78 (November): 44–50.

Tausz, Andrew. 1979. "Computerized Bars: Putting the Byte on Heavyhanded Bartenders." *Canadian Business* 52:29–32.

Taylor, William U., and Thomas J. O'Shea. 1970. "Want Your Story Told? Tell It to a Woman!" *Public Relations Journal* 26 (3): 18–20.

Teahan, Frederick. 1987. Personal communication.

Tebbel, John. 1972. *A History of Book Publishing in the United States.* Vol. 1, *The Creation of an Industry.* New York: Bowker.

————. 1975. *A History of Book Publishing in the United States.* Vol. 2, *The Expansion of an Industry.* New York: Bowker.

————. 1978. *A History of Book Publishing in the United States.* Vol. 3, *The Golden Age between Two Wars, 1920–1940.* New York: Bowker.

————. 1981. *A History of Book Publishing in the United States.* Vol. 4, *The Great Change, 1940–1980.* New York: Bowker.

————. 1987. Personal communication.

Tedlow, Richard S. 1979. *Keeping the Corporate Image: Public Relations and Business, 1900–1950.* Greenwich, Conn.: JAI Press.

Theus, Kathryn T. 1985. "Gender Shifts in Journalism and Public Relations." *Public Relations Review*, Spring, pp. 42–49.

Thrupp, Sylvia. 1933. *A Short History of the Worshipful Company of Bakers.* Croyden, U.K.: Galleon Press.

Thurow, Lester. 1969. *Poverty and Discrimination.* Washington, D.C.: Brookings Institution.

————. 1972. "Education and Economic Equality." *Public Interest* 28 (Summer): 66–81.

————. 1975. *Generating Inequality*. New York: Basic Books.

Tienda, Marta, Shelley A. Smith, and Vilma Ortiz. 1987. "Industrial Restructuring, Gender Segregation, and Sex Differences in Earnings." *American Sociological Review* 52 (April): 195–210.

Time. 1972. "Therapists at the Bar." March 6, p. 52.

Touhey, John C. 1974. "Effects of Additional Women Professionals on Ratings of Occupational Prestige and Desirability." *Journal of Personality and Social Psychology* 29:86–89.

Tradeswomen. 1984. Special issue: *Women in Print*. Vol. 4 (Winter).

Treiman, Donald J., William T. Bielby, and Man-Tsun Cheng. 1988. "Evaluating a Multiple-Imputation Method for Recalibrating 1970 U.S. Census Detailed Industry Codes to the 1980 Standard." In Clifford C. Clogg, ed., *Sociological Methodology 1988*, 18:309–45. Washington, D.C.: American Sociological Association.

Treiman, Donald J., and Heidi I. Hartmann. 1981. *Women, Work, and Wages: Equal Pay for Jobs of Equal Value*. Washington, D.C.: National Academy Press.

Treiman, Donald J., and Donald B. Rubin. 1983. "Developing Multiple Imputation as a Recalibration Tool, with Application to the U.S. Census 1970 and 1980 Occupation and Industry Classifications." Proposal submitted to the National Science Foundation, March.

Treiman, Donald J., and Kermit Terrell. 1975. "Women, Work, and Wages: Trends in the Female Occupational Structure since 1940." In Kenneth C. Land and Seymour Spilerman, eds., *Social Indicator Models*, 157–99. New York: Russell Sage Foundation.

Tuchman, Gay, and Nina Fortin. 1984. "Women Writers and Literary Tradition." *American Journal of Sociology* 90 (July): 72–96.

Tyack, David B., and Myra H. Strober. 1981. "Jobs and Gender: A History of the Structuring of Educational Employment by Sex." In Patricia Schmuck and W. W. Charters, eds., *Education Policy and Management: Sex Differentials*, 131–52. New York: Academic Press.

Tyler, Varro E. 1968. "Clinical Pharmacy: The Need and an Evaluation of the Professional Concept." *American Journal of Pharmaceutical Education* 32 (December):764–71.

Udell, John G. 1978. "Special: The American Newspaper." *IPI Report: Monthly Bulletin of the International Press Institute*, September, pp. 6–10.

Underhill, Lois. 1979. "Talking to Her about Life Insurance." *National Underwriter, Life/Health* 83 (December 29): 11–12.

U.S. Bureau of the Census. 1923. *1920 Census of Population: Occupations*. Vol. 4. Washington, D.C.: Government Printing Office.

————. 1933. *1930 Census of Population: Occupations by State*. Vol. 4. Washington, D.C.: Government Printing Office.

————. 1943. *1940 Census of Population: The Labor Force—Occupations, Industry, Employment, and Income*. Vol. 3. Washington, D.C.: Government Printing Office.

———. 1954. *1950 Census of Population: Occupation by Industry.* Vol. 4, Special Report, pt. 1, ch. C. Washington, D.C.: Government Printing Office.

———. 1956. *1950 Census of Population: Occupational Characteristics.* Vol. 4, Special Report, pt. 1, ch. B. Washington, D.C.: Government Printing Office.

———. 1960a. *1960 Census of Population: Classified Index of Occupations and Industries.* Washington, D.C.: Government Printing Office.

———. 1960b. *Statistical Abstract of the United States: 1960.* 81st ed. Washington, D.C.: Government Printing Office.

———. 1963a. *1960 Census of Population: Subject Reports, Occupational Characteristics.* Final Report PC(2)-7A. Washington, D.C.: Government Printing Office.

———. 1963b. *1960 Census of Population: Subject Reports, Occupation by Industry.* Final Report PC(2)-7C. Washington, D.C.: Government Printing Office.

———. 1963c. *Statistical Abstract of the United States: 1963.* 84th ed. Washington, D.C.: Government Printing Office.

———. 1963d. *1960 Census of Population and Housing.* Vol. 1, *U.S. Summary: Detailed Characteristics of the Population,* pt. 1. Washington, D.C.: Government Printing Office.

———. 1966. *Statistical Abstract of the United States: 1973.* 87th ed. Washington, D.C.: Government Printing Office.

———. 1971. *1970 Census of Population: Classified Index of Industries and Occupations Defined in the U.S. Census.* Washington, D.C.: Government Printing Office.

———. 1972. *1970 Census of Population: Occupation by Industry.* Subject Reports, PC(2)-7C. Washington, D.C.: Government Printing Office.

———. 1973a. *1970 Census of Population: Subject Reports, Occupational Characteristics.* Final Report PC(2)-7A. Washington, D.C.: Government Printing Office.

———. 1973b. *Detailed Occupation of Employed Persons by Race and Sex for the United States: 1970.* Supplementary Report PC(S1)-32. Washington, D.C.: Government Printing Office.

———. 1973c. *Earnings by Occupation and Education.* Subject Report PC(2)8-B. Washington, D.C.: Government Printing Office.

———. 1973d. *Statistical Abstract of the United States: 1973.* 95th ed. Washington, D.C.: Government Printing Office.

———. 1975. *Historical Statistics of the United States: Colonial Times to 1970.* Bicentennial ed., pt. 1. Washington, D.C.: Government Printing Office.

———. 1978. *Statistical Abstract of the United States: 1978.* 99th ed. Washington, D.C.: Government Printing Office.

———. 1979. *Statistical Abstract of the United States: 1979.* 100th ed. Washington, D.C.: Government Printing Office.

———. 1980. *Statistical Abstract of the United States: 1980.* 101st ed. Washington, D.C.: Government Printing Office.

———. 1981a. *1980 Census of Population: Detailed Population Characteristics.* U.S. Summary 1-DA. Washington, D.C.: Government Printing Office.

———. 1981b. *Statistical Abstract of the United States: 1981.* 102d ed. Washington, D.C.: Government Printing Office.

———. 1982a. *1980 Census of Population: Alphabetical Index of Industries and Occupations.* Washington, D.C.: Government Printing Office.

————. 1982b. *1980 Census of Population: Classified Index of Industries and Occupations.* PHC80-R4. Washington, D.C.: Government Printing Office.

————. 1982c. *Statistical Abstract of the United States: 1982–83.* 103d ed. Washington, D.C.: Government Printing Office.

————. 1983a. *Census of Population and Housing, 1980: Public-Use Microdata (A Sample).* Washington, D.C.: Bureau of the Census.

————. 1983b. *Census of Population and Housing, 1980: Public-Use Microdata Samples, Technical Documentation.* Washington, D.C.: Government Printing Office.

————. 1983c. *Statistical Abstract of the United States: 1984.* 104th ed. Washington, D.C.: Government Printing Office.

————. 1984a. *1980 Census of Population: Detailed Occupation of the Experienced Civilian Labor Force by Sex for the United States and Regions, 1980 and 1970.* Supplementary Report PC80-S1-15. Washington, D.C.: Government Printing Office.

————. 1984b. *1980 Census of Population: Subject Reports.* Vol. 2, *Occupation by Industry.* PC80-2-7C. Washington, D.C.: Government Printing Office.

————. 1984c. *1980 Census of Population.* Vol. 2, *Subject Reports: Earnings by Occupation and Education.* Supplementary Report PC80-2-8B. Washington, D.C.: Government Printing Office.

————. 1984d. *1980 Census of Population: Detailed Population Characteristics.* Supplementary Report PC80-1-D1-A. Washington, D.C.: Government Printing Office.

————. 1984e. *Statistical Abstract of the United States: 1985.* 105th ed. Washington, D.C.: Government Printing Office.

————. 1985a. *1982 Census of Manufactures: Industry Series—Newspapers, Periodicals, Books and Miscellaneous Publishing.* MC82-I-27A. Washington, D.C.: Government Printing Office.

————. 1985b. *1982 Census of Retail Trade: Establishment and Firm Size.* RC82-I-1. Washington, D.C.: Government Printing Office.

————. 1986a. *1970–1980 Census Comparability.* Washington, D.C.: Government Printing Office.

————. 1986b. *Statistical Abstract of the United States: 1987.* 106th ed. Washington, D.C.: Government Printing Office.

————. 1987a. *Male-Female Differences in Work Experience, Occupation, and Earnings: 1984.* Current Population Reports, Household Economic Studies Series P-70, no. 10. Washington, D.C.: Government Printing Office.

————. 1987b. *Money Income and Poverty Status of Families and Persons in the United States: 1986.* Washington, D.C.: Government Printing Office.

————. 1989. *The Relationship between the 1970 and 1980 Industry and Occupation Classification Systems.* Technical Paper 59. Washington, D.C.: Government Printing Office.

U.S. Bureau of Labor Statistics. 1948. *Occupational Outlook Handbook.* Bulletin 940. Washington, D.C.: Government Printing Office.

————. 1957. *Occupational Outlook Handbook.* Bulletin 1215. Washington, D.C.: Government Printing Office.

——. 1963. *Occupational Outlook Handbook*. Bulletin 1375. Washington, D.C.: Government Printing Office.

——. 1966. *Impact of Office Automation in the Insurance Industry*. Bulletin 1468. Washington, D.C.: Government Printing Office.

——. 1968. *Industry Wage Survey: Eating and Drinking Places, October 1966–April 1967*. Bulletin 1588. Washington, D.C.: Government Printing Office.

——. 1970. *Occupational Outlook Handbook*. 1970–71 ed. Bulletin 1650. Washington, D.C.: Government Printing Office.

——. 1972. *Occupational Outlook Handbook*. 1972–73 ed. Bulletin 1700. Washington, D.C.: Government Printing Office.

——. 1973a. *Industry Wage Survey: Life Insurance, December 1971*. Bulletin 1791. Washington, D.C.: Government Printing Office.

——. 1973b. *Outlook for Technology and Manpower in Printing and Publishing*. Bulletin 1774. Washington, D.C.: Government Printing Office.

——. 1974a. *Industry Wage Survey: Hospitals, August 1972*. Bulletin 1829. Washington, D.C.: Government Printing Office.

——. 1974b. *Occupational Outlook Handbook*. 1974–75 ed. Bulletin 1785. Washington, D.C.: Government Printing Office.

——. 1976. *Occupational Outlook Handbook*. 1976–77 ed. Bulletin 1875. Washington, D.C.: Government Printing Office.

——. 1978a. *Industry Wage Survey: Banking and Life Insurance, December 1976*. Bulletin 1988. Washington, D.C.: Government Printing Office.

——. 1978b. *Industry Wage Survey: Hospitals, August 1976*. Bulletin 1949. Washington, D.C.: Government Printing Office.

——. 1978c. *Occupational Outlook Handbook*. 1978–79 ed. Bulletin 1955. Washington, D.C.: Government Printing Office.

——. 1979a. *Handbook of Labor Statistics, 1978*. Bulletin 2000. Washington, D.C.: Government Printing Office.

——. 1979b. *Occupational Projections and Training Data*. Bulletin 2020. Washington, D.C.: Government Printing Office.

——. 1979c. *Technology and Labor in Five Industries*. Bulletin 2033. Washington, D.C.: Government Printing Office.

——. 1980a. *Industry Wage Survey: Hospitals and Nursing Homes, September 1978*. Bulletin 2069. Washington, D.C.: Government Printing Office.

——. 1980b. *Occupational Outlook Handbook*. 1980–81 ed. Bulletin 2075. Washington, D.C.: Government Printing Office.

——. 1981. *Labor Wage Survey: Life Insurance, February 1980*. Bulletin 2119. Washington, D.C.: Government Printing Office.

——. 1982a. *Occupational Outlook Handbook*. 1982–83 ed. Bulletin 2200. Washington, D.C.: Government Printing Office.

——. 1982b. *Occupational Projections and Training Data*. Bulletin 2202. Washington, D.C.: Government Printing Office.

——. 1982c. *The Impact of Technology on Labor in Five Industries*. Washington, D.C.: Government Printing Office.

——. 1982d. *Labor Force Statistics Derived from the Current Population Survey: A Databook*. Bulletin 2096. Washington, D.C.: Government Printing Office.

———. 1983. *Handbook of Labor Statistics*. Bulletin 2175. Washington, D.C.: Government Printing Office.

———. 1984a. *Employment Projections for 1995*. Bulletin 2197. Washington, D.C.: Government Printing Office.

———. 1984b. *Occupational Outlook Handbook*. 1984–85 ed. Bulletin 2205. Washington, D.C.: Government Printing Office.

———. 1984c. *Industry Wage Survey: Hospitals, October 1981*. Bulletin 2204. Washington, D.C.: Government Printing Office.

———. 1985. *Employment, Hours, and Earnings, United States, 1904–84*. Vol. 1. Bulletin 1312-12. Washington, D.C.: Government Printing Office.

———. 1986. *Occupational Outlook Handbook*. 1986–87 ed. Bulletin 2250. Washington, D.C.: Government Printing Office.

———. 1987a. *Supplement to Employment and Earnings*. Washington, D.C.: Government Printing Office.

———. 1987b. *The National Industry-Occupation Employment Matrix, 1970, 1978, and Projected 1990*. Bulletin 2086. Washington, D.C.: Government Printing Office.

———. 1989. *Employment and Earnings* 36 (January). Washington, D.C.: Government Printing Office.

U.S. Commission on Civil Rights. 1982. *Health Insurance: Coverage and Employment Opportunities for Minorities and Women*. Clearing House Publication 72. Washington, D.C.: Government Printing Office.

U.S. Department of Commerce. 1954. *Census of Business*. Vol. 1, *Retail Trade Summary Statistics*. Washington, D.C.: Government Printing Office.

———. 1963. *Census of Business*. Vol. 1, *Retail Trade Summary Statistics*. Washington, D.C.: Government Printing Office.

———. 1967. *Census of Business*. Vol. 1, *Retail Trade Subject Report*. Washington, D.C.: Government Printing Office.

———. 1972a. *Census of Manufactures*. Washington, D.C.: Government Printing Office.

———. 1972b. *Census of Retail Trade*. Washington, D.C.: Government Printing Office.

———. 1976. *Women-Owned Business: 1972*. Washington, D.C.: Government Printing Office.

———. 1977a. *Census of Manufactures*. Washington, D.C.: Government Printing Office.

———. 1977b. *Census of Manufacturing*. Subject Statistics, vol. 2, pt. SIC Major Groups 37–34. Washington, D.C.: Government Printing Office.

———. 1982. *Census of Manufactures*. Washington, D.C.: Government Printing Office.

U.S. Department of Commerce, Office of Federal Statistical Policy and Standards. 1980. *Standard Occupational Classification Manual*. Washington, D.C.: Government Printing Office.

U.S. Department of Health and Human Services, Bureau of Health Professions. 1981. *Trends in BHPR Program Statistics—Grants, Awards, Loans: FY 1957–79*. Washington, D.C.: Government Printing Office.

U.S. Department of Health, Education and Welfare. 1970. *Report to the President and the Congress on the Health Profession Education Assistance Program.* Washington, D.C.: Government Printing Office.

U.S. Department of Labor. 1986a. *Projections for 1995: Data and Methods.* Washington, D.C.: Government Printing Office.

————. 1986b. "Rapid Growth Expected in Computer-Related Jobs." New Occupational Outlook Handbook Reports. Press Release, April 21.

U.S. Department of Labor, Employment and Training Administration. 1977. *Dictionary of Occupational Titles.* 4th ed. Washington, D.C.: Government Printing Office.

————. 1981. *Selected Characteristics of Occupations Defined in the Dictionary of Occupational Titles, 4th edition.* Washington, D.C.: Government Printing Office.

————. 1982. *Report 5: Equal Employment Indicators, 1980 Census of Population.* San Francisco: U.S. Department of Labor, Region IX.

U.S. Department of Labor, Employment Service. 1939. *Dictionary of Occupational Titles.* 1st ed. Washington, D.C.: Government Printing Office.

————. 1949. *Dictionary of Occupational Titles.* 2d ed. Washington, D.C.: Government Printing Office.

U.S. Department of Labor, Manpower Administration. 1965. *Dictionary of Occupational Titles.* 3d ed. Washington, D.C.: Government Printing Office.

————. 1968. *Selected Characteristics of Occupations Defined in the Dictionary of Occupational Titles, 3rd edition.* Washington, D.C.: Government Printing Office.

U.S. Department of Labor, Women's Bureau. 1929. *Negro Women in Industry in 15 States.* Bulletin 70. Washington, D.C.: Government Printing Office.

————. 1961. *Life Insurance Selling: Careers for Women as Life Underwriters.* Bulletin 279. Washington, D.C.: Government Printing Office.

————. 1983. *Time of Change: Handbook on Women Workers.* Bulletin 298. Washington, D.C.: Government Printing Office.

————. 1989. "Fillers from the U.S. Department of Labor." *Women and Work* (August 21).

U.S. National Center for Education Statistics. 1972. *Digest of Educational Statistics.* Washington, D.C.: Government Printing Office.

————. 1982. *Digest of Educational Statistics.* Washington, D.C.: Government Printing Office.

————. 1987. *Digest of Educational Statistics.* Washington, D.C.: Government Printing Office.

U.S. Office of Management and Budget. 1987. *Standard Industrial Classification Manual.* Washington, D.C.: Government Printing Office.

Urban and Rural Systems Associates. 1976. *Exploratory Study of Women in the Health Professions.* Vol. 8, *Women in Pharmacy.* San Francisco: Urban and Rural Systems Associates.

Van Breems, Arlene. 1969. "Women in the Money Trades." *Management Review* 59 (5): 56–57.

Veblen, Thorstein. 1899. *The Theory of the Leisure Class.* New York: Macmillan.

Virginia State Board of Education. 1933. "Real Estate Business as a Vocation." *Vocations for Women* 15 (5): 27–29.

Waite, Linda J. 1981. "U.S. Women at Work." *Population Bulletin*, Volume 36, no. 2. Washington, D.C.: Population Reference Bureau.

Walker, Jon, Curt Tausky, and Donna Oliver. 1982. "Men and Women at Work: Similarities and Differences in Work Values within Occupational Groupings." *Journal of Vocational Behavior* 21:17–36.

Wallace, Denise. 1986. "Women: Taking Charge of In-Plants." *In-Plant Reproductions and Electronic Publishing*, January, pp. 37–40.

Wallace, Michael, and Arne L. Kalleberg. 1982. "Industrial Transformation and the Decline of Craft: The Decomposition of Skill in the Printing Industry, 1931–1978." *American Sociological Review* 47 (June):307–24.

Wall Street Journal. 1977. "Bank in San Antonio Told to Alter Hiring or Lose U.S. Awards." May 31, p. 1.

———. 1986. "Corporate Woman." March 24, p. 11D.

Walsh, Dorothy A. 1978. "Up from Programming." *Datamation* 24:227–30.

Walsh, John P. 1989. "Technological Change and the Division of Labor: The Case of Retail Meatcutters." *Work & Occupations* 16 (May): 165–83.

Walsh, Mary Roth. 1977. *Doctors Wanted, No Women Need Apply: Sexual Barriers in the Medical Profession, 1835–1975.* New Haven, Conn.: Yale University Press.

Walshok, Mary Lindenstein. 1981. *Blue-Collar Women.* Garden City, N.Y.: Anchor Books.

Warren, James. 1986. "Old Typographical Union Swallows Pride in Merger to Survive." *Chicago Tribune*, December 30, p. 4.

Weaver, David H., and G. Cleveland Wilhoit. 1986. *The American Journalist.* Bloomington: Indiana University Press.

Weber, Max. 1978. *Economy and Society.* Vol. 2. Berkeley: University of California Press.

Weber, Virginia Gibbs, and Walter W. Seifert. 1966. "National Survey Explores Role of Women in Public Relations." *Public Relations Journal* 22 (July):33–34.

Webster, Josephine M. 1979. "The Winds of Change." *NABW Journal*, September-October, pp. 10–13.

Wendroff, Michael. 1980. "Should We Do the Book?" *Publishers Weekly* 218 (August 15): 24–30.

Werneke, Diane. 1982. *Women and Microelectronics: The Impact of the Chip on Office Jobs.* Geneva: International Labor Office.

Wetzel v. Liberty Mutual Insurance Company. 1974, 1978. 372 F. Supp. 1146 (1974); 449 F. Supp. 397 (1978).

Wexler, Beatrice L. 1980. "Staunch Support for Women's Marketing." *Managers Magazine* 55 (8): 5–6.

Weyr, Thomas. 1980. "Minorities in Publishing." *Publishers Weekly* 218 (October 17): 31–35.

White, Harrison. 1970. *Chains of Opportunity.* Cambridge, Mass.: Harvard University Press.

Williams, Christine. 1989. *Gender Differences at Work: Women and Men in Nontraditional Occupations.* Berkeley: University of California Press.

Williams, Lena. 1987. "Black and Female, and Now Deemed Effective." *New York Times*, June 30, p. A23.

Wilson, Jean Gaddy. 1989. "Women, Men and Media." *New Directions for News*, May.

Wolfe, Tom. 1970. *Mau-Mauing the Flak Catchers*. New York: Farrar, Straus & Giroux.

Wright, John W. 1984. *The American Almanac of Jobs and Salaries*. New York: Avon Books.

Youngken, Heber W., Jr. 1968. "Report on the Committee on Future Enrollment Problems of the American Association of Colleges of Pharmacy." *American Journal of Pharmaceutical Education* 32 (August): 448–50.

Zimbalist, Andrew. 1979. "Technology and the Labor Process in the Printing Industry." In Andrew Zimbalist, ed., *Case Studies on the Labor Process*, 103–26. New York: Monthly Review Press.

Zimmerman, Bill. 1983. "There Are No Tears in Our Office!" *Insurance Sales*, June, pp. 34–35.

Name Index

Page numbers in italic type refer to figures and tables.

Abbott, Edith, 34, 67*n*30, 278
Abrahamson, Mark, 40
Ames, Linda J., 319
Anderson, Karen T., 34, 65*n*14, 76
Arnold, Carolyn L., 14, 15, 30, 34, 43, 47, 52, 81, 145, 153, 154, 158, 169, 170
Arrow, Kenneth, 186
Ashenfelter, Orley, 37, 38, 159
Attewell, Paul, 178

Baker, Elizabeth F., 242, 278, 280, 309
Baran, Barbara, 231, 234, 237, 240*n*9
Baron, Ava, 279, 283, 291
Baron, James N., 26*n*6, 36, 40, 47, 49, 56, 57, 72, 77, 104, 157, 235, 273*n*10, 304, 319, 320*n*3
Becker, Gary, 37, 159
Beechey, Veronica, 58
Beller, Andrea, 6, 16, 68*n*37, 160, 321*n*10
Bergmann, Barbara R., 36, 56, 310, 317
Berryman, Susan E., 38, 180
Bianchi, Suzanne M., 6, 16, 20, 272*n*1
Bielby, Denise D., 49, 65*n*13, 72, 110*n*21
Bielby, William T., 26*n*6, 36, 40, 49, 65*n*13,

72, 77, 104, 110*n*21, 157, 235, 273*n*10, 304, 319, 320*n*3
Binkin, Martin, 39
Bird, Chloe E., 22, 87, 145–66
Blau, Francine D., 11, 16, 21, 65*n*5, 68*n*38, 72, 211, 218, 304, 314, 321*n*10
Blauner, Robert, 286
Blum, Linda, 319
Bose, Christine E., 38, 186
Boylan, Ross, 64*n*1
Braverman, Harry, 43, 65*n*10
Burbridge, Lynn, 316
Burris, Beverly H., 298*n*16, 321*n*14
Burstein, Paul, 317

Caplette, Michele, 94, 95, 96, 97, 98, 102, 103, 105, 106, 108*n*, 109*n*17
Carey, Max, 42, 57, 250
Carter, Michael J., 43, 107, 194, 237
Carter, Susan Boslego, 43, 107, 194, 237
Catanzarite, Lisa M., 30, 34, 35, 37, 76
Cobble, Dorothy Sue, 13–14, 27*n*11, 52, 76, 242, 243, 244, 246–47, 251, 311, 313
Cockburn, Cynthia, 35, 37, 280, 282, 285,

371

Cockburn, Cynthia (*cont.*)
   291, 298n16, 309, 310, 312, 321n11
Cohn, Samuel, 12, 36, 37, 56, 65n14, 74,
   284, 310, 312
Collins, Randall, 217
Collins, Sharon, 49, 67n29, 321n15
Corcoran, Mary, 308
Cornfield, Daniel B., 231, 237, 283, 284,
   286, 290, 293
Coser, Lewis, 93, 94, 95, 97, 101, 104, 105

Darity, William, 36, 56, 310
Davies, Margery W., 11, 12, 26n8, 51, 56,
   322n19
Dertouzos, James N., 276, 283, 290, 295,
   296n3
Dessauer, John, 98–99, 104
Detman, Linda A., 22, 23, 52, 241–55
Doeringer, Peter B., 30, 35, 36, 40, 64n3
Donato, Katharine M., 22, 27n18, 75, 76,
   129–43, 167–82
Dubnoff, Steven, 171, 173, 178
Duncan, Beverly, 26n2, 70, 78, 314
Duncan, Otis Dudley, 26n2, 70, 78, 314

Edwards, Richard, 26n10
England, Paula, 11, 36, 37, 38, 308
Epstein, Cynthia Fuchs, 72
Evans, Sara M., 319

Farber, Henry S., 290
Ferber, Marianne A., 211, 218
Fields, Judith, 40, 57
Figart, Deborah M., 310, 317
Filer, Randall K., 66n16, 246, 273n14
Folbre, Nancy, 26n5
Freeman, Richard B., 56

Gerson, Judith M., 63
Glazer, Nona Y., 50, 66n21
Granovetter, Mark S., 41, 188
Greenbaum, Joan M., 168, 169, 170, 178,
   179, 182n8
Gross, Edward, 5, 11, 320

Hacker, Sally L., 287, 317
Harlan, Sharon, 38, 102, 136, 194
Hartmann, Heidi I., 4, 10, 13, 15, 21,
   26n6, 36, 37, 44, 54, 67n27, 72, 80, 107,
   189, 194, 212, 236, 279, 305, 309, 310,
   311, 317

Hochschild, Arlie R., 51, 132, 139, 161, 197
Hodge, Robert W., 30, 31, 64n2, 65n7,
   67n28, 203n6
Hout, Michael, 67n29
Hudis, Paula M., 30, 250

Jacobs, Jerry A., 5, 11, 16, 30, 37, 42, 59,
   66n16, 314
Jencks, Christopher, 38
Jones, Jacqueline, 34, 37

Kalleberg, Arne L., 285, 290, 293, 294,
   296n3
Kanter, Rosabeth M., 36, 106, 108n3, 139,
   156, 166n10, 187, 188
Kessler-Harris, Alice, 9, 15, 16, 34, 35, 49,
   51, 65n6, 153, 161, 183, 312
Konrad, Allison M., 36
Kraft, Philip, 168, 169, 170, 171, 173, 178,
   180, 182n9
Kulis, Stephen, 58

Laslett, Peter, 257, 259, 272n4
Leidner, Robin, 51, 52, 67n32, 186, 187,
   189, 193, 195, 198, 203nn5,13
Leonard, Jonathan S., 76, 316
Lieberson, Stanley, 30, 31, 38, 49,
   65nn6,7,14, 67n29
Lipset, Seymour M., 275, 290, 291, 293
Lorence, Jon, 65n13
Lynton, Edith F., 55, 57, 77, 157, 163
Lyson, Thomas A., 30, 35

McCreary, Lori, 11, 36, 37, 38
Malveaux, Julianne, 76
Markham, William T., 58
Martin, Susan E., 38, 47
Medhoff, Richard L., 56
Merton, Robert K., 319
Milkman, Ruth, 34, 35, 36, 56, 65nn9,13,14,
   263, 312
Miller, Ann R., 182n7
Miller, Karen A., 58
Mincer, Jacob, 38
Morantz-Sanchez, Regina M., 16
Murolo, Priscilla, 44

Nelkin, Dorothy, 273n13
Nelson, Barbara J., 319
Nesbitt, Paula D., 49, 66n22, 135, 143n6,
   318

Newman, Andrew E., 36, 40, 47

O'Farrell, Brigid, 38, 102, 136, 194, 321n15
Olzak, Susan, 30
Oppenheimer, Valerie, 8, 9, 36, 40, 42, 43, 50, 51, 140, 212
Osterman, Paul, 97, 110n23, 321n7

Padavic, Irene, 65nn12,13, 66n17, 305, 316
Pettigrew, Thomas F., 70, 88nn2,3
Pfeffer, Jeffrey, 36
Phelps, Edmund S., 186
Phillips, Anne, 321n17
Phipps, Polly A., 22, 44, 46, 74, 87, 111–43, 184, 225–40
Pinchbeck, Ivy, 242
Piore, Michael J., 30, 35, 36, 40, 64n3
Polachek, Solomon, 38
Powell, Walter, 93, 94, 97, 98, 99, 100, 101, 104, 108, 109nn11,13

Reskin, Barbara F., 4, 6, 10, 21, 22, 23, 26n6, 37, 54, 65n12, 66n17, 72, 75, 89n6, 93–110, 108n3, 126n, 189, 205–23, 236, 257–74, 310, 316, 322n17
Riley, John W., Jr., 186, 190, 198
Ritzer, George, 112
Romano, Frank, 280, 281, 288, 289, 292
Roos, Patricia A., 6, 22, 23–24, 47, 56, 57, 74, 75, 108n3, 172, 182n2, 275–98, 297n9
Rose, Sonya O., 36, 43
Rosenbaum, J. A., 194
Rosenfeld, Rachel, 60
Ross, H. Laurence, 226, 227, 228, 229, 240n3
Rossi, Peter H., 38
Rotella, Elyce J., 11, 12, 30, 36, 37, 42, 53, 57, 231, 304, 322n19
Rule, James, 178

Rytina, Nancy F., 6, 16, 20, 272n1

Schroedel, Jean Reith, 36
Scott, Joan W., 9, 12, 36, 65n10, 317–18
Shaeffer, Ruth G., 55, 57, 77, 157, 163
Sigelman, Lee, 40
Simpson, Ida Harper, 35, 43, 66n15
Snyder, David R., 30, 250
Sokoloff, Natalie J., 6, 7, 26n4, 34, 75, 76
Spaeth, Joe L., 149
Starr, Paul, 34
Steiger, Thomas, 22, 23, 89n6, 257–74
Steinberg, Ronnie J., 66n16, 319, 320
Stolzenberg, Ross, 37, 310
Strober, Myra H., 14, 15, 30, 34, 35, 37, 43, 47, 50, 52, 76, 81, 145, 153, 154, 158, 169, 170, 310
Strom, Sharon H., 12, 310
Szafran, Robert F., 156, 159, 166n12

Talbert, Joan, 186
Taylor, Barbara, 321n17
Thomas, Barbara J., 22, 183–203, 205–23
Thurow, Lester, 30, 35, 58, 64n2, 65n7, 66n15
Tienda, Marta, 42, 270
Treiman, Donald J., 21, 27n14, 80
Tuchman, Gay, 104

Waite, Linda J., 10, 38
Walczak, David, 112
Walker, Jon, 38
Wallace, Michael, 285, 293, 294
Walshok, Mary L., 36
Weber, Max, 94
White, Harrison, 65n5
Williams, Christine, 34, 38

Zimbalist, Andrew, 65n10, 285

Subject Index

Page numbers in italic type refer to figures and tables.

absentee rates, 36, 49, 65n13

accountants, 11, 20, 22, 34, 40, 41, 45, 53, 60, 61, 62, 67n27, 278, 303, 305, 306

administrative-support occupations, 5, 145, 179

affirmative action, 49, 54, 57, 127n15, 166n13, 305, 316; in baking, 264, 273n19; in banking, 155, 159–60, 161, 163, 164, 166n13; black women and, 76; and consent decrees, 321nn13,15; importance of, 319–20, 321nn8,15; in insurance, 236; and managerial occupations, 55, 317; in public relations, 139; in publishing, 105, 106; and systems analysis, 176, 179; and typesetting, 298n19; women in visible positions due to, 76–77, 133, 136–39

age, 12, 23, 57, 58; of insurance adjusters, 235; in public relations, 135; in typesetting, 292, 293

antidiscrimination regulations, 6, 53, 54–55, 159–60, 196, 236, 303, 304, 305, 312, 321n14; enforcement of, 196, 237, 305, 316–17; at state level, 54

apprenticeship programs, 273n19, 275, 290, 292, 295

attitudes, sex-role, 203n7; and bartending, 243, 252, 254; changes in, 23, 52–53, 216, 304; and real estate sales, 212–13, 215. *See also* sex stereotypes

auditors, 20, 22, 40, 45, 67n27

authority, of managers, 163, 164

authors, 104, 110n22, 281

automation, 317–18; in baking, 67n31, 261–63, 270; in banking, 150–51; in bartending, 248–49, 255nn9,10; in insurance claims, 231, 234, 238, 239. *See also* computerization; mechanization; technological change

autonomy, 15, 23, 38, 42, 44, 47, 48, 73–75, 138, 303, 308, 317; of book editors, 100, 107; in insurance claims, 227, 228, 230, 234, 240n9; of real estate agents, 222; of typesetters, 275, 287, 290–91. *See also* control

bakers, 3, 20, 22, 45, 47–48, 49–50, 56, 59, 61, 63, 67n31, 73, 76, 78, 87, 89n6, 257–74, 303, 306, 312, 320n1

baking-off, 48, 58, 73, 258, 261, 265, 266–68, 269, 307, 320n2

banking: branch, *148*, 149, 150, 152–53, 154, 157, 158, 163–64; jobs in, 35, 54, 57, 58, 136, 236, 305, 311; managers, 22, 45, 46, 47, 50, 51–52, 53, 55, 59, 77, 87, 145–66, 304, 306, 321*n*12; tellers, 14–15, 34, 43, 47, 52, 59, 62, 78, 81, 89*n*11, 153–54
bartenders, 3, 20, 22, 42, 46, 47, 49, 52, 54, 56, 57, 59, 60–61, 63, 76, 77–78, 79, 84, 85, 86, 87, 241–55, 242, *250*, *251*, 303, 304, 311, 312, 321*n*16
black men, 5, 6, 25*n*1, 34
blacks, 5, 7, 89*n*5, 321*n*13; and labor queues, 30, 32, 33, 65*nn*8,14; nominal integration of, 70; and protected markets, 67*n*29; in public relations, 138; in publishing, 106; resistance, of whites, to, 65*n*14; sex segregation among, 6. *See also* race
black women, 5–6, 25*n*1, 34, 35, 321*n*16; ghettoization of, 75–76. *See also* non-white women
blue-collar jobs, 5, 8, 8, 22, 66*n*17, 275, 286, 292, 317; male, and masculinity, 34, 38, 281, 285; women's gains, in male, 20, 34, 291, 321*n*15. *See also* craft occupations
book editors, 27*n*16, 42, 47, 49, 50, 51, 54, 56, 57, 59, 61, 75, 77, 78, 87, 93–110, 303, 304, 306, 311, 312
bookkeepers, 11, 62, 220
broadcast reporters, 53, 55, 77, 303, 311
bureaucratization, 9, 11, 132, 318
bus drivers, 3, 20, 22, 45, 61, 62, 82, 84, 85, 86, 87, 90*n*14, 301, 306; on municipal transit, 76; school, 48, 59, 63, 76, 78, 86, 320*n*2
business administration majors, 151, 152, 162, *162*

career ladder (promotion), 23, 38, 42, 43, 44, 48, 73, 82, 87, 103, 105, 109*n*6, 110*n*23, 138–39, 149, 150, 152, 155, 164–65, 191, 303, 308, 317, 321*nn*7,12,13; in bank management, 152–57, 162, 163, 164–65, 306, 321*n*12; in editing and reporting, 101, 102; in insurance sales, 188, 190–91; and job title, 68*n*37, 160; in public relations, 138, 142; sex discrimination and, 54, 139, 154; for women in feminizing occupations, 86–87
case studies, 21–24, 46; generalizability of, 22, 313; guidelines in, 21–24, 325–30; research methods in, 23–24; results of,

on earnings, 82–87, *83*, *84*; vs. statistical analysis, 21, 22
cashiers, 11, 26*n*9, 315
Census Bureau, 16; data on turn of century, 26*n*5; misleading data of, 319–20; 1980 census data, 3, 4; occupational classification by, 20, 26*n*6, 27*nn*12,14,15,18, 71–72, 143*nn*3,10,11,14, 165*n*1, 170, 179, 272*nn*1,9, 285, 297*n*10, 298*n*17
certification, 23, 59–60. *See also* licensing
chains, 57, 77; bakery, 58, 261, 265, 266–68, 273*n*15; drugstore, 114, 115, 119, 123, 125, 126, 304; of eating and drinking establishments, 249, 252
child care, 268. *See also* women with children
Civil Rights Act (1964), 247, 254; Title VII, 54, 110*n*23, 245, 246, 273*n*10, 311
civil rights movement, 52, 55, 304
clergy, 66*n*22, 318
clericalization, 43–44, 50, 67*n*35, 95, 116, 181, 303–4; of insurance adjusting, 225, 230, 234, 240*n*9, 303; of insurance sales, 191, 194–95; and skill level, 322*n*17; of systems analysis, 181; of typesetting, 284–85, 288, 303
clerical work, 5, 9, 14, 22, 26*n*9, 43, 59, 65*n*9, 75–76, 153, 169, 179, 191, 217, 225, 320*n*6, 321*n*12, 322*n*17; feminization of, 11–12, 15, 20, 30, 51, 56, 78, 81
coders, computer, 43, 59, 169, 179, 180
collective action, 54, 55, 106, 160, 310, 311, 316–17, 321*n*16
colleges and universities: courses at, 140, 201, 203*n*14, 217, 218, 222, 228; degrees from, 60, 140, *162*, 180–81, 196, 199; graduate and professional programs of, 53, 60, 180–81; majors at, 44, 142, 151–52, 159; students of, 66*n*23; teaching in, 43. *See also* education; training
commercial: banking, 152, 154, 155, 164, 165*nn*3,4; insurance sales, 192; printing, 277, 281, 284, 285–86, 287–88, 292, 294, 295, 296–97*n*4; real estate, 74, 76, 207, 212–13, 223*n*7, 312
commissions, 58, 63; in insurance sales, 185, 194, 199–200; in real estate sales, 207, 215, 220
communication skills, 50–51, 177, 289, 304
comparable worth. *See* pay equity
competition, 47, 151, 159, 161, 164, 209, 229, 296*n*3, 311

composing room, 280, 282–83, 284–85, 287, 290, 291, 295, 297–98nn12,13. *See also* typesetters and compositors

computer: industry, 43, 167–82; operators, 20, 170, 178, 179; programming, 43, 59, 167, 168–70, 178–79, 182n8; science degrees, 60, 180; systems analysts, 27n18, 41, 62, 167–82, 168; technicians, 178

computerization, 44, 46, 47, 59, 74, 301, 318; in banking, 150–51; in bars, 255n9; in insurance claims, 231–32, 233, 234, 235, 240n9; in pharmacy, 116, 117; in typesetting, 280, 281, 290

conglomerization, 75, 98–99, 100, 107, 108, 110n24, 209, 215, 296n3

construction, 8, 40, 41, 65n8, 174, 182n5

consumers, 59, 160–61. *See also* female customers (clientele)

control, 252, 283, 285, 287, 290–91, 311. *See also* autonomy

corporations (corporate), 57–58, 101, 107, 114, 123, 130–31; bank managers, 152; in-house printers, 277, 285–86, 289, 294; public relations specialists, 135, 136, 138–39

craft occupations, 5, 20–21, 43, 56, 257, 275, 286, 312. *See also* blue-collar jobs; *and see* specific occupations

cultural barriers, 252, 253

custom, 36, 38, 242, 308, 310

data-entry clerks (keypunch operators), 62, 76, 170, 179. *See also* coders, computer

data processing, 154; managers, 175

Depression, 15–16, 35, 52, 65nn8,9, 78, 153, 183

deregulation, 46, 147, 149–50, 151, 159, 304

desegregation, 16–21, 17–18, 25, 77; causes of, 302–7; and earnings, 79–87; and job-level integration, 69–90, 302; misleading inference from data on, 319–20; prospects for, 314–19; real vs. nominal, 70–72, 306, 317–18. *See also* integration, sex

deskilling, 303; in baking, 263, 269, 270, 274n22; in bartending, 248–49, 255nn9,10; of computer specialists, 178–79, 182n2; and earnings, decline in, 46, 81; and feminization, 11–12, 15, 43, 235, 285–86, 298nn16,18, 317–18, 322nn18,19; in typesetting, 285–86, 287, 291, 295, 298nn14,18

detailed occupations, 11, 16, 20, 22, 26n3, 27n14, 88; defined, 26n6

devaluation of women's work, 38–39, 47, 285, 321n17

Dictionary of Occupational Titles (DOT), 22, 171–72, 177, 182n7, 223n2, 232, 258, 259, 274n22, 287, 325

discrimination. *See* ethnic discrimination; race, discrimination by; sex discrimination

division of labor, 26n10, 43, 59, 238, 318; in baking, 261, 263, 266, 269, 271; in banking, 164; in computer programming, 169, 170, 178–79; by sex, 72, 73, 88, 134–35, 306

domestic responsibilities, 63, 308

earnings, 22, 23, 38, 66n24; annual, 83, 89n10; change in relative, 66n25; and desegregation, 79–87, 310; differential, and employer cost cutting, 53–57, 104, 105; and feminization of occupations, 12, 13, 36–37, 42, 44, 62–63, 74, 104; maximization of, 308; as negatively related to proportion of females in occupations, 21, 80–81; as premium, for male workers, 37; and tips, 47, 251. *See also* commissions

earnings, by occupation: bakers, 263, 264, 266, 267–69, 270, 271, 271; bank managers, 158, 160; bank tellers, 82, 89n11; bartenders, 84, 85, 251–52, 251, 253–54; bus drivers, 82, 84, 85, 86, 90n14; computer occupations, 170; editors and reporters, 84–85, 89–90n13, 97; financial managers, 157; insurance adjusters, 74, 82, 84, 85, 86; insurance claims workers, 235–39, 235, 238; insurance examiners, 82, 84, 85, 239n1, 240n9; insurance investigators, 82; insurance sales, 82, 190, 192, 194, 196, 199–201, 200, 203n10; pharmacists, 82, 84, 85, 86, 123–24, 124, 125; public relations, 84, 86, 134, 135, 141, 143n6; publishing, 94, 95, 102, 104, 105, 109nn9,14,15; real estate agents and brokers, 84, 85, 86, 207, 208, 211, 212, 219–20, 222, 223n5; systems analysts, 172–76, 174, 181, 182n6; typesetters and compositors, 89n7, 275, 282, 283–84, 287, 293–94, 293, 295; waiting occupations, 13–14, 85, 251–52

earnings, decline of, 43, 44–47, 80, 303, 307; family, 301; men's, 80, 84–85, 88,

89*n*13; and resegregation, 314, 318; and within-occupation segregation, 73–75

earnings ratio: weekly or hourly, 89*n*10; women to men in same occupation, 23, 35–36, *45*, 62, 79–80, 82–85, 83, *84*, 88, 89–90*nn*11,13, 124, *124*; women to other-occupation men workers, 86, 89*nn*9,10; women to other-occupation women workers, 85–86, 88, 89*n*11, 162–63, 181, 199–201, 220, 251–52, 268, 305, 307, 318, 321*n*10. *See also* wage gap

economic equality, 6, 23, 69, 71, 79–88, 270–71, 302, 306–7, 317, 319

economic theory (neoclassical), 35, 307–8. *See also* human capital, explanation of

editors, 22, 43, 143*n*10, 287; copy-, 95, 109*n*20; editorial assistants, 95, 96–97, 102, 103, 105, 109*n*20, 321*n*7; freelance, 104, 109–10*n*20, lower-level jobs, 101, 106; and reporters, 27*n*16, 46, 54, 63, 84–85, 89–90*n*13, 142*n*1, 311. *See also* book editors; publishing

education, 22, 23, 36, 40, 42, 43, 49, 60–61, 305, 315; for bank jobs, 151–52, 161; and degrees awarded to women, *60*, *121*, 180; federal funding of, 42, 60, 111, 117, 118, 120–22, 125, 127*nn*11,12; for insurance adjusters, 227; for insurance sales, 185, 190, 196, 199, 201, 203*n*14; and level of earnings, 44, 45–46, 61, 62; for public relations, 75, 134, 135, 136; for real estate, 60, 208, 217–18, 222; sex equity in, 53, 318–19; for systems analysis, 180–81; of typesetters and compositors, 60, 275, 286, 291–92, 295. *See also* colleges and universities; training; *and see* specific types of schools and degrees

"emotional work," 51; by bank managers, 161; in insurance sales, 51, 63, 67*n*32, 197–98; in public relations, 51, 132, 139–40, 143*n*15

employers, 73, 76–77, 213–14, 218, 282, 309–12, 316; equal-employment practices by, 55, 105, 304; ranking of sexes by, 31–38, 33, 48–58, 65*nn*10,11,12, 305, 307–8, 315–16; resistance of, to hiring women, 222. *See also* preference for men; sex-specific demand for women

enforcement, of equal employment regulations, 54, 106, 159, 196, 237, 305, 315, 316–17, 319

entrepreneurial opportunities, 46, 73, 75, 114, 116, 122, 123, 125, 127*n*18, 190, 220–21, 304, 318. *See also* self-employment

Equal Employment Opportunity Commission (EEOC), 54, 68*n*37, 77, 138, 159, 164, 189–90, 196, 199, 236–37, 240*n*11

equal pay, 56, 63, 71, 199–200, 220, 313, 318–19. *See also* economic equality; pay equity

Equal Pay Act (1963), 53, 69, 154

ethnic discrimination, 56, 314, 320*n*5

Executive Order: 11246, 54, 138, 166*n*13, 236; 11375, 159–60, 236

executives, 3, 156, 165*n*1, 190. *See also* management, top

experience, of labor force, 36, 49, 315

federal agencies: Federal Communications Commission (FCC), 55, 77; Federal Deposit Insurance Corporation (FDIC), 147, 149; Health, Education and Welfare, 117, 122; Health Professions and Manpower Training, Bureau of, 118, 120; Internal Revenue Service, 208; Occupational Safety and Health Administration, 273*n*13; U.S. Commission on Civil Rights, 203*n*11, 236, 237; Women's Bureau, 30, 34. *See also* Equal Employment Opportunity Commission; Office of Federal Contract Compliance Programs

federal contractors. *See* Office of Federal Contract Compliance Programs

federal statutes: Educational Amendment of 1972, Title IX, 35, 60; Fair Labor Standards Act (1966), 46, 251; Health Manpower Act (1971), 120; Health Profession Educational Assistance Act (HPEAA) (1963), 120; tax-law changes, 46, 208–9

female customers (clientele), 49–50, 52, 59, 66*n*21, 77, 104, 135–36, 160–61, 186, 192, 197–98, 203*n*12, 253, 279, 303, 304

female-dominated occupations, 136, 163, 315; growth of, 315; increased feminization of, 21, 314; low pay in, 314; and men's entry into, 16, *18*, 21, 35

feminization, of occupations, 11–15, 21, 64, 66*n*19, 269, 296*n*2; and their abandonment by men, 317–18, 322*n*18; in Britain, 12, 35, 56, 74; causes of, 302–6, 310–12, 317–18; and declining earnings, 44–47, 74, 237, 239, 293–94, 314; effect of, on earnings

feminization, of occupations (*cont.*)
  gap among women, 85–86; effect of, on
    women's vs. men's earnings, 79–85; and
    nonincome progress of women, 86–87; and
    queueing, 29–68, 307–9; and technologi-
    cal change, 43–44, 74, 294–96, 317–18,
    322n19. *See also* desegregation; integra-
    tion, sex; resegregation; *and see* specific
    occupations
financial managers, 27n17, 45, 60, 62, 152,
    162, 165n1, 305
flexible work schedules, 63, 201–2, 218–19
food-service industry, 13, 27n13; and bakers,
    259, 261, 268–69, 273n21
franchises, 57–58, 166n9, 215–16, 217, 252
full-time jobs, 46, 72, 73, 86, 89n6, 274n23

gender: queues, 35–38, 305, 306, 309–13;
    -role socialization, 102, 103, 139, 197–98,
    212–13, 221; solidarity, 37, 309; as type,
    297n8. *See also* ideology, gender; sex labels;
    sex stereotypes
ghettoization, 25, 72–78, 88, 306; defined,
    71; in insurance adjusting, 239; in insur-
    ance sales, 193; vs. integration or resegre-
    gation, 70, 79, 89n4; in professions, 318;
    in public relations, 75, 76–77, 79, 134–35,
    306; in publishing, 75, 77, 78, 95–97, 104,
    306. *See also* industrial segregation by sex;
    job segregation by sex; specialties

harassment, 56, 253
hiring, 38; by women, 58, 316. *See also*
    recruitment
hospital(s), 57; pharmacies in, 75, 111,
    112, 114, 115, 116–19, 123, 124, 125–
    26, 127n8, 306; public relations in, 75,
    134, 136
human-capital: explanation of, 35–38; invest-
    ments in, 35, 308

ideology, 319–20; gender, 12, 57, 139–40,
    176, 242, 244, 279, 282, 285, 289, 308.
    See also attitudes, sex role; sex labels; sex
    stereotypes
immigrants, 15, 65nn6,7
independent contractors, 74, 206–7, 208–9,
    215, 218–20, 222
industrial change (transformation), 6, 7–10,
    7, 304; in baking, 262, 265; in banking,
    146–51, 157, 165n4, 166nn8,9; in insur-
    ance, 228–29, 233; in pharmacy, 111–12,

    123, 125–26; in publishing, 93–95, 98–
    101; in real estate, 208–9, 215. *See also*
    occupational change (deterioration)
industrial growth: in banking, 147–49, 150,
    157–59, 164, 166n6; in bartending, 250–
    51; in health care, 118, 125; in insurance
    sales, 184, *184*, 190, 193–99; in publish-
    ing, 98–99, 100–101, 103; in real estate,
    205–6, *206*, 214–16; in systems analy-
    sis, 167–68, 175–76. *See also* job growth;
    occupational growth
industrial segregation by sex (industrial distri-
    bution by sex), 40, 57, 75, 306; in baking,
    260, 262–63; in bus driving, 76; in phar-
    macy, *112, 113,* 114–16; 118–19, 124; in
    public relations, 136, *137*; in publishing,
    95; in systems analysis, 172, 173–74, *173*;
    in typesetting, 276–77, *277,* 285–86, 293
informal barriers, 164, 189, 214
insurance adjusters, 3, 20, 22, 27n13, 42,
    43–44, 46, 50, 52, 53, 55, 56, 57, 59, 62,
    63, 66n21, 67nn26,35, 74, 75, 78, 82, 84,
    85, 86, 225, 226–32, *226,* 234–40, 239n1,
    240nn3,7,8, 303, 306, 311, 313; outside vs.
    inside, 230, 234, 236, 237, 238, 239, 312
insurance examiners, 3, 22, 42, 43, 44, 46,
    56, 57, 59, 62, 63, 67n35, 74, 75–76, 78,
    82, 84, 225, 232–37, *226,* 235, 238, 239n1,
    240nn7,10, 303, 306, 311
insurance investigators, 3, 27n13, 78, 82,
    85, 225
insurance jobs, 35, 58, 172, 174, 305
insurance sales, 22, 42, 45, 49, 50, 51, 54,
    55, 63, 67n32, 77, 82, 183–202, 203n1,
    304; agents vs. brokers in, 184; underwriters
    and, 225, 226
integration, sex, 49, 157, 304; in baking, 269,
    306; of bartenders, 77–78; of bus drivers,
    306; in computer occupations, 170; gender-
    based, 304; genuine, defined, 71, 70–79,
    87–88, 238; in insurance claims, 238; in
    insurance sales, 194–95; and new rankers,
    57; prospects for, 313–19; real vs. nomi-
    nal, 70–72, 87–88, 306, 319–20. *See also*
    desegregation
interpersonal relations, 50–51, 77, 103, 104,
    139–40, 161, 177, 248, 289

job assignment, 38, 54; in baking, 264; in
    banking, 155, 156–57; by women, 58
job attractiveness, 61, 316; of baking-off, 266–
    67, 320n2; of bank management, 158, 163;

of bartending, 250–51; of book editing, 101–2, 103; of computer programming, 170; declining, 42–43, 66n20, 234, 302–3, 304–5, 306, 311; of insurance claims, 225–26; of insurance sales, 187–88, 194–96, 199–202; of pharmacy, 116, 121, 122–24, 126; of public relations, 140–41; as ranked differently by women and men, 38–39; of real estate, 215, 216; of systems analysis, 175–76, 179–81; to women, of feminizing occupations, 60–63, 305

job growth, 23, 39–41, *41*, 66n19, 301, 302–3, 312, 315; in baking, 259, 265; in bank management, *146*, 147–49; in bartending, 249, 254; in insurance claims, 235; in insurance industry, 225; in real estate, 205, 206. *See also* industrial growth; occupational growth

job loss, 23, 66n19, 166n8, 315; in baking, 262, 268, 303; in typesetting, 275–77, 276, 287, 296

job posting, 105, 156, 196, 264

job queues, 29, 30–35, 38–48, 56, 66n20, 307, 308, 309, 315; reordering of, 42–49, 101–2, 116, 123, 125–26, 158, 194, 215, 234, 317–18; shape of, 31, 32, 39–42; and within-occupation segregation, 73; women's share, changes in, 39, 43, 302–3, 305–6, 315

job security, 38, 42, 44, 47, 48, 303; in bank management, 158; in editing, 101, 107; in typesetting, 282–83, 289, 290.

job segregation by sex, 26n6, 70–77, 306, 312; in baking, 73, 262–63; in banking, 153–57; in bartending, 253; in bus driving, 76; in insurance claims, 235; in insurance sales, 191–93; within occupations, 57, 68n37, 69, 71, 72–78, 87–88, 88n1, 89n4, 302, 306, 312, 319; in pharmacy, 124; in public relations, 134–36; in publishing, 95–97; in real estate sales, 210–11; in systems analysis, 178; in typesetting, 285–86. *See also* ghettoization; segregation.

journalism, 44, 53, 60, 80, 140, 305, 312; and majors in, 140–41, 142

labor costs, 35–38, 315; in banking, 146; buffering from, 37; changing, associated with each sex, 53–57; cutting, 65n10, 104, 196, 281, 282, 311; and division of labor, 178–79; and feminization, 12–13, 53–57, 64, 196, 235–36, 303–4, 310–11; and inde-

pendent contractors, 209, 215; in printing, 281, 295; and technological change, 43, 44, 281, 295. *See also* earnings

labor demand, 295; in bank management, 157–58, 163; in commercial printing, 295; and feminization, 11, 39, 58–59, 68n38, 89n8, 305, 312; and specialties, 76–77; in systems analysis, 175–76. *See also* job growth; labor shortages; sex-specific demand for women

labor force participation of women, 3, 9–10, *10*, 26n5, 166n10, 301, 315; and marriage, 58

labor market, 23, 78, 267, 307, 308–9; defined, 64n1; internal, 321n14; as ordered by sex, 309–13; in pharmacy, 119–21; in publishing, 103

labor queue(s), 29, 30–68, 304, 306, 307, 308, 309, 315, 320n5; gender queues and, 309–13, 315; shape of, 31, 32; within-occupation segregation, 73

labor shortages, 34–35, 39–42, 49, 52, 53, 65n6, 82, 116, 120, 153, 198, 215, 302–3, 304, 315, 320n2. *See also* labor demand; labor supply, female; labor supply, male; male workers, shortage of

labor supply, female, 320n4; in baking, 270; in banking, 161–63, 166n11; and demand, 58–59, 89n8, 305; increase in, 305–6; in insurance claims, 236; in public relations, 140–41; in publishing, 102–3; in real estate sales, 216–21; in systems analysis, 179–81

labor supply, male, 42, 52; in banking, 153–54, 158, 161; in bartending, 243; control over, 56; decline in, 302–3, 320n2; in insurance sales, 190–91, 195–96, 198; in pharmacy, 116, 119–20, 122–24; in public relations, 133–34, 141; in publishing, 98, 101–2, 107; in real estate, 215; in systems analysis, 175–76

law, 3, 40, 42, 43, 44; female specialties in, 72

lawsuits. *See* litigation

legal barriers, 244–45, 254

librarians, 5, 9, 11, 16, 35, 63

licensing, 23, 120, 127nn7,14, 303; of insurance adjusters, 228; of insurance agents, 185, 192, 203n11; of pharmacists, 127n14; of real estate agents, 208, 210, 217–18; of real estate brokers, 211, 217, 222

life insurance, 34, 44, 183, 184, 186, 192, 198, 226, 232, 233 litigation, 54–55, 105–6, 196–97, 199, 236, 244–47, 252, 264, 303, 312, 317; against media, 56; *Kraszewski et al. v. State Farm Insurance*, 55; *Krause v. Sacramento Inn*, 245; *Liggett v. Baldridge*, 113–14; *McCriminon v. Daley*, 245; *Martin v. Wilks*, 316; *North Dakota State Board of Pharmacy v. Snyder's Drug Stores, Inc.*, 114; *Sail'er Inn, Inc. v. Kirby*, 245; *Wetzel v. Liberty Mutual Insurance Co.*, 55, 236

lobbyists, 132–33, 138, 143nn11,12

low-wage jobs, 43, 48; in baking, 267; in publishing, 94, 100, 101, 102, 104

male-dominated occupations: abandonment of, to women, 42–49, 279, 295–96, 305, 317–18, 321n11; coaching, 35; in female industries, 102; job growth in, 315; printing as, 278, 281, 282, 285, 291; public relations specialists in, 136; resistence of, to women's entry, 19, 20–21; and shortages of white males, 34; women's gains in, 5, 6–7, 16–21, 17–19, 22, 29, 69–70, 313–14, 319–20; women's gains and queueing processes, 39–64

males: image of, 196; informal groups of, 188; power of, 37, 108n3, 188, 189, 308

male workers: and coalitions with employers, 309–10, 316; and declining preference for, 52–53, 59; and exclusion of women, 164, 188, 189, 214; exclusively male jobs valued by, 38–39; flight of, 42–49, 279, 295–96, 305, 317–18, 321n11; replacement of, by lower-paid women, 283–84, 285, 295; resistance of, to women, 36–37, 53, 55–56, 66n17, 76, 96, 115, 188–89, 213–14, 244–47, 264, 281–82, 283, 304, 309–10, 312–13, 316; resistance of, to women, declining, 55–57, 304–5, 309; shortage of, 101–2, 133–34, 175–76, 235, 302–3. *See also* harassment

management: barriers to top, 155; entry-level, 155; lower, 160, 165; middle, 149, 155, 156, 158, 164; titles in, without job change, 160; top, 139, 155, 156, 164–65, 189–90, 198, 306; training in, 154, 158, 162, 163

managerial occupations (managers), 5, 9, 11, 14, 20, 22, 53, 55, 58, 59–60, 315, 317; in banking, 145–66; in computer occupations, 170–71; in insurance sales, 185, 189–91; in pharmacy, 115; and promotion, 87; in

public relations, 134, 138, 142–43n3; in publishing, 104, 105, 106, 108n3, 110n24; in real estate sales, 211; service-providing, 51, 150, 151, 160–61, 311; sex segregation within, 57, 68n37, 72, 77

manufacturing, 8; print production workers, 277; systems analysts, 172; wages in, 12, 81

marriage, 35; as bar to employment for women, 12, 13; delay of, 52

married women: forced resignation of, 12; labor force participation of, 9–10, 58; in real estate, 220. *See also* women with children

masculinization of occupations, 15–16, 35, 67n30

master's degrees, 60, 152; in computer science, 180; M.B.A.'s, 152, 159, 161–62, 305

mechanization, 9, 51, 67n31, 315

media, 3–4, 304, 319; and printing industry, 278

medical profession (physicians), 3, 16, 42, 43, 44, 112, 122, 125, 318; and healers, midwives, 16, 112

medical school, 34, 42, 44, 318

military, 34, 35, 39

mining, 8, 15, 174, 236

minorities, 34, 159, 164, 176, 321nn14,15,16

mixed-sex occupations, 22, 29

mobility, 15, 44, 76, 228, 317; declining, 47, 101, 109n19, 175, 176; of secretaries, 188. *See also* career ladder (promotion)

National Organization for Women (NOW), 54, 106, 160

networking, 164, 188, 189, 192, 196, 214, 267, 305

newspaper(s), 43, 54, 73–74, 77, 78, 89n7, 276, 296n3, 311; typesetters and compositors on, 277, 280–87, 293–95, 312

9to5, 105

nonresidential real estate, 207, 208, 210, 212–14, 223nn5,7

nonunionized labor, 251, 281, 291

nonwhite women, 5–6

nursing, 5, 9, 11, 16, 62, 66n20, 76, 77, 122, 125, 127n16, 192, 315

occupational change (deterioration), 6, 8–10, 23, 56, 234, 317–18; in baking, 261–63,

265, 267; in bank management, 146, 148–49, 152–53, 157–58, 163–64, 165n1, 261–63, 265, 267; in bartending, 247–54; in book editing, 99–101; in insurance adjusting, 228–32; in insurance claims, 234–36; in insurance examining, 232, 233–34; in insurance sales, 194–95, 197–98, 199; in pharmacy, 113, 116, 117–18, 123, 125–26; in public relations, 132; in real estate sales, 208–9, 215; in systems analysis, 177–79, 181; in typesetting, 275–96. *See also* deskilling; industrial change (transformation); job attractiveness; technological change

occupational classification system, 27nn12,14; and job titles, 160. *See also* Census Bureau

occupational entry, 59, 154, 196, 198, 217–18, 250, 252, 267, 273n18. *See also* recruitment

occupational groups: detailed, 11; distribution of, by sex and race, 4, 5; major, 11

occupational growth, 40, 302–3. *See also* job growth

Occupational Outlook Handbook, 22, 59, 119, 152, 177, 182n7, 194, 217, 236, 247, 255n6, 262, 325, 326

occupational segregation, 17–18; costs of, 311–12; deceptiveness of data on, 319–20; decline in, 16–21; extent of, 5, 11, 16, 25–26nn2,6,7,10, 109n5, 313–14; human-capital theory of, 308–9; and job growth, 40–41; vs. job-level segregation, 26n6, 69–70, 88n1, 320; and labor shortages, 34; persistence of and change in, 3–27, 301, 318–20; and queueing theory, 30, 35–38, 307–9; and wage gap, 319. *See also* desegregation; industrial segregation by sex; integration, sex; job segregation by sex; *and see* specific occupations

occupations: with disproportionate increase of women, 17–18, 22, 27nn13,16,18, 234, 302–7, 313–14; with only small gains by women, 19; wage–sex ratios within, 35–36

office clerks, 11, 26n9, 62, 72, 315

Office of Federal Contract Compliance Programs (OFCCP), 54–55, 106, 159–60, 166n13, 236–37, 303

operations researchers and analysts, 20, 27n18, 63, 167–82, 168, 170, 179

organization: by age, 57; and hierarchy, 306; leadership of, 57; by size, 58, 172–73

part-time work, 22, 23, 48, 58, 63, 68n39, 73, 75, 84, 86, 90n14; in baking, 89n6, 267, 268, 269, 270–71, 273nn18,20; in bartending, 84, 86, 249, 255n5; in bus driving, 84, 86; in insurance sales, 84, 201–2; in pharmacy, 84, 86, 124–25; in public relations, 84, 86; in real estate sales, 84, 208, 219

pay equity, 319; National Committee on, 80, 90n13

performance, women's in sex-atypical jobs, 49, 65n13, 199, 316

personnel and labor relations specialists, 20, 67n29, 138, 154, 303

pharmaceutical technicians, 117, 119, 126n5, 127n7

pharmacists, 3, 46, 47, 50, 53, 57, 60–62, 75, 82, 84, 85, 86, 111–27, *111, 113, 121, 124,* 301, 303, 304, 305; clinical, 118, 119, 125

pharmacy schools, 42, 49, 112, 115, 117, 118, 120; enrollment of, 120–22, *121,* 125; federal grants to, 127nn7–9,13,14,16

policy, public and political, on equal employment practices, 316, 318–19, 320

power, 252, 290–91, 309–10; base, 56, 312; group, 25

preference for men, 36–38, 41, 303, 309–10; decline in, 52–53, 59; in insurance sales, 186, 187–88; in publishing, 105. *See also* gender, queues

preference for women. *See* sex-specific demand for women

preferences: employers', 31–32, 32, 33, 53, 307–8; workers', 32–33, 38–39, 66n16, 270, 307–8. *See also* job queues

prestige, 23, 38, 39, 63, 308; of bank managers, 145, 153, 157, 158, 163, 164; of bartenders, 251; of computer occupations, 170; declining, 47, 48, 303; and feminization, 47, 80, 314, 318; of insurance adjusters, 228; of pharmacists, 122, 123, 127n16, 303; of public relations specialists, 134–35, 140; of publishing jobs, 93–94, 95, 99, 303; of typesetters, 282, 286, 293

productivity, 35, 36, 37, 38, 40, 150, 231, 233, 234, 249, 308, 311; of men vs. women, 48–49, 77, 186, 196, 199, 303–4, 312, 320n3

professional and trade associations, 214; American Banking Association, 159;

professional and trade associations (*cont.*)
American Bartenders' Association, 250,
252; American Council on Public Relations, 132; American Institute of Baking
(AIB), 272nn2,3; American Medical
Association, 16; American Newspaper
Publishers Association (ANPA), 276, 312;
American Pharmaceutical Association, 42,
118, 120, 127n7; International Association
of Business Communicators (IABC), 134,
143n9; Life Insurance Marketing and Research Association (LIMRA), 190, 194,
197, 200; Life Office Management Association (LOMA), 233; National Association of
Bank Women (NABW), 154, 155; National
Association of Manufacturers (NAM), 131,
321n8; National Association of Printers
and Lithographers, 291, 297n7; Public
Relations Society of America (PRSA), 132,
143n9
professional jobs, 5, 8, 9, 22, 42, 53, 59–60,
318; and affirmative action, 55; black men
vs. women in, 25n1; rift between women
with, and others, 317
professional schools: enrollment in, 42, 53,
117, 318; funding of, 127n17; of health,
127n17. *See also* specific professions
professional services, 136; of pharmacists, 112,
116–17, 125; of systems analysts, 174
promotion. *See* career ladder (promotion);
mobility
protected niches. *See* restricted markets
protective labor laws, 52, 54, 56, 242–47,
255n4, 272–73n10, 303
public relations, 20, 22, 48, 49, 50, 51, 53,
55, 58, 63, 75, 76–77, 79, 84, 86, 101,
129–43, 133, 135, 137, 141, 303–4, 306;
communications-expert specialty in, 48,
50, 75, 134; external, 132; internal, 132,
143n10; in schools, 134
publishing, 34, 49, 50, 54, 56, 57, 58, 93–
110, 305; educational, 95, 97, 103, 104,
106, 107, 108n2, 109n12; paperback, 95,
97, 98, 104; sales jobs in, 96, 97; school,
97, 104, 106, 109n15; scholarly, 75, 94,
95, 96, 97, 109n11; trade, 94, 95, 97, 98,
100, 106, 107, 108nn1,2

qualifications (qualified labor pool), 49, 61,
65n4, 67n28; in baking, 259; in banking,
158–59, 161–63; in computer sciences,

180–81; for insurance adjusters, 227–
28; for insurance examiners, 232–33; in
insurance sales, 196; in pharmacy, 122,
127n14; in printing, 292, 294; in publishing, 102–3, 107; in real estate sales, 216;
and women's changes in share, 39, 40–43,
302–3, 305–6. *See also* education; labor
supply, female; labor supply, male; training;
training requirements
queues (queueing), 320n4; and changing
occupational composition of, 29–68, 306;
defined, 31; and intensity of rankers' preferences, 31–33, 33, 315; and mismatches in,
34–35; model of, 25; ordering of elements,
31; and prospects for integration, 314–19;
shape of, 31, 32, 39–42, 315; structural
properties of, 31–33, 39, 315; theory of, 25,
307–13; and within-occupation segregation,
73–78; of women, for sex-atypical jobs,
305. *See also* gender, queues; job queues;
labor queue(s)

race, 320n5; desegregation by, 70, 88–
89nn2,3,5; discrimination by, 56, 105;
index of occupational segregation by, 5,
25–26n2; integration by, 37; occupational
distribution by, 4; and occupational segregation, 5–6, 7, 37, 320; and queueing
theory, 30, 34, 35, 304; residential segregation by, 70, 78, 314; segregation by, 70,
88nn2,3, 314
real estate agents and brokers, 3, 22, 24, 40,
41, 42, 43, 45, 46, 49, 51, 56, 57, 58–59,
60, 61, 62, 63, 72, 74–75, 76, 77, 78, 84,
85, 86, 186, 205–23, 206, 208, 210, 212,
304, 305, 306; brokers defined, 207, 211;
commercial, 74, 76, 207, 212–13, 223n7;
312; residential, 56, 59, 61, 63, 74–75, 77,
78, 207, 209, 210, 211, 212, 214–21, 222,
303, 312
recruitment, 39, 59, 305; in insurance sales,
188–91, 193, 196, 198–200, 202; in real
estate sales, 217; in typesetting, 292
regulation, 301–2; in banking, 146–47, 151;
need for, 319; in real estate, 208–9. *See
also* affirmative action; enforcement; litigation; regulatory agencies; *and see* specific
agencies and laws
regulatory agencies, 23, 54, 55, 76, 159, 198,
203n11, 306, 311, 312–13, 316–17, 319.
See also enforcement; Equal Employment

Opportunity Commission; Office of Federal
Contract Compliance Programs
reporters, 22, 27n16, 34, 44, 53, 54, 55,
56, 77, 84, 87, 287. *See also* editors, and
reporters
resegregation, 25, 88, 225, 238–39, 305, 306;
defined, 70, 71, 78–79, 314
residential segregation, 70, 78, 314
restricted markets, 49, 67n29, 321n15
retail sector, 57; baking, 50, 63, 73, 76, 78,
259, 261, 265–69, 303, 320n1; banking,
145, 154, 164; buyers, 20; pharmacies, 46,
47, 50, 56, 58, 75, 87, 111, 112–16, 117,
119, 122–23, 126, 126n4, 304, 306, 315;
sales, 76, 186, 315; trade, 182n5
rewards: change in, 23, 42, 44–48, 303, 317;
noneconomic, 37, 66n16, 86, 107, 308.
See also earnings; *and see* specific rewards
such as autonomy; job security
role partners, 104, 304. *See also* female
customers (clientele)
routinization, 74, 116, 123, 194–95, 225,
229–31, 234–35, 237, 239, 240n9, 318

sales occupations, 5, 20, 22, 179, 185–86;
automobile, 50; in baking, 261; in pharmaceuticals, 113, 126n3; in printing, 278–79;
in publishing, 49, 96, 97, 103, 108n4; and
soft sell, 197–98, 199. *See also* insurance
sales; real estate agents and brokers
secretaries, 200, 220, 278; in insurance, 188;
in publishing, 95, 96, 105; as typesetters,
283, 292
segregation: and sex differences, 52; vertical,
74, 78, 154–57, 306. *See also* ghettoization;
industrial segregation by sex; job segregation
by sex; occupational segregation; specialties;
and see specific occupations
self-employment, 115, 122–23, 220–21,
223n8, 254. *See also* entrepreneurial
opportunities
semiprofessions, 5, 9, 11, 15–16, 25n1,
66n20, 76, 141, *141*
semiskilled occupations, 20, 34
seniority, 12, 34, 46; rules of, 36
service: banking and, 77, 146, 147, 150, 151,
160–61, 311; occupations, 5, 8, 8, 20,
22, 51, 268; -producing industries, 7, 8,
39–40, 140, 301, 302
sex composition, 16–21, 27n14, 71–72,
313–14; changes in, 301, 319; conditions

fostering change in, 21–24; and earnings,
80–82; employer-worker coalitions and,
309–12; and job queues, 35, 38–39, 39–48,
308; of labor force, 10, *10*, 58; and labor
queues, 35–38, 48–64; and occupational
characteristics, 22, 23, 24; queueing and,
29–68; of specialties within occupations,
24, 25, 49–50; and structural change, 25
sex composition by occupation: baking, 257,
258, *260*, 265–71, 272n1; bank management, 145, *146*, 163–64; bartending,
241–54, *242*, *250*; computer occupations,
169–71; insurance claims, 225, 226; insurance examiners, 232; insurance sales,
183–84, *184*, 187–88, 193–202, *195*; .
pharmacy, 111–17, *112*, *113*, 119; public
relations, 129–30, 133–40, *133*, *137*, 142;
publishing, 95, 96–98; real estate, 205–6,
206, 209–10; real estate specialties, 210–
16, *210*, 223n1; sales, 186; systems analysis,
167–68, *168*, 170; typesetting, 275–79,
276, 277, 281–86, 287, 288–89, 296,
297n8
sex differentiation, 4–5, 37, 49–50, 65n13,
104, 203n4, 310; and earnings, 69; and soft
sell, 197–98
sex discrimination, 38, 48, 52, 308, 320n3;
in baking, 264; in banking, 155–56, 164;
as barred in education, 60; in bartending, 245; costs of, 53, 160, 303; declining,
52–57, 304, 305, 315–16; declining, in
banking, 159–60; declining, in publishing,
96, 105–7; and earnings, 81; in graduate
and professional programs, 53; in insurance
jobs, 54–55, 67n35; in insurance sales,
185–91, 196–200, 202; and labor costs,
37–38, 196, 311; and misrepresentation
of job requirements, 196; in newspaper
reporting, 56; in promotions, 54, 139, 154;
prospects for reduction of, 315–17; in publishing, 103; in real estate, 213–14, 216,
222; in retail pharmacy, 115; in typesetting,
281–283, 298n14; by unions, 56, 243–44,
246, 291
sex-discrimination charges, 23, 54–55, 67–
68n36, 303; in baking, 264; in banking,
160; in insurance adjusting, 55, 236; in
insurance sales, 196; in newspaper publishing, 56; and promotions, 139, 154; in
public relations, 139; in publishing, 105–6,
107. *See also* litigation

sex labels, 36, 50, 51–52, 67n33, 74, 135, 212, 215, 237, 263, 266–67, 282, 285, 296, 303, 304, 305, 310, 313, 320, 322n19

sex-specific demand for women, 58–60, 68n37, 76–78, 303–4, 305, 308–9; in baking, 270; in bank management, 303; in bartending, 252, 253, 254; in insurance sales, 193, 195–96; in public relations, 133–40, 142; in publishing, 98, 103–5; in residential real estate, 214–16; in systems analysis, 176, 177, 181; in typesetting and composition, 295–96

sex stereotypes, 36, 38, 48, 50–52, 65n12, 67n34, 77, 108n3, 304, 308, 322n19; and bartending, 244, 248, 304; in books, 106; and insurance sales, 185–91, 198; and residential real estate sales, 221; and service banking, 160–61; and systems analysis, 177, 181

skills, 59–60, 104; female-labeled, 74, 135; and change in mix of, 23, 47–48, 251, 298n16; and mix, by sector, 286–89. See also deskilling

social work, 5, 9, 11, 16, 35, 63, 67n29, 143n5

specialties, 24, 71, 318; in banking, 152–55, 155–56, 166n10; ghettoization (segregation) by, 72, 73–76, 88, 306, 312, 313; in insurance sales, 193; and lower earnings for women, 81; predominantly male, 76; rejected by men, 73–74; in public relations, 75, 134–35; in real estate, 207, 208, 210–14, 210, 216, 222, 306; resegregation of, 78; in systems analysis, 50–51, 75, 178, 179, 182, 306; in typesetting, 72, 73–74, 76. See also ghettoization; segregation

staff vs. line jobs, 138–39, 154, 176

systems analysts, 21, 27n18, 41, 43, 45, 50–51, 53, 59, 60, 61, 63, 75, 167–82, 303, 304, 305, 306

tasks, 50, 317; shifted to others, 66n21, 287. See also division of labor

teachers, 5, 9, 11, 15, 62, 66n20, 77, 78, 192; black, 37, 76; as editors, 97, 109n15; in public schools, 14, 42

technicians: computer, 178, 179; in pharmacy, 117; in public relations, 134, 135, 140, 142

technological change, 23, 43, 315; in baking, 261–62, 269–70; in banking, 150–51,

153; and computer work, 168–71, 175; and feminization, 15, 43, 47, 73–74, 234, 239, 294–95, 296, 303, 317–18, 322n19; in food and drink industry, 249; in insurance claims, 225, 234, 237, 239, 315; in insurance sales, 194–95; in pharmacy, 117–18, 119, 123; in systems analysis, 178–79; in typesetting, 275, 276, 279–96, 298n13, 311. See also automation; mechanization

telegraph operators, 12–13

telephone: operators, 12–13, 78; work, 230–31

tenure: bar to, 284; median, by occupation, 57

Title VII. See Civil Rights Act (1964)

tokenism, 156

trainees, 74; in insurance sales, 185, 196, 197, 199, 200; in typesetting, 283–84

training: in baking, 259, 270, 272n3; in banking, 151–52, 155–56, 160, 161; in bartending, 250; in insurance adjusting, 228; in insurance examining, 232–33; in insurance sales, 201; on-the-job, 201, 228, 250, 259; on-the-job vocational, 35, 36–37, 40; in publishing, 103; in real estate sales, 217; sex equity in, 318–19; in systems analysis, 176, 180–81; in typesetting, 283, 291–92; and women seeking, for male occupations, 304, 305

training requirements, 23, 40–41, 43, 59–61; in banking, 159, 161; for computer programmers, 180; in insurance sales, 185, 196; for real estate brokers, 217; for real estate sales, 208, 217; in systems analysis, 180

turnover rates, 36, 41–42, 49, 53, 57, 65n13; of bartenders, 249–50; high, 312; of insurance adjusters, 228, 237; in publishing, 103, 109n19

typesetters and compositors, 20, 22, 24, 43, 45, 46, 47, 50, 53, 56, 57, 59, 60, 66n19, 72, 73–74, 76, 89n7, 275–98, 301, 303, 304, 306, 312; defined, 296n1

typists (typing), 11, 62; in printing, 288; skills, 281, 282; and typewriter, 12, 26n8, 57

unemployment, 22, 30

unions, 22, 23, 48, 52, 74, 243, 246, 253, 264, 267, 273nn14,17,20, 292, 293–94; American Newspaper Guild, 56; Bakery, Confectionery and Tobacco Workers Union, 56, 261, 263, 264; Cigar Makers

International Union, 15; Communications Workers of America, 291; Hotel and Restaurant Employees and Bartenders' International, 56, 243, 244, 245–46, 254; International Typographical Union (ITU), 56, 74, 275, 279, 283, 290–91, 292, 295, 311, 312; loss of power of, 246, 290–91; Newspaper Guild, 56; resistance of, to women in, 56, 76, 78, 243–44, 245–46, 247, 254, 279, 283, 291, 295, 304, 312, 313, 321n16; women vs. men in, 15, 282–84, 295, 296, 307, 311
U.S. Supreme Court, 52, 113–14, 244–45, 316

vacancy-chain model, 65n5
video display terminals (VDTs), 44, 47, 50, 276, 280, 283, 295

wage gap: 12, 13, 14, 56, 303; and comparable worth, 318–19; and desegregation, 306–7; and feminization, 15, 44–47, 45, 48, 53, 61–63, 62, 80–87, 88; and gender queues, 35; and job queues, 35, 39; and male resistance to women workers, 36–37, 283–84; and occupational distribution, 5; within occupations, 25, 35–36, 66n16, 68nn37,39, 69, 72, 73, 74–75, 76, 82, 83, 88; reduction of, 318–19; and technological change, 43, 318. *See also* earnings ratio
waiting occupations, 13–14, 15, 63, 243, 252, 315; assistants in, 21
wars, 34, 35. *See also* World War I, World War II
white-collar employment, 8, 8, 284–85, 317
white men, 34, 65n14, 315, 320

white women, 34, 35, 65n14
wholesale: baking, 67n31, 258, 259, 261–64, 273n11, 307, 312; buyers, 20; sales, 186; trade systems analysts, 174
women's groups, 54, 105, 106, 107, 138, 160, 303
women's liberation movement, 6, 50, 52, 53, 104, 105, 106, 216, 252, 304, 316, 317. *See also* collective action
women with children, 35, 38, 268, 270; in baking, 268; as freelancers, 109n16; in insurance sales, 201, 203n13; labor force participation of, 9, 10; in pharmacy, 125; in real estate sales, 216, 218–19
working conditions, 22, 23, 35, 38, 42, 43, 58, 72, 116, 215, 302, 317; in baking, 258; and queuing, 308; in typesetting and composing, 284–85, 295. *See also* work reorganization; work setting
work reorganization, 23, 43–44, 49, 51, 58, 67n27, 303, 311, 317–18, 322n19; in banking, 149–51, 153; in book editing, 99–101, 107; and earnings, 81; in pharmacy, 116, 123; and sex-label change, 313; in systems analysis, 177–78; in typesetting, 279–96. *See also* automation; clericalization; industrial change (transformation); occupational change (deterioration); routinization; technological change
work setting, 22–24, 88, 123, 134, 317, 319; of baking, 259–69; of bartending, 249; of systems analysis, 172; and women in separate, 321n12
World War I, 14, 34, 35, 51, 78, 243
World War II, 15, 34, 42, 52, 78, 183, 243

About the Authors

Barbara F. Reskin is a Professor of Sociology at the University of Illinois. She became interested in sex segregation as the Study Director of the National Academy of Sciences Committee on Women's Employment and Related Social Issues. She has written on sex inequality in science, the courts, and the workplace, including *Sex Segregation in the Workplace: Trends, Explanations, Remedies* and *Women's Work, Men's Work: Sex Segregation on the Job* (with Heidi Hartmann). She was the third Cheryl Allyn Miller Lecturer on Women and Social Change, and has been a Fellow at the Center for Advanced Study in the Behavioral Sciences. Her research combines scholarly and political interests in the social and organizational forces that maintain women's subordination and in mechanisms to reduce inequality.

Patricia A. Roos is an Associate Professor of Sociology at Rutgers University. She has long been interested in sex and ethnic stratification. In 1985 she published *Gender and Work: A Comparative Analysis of Industrial Societies* (SUNY Press). Other related publications in gender and work have appeared in the *American Sociological Review*, the *American Journal of Sociology, Social Science Research*, and elsewhere. Her current research includes an ongoing interest in the feminization of typesetting/composition and work with Barbara Reskin on the determinants of changing occupational sex composition for the full set of detailed occupations in the 1980 Census.

Katharine M. Donato is an Assistant Professor of Sociology at Louisiana State University. She received her Ph.D. from the State University of New York at Stony Brook in 1988, and was a postdoctoral fellow at the Population Research Center at the University of Chicago and the National Opinion Research Corporation before going to

Louisiana. She has done research on the international migration patterns of women. She is currently applying queueing theory to the labor force participation of minority women since 1960 and examining the consequences of U.S. immigration reform for Mexican migrants.

Polly A. Phipps is a sociologist at the Bureau of Labor Statistics in Washington, D.C. She is part of an interdisciplinary group of social scientists conducting research on cognitive aspects of survey methodology. She received her Ph.D. from the University of Michigan, where she was the Associate Director of the Detroit Area Study in 1987 and 1988. Her current interests include the relationship between industrial change and male and female wages, and the adequacy of administrative remedies in employment-discrimination complaints.

Barbara J. Thomas is a Ph.D. candidate in Sociology at the University of Illinois-Urbana. With Robert Schoen she has investigated "who marries whom" in terms of such characteristics as age, educational attainment, race and ethnicity, and religion in both 1970 and 1980. She is also interested in sex segregation in the labor force, especially in sales occupations. Her doctoral dissertation, by examining sex and race differences in occupational exit and entry in the early 1980s, examines—among other questions—to what occupations men are moving.

Chloe E. Bird is a Ph.D. candidate in Sociology at the University of Illinois-Urbana. For several years she has been studying sex segregation in occupations. She has also examined the impact of gender roles on health. Her doctoral dissertation analyzes occupational sex segregation and earnings inequality among physicians, dentists, and veterinarians.

Linda A. Detman is a Ph.D. candidate in the Department of Sociology at the University of Illinois-Urbana. She has presented co-authored work on small-group experience in graduate school and the impact of a new computer system on undergraduates' learning experiences. She is interested in women and work, technology's impact on work, social problems, and the media. She is currently investigating the representation of women's work in magazine advertisements.

Thomas Steiger is an Assistant Professor of Sociology and Social Work at Indiana State University. He received his Ph.D. from the University of Illinois-Urbana, and has published a recent article from his doctoral dissertation on the labor process in the construction industry. His current research focuses on the predominantly female labor reserve and the relationship between its exclusion from and inclusion in the workplace and the reproduction of social class.